The Rights of Minority Cultures

The Rights of Minority Cultures

EDITED BY

Will Kymlicka

OXFORD
UNIVERSITY PRESS

OXFORD
UNIVERSITY PRESS
Great Clarendon Street, Oxford OX2 6DP
Oxford University Press is a department of the University of Oxford.
It furthers the University's objective of excellence in research, scholarship,
and education by publishing worldwide in
Oxford New York
Athens Auckland Bangkok Bogotá Buenos Aires Calcutta
Cape Town Chennai Dar es Salaam Delhi Florence Hong Kong Istanbul
Karachi Kuala Lumpur Madrid Melbourne Mexico City Mumbai
Nairobi Paris São Paulo Singapore Taipei Tokyo Toronto Warsaw
with associated companies in Berlin Ibadan
Oxford is a registered trade mark of Oxford University Press
in the UK and in certain other countries
Published in the United States
by Oxford University Press Inc., New York

First published in hardback and paperback 1995
Reprinted as paperback 1996, 1999
Reprinted in hardback and paperback 1997
Reprinted in paperback 2000

British Library Cataloguing in Publication Data
Data available
Library of Congress Cataloging in Publication Data
Data available
ISBN 0-19-878100-8
ISBN 0-19-878101-6 (Pbk)
Typeset in Plantin
Printed in Great Britain
on acid-free paper by
Bookcraft Ltd,
Midsomer Norton, Somerset

Contents

Notes on Contributors

S. JAMES ANAYA is Professor of Law at the University of Iowa, and a 1983 graduate of Harvard Law School. He is the author of *Indigeneous Peoples in International Law* (Oxford University Press, forthcoming) and several other publications on indigenous peoples and human rights. He was previously director of the Legal Advocacy Project of the National Indian Youth Council, a non-governmental organization in consultative status with the United Nations.

ALLEN BUCHANAN is Grainger Professor of Business Ethics and Professor of Philosophy at the University of Wisconsin-Madison. He is the author of *Secession: The Morality of Political Divorce* (Westview Press, 1991), *Marx and Justice* (Methuen, 1982), *Ethics, Efficiency and the Market* (Rowman and Allenheld, 1985), and co-author (with Dan Brock) of *Deciding for Others* (Cambridge University Press, 1989).

JOSEPH H. CARENS is Professor of Political Science at the University of Toronto. He is the author of *Equality, Moral Incentives and the Market* (University of Chicago Press, 1980), and editor of *Democracy and Possessive Individualism* (State University of New York Press, 1993). He is currently completing work on a book tentatively titled *Migration, Morality, and Political Community.*

NATHAN GLAZER is Professor of Education and Sociology at Harvard University, emeritus since 1993. He is the co-author (with Daniel P. Moynihan) of *Beyond the Melting Pot* (MIT Press, 1963, 1970), and author of *Affirmative Discrimination: Ethnic Inequality and Public Policy* (Basic Books, 1975, 1978), *Ethnic Dilemmas: 1964-1982* (Harvard University Press, 1983), and *The Limits of Social Policy* (Harvard University Press, 1988). He has been co-editor of the journal *The Public Interest* since 1973.

LESLIE GREEN is a Professor at Osgoode Hall Law School and in the Department of Philosophy at York University, Toronto. He is the author of *The Authority of the State* (Oxford University Press, 1988), co-editor (with A. Hutchinson) of *Law and the Community* (Carswell, 1989), and of other works in legal and political theory.

MICHAEL HARTNEY has taught philosophy at McMaster University, and at the Universities of Ottawa and Western Ontario. His areas of interest include legal theory, judicial review, and collective rights. He has published a translation of Hans Kelsen's *General Theory of Norms* (Oxford University Press, 1991), and is now writing a book on Kelsen's legal philosophy for Oxford University Press.

DARLENE M. JOHNSTON (BA, Queen's University, LLB, University of Toronto) is an Assistant Professor in the Common Law Section of the Faculty of Law at the University of Ottawa. She belongs to the Chippewas of Nawash First Nation, and is currently engaged in land claims research on behalf of the Chippewas of Nawash and Saugeen First Nations. She is the author of *The Taking of Indian Lands in Canada: Consent or Coercion?* (University of Saskatchewan Native Law Centre, 1989).

CHANDRAN KUKATHAS teaches in the Department of Politics, University College, University of New South Wales at the Australian Defense Forces Academy. He is the author of *Hayek and Modern Liberalism* (Oxford University Press, 1989), co-author (with Philip Pettit) of *Rawls: A Theory of Justice and its Critics* (Polity, 1990), and editor of *Multicultural Citizens: The Philosophy and Politics of Identity* (Centre for Independent Studies, 1993).

AREND LIJPHART is Professor of Political Science at the University of California, San Diego. He is the author or editor of more than a dozen books, including *Democracy in Plural Societies: A Comparative Perspective* (Yale University Press, 1977), *Democracies: Patterns of Majoritarian and Consensus Government in Twenty-One Countries* (Yale University Press, 1984), *Power-Sharing in South Africa* (Institute of International Studies, 1985), *Parliamentary versus Presidential Government* (Oxford University Press, 1992), and *Electoral Systems and Party Systems: A Study of Twenty-Seven Democracies* (Oxford University Press, 1994).

AVISHAI MARGALIT is Professor of Philosophy at the Hebrew University of Jerusalem. He is the co-author (with Moshe Halbertal) of *Idolatry* (Harvard University Press, 1992), and co-editor (with Edna Ullman-Margalit) of *Isaiah Berlin: A Celebration* (University of Chicago Press, 1991). His book *The Decent Society* is forthcoming from Harvard University Press.

EPHRAIM J. NIMNI is Professor of Politics at the University of New South Wales. He was born in Buenos Aires, studied in Jerusalem and the United Kingdom, and has taught Sociology and Political Science at the Universities of Hull, Keele, and Woolwich. In 1991-92, he was a Jean Monnet Fellow at the European University Institute in Florence. He is the author of *Marxism and Nationalism: Theoretical Origins of a Political Crisis* (Pluto Press, 1991, 1994), and *Ethnicity and the Nation-State* (forthcoming).

BHIKHU PAREKH is Professor of Political Theory at the University of Hull. He is the author of *Contemporary Political Thinkers* (Martin Robertson, 1982), *Colonialism, Tradition and Reform* (Sage, 1989), *Hannah Arendt and the Search for a New Political Philosophy* (Macmillan, 1981), *Marx's Theory of Ideology* (Johns Hopkins, 1981), and *Gandhi's Political Philosophy: a critical examination* (Macmillan, 1989). He served as Deputy Chair of the Commission for Racial Equality in Britain between 1986 and 1990.

ANNE PHILLIPS is Professor of Politics at London Guildhall University. She is the author of *Engendering Democracy* (Polity, 1991), *Democracy and Difference* (Penn State Press, 1993), and the forthcoming *Politics of Presence* (Oxford University Press). She is also the editor of *Feminism and Equality* (New York University Press, 1987), and co-editor (with Michèle Barrett) of *Destabilizing Theory: Contemporary Feminist Essays* (Polity, 1992).

JOSEPH RAZ is Professor of the Philosophy of Law, Oxford University, and Fellow of Balliol College. He is the author of *Practical Reason and Norms* (Hutchinson, 1975), *The Authority of Law* (Oxford University Press, 1979), *The Morality of Freedom* (Oxford University Press, 1986) and *Ethics in the Public Domain* (Oxford University Press, 1994).

VERNON VAN DYKE is Professor Emeritus of Political Science at the University of Iowa. His works include *Political Science: A Philosophical Analysis* (Stanford University Press, 1960); *Human Rights, the United States and the World Community* (Oxford University Press, 1970); *Human Rights, Ethnicity and Discrimination* (Greenwood, 1985); *Equality and Public Policy* (Nelson-Hall, 1990), and *Ideology and Political Choice* (Chatham House, 1995).

JEREMY WALDRON is Professor of Law and Philosophy and Chair of the Jurisprudence and Social Policy Program at the School of Law, University of California, Berkeley. Educated in New Zealand and at Oxford, he has written extensively on liberalism, rights, property, and social justice. He is the author of *The Right to Private Property* (Oxford University Press, 1988) and *Liberal Rights: Collected Papers 1981-1991* (Cambridge University Press, 1993), and editor of *Theories of Rights* (Oxford University Press, 1984).

MICHAEL WALZER is a Professor of Social Science at the Institute for Advanced Studies in Princeton, and co-editor of *Dissent*. He is the author of *Just and Unjust Wars* (Penguin, 1977), *Spheres of Justice: A Defense of Pluralism and Equality* (Blackwell, 1983), and *What It Means To Be An American* (Marsilio, 1993). He is currently writing about issues of ethnicity, nationalism, pluralism, multiculturalism, toleration, and civil society.

IRIS MARION YOUNG teaches ethics and political philosophy in the Graduate School of Public and International Affairs at the University of Pittsburgh. She is the author of *Justice and the Politics of Difference* (Princeton University Press, 1990), and *Throwing Like a Girl and Other Essays in Feminist Philosophy and Social Theory* (Indiana University Press, 1990). She is currently working on a book on the ideals and problems of democratic communication across group differences.

Introduction

WILL KYMLICKA

Many people hoped that the end of the Cold War would lead to a more peaceful world. Instead, the ideological conflict between capitalism and communism has been replaced with an upsurge in conflicts between ethnic and national groups. Throughout the world, minorities and majorities clash over such issues as language rights, federalism and regional autonomy, political representation, religious freedom, education curriculum, land claims, immigration and naturalization policy, even national symbols such as the choice of national anthem or public holidays.

Resolving these disputes is perhaps the greatest challenge facing democracies today. In Eastern Europe and the Third World, attempts to create liberal democratic institutions are being undermined by violent nationalist conflicts. In the West, volatile disputes over the rights of immigrants, indigenous peoples, and other cultural minorities are throwing into question many of the assumptions which have governed political life for decades. Since the end of the Cold War, ethnocultural conflicts have become the most common source of political violence in the world, and they show no sign of abating.

These conflicts have been studied intensively by sociologists and political scientists.[1] But, until very recently, they have been almost entirely neglected by Western political theorists. Although the Anglo-American world has witnessed a much-celebrated 'rebirth' of normative political philosophy in the 1970s and 1980s—including important new theories of justice, freedom, rights, community, and democracy[2]—the sorts of issues raised by minority cultures have rarely entered these discussions.

This is surprising, since these conflicts raise difficult questions about some of our most basic political principles. For example, most people today subscribe to the ideal of 'democracy'—that is, most people accept that the political authorities governing a particular community should be accountable to its citizens through periodic elections. But this, by itself, does not tell us where the boundaries of a particular community should be drawn. Nor does it tell us how political powers should be distributed between different levels of government (municipal, regional, federal, international).

Yet these are precisely the sorts of questions often in dispute in ethnocultural conflicts, as minorities seek to redraw boundaries or redistribute powers so as to become more 'self-determining'. The value of democracy to a group may differ dramatically depending on how these questions are answered. Rather than tackle these questions directly, however, most contemporary theorists of democracy simply take for granted that the boundaries and powers of a political community have already been settled.

A related question concerns immigration. Democratic theory is typically phrased in terms of the political rights of citizens, but this, by itself, does not tell us who should be allowed to become a citizen. Some countries accept few immigrants, and require a high degree of cultural integration before allowing immigrants to gain citizenship. Other countries have a more open immigration and naturalization policy. These policies are another source of ethnocultural conflict that is largely ignored by political theorists, since the membership of political communities is typically taken as settled within liberal-democratic theory.

Or consider language policy. Liberal theorists debate the role of public education in promoting individual freedom, but in what language should public education be provided? What language should be used in the courts, or when public services are provided? The extent to which these rights and opportunities promote someone's freedom depends, at least in part, on whether they are available in her own language. Similarly, theorists debate the role of shared political deliberations in promoting a sense of community, but in what language should these deliberations be conducted? Are common political deliberations possible in a multilingual society?

Language issues are arguably central to both individual freedom and political community, and questions about language policy are at the heart of ethnocultural conflict in many parts of the world. Yet contemporary political theorists have rarely answered, or even asked, these questions. As Brian Weinstein noted, political theorists have had a lot to say about 'the language of politics'—that is, the symbols, metaphors and rhetorical devices of political discourse—but have had virtually nothing to say about 'the politics of language'—that is, decisions about which languages to use in political, legal, and educational forums.[3]

In short, ethnocultural conflicts often centre on questions which political theorists have simply ignored, from the boundaries and powers of political communities to language rights and immigration and naturalization policies. In the absence of accepted principles, these conflicts are often decided on the basis of brute power—that is, whether the majority has the power to subdue the aspirations of minority cultures, or whether the minority has the power to upset the *status quo*, and wring political concessions for itself. There is very little sense of what would be a just or fair solution to these conflicts.

However, over the last few years, many of the issues raised by ethnocultural movements have come to the foreground of political theory.[4] In part, people are looking to political theory to shed light on these conflicts, and help us identify morally defensible and politically viable solutions to them. But there is also a recognition that these issues can shed light on some of the basic concepts and principles of political theory. Thinking about these issues helps us see that our traditional understandings of liberty, equality, democracy, and justice may rest on unstated assumptions about the ethnic or cultural make-up of the country, assumptions which may be inapplicable in the context of multi-ethnic or multinational states.

This collection brings together seventeen of the most important recent articles by political and legal theorists which explore these normative issues. In selecting these articles, I have tried to choose topics that are unlikely to be covered in more general courses on ethics or applied ethics. For example, at the meta-ethical level, virtually every undergraduate reader in moral philosophy includes a section on moral relativism.[5] Similarly, most applied ethics textbooks include a section on affirmative action for racial minorities or women. While these topics are raised in a number of the articles in this reader, the primary focus is on issues that are more specific to minority cultures, and to the accommodation of cultural differences. These seventeen articles represent just a small fraction of the rapidly growing literature on the rights of minority cultures. The 'Guide to Further Reading' at the end of the volume provides a more comprehensive bibliography.

In focusing on the accommodation of cultural differences, I am taking for granted that a minimal level of tolerance and good will exists amongst the various groups within a state. Needless to say, in many parts of the world, minority groups face enormous discrimination and persecution, even genocide or 'ethnic cleansing', and so are fighting for the minimal set of basic civil and political rights which are at the heart of traditional liberal-democratic theory. For these groups, the sorts of issues addressed here—like language rights, regional autonomy, or group representation—may seem like utopian ideals.

But it is increasingly clear that ethnocultural conflicts have not been resolved simply by ensuring respect for basic individual rights. Minority groups throughout the West are seeking greater recognition and accommodation of their cultural differences. They may even seek to secede, if they think their aspirations cannot be met within the existing state. Of course, every ethnocultural conflict has its own unique history, which makes it difficult to attempt generalizations about the moral principles involved. But there are some basic questions regarding the meaning of freedom and justice in a multi-ethnic state which continually arise in these disputes. These are the issues addressed in this volume.

The collection is organized around five general issues: the place of minority cultures in the Western political tradition; the nature and value of cultural membership; the forms or models of cultural pluralism; the relationship between individual and group rights; the political representation of minority groups. The collection concludes with a section discussing four specific controversies that help illustrate these general themes—namely, debates over international law, religious toleration, immigration, and secession.

1. Minority Cultures in Western Political Theory

One of the pioneers in the study of the rights of ethnic groups is Vernon Van Dyke, and his 1977 article still provides a useful summary of the sorts of challenges minority cultures raise for political theory.[6] As Van Dyke shows, the neglect of minority cultures is not a new phenomenon, but has deep roots in the Western political tradition.

Van Dyke focuses in particular on the liberal tradition, and its assumption that the fundamental issue for political theory is the proper relation between the individual and the state. He argues that the relentless individualism of the traditional liberal approach makes it incapable of explaining some of the inherently collective features of political life, including the formation of the state itself or the drawing of political boundaries. To answer these questions, Van Dyke suggests, liberals typically, but implicitly, introduce assumptions about the way individuals are organized into groups. Hence liberal theorists have often taken for granted that citizens feel themselves to constitute a distinct group, sharing a common language and a common desire to live together, and that this community has organized itself into a state through some form of 'social contract'.

The problem, Van Dyke notes, is that in many countries two or more ethnocultural communities cohabit a single state. According to recent estimates, the world's 184 independent states contain over 600 living language groups and 5,000 ethnic groups. In very few countries can the citizens be said to share the same language, or belong to the same ethno-national group.[7] Because liberalism ignores the group basis of political life, Van Dyke argues, it is blind to the injustices suffered by minority cultures, which can only be rectified by supplementing liberalism with a theory of collective rights.

Van Dyke argues that the flaw in the liberal tradition is its individualism, which cannot accord any status to groups between the individual and the state. Yet, as the article by Ephraim Nimni notes, we find a very similar pattern in the Marxist tradition. Indeed, Marxists have, if anything, been more indifferent or hostile to the claims of minority cultures. Marx and Engels accepted the right of 'the great national subdivisions of Europe' to independence, and hence supported the unification of France, Italy, Poland, and Germany; and the independence of England, Hungary, Spain, and Russia. But they rejected the idea that the smaller 'nationalities' had any such right, such as the Czechs, Croats, Basques, Welsh, Bulgarians, Romanians, and Slovenes. These smaller 'nationalities' were expected to assimilate to one of the 'great nations', without the benefit of any minority rights, whether it be language rights or national autonomy.

Socialist hostility to minority rights is often explained in terms of its commitment to 'internationalism'. As Marx famously said in *The Communist Manifesto*, the proletariat have no nationality—they are workers of the world. Marxists often view cultural or national divisions as temporary stopping-points on the way to being citizens of the world.

So it seems that liberal individualism and socialist internationalism have both led to a denial of the rights of minority cultures. In both cases, however, this denial is exacerbated by an ethnocentric denigration of smaller cultures, and a belief that progress requires assimilating them into larger cultures. Compare the following quotes from J. S. Mill and Engels:

> Experience proves it is possible for one nationality to merge and be absorbed in another: and when it was originally an inferior and more backward portion of the human race the absorption is greatly to its advantage. Nobody can suppose that it is not more beneficial to a Breton, or a Basque of French Navarre, to be brought into the current of the ideas and feelings of a highly civilised and cultivated people—to be a member of the French nationality, admitted on equal terms to all the privileges of French citizenship . . . than to sulk on his own rocks, the half-savage relic of past times, revolving in his own little mental orbit, without participation or interest in the general movement of the world. The same remark applies to the Welshman or the Scottish Highlander as members of the British nation.[8]
>
> There is no country in Europe which does not have in some corner or other one or several fragments of peoples, the remnants of a former population that was suppressed and held in bondage by the nation which later became the main vehicle for historical development. These relics of nations, mercilessly trampled down by the passage of history, as Hegel expressed it, this ethnic trash always become fanatical standard bearers of counterrevolution and remain so until their complete extirpation or loss of their national character, just as their whole existence in general is itself a protest against a great historical revolution. Such in Scotland are the Gaels... Such in France are the Bretons... Such in Spain are the Basques.[9]

For both liberals and Marxists in the nineteenth century, the great nations, with their highly centralized political and economic structures, were the carriers of historical development. The smaller nationalities were backward and stagnant, and could only participate in modernity by abandoning their national character and assimilating to a great nation. Attempts to maintain minority languages were misguided, for German was 'the language of liberty' for the Czechs in Bohemia, just as French was the language of liberty for the Bretons, and English was the language of liberty for the Québécois in Canada.[10]

N.B. This sort of view was very widespread in the nineteenth century. Indeed, Hobsbawm claims that it is 'sheer anachronism' to criticize Mill or Marx for holding it, since it was shared by virtually all theorists in the nineteenth century, on both the right and left. This view provided a justification not only for assimilating minorities within European states, but also for colonizing other peoples overseas.[11]

It is this conception of historical development, more than anything else, which has shaped traditional liberal and Marxist opposition to the rights of minority cultures. It seems misleading, then, to explain this opposition in terms of liberal 'individualism' or socialist 'internationalism'. Instead, it reflects a rather blatant form of ethnocentric nationalism. Mill and Marx did not reject all group identities between the individual and the state. Rather, they privileged a particular sort of group—the 'great nation'—and denigrated smaller cultures. They did not express an indifference to people's cultural identities or group loyalties. Rather, they insisted that progress and civilization required assimilating 'backward' minorities to 'energetic' majorities.

This assumption—which was central to most discussions of minority cultures in the nineteenth century, and the first part of the twentieth[12]—has gradually been abandoned. The claim that the Czechs were incapable of participating in the modern world except by assimilating into the German nation has been proven wrong. The Flemish, Québécois, and Basques have also successfully resisted assimilation, and now form vibrant modern societies. But the influence of this nineteenth-century view remains with us, I believe, and unconsciously continues to affect how many people respond to minority rights.[13] Given the way the Western political tradition has either neglected or denigrated the claims of minority cultures, theorists today are increasingly recognizing that we need to examine these issues anew, starting from scratch, as it were. The remaining essays in the collection can be seen as steps in that direction.

2. Cultural Membership

In rethinking the issue of minority rights, the first task is to come to a clearer understanding of the nature of cultural groups, and the value of belonging to such groups. What role do these groups play in people's lives, and how are people affected if these groups become subject to assimilation or other forms of instability?

Avishai Margalit and Joseph Raz argue that membership in a 'pervasive culture' is crucial to people's well-being for two reasons. The first is that cultural membership provides people with meaningful choices about how to lead their lives, in the sense that 'familiarity with a culture determines the boundaries of the imaginable'. Hence if a culture is decaying or discriminated against, 'the options and opportunities open to its members will shrink, become less attractive, and their pursuit less likely to be successful'.

Of course, the members of a decaying culture could integrate into another culture, but Margalit and Raz argue that this is difficult, not only because it is 'a very slow process indeed', but also because of the role of cultural membership in people's self-identity. Cultural membership has a 'high social profile', in the sense that it affects how others perceive and respond to us, which in turn shapes our self-identity. Moreover, cultural identity is particularly suited to serving as the 'primary foci of identification', because it is based on belonging not accomplishment:

> Identification is more secure, less liable to be threatened, if it does not depend on accomplishment. Although accomplishments play their role in people's sense of their own identity, it would seem that at the most fundamental level our sense of our own identity depends on criteria of belonging rather than on those of accomplishment. Secure identification at that level is particularly important to one's well-being.

Hence cultural identity provides an 'anchor for [people's] self-identification and the safety of effortless secure belonging'. But this in turn means that people's self-respect is bound up with the esteem in which their national group is held. If a culture is not generally respected, then the dignity and self-respect of its members will also be threatened.[14]

Jeremy Waldron rejects these claims, and insists that defenders of minority rights exaggerate our dependence on particular cultural groups. He defends what he calls the 'cosmopolitan alternative'. On this view, people can pick and choose 'cultural fragments' that come from a variety of ethnocultural sources, without feeling any sense of membership in or dependence on a particular culture. In the modern world, people live 'in a kaleidoscope of culture', moving freely amongst the products of innumerable cultural traditions. Each person's life incorporates a melange of such cultural fragments, including, say, Inuit art, Chinese food, German folklore, and Judeo-Christian religion.

Indeed, Waldron questions whether there really are such things as distinct cultures. The globalization of trade, the increase in human mobility, and the development of international institutions and communications have made it impossible to say where one culture begins and another ends. The only way to preserve a distinct culture intact, he argues, would be to artificially cut it off from the general course of human events. As Waldron puts it, the only way to preserve the 'authenticity' or 'integrity' of a particular culture would be to adopt a wholly inauthentic way of life—one which denied the overwhelming reality of cultural interchange and global interdependence.[15]

Waldron takes himself to be criticizing 'communitarian' conceptions of the self, which view people as embedded in particular cultures, in contrast to more liberal conceptions of the self, which emphasize the ability of individuals to question and revise inherited ways of life. And many commentators have supposed that defenders of minority rights are likely to endorse the communitarian critique of liberal individualism.[16]

Yet it is interesting to note that Raz and Margalit view themselves as liberals, and share Waldron's commitment to the importance of human freedom.[17] Indeed, their views may not be as far apart as they initially seem. For it is possible to read Waldron as objecting primarily to the idea that our choices and self-identity are defined by our ethnic descent. For example, he suggests that a Québécois who eats Chinese food and reads Grimm's Fairy Tales to her child while listening to Italian opera is living in 'a kaleidoscope of cultures', since these cultural practices originated in different ethnic groups.

Raz and Margalit, on the other hand, argue that cultures should be defined in terms of such things as a common language and shared history, and these do not preclude the incorporation of new ideas and practices from other parts of the world. On this view, the Québécois form a distinct culture in North America because of their distinct language and history. The fact that some Québécois now eat Chinese food and listen to Italian opera does not mean that they cease to form a distinct culture. It simply means that the 'encompassing group' they belong to is an open and pluralistic one, which borrows whatever it finds worthwhile in other cultures, integrates it into its own practices, and passes it on to their children.

Waldron worries that this process of cultural interchange will be dramatically hindered if we accept the principle that the 'authenticity' of minority cultures should be protected through minority rights. But defenders of minority rights are rarely seeking to preserve their 'authentic' culture, if that means living the same way that their ancestors did centuries ago, unable to learn from other peoples and cultures. What the Québécois or Flemish want, for example, is to preserve their existence as a culturally distinct group—always adapting and transforming their culture, of course, but resisting the pressure to abandon entirely their group life and assimilate into the larger society. In short, these minority cultures wish to be cosmopolitan, and embrace the cultural interchange Waldron emphasizes, without accepting Waldron's own 'cosmopolitan alternative', which denies that people have any deep bond to their own language and cultural community.[18]

3. Forms of Cultural Pluralism

While theorists disagree over the importance of cultural identity, very few today would endorse Engels's view that minority cultures and languages should be suppressed with 'iron ruthlessness'. There is broad agreement that cultural identities should be tolerated and accommodated, at least to some degree, in a free and democratic society.

But what does it mean to accommodate cultural identities? Both Nathan Glazer and Michael Walzer distinguish two broad forms or models for accommodating ethnocultural diversity. One model rests on the 'non-discrimination principle'. On this view, cultural identity should neither be supported nor penalized by public policy. Rather, the expression and perpetuation of cultural identities should be left to the private sphere.

As Walzer notes, this model is, in effect, an extension of the way religious minorities are treated in liberal states. In the sixteenth century, European states were being torn apart by conflict between Catholics and Protestants over which religion should rule the land. These conflicts were finally resolved, not by granting special rights to particular religious minorities, but by separating church and state, and entrenching each's individual freedom of religion. Religious minorities are protected *indirectly*, by guaranteeing individual freedom of worship, so that people can freely associate with other co-religionists, without fear of state discrimination or disapproval.

The non-discrimination model extends this principle to ethnocultural differences as well. Ethnic identity, like religion, is something which people should be free to express in their private life, but which is not the concern of the state. The state does not oppose the freedom of people to express their particular cultural attachments, but nor does it nurture such expression—rather, as Glazer elsewhere puts it, the state responds with 'salutary neglect'.[19] The members of ethnic and national groups are protected against discrimination and prejudice, and they are free to try to maintain whatever part of their ethnic heritage or identity they wish, consistent with the rights of others. But their efforts are purely private, and it is not the place of public agencies to attach legal identities or disabilities to cultural membership or ethnic identity.

The second model, by contrast, involves public measures aimed at protecting or promoting an ethnocultural identity. These measures include language rights, regional autonomy, land claims, guaranteed representation, veto rights, etc. Walzer calls this the 'corporatist' model, Glazer calls it the 'group rights' model. This model requires that the government identify specific groups, and perhaps even assign individuals to those groups, in order to determine who should exercise these group rights.

This distinction between 'non-discrimination' and 'group rights' is a familiar one in the literature. But the distinction is often difficult to draw in practice. According to Walzer, the non-discrimination model involves a 'sharp divorce of state and ethnicity'. The state stands above all the various ethnic and national groups in the country, 'refusing to endorse or support their ways of life or to take an active interest in their social reproduction'. Instead, the state is 'neutral with reference to [the] language, history, literature, calendar' of these groups. He says the clearest example of such a neutral state is the United States.[20]

But is the United States neutral with respect to language, for example, or history, or the calendar? English is the language of public schools in the United States, and of court proceedings, and of welfare agencies. Government legislation and regulations are printed in English. Immigrants to the United States are required to learn English before acquiring citizenship, and to learn something about the history of the country. Children in the United States are also legally required to learn English and American history. Every country must make these sorts of decisions about government languages, school curricula, and naturalization policies.[21] They must also make decisions about public holidays, which in Western countries (including the United States) have almost invariably accorded with the Christian calendar (for example, schools and government offices are closed on Sundays, Easter and Christmas are holidays, etc.).

N.B. What Walzer calls the 'neutral state' can be seen, in effect, as a system of 'group rights' that supports the majority's language, history, culture, and calendar. Government policy systematically encourages everyone to learn English, and to view their life-choices as tied to participation in English-language institutions.[22] This is a system of 'non-discrimination', in the sense that minority groups are not discriminated against within the mainstream institutions of the majority culture, but it is not 'neutral' in its relationship to cultural identities.

Conversely, what Glazer calls the 'group rights' model can be seen, in effect, as a more robust form of non-discrimination. After all, when Spanish-speakers in the United States or francophones in Canada seek language rights, they are not asking for some sort of special 'group right' not accorded to English-speakers. They are simply asking for the same sort of rights taken for granted by the majority culture.

Glazer and Walzer raise a number of important worries about the possible impact of endorsing minority rights, including the heightened potential for ethnic conflict. According to Glazer, the non-discrimination model is appropriate whenever the government aims at integrating disparate groups into a single national culture, based on a common language, shared history, and political institutions. On the other hand, the group rights model is appropriate if a society operates on the assumption 'that it is a confederation of groups, that group membership is central and permanent, and that the divisions between groups are such that it is unrealistic or unjust to envisage these group identities weakening in time to be replaced by a common citizenship'.

On Glazer's view, then, the choice between non-discrimination and group rights is really a choice between forming a common national culture, or accepting the permanent existence of two or more national cultures within a single state. Glazer insists that the United States has firmly adopted the former as its goal, and indeed it has had enormous success in integrating people of many different races and religions into its common culture. Yet in many parts of the world this sort of integration seems unthinkable, and minority groups are insistent on viewing the larger state as a 'confederation of groups'.

What explains this difference? According to Walzer, the key reason why the non-discrimination model has worked in the United States, despite its inherently integrative dynamic, is that the ethnic minorities are *immigrant* groups. Immigrants have made a painful choice to leave their original culture, and know that the success of their decision will depend on integrating into the mainstream of their new society. Walzer calls this 'New World' pluralism, where ethnic diversity arises from the voluntary decisions of individuals or families to uproot themselves and join another society.[23]

This is very different, Walzer argues, from 'Old World' pluralism, where minority cultures are territorially concentrated, settled on their historic homelands. These groups find themselves in a minority position, not because they have uprooted themselves from their homeland, but because their homeland has been incorporated within the boundaries of a larger state. This incorporation is usually involuntary, resulting from conquest, or colonization, or the ceding of territory from one imperial power to another. Under these circumstances, minorities are rarely satisfied with non-discrimination and eventual integration. What they desire, Walzer says, is 'national liberation'—that is, some form of collective self-government, in order to ensure the continued development of their distinct culture.

Of course, as Walzer notes, there are some minority groups in the New World which are not immigrant groups, and indeed which fit the Old World pattern. For example, the indigenous peoples of North America were colonized or conquered, and their homelands involuntarily incorporated into a larger state. The Québécois and Puerto Ricans were also involuntarily incorporated into Canada and the United States respectively. And these groups indeed bear out Walzer's hypothesis, since they have strongly resisted integration, and are the only groups which have generated nationalist movements within North America.[24]

This points to an important ambiguity in the fashionable term 'multiculturalism'. This term is often used to cover all forms of ethnic diversity, but, as Walzer shows, there is a profound difference between the sort of diversity created by the voluntary immigration of individuals and families, and the sort of diversity created by involuntarily incorporating entire cultures which have no desire to give up their status as separate and self-governing peoples. As we will see below, some immigrant groups have raised their own demands for certain sorts of 'group rights', and are dissatisfied with the non-discrimination model (see 'Controversies' below). But they are generally seeking a renegotiation of the terms of integration, so as to allow for greater accommodation of their ethnic particularity within the dominant institutions of the mainstream society. They are not rejecting integration entirely and seeking the sort of self-government associated with 'Old World' national groups.

The two models, then, are typically associated with different sorts of groups—immigrants and incorporated cultures—and two different sorts of aims—integration and self-government. In her article, Iris Marion Young attempts to describe another option, which she calls the 'relational' theory of difference. According to Young, discussions of multi-ethnic states too often alternate between two extremes—assimilation (which she associates with liberal individualism) and separatism (which she associates with xenophobic nationalism). The former denies the reality of cultural differences, and the need for their political expression; the latter defines cultural differences exclusively, as 'the Other'. Separatists define themselves as not only different from, but as entirely opposed to, and superior to, the members of other cultures. The inevitable result is to encourage secession, or at any rate to preclude meaningful co-operation and interchange between groups.

Young's 'relational' account of difference attempts to accommodate the reality of cultural differences, while still encouraging interdependence, and promoting a more fluid and permeable conception of the boundaries between groups. Part of the solution, she argues, is to create a 'heterogenous public'—one which brings groups together as groups, and which encourages the expression of group differences, but within common institutions and a shared commitment to the larger political order.[25] She then applies this account to two case studies—the disintegration of the former Yugoslavia, where nationalist separatism undermined any possibility of mutual co-operation, and Maori demands for 'biculturalism' in New

Zealand, which she sees as a promising, if incomplete, instantiation of the 'relational' conception of cultural diversity.

There are almost as many models of cultural diversity as there are multi-ethnic states. Each such state has developed its own unique response to cultural diversity, and recent studies provide many interesting examples of the successes and failures of particular policies and institutions.[26] To some extent, recent theoretical accounts of minority rights are still trying to assimilate the rich variety of political experiments involving minority rights around the world. As Young rightly insists, we shouldn't be locked into preconceived beliefs about how states must be structured, or into over-simplified dichotomies of assimilation or separation.

4. Individual Rights and Group Rights

Both Van Dyke and Glazer describe minority rights as 'group rights' or 'collective rights'. For many people, the idea of 'group rights' is both mysterious and disturbing. For how can groups have rights that are not ultimately reducible to the rights of their individual members? And if groups do have rights, won't these rights inherently conflict with individual rights?

In her article, Darlene Johnston surveys recent analyses of group rights, to see how the term 'group' is defined, and in what sense these groups have rights.[27] She notes that on most accounts of group rights, the relevant sorts of groups are 'natural' or 'involuntary' ones, in that people are typically born into them. Moreover, these groups are bound together by significant and 'multidimensional' relationships of mutual interdependence, recognition, and obligation.

'Groups', then, must be distinguished both from artificial or random categories of people who have no shared life together, such as people whose last name begins with K, and from voluntary associations or contractual associations, such as recreational groups or business firms. According to Johnston, once we recognize the extent to which people's well-being is tied up with the groups they belong to, then we should recognize the existence of certain group rights, not reducible to individual rights, including the right to self-preservation. She then applies this theory to the case of native Indians in Canada, and argues that the group right to self-preservation provides important support for their land claims.[28]

Michael Hartney offers a more critical perspective on group rights. He accepts that membership in a group or community is often of great value to individuals, but argues that this claim does not by itself show that groups should have rights. He points to a number of potential confusions in discussing collective rights, including different senses of 'rights' (for example, legal versus moral rights), and different senses of 'collective' (for example, rights can be exercised collectively, or be exercised to seek a collective benefit). But in all these cases, he argues, the moral justification for a particular right rests on its value to particular individuals, and so it is a mistake to say that the right 'inheres' in the group. Moreover, talk of group rights is dangerous. According to Hartney, saying that we are limiting individual rights in the name of group rights obscures the real situation, which is that we are giving precedence to some individuals' interests over others.

Both Johnston and Hartney raise familiar questions about the priority (moral, ontological, formative) of the individual and the community, and hence about the relative priority of individual rights and collective rights. Yet, as Hartney notes in passing, there are two importantly different cases here. In some cases, a minority culture is demanding rights against the larger society, to protect it from the economic or political decisions of the larger population. In other cases, a minority culture is demanding rights against its own members, to protect its traditional way of life against individual dissent.

Both of these are often described as group rights or collective rights, but they raise quite different issues. The former concerns the relationship between groups, and the claim is that justice between minority and majority cultures requires certain 'collective rights' which reduce the minority's vulnerability to the decisions of the majority. The latter concerns the relationship between the group and its own members, and the claim is that cultural self-preservation requires certain 'collective rights' which limit the freedom of individual members to reject or revise traditional ways of life. To distinguish these two sorts of claims, we could call the former 'external protections', and the latter 'internal restrictions'.[29]

These two claims often go together, but they need not. For example, Chandran Kukathas defends the right of minority cultures to impose many internal restrictions on the freedom of their members, so long as members retain one essential liberty—the right to exit. He recognizes the possibility that this may lead to injustice—for example, a group may deny education or economic opportunities to women, or may discriminate on the basis of sexual orientation or religious belief. But he thinks that the right to exit reduces the danger of such injustice, and that any attempt to force minority cultures to reorganize themselves in accordance with liberal-egalitarian norms would be intolerant.

Yet Kukathas is sceptical of the view that minorities have any claim to special powers or resources to provide external protections *vis-à-vis* the larger society. To provide such external rights, he argues, would artificially fix what would naturally be fluid and constantly changing boundaries between groups, and would also change the nature of the power relations within each group.

In his article, Leslie Green defends what is essentially the opposite position to Kukathas. He accepts that minority cultures often have a legitimate claim to external protections, so as to promote the good of cultural membership. But he insists that the very same reasons which argue in favour of external protections for minority cultures also argue against internal restrictions against dissenting members within the group (what he calls 'internal minorities'). Just as minority cultures should be protected from pressure to assimilate to the majority culture, so internal subgroups should not be forced to comply with the traditional norms and practices of the group. For example, women or homosexuals within a minority culture should not be oppressed or discriminated against. In contrast to Kukathas, Green explicitly rejects the view that the right to exit makes such unjust treatment permissible.

It is interesting to note that both Kukathas and Green view themselves as liberals. And indeed one way to characterize this dispute is in terms of two competing accounts of what the fundamental value is within liberal theory. For some people, the fundamental liberal value is tolerance, including tolerance of non-liberal groups (so long as they allow a right of exit). For others, the basic liberal value is autonomy, and so a liberal state should ensure that all citizens have the liberties and resources needed to make informed decisions about the good life, including the right to question and revise traditional cultural practices.

There is in fact a lively debate amongst contemporary liberals about whether autonomy or tolerance has pride of place within liberal theory. This contrast is described in different ways—for example, a contrast between 'Enlightenment' and 'Reformation' liberalism, or between 'comprehensive' and 'political' liberalism, or between 'Kantian' and '*modus vivendi*' liberalism.[30] Underneath all these contrasts is a similar concern—namely, that there are many groups within the boundaries of liberal states which do not value personal autonomy, and which restrict the ability of their members to question and dissent from traditional practices. Basing liberal theory on autonomy threatens to alienate these groups, and undermine their allegiance to liberal institutions, whereas a tolerance-based liberalism can provide a more secure and wider basis for the legitimacy of government. Yet basing liberalism on tolerance abandons the traditional liberal concern with individual freedom of choice, and threatens to condemn individuals or subgroups within minority cultures to traditional roles that may be unsatisfying and indeed oppressive. The debate between Kukathas and Green, therefore, provides a concrete illustration of an important debate within liberal political philosophy more generally.

5. Minority Cultures and Democratic Theory

One of the most common demands of minority cultures is for greater representation within the political process. In some cases, this is simply a demand that mainstream political parties be made more inclusive, by reducing the barriers which inhibit the members of minority groups from becoming party candidates or leaders (for example, public funding of nomination campaign expenses, or establishing search committees within each party to help identify and nominate potential candidates from minority groups).

But there is also increased interest in the idea that minorities should be guaranteed a certain level of representation in the political process. Arend Lijphart discusses one of the more familiar forms of group-based political representation—namely, consociationalism. Under a scheme of consociational democracy or 'power-sharing', each group is guaranteed a place in the cabinet, which therefore becomes a 'grand coalition', as well as a degree of proportionality in other areas of the political and bureaucratic process. Moreover, minority groups have a veto over certain basic issues that affect their vital interests.

Lijphart argues that this system helps ensure basic fairness in political decision-making, and prevents democracy from degenerating into a system of majority tyranny.[31] But one danger with consociationalism, or any other form of group representation, is that it requires someone to decide what the relevant groups are, and who belongs to which group. In some cases, this may be relatively uncontroversial, but in other cases it may be a source of great conflict, and of manipulation. Lijphart discusses the case of apartheid in South Africa, where people were officially assigned to artificial ethnic and racial categories as part of the general system of white domination. To avoid this danger, Lijphart discusses an alternative form of consociationalism, in which groups would be free to organize themselves into separate political parties, which would then be elected on the basis of a system of proportional representation. This, he argues, would combine the benefits of minority representation with the benefits of authentic and consensual, rather than coercively imposed, group self-identification.

Lijphart describes this alternative as a form of 'self-determination', in contrast to the traditional consociational pattern which involves the 'pre-determination' of groups. As Lijphart notes, this usage of 'self-determination' is very different from the more familiar idea of 'national self-determination', in which a national minority seeks greater self-government, either through an independent state or some other form of territorial autonomy. Demands for national self-government reflect a desire to reduce the power of the larger state over the national minority, either through secession or decentralized federalism. National self-determination involves taking power away from the central legislature and giving it to some other body which is controlled by the national minority. What Lijphart refers to as 'self-determination', by contrast, involves giving self-identified groups greater influence *within* the central legislature. It gives more power to the minority within the central legislature, rather than giving national minorities more power to govern themselves separate and apart from the central legislature.[32]

Anne Phillips discusses similar issues from a feminist standpoint. She notes that contemporary feminist theory has decisively rejected the 'abstract individualism' of liberal theory, which ignores or denies the profound (and profoundly different) ways that people are shaped by their physical embodiment and social environment. This has led many feminists, like Iris Marion Young, to insist on the need for proper representation of social groups, such as ethnic and racial minorities, as well as women and other disadvantaged groups.[33] But Phillips, like Lijphart, worries about how these groups are defined, and whether group representation will encourage the 'freezing' or 'closure' of group identities, and discourage people from adopting a wider perspective that takes into account the interests of other groups, and the common good of the society.

Moreover, Phillips raises important questions about accountability within group-based quota systems which guarantee a certain number of seats in the legislature for the members of various groups. There is often no mechanism to hold these legislators accountable to the members of the group they supposedly represent, and no way to determine what the group's members actually want. As Phillips puts it, 'Accountability is always the other side of representation, and, in the absence of procedures for establishing what any group wants or thinks, we cannot usefully talk of their political representation'.

While expressing scepticism about recent proposals for group representation, Phillips none the less insists that the underrepresentation of minority groups is a serious issue that must be addressed if political decisions are to be fair, and democratic procedures are to be legitimate.[34]

6. Controversies

The final articles discuss four specific debates about the rights of minority cultures, which help illustrate some of the broader themes and perspectives discussed in the other articles. James Anaya discusses recent attempts to entrench minority rights within international law, including international declarations of human rights. As he notes, existing international law, particularly since World War II, has been based primarily on the non-discrimination model (see 'Forms of Cultural Pluralism' above). There is relatively little recognition in international law of substantive minority rights, such as rights to self-government.

It is interesting to note that minority rights did receive some international recognition under the 'minority protection' scheme of the League of Nations. However, this scheme was badly abused by the Nazis, who encouraged German minorities in Czechoslovakia and Poland to escalate their demands for minority rights. When the Czechoslovak and Polish governments were unable or unwilling to accept these demands, the Nazis used this as a pretext for invasion. As a result, when the United Nations adopted its Universal Declaration of Human Rights, all references to the rights of ethnic and national minorities were deleted. The hope was that the new emphasis on 'human rights'—and in particular, the principle of non-discrimination—would resolve minority conflicts. Rather than protecting vulnerable groups directly, through special rights for the members of designated groups, cultural minorities would be protected indirectly, by guaranteeing basic civil and political rights to all individuals regardless of group membership.

However, it has become increasingly clear that existing human rights standards are simply unable to resolve some of the most important and controversial questions relating to cultural minorities. The right to free speech does not tell us what an appropriate language policy is; the right to vote doesn't tell us how political boundaries should be drawn, or how powers should be distributed between levels of government; the right to mobility doesn't tell us what an appropriate immigration and naturalization policy is. These questions have been left to the usual process of majoritarian decision-making within each state. The result has been to render cultural minorities vulnerable to significant injustice at the hands of the majority, and to exacerbate ethnocultural conflict.

As a result, there is increasing interest at the international level in supplementing traditional human rights principles with a theory of minority rights. For example, the Conference on Security and Cooperation in Europe adopted a declaration on the Rights of National Minorities in 1991, and established a High Commissioner on National Minorities in 1993. The United Nations has been debating both a Declaration on the Rights of Persons Belonging to National or Ethnic, Religious and Linguistic Minorities (1993), and a Draft Universal Declaration on Indigenous Rights (1988). The Council of Europe adopted a declaration on minority language rights in 1992 (the European Charter for Regional or Minority Languages).[35]

Yet, as Anaya discusses, there are serious impediments to this project of incorporating minority rights into international law. Many minority demands are tied to claims of historical sovereignty. For example, many indigenous peoples claim that they were involuntarily incorporated into larger states, and that their historical rights of self-government should now be restored. But it would be difficult, and potentially destabilizing, for international law to accept such an argument, since the origins of virtually every state, and virtually every political boundary, are tainted by conquest or other injustices.

Other minority demands are based on the idea that the right to a cultural identity should itself be one of the basic human rights. But, Anaya argues, this idea contradicts the essential individualism of Western political theory, which views human rights as rights that are independent of group membership. Moreover, claims to self-government challenge traditional conceptions of state sovereignty. Hence, Anaya concludes, it is unlikely that ethnic and national minorities will get much support in the near future from international law.

Bhikhu Parekh discusses what is perhaps the most famous dispute in recent years relating to a minority culture—namely, demands by Muslims in Britain (and elsewhere) for the banning of Salman Rushdie's *The Satanic Verses*, and their response to the *fatwa* (death sentence) imposed on Rushdie by the Islamic rulers in Iran.[36] It was this case, perhaps more than any other single event, which has led people in the West to think carefully about the nature of 'multiculturalism', and the extent to which the claims of minority cultures can or should be accommodated within a liberal-democratic regime.

The *fatwa* was almost universally condemned in the West, including by many Muslim groups. Yet, Parekh argues, the fact that Rushdie's book was found blasphemous and offensive to many Muslims is significant, and raises important issues about the nature of a multi-ethnic society. In particular, Parekh raises four issues: (i) whether the integration of immigrants is a one-way process, in which immigrants are expected to learn and accept the norms and customs of the host society, or a two-way process of accommodation, in which the members of the host society also learn and respect the norms and customs of the immigrants; (ii) whether Western democracies are truly 'neutral' in their treatment of religious groups, or whether there is not an implicit or explicit privileging of Christianity—for example, in the choice of public holidays, or other public symbols and laws; (iii) whether laws against libel, which currently only protect individuals, should be extended to protect groups from various forms of defamation or hate speech; (iv) whether traditional accounts of the moral grounds of free speech have not focused too much on the benefits to the speaker, and ignored some of the costs and harms which may fall on the listener.

Parekh suggests that while the Rushdie affair may subside, these four issues will grow in importance as Western countries become more multi-ethnic and multiracial as a result of immigration. While immigrant groups rarely if ever seek the same sort of national self-government sought by incorporated cultures, it is increasingly clear that they none the less are not necessarily satisfied with the traditional non-discrimination model.

Given the many controversies and conflicts which arise in multi-ethnic and multinational states, some people have expressed a nostalgia for the sort of culturally homogeneous political units which supposedly existed in earlier times, before the rise of multination empires and of transnational migration. In reality, culturally homogeneous polities have always been the exception rather than the rule, a testament to the ubiquity of both military conquest and long-distance trade in human history.[37]

However, while multi-ethnic states are the norm, there are ways that states can attempt to limit or reduce ethnocultural diversity. One obvious technique is forced expulsion (or 'ethnic cleansing'), like the expulsion of ethnic Germans from Czechoslovakia after World War II, or of Asians from Uganda in the 1970s. This is firmly prohibited by international human rights doctrines, although it still occurs, as recent events in the former Yugoslavia show.

But there are at least two other techniques for limiting ethnocultural diversity that need not violate human rights. First, a country with a territorially concentrated minority group—like the former Czechoslovakia—can allow or encourage secession, so that a single multination state becomes two states, each with a higher degree of cultural homogeneity. Second, a country that is more or less culturally homogeneous, like Iceland, can try to maintain its homogeneity by closing its borders to immigrants. The final two papers in the collection address the morality of secession, and of limiting immigration.

Allen Buchanan argues that there are some circumstances when a territorially concentrated minority culture can legitimately demand a right to secede. However, he thinks that this is a very limited right. In particular, he rejects the idea that a minority culture can secede simply to more fully express or develop its distinct culture. He argues that 'cultural preservation' can only justify secession if the culture is literally imperiled—condemned to assimilation—and if there are no alternative means to protect the culture within the larger state (for example, through federalism, or other minority rights). It is impossible for every ethnocultural group to have its own state, Buchanan argues, given the scarcity of territory and the intermingling of cultures, and so stringent conditions must be placed on groups that demand such a state.[38]

In any event, secession will rarely if ever achieve complete homogeneity. The breakup of Czechoslovakia still leaves Slovak and German minorities in the Czech Republic, and Czech and Hungarian minorities in Slovakia, amongst other minorities. If Quebec were to secede, so as to protect and promote the Québécois culture, the new state would have several indigenous peoples within its borders (including the Mohawks, Cree, and Inuit), as well as a long-settled anglophone community, and immigrant groups from all over the world. So even if we accept that secession is sometimes a legitimate option for minority cultures, this will just rearrange which groups fall within which states. It cannot create a world of homogeneous states.

Short of ethnic cleansing, it is difficult for states to reduce the existing degree of ethnocultural diversity. But states can at least limit new sources of ethnocultural diversity, by closing their borders to immigration. The scope of immigration into Western countries increased dramatically in the post-war era, as states sought to expand their workforces.[39] But many countries are now cutting back on their immigration levels, and some countries never accepted the idea that foreigners should be able to take up residence in their countries and become citizens.

The right of states to determine their own immigration levels is widely accepted, both under international law and by the general public. And the fear that an influx of immigrants may change the cultural fabric of the country is often taken as a legitimate reason for restricting the number of immigrants. But as Joseph Carens discusses, there are serious moral questions about this practice of closing borders. Indeed, Carens argues that basic liberal principles of freedom and equality preclude any limits on immigration, other than minimal restrictions to maintain public order. He examines three of the most popular theoretical foundations for liberalism—namely, utilitarianism, Nozick's libertarianism, and Rawls's liberal egalitarianism—and argues that none provide any grounds for restricting the right of aliens to enter and take up residence in a country, share in its wealth, and participate in its political process. The rights of citizenship, he argues, should be a basic right available to all who desire them, not a privilege granted only to those who happen to be born in that country.[40]

If Buchanan and Carens are right, then we cannot hope to avoid ethnocultural diversity by closing or redrawing borders. We have no choice but to learn to live with cultural pluralism, and to devise strategies for coexistence that are consistent with principles of freedom, justice, and democracy.

Notes

1. See, for example, Ted Gurr, *Minorities at Risk: A Global View of Ethnopolitical Conflict* (Institute of Peace Press, Washington, 1993); Donald Horowitz, *Ethnic Groups in Conflict* (University of California Press, Berkeley, 1985); Joseph Montville (ed.), *Conflict and Peacemaking in Multiethnic Societies* (Lexington Books, Washington, 1990).
2. For surveys of this work, see Raymond Plant, *Modern Political Thought* (Blackwell, Oxford, 1991), and my *Contemporary Political Philosophy* (Oxford University Press, Oxford, 1990).
3. Brian Weinstein, *The Civic Tongue: Political Consequences of Language Choices* (Longman, New York, 1983): 7–13. Language rights are a cause of political conflict in Canada, Belgium, Bulgaria, Spain, Sri Lanka, the Baltics, Turkey, and many other countries (Horowitz, *Ethnic Groups*: 219–24).
4. The rights of minority cultures are often raised as part of a broader discussion of 'the politics of difference', which includes gender, sexual orientation, disability, etc. See, for example, Iris Marion Young, *Justice and the Politics of Difference* (Princeton University Press, Princeton, 1990); Martha Minow, *Making all the Difference: Inclusion, Exclusion and American Law* (Cornell University Press, Ithaca, 1990); William Connolly, *Identity/Difference: Democratic Negotiations of Political Paradox* (Cornell University Press, Ithaca, 1991).
5. For a recent discussion of cultural relativism, see Amy Gutmann, 'The Challenge of Multiculturalism to Political Ethics', *Philosophy and Public Affairs* 22/3 (1993): 171–206. On affirmative action, see Michel Rosenfeld, *Affirmative Action and Justice: A Philosophical and Constitutional Inquiry* (Yale University Press, New Haven, 1991); Robert Fullinwider, *The Reverse Discrimination Controversy* (Rowman and Allenheld, Totawa, 1980).
6. Van Dyke published a number of articles throughout the 1970s and 1980s on the rights of minority cultures, at a time when few people saw these as important issues for political theory. In addition to the article reprinted here, see, for example, 'Human Rights and the Rights of Groups', *American Journal of Political Science* 28 (1974): 725–41; 'Justice as Fairness: for Groups?', *American Political Science Review* 69 (1975): 607–14; 'Collective Rights and Moral Rights: Problems in Liberal-Democratic Thought', *Journal of Politics* 44 (1982): 21–40; and *Human Rights, Ethnicity and Discrimination* (Greenwood, Westport, 1985).
7. For these estimates (and their imprecision), see Gurr, *Minorities at Risk*, ch. 1; Gunnar Nielsson, 'States and "Nation-Groups": A Global Taxonomy', in Edward Tiryakian and Ronald Rogowski (eds.), *New Nationalisms of the Developed West* (Allen and Unwin, Boston, 1985): 27–56; Leslie Laczko, 'Canada's Pluralism in Comparative Perspective', *Ethnic and Racial Studies* 17/1 (1994): 20–41. Iceland and the Koreas are commonly cited as two examples of countries which are more or less culturally homogenous.
8. J. S. Mill, *Considerations on Representative Government* (1861), in *Utilitarianism, On Liberty, Considerations on Representative Government*, ed. H. B. Acton (J. M. Dent and Sons, London, 1972): 395. Mill also opposed the attempts of the

Québécois to maintain a distinct francophone society in Canada, and encouraged their assimilation into the more 'civilized' English culture. See Bhikhu Parekh, 'Decolonizing Liberalism', in Alexsandras Shiromas (ed.), *The End of 'Isms'?* (Blackwell, Oxford, 1994): 91.

9. Engels, 'Hungary and Panslavism' (1849), reprinted in full in Marx and Engels, *The Russian Menace to Europe*, ed. Paul Blackstock and Bert Hoselitz (Free Press, Glencoe, 1952), and quoted in Nimni's article in this volume.
10. See also Engels's claim that when Germany governed the Czechs and Slovenes, it 'bound these tiny, crippled powerless little nations in a great Empire, and thereby enabled them to take part in an historical development which, if left to themselves, would have remained entirely foreign to them! To be sure such a thing is not carried through without forcibly crushing many a delicate little national flower'. It was not only the right of the German nation to 'subdue, absorb, and assimilate' smaller nationalities, but also its historical 'mission', and a sign of its historical 'vitality'. As Engels put it, 'By the same right under which France took Flanders, Lorrain and Alsace, and will sooner or later take Belgium—by that same right Germany takes over Schleswig; it is the right of civilisation as against barbarism, of progress as against stability. . . [This] is the right of historical evolution'. See Engels, 'Democratic Panslavism', in *The Russian Menace*: 76, and 'The Danish-Prussian Alliance', quoted in Ian Cummings, *Marx, Engels and National Movements* (Croom Helm, London, 1980): 45–6.
11. E. J. Hobsbawm, *Nations and Nationalism since 1780: Programme, Myth and Reality* (Cambridge University Press, Cambridge, 1990): 35. On the way this attitude toward minority cultures supported European colonialism, see Parekh, 'Decolonizing Liberalism', and Tzvetan Todorov, *On Human Diversity: Nationalism, Racism and Exoticism in French Thought* (Harvard University Press, Cambridge MA, 1993), ch. 3.
12. There were countervailing trends within the Western political tradition. In particular, there were the Austro-Marxists, like Otto Bauer, and the English Pluralists, like Figgis and Laski. On Bauer, see Nimni, *Marxism and Nationalism: Theoretical Origins of a Political Crisis* (Pluto Press, London, 1994), chs. 6–8; Ronnie Munck, 'Otto Bauer: Towards a Marxist Theory of Nationalism', *Capital and Class* 25 (1985): 84–97. For a collection of writings on minority rights that includes selections from the English Pluralists, see Julia Stapleton (ed.), *Group Rights* (Thoemmes Press, Bristol, 1995). See also David Nicholls, *The Pluralist State: The Political Ideas of J. N. Figgis and his Contemporaries* (2nd edn., St. Martin's Press, New York, 1994).
13. For example, contemporary discussions of the status of indigenous peoples often bear a striking resemblance to earlier discussions about the status of European minorities. The assumption that modernization requires assimilation is still commonly made in the context of the Indian peoples in North America, or hill tribes in Asia.
14. Similar arguments are made in Charles Taylor, 'The Politics of Recognition', in *Multiculturalism and the 'Politics of Recognition'*, ed. Amy Gutmann (Princeton University Press, Princeton, 1993), and Yael Tamir, *Liberal Nationalism* (Princeton University Press, Princeton, 1993). For other accounts

of the value of cultural identity, see David Miller, 'In Defense of Nationality', *Journal of Applied Philosophy* 10/1 (1993): 3–16; James Nickel, 'The Value of Cultural Belonging', *Dialogue*, 33/4 (1994): 635–42.

15. See also George Kateb, 'Notes on Pluralism', *Social Research* 61/3 (1994): 512–37.
16. For a general survey of the liberal-communitarian debate, see Shlomo Avineri and Avner De-Shalit (eds.), *Communitarianism and Individualism* (Oxford University Press, Oxford, 1992). For three discussions which interpret the debate over minority rights in terms of this broader liberal-communitarian debate, see Adeno Addis, 'Individualism, Communitarianism and the Rights of Ethnic Minorities', *Notre Dame Law Review* 67/3 (1992): 615–76; Marlies Galenkamp, *Individualism and Collectivism: The Concept of Collective Rights* (Rotterdamse Filosofische Studies, Rotterdam, 1993), and Darlene Johnston's article in this volume.
17. For their broader accounts of liberal theory, see Raz, *The Morality of Freedom* (Oxford University Press, Oxford, 1986), and Waldron, *Liberal Rights* (Cambridge University Press, Cambridge, 1993). See also Margalit and Moshe Halbertal, 'Liberalism and the Right to Culture', *Social Research* 61/3 (1994): 491–510.
18. I discuss this further in *Multicultural Citizenship: A Liberal Theory of Minority Rights* (Oxford University Press, Oxford, 1995), ch. 5.
19. Glazer, *Affirmative Discrimination: Ethnic Inequality and Public Policy* (Basic Books, New York, 1975): 25.
20. Walzer, 'Comment', in *Multiculturalism and the 'Politics of Recognition'*: 100–1. See also Walzer, *What it Means to be an American* (Marsilio, New York, 1992): 9.
21. This shows, I think, that the analogy with religion does not work. It is possible for the state to avoid adopting an official religion. But the state cannot avoid promoting a particular culture and cultural identity when it adopts official languages, public holidays, or citizenship tests. For a more detailed discussion, see my *Multicultural Citizenship*, chs. 5–6.
22. Some neo-conservatives have viewed this as an important argument for a minimal state. Since government schools or public services inevitably involve reproducing a particular cultural identity, a state which has little or no role in providing public services, or in regulating public education or naturalization, will be most tolerant of minority cultures. See, for example, John Gray, 'The Politics of Cultural Diversity', in *Post-Liberalism: Studies in Political Thought* (Routledge, London, 1993).
23. Glazer elsewhere makes a similar point, arguing that the non-discrimination model is particularly appropriate in the context of immigrant groups. See *Ethnic Dilemmas: 1964–1982* (Harvard University Press, Cambridge, 1983), chs. 7, 14.
24. It is a puzzling feature of Walzer's article that, while he emphasizes the difference between voluntary immigrants and involuntarily incorporated national groups, he none the less concludes by arguing that even non-immigrant groups in the United States should accept and live by the non-discrimination model, and relinquish any aspirations for 'national liberation'. I discuss this in *Multicultural Citizenship*, ch. 4.

25. For a more extensive discussion of this idea of a 'heterogenous public', see Young's *Justice and the Politics of Difference*.
26. For surveys of minority rights claims worldwide, see Jay Sigler, *Minority Rights: A Comparative Analysis* (Greenwood, Westport, 1983); Van Dyke, *Human Rights, Ethnicity and Discrimination*; F. Capotorti, *Study on the Rights of Persons Belonging to Ethnic, Religious and Linguistic Minorities* UN Doc. E/CN 4/Sub.2/384 Rev. 1 (United Nations, New York, 1979); Hurst Hannum, *Autonomy, Sovereignty, and Self-Determination: The Adjudication of Conflicting Rights* (University of Pennsylvania Press, Philadelphia, 1990); and Hannum (ed.), *Documents on Autonomy and Minority Rights* (Martinus Nijthoff, Boston, 1993).
27. Influential analyses and defences of the idea of group rights include Ronald Garet, 'Communality and Existence: The Rights of Groups', *Southern California Law Review* 56/5 (1983): 1001–75; Frances Svennson, 'Liberal Democracy and Group Rights: The Legacy of Individualism and its Impact on American Indian Tribes', *Political Studies* 27/3 (1979): 421–39; Van Dyke, *Human Rights, Ethnicity, and Discrimination*; Michael McDonald, 'Questions about Collective Rights', in D. Schneiderman (ed.), *Language and the State: The Law and Politics of Identity* (Les Editions Yvon Blais, Cowansville, 1991); id., 'Should Communities Have Rights? Reflections on Liberal Individualism', *Canadian Journal of Law and Jurisprudence* 4/2 (1991): 217–37. See also the various essays in *Canadian Journal of Law and Jurisprudence* 4/2 (1991), a special issue devoted to 'Collective Rights'; and Denise Réaume, 'Individuals, Groups, and Rights to Public Goods', *University of Toronto Law Journal* 38/1 (1988): 1–27.
28. For a related discussion, see Allen Buchanan, 'The Role of Collective Rights in the Theory of Indigenous Peoples' Rights', *Transnational Law and Contemporary Problems* 3/1 (1993): 89–108.
29. I discuss the distinction between these two sorts of 'collective rights' in more detail in *Multicultural Citizenship*, ch. 3.
30. For these contrasts, see William Galston, 'Two Concepts of Liberalism', *Ethics* 105/3 (1995); John Rawls, *Political Liberalism* (Columbia University Press, New York, 1993); Donald Moon, *Constructing Community: Moral Pluralism and Tragic Conflicts* (Princeton University Press, Princeton, 1993); Charles Larmore, *Patterns of Moral Complexity* (Cambridge University Press, Cambridge, 1987). I discuss this debate in 'Two Models of Pluralism and Tolerance', *Analyse & Kritik* 14/1 (1992): 33–56, reprinted in *Toleration*, ed. David Heyd (Princeton University Press, Princeton, forthcoming).
31. Lijphart has developed this argument in various works, including *The Politics of Accommodation*, (2nd edn., University of California Press, Berkeley, 1975); *Democracy in Plural Societies* (Yale University Press, New Haven, 1977); and *Power-Sharing in South Africa* (Institute of International Studies, Berkeley, 1985).
32. As Lijphart notes, these two forms of 'self-determination' are not mutually exclusive. National groups can seek both a greater decentralization of power, and a greater share of power within the central legislature. Yet there is at least a potential conflict here, particularly if the decentralization of power only

applies to certain groups within society. For example, if Quebec is granted self-government powers not given to other provinces in Canada, so that Quebec is exempt from federal legislation that applies to other provinces, then it would seem that Quebec should have less representation in the federal legislature. The less a group is governed by the central legislature, then presumably the less representation it requires in it. This explains why Puerto Rico—a self-governing commonwealth within the United States—has only limited representation within the American Congress. I discuss this issue in more detail in *Multicultural Citizenship*, ch. 7.

33. See Young, *Justice and the Politics of Difference*.
34. Phillips has developed her views at greater length in *The Politics of Presence* (Oxford University Press, Oxford, 1995).
35. For discussions of the history of minority rights in international law, including the profound shift between the League of Nations and the United Nations, see Inis Claude, *National Minorities: An International Problem* (Harvard University Press, Cambridge MA, 1955); Patrick Thornberry, *International Law and the Rights of Minorities* (Oxford University Press, Oxford, 1991); and W. McKean, *Equality and Discrimination Under International Law* (Oxford University Press, Oxford, 1983). For recent developments, see also Natan Lerner, *Group Rights and Discrimination in International Law* (Martinus Nijhoff, Dordrecht, 1991); and Arie Bloed, 'The CSCE and the Protection of National Minorities', *CSCE ODHIR Bulletin* 1/3 (1994): 1–4.
36. For an overview of the Rushdie affair, see Daniel Pipes, *The Rushdie Affair: The Novel, the Ayatollah, and the West* (Birch Lane Press, New York, 1990). For a collections of essays by political theorists inspired, in part, by reflections on this affair, see John Horton (ed.), *Liberalism, Multiculturalism and Toleration* (St. Martin's Press, New York, 1993).
37. On the reality of cultural heterogeneity throughout history, and its causes, see William McNeill, *Polyethnicity and National Unity in World History* (University of Toronto Press, Toronto, 1986). However, as McNeill notes, the Western political theory tradition has almost always taken the (more or less) homogeneous city-states of Ancient Greece or Renaissance Italy as the essential or standard model of the political community. On the assumption of cultural homogeneity in Western political thought, see Kenneth McRae, 'The Plural Society and the Western Political Tradition', *Canadian Journal of Political Science* 12/4 (1979): 675–88; and the essays by Walzer and Van Dyke in this volume.
38. For a more permissive account of the right to secede, see Daniel Philpott, 'In Defense of Self-Determination', *Ethics* 105/2 (1995): 352–85; David Gauthier, 'Breaking-Up: An Essay on Secession', *Canadian Journal of Philosophy* 24/3 (1994): 357–72. See also my review of Buchanan in *Political Theory* 20/3 (1993): 527–32.
39. On the ever-increasing scale of this migration, see Stephen Castles and Mark Miller, *The Age of Migration: International Population Movements in the Modern Age* (Macmillan, Basingstoke, 1993).
40. For other defenders of open borders, see James Hudson, 'The Philosophy of Immigration', *Journal of Libertarian Studies* 8/1 (1986): 51–62; Timothy King,

'Immigration from Developing Countries: Some Philosophical Issues', *Ethics* 93/3 (1983): 525–36; Veit Bader, 'Citizenship and Exclusion: Radical Democracy, Community and Justice', *Political Theory* 23 (1995): 211–46. For defenders of (partially) closed borders, see Michael Walzer, *Spheres of Justice: A Defence of Pluralism and Equality* (Blackwell, Oxford, 1983), and Donald Galloway, 'Liberalism, Globalism, and Immigration', *Queen's Law Journal* 18 (1993): 266–305. Carens himself has developed, and partially modified, his position. See, for example, 'Democracy and Respect for Difference: the case of Fiji', *University of Michigan Journal of Law Reform* 25/3 (1992): 547–631.

I Historical Background

1 The Individual, the State, and Ethnic Communities in Political Theory

VERNON VAN DYKE

Since the time of Hobbes and Locke, liberal political theorists have made it their primary purpose to explore relationships between the individual and the state.[1] Problems in these relationships pervade the writing of academic theorists, and pronouncements about them are central features of historic documents. The truths that Thomas Jefferson held to be self-evident are truths concerning the individual and the state: all men have inalienable rights, and governments derive their just powers from the consent of the governed. Similarly, the French revolutionaries, though also concerned with the nation, proclaimed the rights of man and of the citizen. The tradition is carried on in contemporary international declarations and covenants on human rights, for—with certain exceptions—the rights enumerated are the rights of individuals in relation to the state.

The argument here will be that the liberal conception—an individualist conception—is unduly limited. It is not enough to think in terms of two-level relationships, with the individual at one level and the state at another; nor is it enough if the nation is added. Considering the heterogeneity of mankind and of the population of virtually every existing state, it is also necessary to think of ethnic communities and certain other kinds of groups, and to include them among the kinds of right-and-duty-bearing units whose interrelationships are to be explored. The question is whether ethnic communities that meet certain criteria should be considered units (corporate bodies) with moral rights, and whether legal status and rights should be accorded to them.

This article was stimulated by discussions in a seminar that I conducted in 1975–76 in connection with the residential fellowship program of the National Endowment for the Humanities. I wish to thank the Fellows who participated, and particularly Malcolm Byrnes (Southern University), Craig R. Goodrum (University of Texas Law School), Rockne M. McCarthy (Trinity Christian College), and Roger N. Pajari (Georgia Southern College). I have benefited also from suggestions offered by colleagues, notably Lane Davis and John Nelson.

Vernon Van Dyke, 'The Individual, the State, and Ethnic Communities in Political Theory', *World Politics*, Vol. 29/3 (1977), pp. 343–69. Reprinted by permission of The Johns Hopkins University Press, Baltimore/London.

The first step in the argument, after the definition of crucial terms, is to show that the liberal emphasis on the individual even precludes a proper theory of the state, which suggests in principle that liberalism cannot be trusted to deal adequately with the question of status and rights for ethnic communities, most of which are minorities within the state. The second step is to cite practices relating to ethnic communities and other groups—practices that at the very least raise questions about the adequacy of the liberal individualistic prescription. They suggest that liberalism needs supplementing. The third step elaborates on the second, citing the right of nations or peoples to self-determination as the right of groups rather than of individuals, and therefore as a right for which liberalism does not offer a clear basis. In some cases the rights that groups exercise are perhaps reducible to individual rights and can thus be brought within the framework of liberal theory, but in other cases the rights belong to groups as corporate units. The fourth step is to note an implication of the third: that the usual assumption that the consent of the governed is the consent of individuals is open to question, and that the consent that counts may come from groups. The final step is to ask what difference it makes if ethnic communities and other groups, in addition to individuals, are acknowledged as right-and-duty-bearing units.

The Meaning of Crucial Terms

By ethnic community I mean a group of persons, predominantly of common descent, who think of themselves as collectively possessing a separate identity based on race or on shared cultural characteristics, usually language or religion; they may or may not think of themselves as a nation, a concept with stronger implications for political autonomy or independence.

In asking whether ethnic communities should be considered to have rights, I am asking about moral rights—that is, about morally justified claims.[2] Whether a claim is morally justified is, I assume, a question for individual judgment, though of course many persons need to concur in the judgment before meaningful social recognition of the claim is likely to occur. In fact, one of the common issues in politics is whether a justified moral claim (a moral right) exists that ought to be reinforced by law—that is, by being made a legal right as well.

The above implies that rights may be moral or legal, or both. To classify them in additional ways is to raise questions, some of which will be argued below. Rights may belong either to individuals or to groups as units. I do not have an exhaustive list of the kinds of groups that ought to be considered in this connection. I would surely include the following as potential or actual right-and-duty-bearing units: ethnic communities, nations, and the populations of political dependencies and sovereign states. I would also include trade unions, though they do not figure in my present argument. I would exclude chance aggregations and even social and economic classes, considered as such; they may have group interests, but not group rights. What to say about other sorts of groups is a question that I leave unexplored.

Rights that belong to individuals may go to them either as human beings or as members of a group. The Universal Declaration of Human Rights enumerates rights of the first sort; they go to 'everyone . . . without distinction of any kind, such as race, color, sex, language, religion, political or other opinion, national or social origin, property, birth or other status.' No comparable enumeration exists of rights of the second sort, going to individuals as members of a group; they are illustrated by the right to vote, which as a rule goes only to citizens.

Rights that belong to a group may be either derivative or intrinsic. A group right is derivative if it is delegated by one or more original holders of the right—for example, the members of the group, or perhaps the state; it is intrinsic if it is aboriginal to the group. To hold that a group right is derivative, and most particularly to hold that it is derived from individuals, is compatible with liberal individualistic theory, for the group right is then reducible to an individual right. To hold that a group right is intrinsic, however, requires a modification of individualism in some degree.

The statement that groups have moral and legal rights (are right-and-duty-bearing units) inevitably threatens to revive the old question whether there is such a thing as a real 'Group-Person' with human qualities such as a mind or a spirit.[3] I reject the thought, but will not argue the question in this brief statement of crucial definitions. What I have in mind is suggested by the idea of a corporation, which has rights and liabilities distinct from those of the persons composing it. It is suggested, for that matter, by the state itself, for *it* is a kind of corporation. At the same time, ethnic communities are unlike corporations in that they are not the creatures of law or the state. They come into existence—as nations sometimes do—independently of the state, raising the question whether they may have moral rights and a capacity to advance moral claims regardless of their legal status.

Liberal Theory on the Individual and the State

Among liberal political theorists, the focus on the individual and the state is so prominent and obvious that it seems almost superfluous to cite supporting evidence. But the focus is important, and so is the related fact that the emphasis on individualism leaves liberals without a proper theory of the state.

Both the focus and the related fact are apparent in works stressing the idea of the social contract. Hobbes and Locke, for example, make it clear that individuals (men, in fact) are parties to the contract—men who act for themselves and presumably for associated women and children. They do not act as representatives of ethnic or other groups. According to Hobbes, 'A commonwealth is said to be instituted when a multitude of men do agree. . . .'[4] Hobbes provided no place for associations or groups at the intermediate level between the individual and the commonwealth. As Sabine puts it, 'There is [for Hobbes] no middle ground between humanity as a sand-heap of separate organisms and the state as an outside power. . . .'[5] Similarly, Locke spoke of an 'original compact [through which] any number of men . . . make one community or government wherein the majority have a right to act and conclude the rest.'[6] Later, Rousseau too spoke of a number of men establishing the state through a social compact; and he was explicit about eliminating associations intermediate between the individual and the state, holding that 'if . . . the general will is to be truly expressed, it is essential that there be no subsidiary groups within the State. . . .' Each citizen was to 'voice his own opinion and nothing but his own opinion.'[7]

The most recent major exponent of a contractarian point of view, John Rawls, likewise assumes that the parties in the original position, who work out the principles of justice, are individuals who speak for themselves. Moreover, the justice that they seek is only for individuals. Rawls shows concern for social classes (that is, for 'the least advantaged'), but he does not raise the question whether ethnic communities should be considered as entities with claims to justice.[8]

Emphasis on the individual is not confined to those who assume a social contract. In speaking of the greatest good of the greatest number, utilitarians obviously have individuals in mind. Those who focus on the common good or on the nature of political obligation are thinking of individuals. Those who speak of the consent of the governed usually take it as an obvious assumption that the consent is to come from individuals. Those who deal with the concepts of one man–one vote, one vote–one value, and of majority rule, clearly have individuals in mind. And references to equality can be assumed to be references to the equality of individuals unless it is specified otherwise, as in references to the sovereign equality of stress.

Stressing individualism, liberals have no proper theory of the state. As indicated above, Hobbes spoke of a 'multitude of men,' and Locke of 'any number of men,' making a covenant. Neither attempted to characterize the men—not saying, for example, whether the men shared a common language or religion. They evidently thought of the question how some men acquired a moral right to make a covenant that would bind dissenters, for they both specified that the covenant was to have unanimous consent—not asking how probable it was that unanimous consent could be obtained. They did not bother, however, to say how women and children came to be bound. Rousseau's solution to the problem was in a way more forthright. He stated that those who did not consent became foreigners and could leave; if they remained, consent was implied.[9] At the same time, Rousseau's solution assumes that those making the contract somehow had a right to impose change on others.

More recent liberal authors handle the problem in different ways. Ernest Barker, considering Locke's position, says that two steps are necessary to a social contract: preceding the contract that establishes a government is an earlier contract that establishes a society. 'There must already be something in the nature of an organized community' before there can be a contract.[10] This is an ingenious, if not a disingenuous, solution to the problem; it suggests infinite regress. Rawls' solution to the problem is simpler: he just takes the state for granted, as a kind of happening, and goes on from there.

Some associate the state with the nation. That is the case with John Stuart Mill and with Ernest Barker (when speaking for himself and not commenting on Locke). Both are concerned, as Barker puts it, with the maximum development of the capacities of the greatest number of individuals, and both therefore favor a democratic state. Thus, they are concerned about the conditions prerequisite to democracy, and this leads them to insist that the boundaries of the nation should determine the boundaries of the state. Mill's statement, descriptive in form but prescriptive in intent, is as follows:

> Free institutions are next to impossible in a country made up of different nationalities. Among a people without fellow-feeling, especially if they read and speak different languages, the united public opinion, necessary to the working of representative government, cannot exist. . . . [I]t is in general a necessary condition of free institutions that the boundaries of governments should coincide in the main with those of nationalities.[11]

Barker also is both descriptive and prescriptive. '[M]ost States,' he says, 'are what we call "national States."' The assertion was highly questionable when he made it (his book was published in 1951), and it surely is untrue today. Speaking of the United Kingdom, he equated it with England. He spoke of the 'general structure of English life,' and said that 'we start from the primary fact of the existence of national society.'[12]

> The reason why the nation is generally the basis of a State is simple. There must be a general social cohesion which serves as it were, as a matrix, before the seal of legal

association can be effectively imposed on a population. If the seal of the State is stamped on a population which is not held together in the matrix of a common tradition and sentiment, there is likely to be a cracking and splitting, as there was in Austria-Hungary.[13]

Barker acknowledges that 'the modern State is not always a unitary national society. It may contain national minorities. . . .'[14] But, rather than adjusting his theory to this fact, he treats it as an 'addition,' tacked on and left as an anomaly.

Though Barker thinks that the state should be based on a national society, he does not grant the nation a moral right to statehood any more than he accepted Locke's apparent assumption that 'any number of men' in a state of nature had a moral right to make a contract of government without having made a prior contract of society. In fact, Barker refuses to attribute moral rights (or what he calls 'quasi-rights')[15] to groups of any sort. Aggregations of individuals may form groups, such as trade unions, and carry on activities; and the aggregations may be regarded as bodies or 'wholes.' But they are not to be regarded as persons, and not to be accepted as possessing moral claims or 'quasi-rights.' Moral rights belong only to individuals. If the state were regarded as a moral person, *étatisme* would be fostered and might issue in 'a philosophy of the total and engulfing State whose will is the peace—and the tomb of its members.'[16] If groups other than the state were regarded as moral persons, the authority of the state would be threatened. According to Barker, the state, and nonstate groups, are to be legal persons only. How 'any number of men,' or a nation, acquires a moral right to establish a state is a question left without a satisfactory answer. And the point has an implication: those who do not see a moral basis for the establishment of the state are not likely to see a moral basis for the claims of ethnic communities.

One wonders what Barker's answer would have been had he thought of the question whether, in international politics, one state might in principle have a moral claim against another, or whether the people of a colony might collectively have a moral claim against their imperial overlord. For that matter, one wonders what his answer would have been if he had thought of the question whether the citizens of a state, who in his eyes constitute a corporate unit with collective legal rights and responsibilities while it exists, also constitute a corporate unit with a collective moral right to re-establish the state if it were somehow dissolved. To be consistent, he would have had to say no to all these questions—unless in the third case he chose to suggest a prior contract of society. He concedes moral rights to individuals, but offers no basis for saying that some individuals have a moral right to impose change on others or to restrict their liberty.

Historic Precedents and Contemporary Practices

Historic precedents exist and contemporary practices are followed that go against the liberal individualistic position. They reflect the grant of both legal and moral rights to groups. In some cases, it seems clear that the group rights are not reducible to individual rights. In other cases the question can be answered, in a Kuhnian sense, in terms of the paradigm one adopts. Those who insist on an individualistic paradigm can find a basis for arguing that what is ostensibly a group right is reducible; and those who reject an individualistic paradigm as inadequate can contend (as I do) that it is preferable to adopt a more complex paradigm permitting individual and group rights, both legal and moral, to exist side by side.

The great historic precedent, of course, is the establishment of the state itself. As suggested above, the notion that all individuals somehow consent to the jurisdiction of the state is an obvious fiction. A more tenable position (though none is entirely satisfactory) is that human needs exist at various levels (for example, at the level of the individual and at the level of the community), and that the existence of needs implies a right to meet them. Essentially the same principle can be expressed in terms of the good: that the good can be sought for units at various levels, and that there is a right to promote the good.[17] This principle justifies individual rights, and it also justifies the rights of communities, including the communities (or the communities of communities) that constitute states. At no level are the rights absolute. At each level and between levels, rights and their exercise are limited by other rights. Within limits reached after considering the relevant rights, the meeting of the needs of the community—or the promotion of the good of the community—justifies restrictions on the behavior of individuals, whether they consent or not.

Precedents in specific circumstances were set in connection with the American and the French Revolutions. In the same Declaration in which Jefferson and his associates proclaimed the inalienable rights of all men, they also proclaimed the right of 'one People to dissolve the Political Bands which have connected them with another, and to assume . . . the separate and equal Station to which the Laws of Nature and of Nature's God entitle them. . . .' The wording permits a choice between paradigms. Jefferson spoke of 'one People' and of 'them.' Those impressed by the term 'them' can say that the Laws of Nature and Nature's God conferred the right on individuals severally, who then acted through representatives in exercising it. Those impressed by the term 'one People' can say that the right was conferred aboriginally on the community as a kind of corporate unit, and that the right of individuals was simply to participate in the decision of the corporation.

The French revolutionaries were clearer. They proclaimed the rights of man, but they also proclaimed that 'all sovereignty resides essentially in the nation.' The statement presumably means that the nation has a collective right to act as a unit, and the word 'essentially' suggests that the right is intrinsic, not delegated by individuals and not reducible.

Elsewhere, I have described contemporary practices with regard to the legal rights of groups.[18] Ethnic communities are sometimes treated as political units within countries, both through territorial delimitations and through the use of separate electoral rolls. Thus, communities as units are accorded representation in the various branches of government. Different communities sometimes live under different sets of laws—for instance, in the field of family law. It is not at all uncommon for ethnic communities to operate their own school systems, with tax support. Ethnic communities in many countries are differentially treated with respect to rights of property and residence; it is not only a question of territorial reservations for the indigenous but also a question of special measures designed to make it possible for the communities to preserve their distinctive identity. And in the case of less advanced groups, or of groups that have suffered discrimination, it is now not uncommon to give them a right to expect special measures (affirmative action) designed to promote their equality, e.g., in the economic and educational realms.

Of the various questions that attend these practices, two will be considered here. The first concerns reducibility: whether the communities have the rights as units, and whether the rights of the communities are reducible to the rights of individuals as members. The second is whether the legal rights should be thought of as reflecting moral claims. I will argue that the communities have the rights as units, that in some cases the rights are irreducible, and that in principle they may well reflect moral claims.

With respect to the first question, some of the clearest illustrations come from British colonial practices. In setting up legislative councils in colonies, the British regularly faced the problem of disparate ethnic communities—a relatively small but economically and politically powerful European (mainly British) community, one or more 'native' communities, and perhaps a non-European immigrant community (for instance, in East Africa, an Asian community). Cultural differences were often acute. In such circumstances, the British thought explicitly in terms of communities, and perhaps in terms of 'interests.' In Tanganyika, for example, they thought in terms of three communities: European, Asian, and African—in 1948 numbering 11,000, 57,000, and 7 million, respectively. A British commission charged with recommending a system of representation at the end of World War II apparently did not even think of assuming that what should be represented were individual inhabitants. Instead, it thought in terms of the 'claims of the communities' and the relative importance of those claims. Further, professing an inability to assess their relative importance, it saw 'no logical alternative to equal representation.'[19] There would be what other British spokesmen have called 'parity'; that is, each community would count as one. There would be a 'partnership' of communities in a 'multiracial' society.[20] The words implied that the communities would retain their separate identities, being treated as distinct units. Individuals would have the right to help elect the representatives of the community to which they belonged. The British did this kind of thing not only in Tanganyika, but in other dependencies as well.[21]

That the British conferred legal rights on the communities as units is plain. And it is difficult to see how the community rights can be reduced to individual rights. The best reductionist argument would presumably be that each voter, or each adult inhabitant, was given a right to expect that his or her racial group would be represented as indicated. Individualists would be uncomfortable in making the argument, however, if their individualism included even an elementary variety of egalitarianism, for the arrangement made each European equivalent to about 4 Asians or about 636 Africans. It is much more comfortable and sensible to hold that the British looked at the problem of representation much as they and others look at it in international politics. Between states, regardless of their size, the problem of representation is solved by the parity rule: one state-one vote. The British simply treated the communities of Tanganyika like states.

Practices analogous to those followed in British colonies are followed today in a number of countries. Fiji provides an example—not surprisingly, perhaps, for it was a British dependency not long ago. Its population is racially divided. Approximately 50 percent are Indian, 42 percent Fijian, and 8 percent European and other. Voters register on racial electoral rolls, and each racial group has a quota of seats in the two houses of the central legislature. The House of Representatives consists of 52 members, with Indians, Fijis, and Europeans and others entitled to 22, 22, and 8 seats, respectively. No provision exists for changing the quotas as the distribution of the population changes. Again, a reductionist could argue that the arrangement gives each voter or adult a right to expect that his or her group will be represented as indicated, and the departure from the requirements of egalitarianism is not so egregious as in Tanganyika. Moreover, the third racial roll (European and other) is not strictly a community roll, though the British are the dominant element. At the same time, a modification of the international analogy applies in a credible way: the Fijian constitution (conferred by Britain) assumes the existence of three communities and assures them representation as such. The right of the individual is to participate in selecting those who represent not individuals, but the community.

In Fiji, five-sixths of the land is owned by over 6,600 Fijian land-owning units and is administered by a Native Land Trust Board. The constitution includes special protection for this arrangement, providing that any bill affecting it must be approved by at least 6 of the 8 Senators appointed in accordance with the advice of the Great [Fijian] Council of Chiefs.[22] The arrangement is obviously communal, giving land rights to the community as such on a collective, corporate basis. To seek to reduce these communal rights to individual rights is to strain to preserve a paradigm that does not fit.

In Belgium, the linguistic communities have rights. The constitution itself says that 'Belgium comprises three cultural communities. . . . Each community enjoys the powers invested in it by the Constitution or by such legislation as shall be enacted by virtue thereof.' Clearly, each community is here treated as a unit—potentially as a right-and-duty-bearing unit. The cultural communities are identified by language. Each has its own region, and a fourth region (Brussels-Capital) is bilingual. Within each region language regulations prevail. The language of instruction in the schools, for example, must be the language of the region if tax support is to be forthcoming and if diplomas granted are to be recognized. The Belgians speak specifically, in official publications, of assuring 'the territorial integrity of the cultural communities.'[23] According to the constitution,

> The boundaries of the four regions may only be altered or amended by an act of Parliament passed on a majority vote in each linguistic group of each of the Houses, on condition that the majority of the members of each group are present and that the total votes in favour within the two linguistic groups attain two-thirds of the votes cast.

French and Dutch Cultural Councils are established, made up respectively of the French- and Dutch-speaking members of Parliament, and limited legislative powers are devolved upon them. The constitution specifies that 'with the possible exception of the Prime Minister, the Cabinet comprises an equal number of French-speaking and Dutch-speaking Ministers.' Clearly, these provisions confer rights on the communities as units. Determined individualists can of course argue that the community rights are reducible to individual rights, and that the moral claim is that of individuals rather than of the group. The argument would be that individuals have a right to expect that the territorial integrity of their linguistic community will be maintained, that within their region their language will be used, and that members of their linguistic community will share in governmental offices. In contrast, those who accept a paradigm including group rights can say that when the Belgians themselves officially speak of the rights of communities, it is gratuitous to allege that this cannot be what they mean, and that the rights really go to individuals. Moreover, the requirements that the language of the community be used and that the linguistic communities be represented in the Cabinet are not suggestive of individualism.

Community rights are recognized even in the United States. Individualism is dominant, of course, but there are exceptions to it and inconsistencies in it; and references to groups and their rights are increasing. The clearest case is that of the Indian tribes—'subordinate and dependent nations,' enjoying those powers of sovereignty that Congress has not taken away.[24] Legislation concerning the Indians reflects different and contradictory principles, but some of it assumes that the tribes are like sovereign states in being irreducible right-and-duty-bearing units.

In the United States, courts refer increasingly to groups. In 1938 the Supreme Court spoke of the possibility that 'prejudice against discrete and insular minorities' might call for especially searching judicial inquiry.[25] Subsequently, the Court noted that 'the economic rights of an individual may depend for the effectiveness of their enforcement on rights in the group, even though not formally corporate, to which he belongs.'[26] In one of the landmark cases on school integration, a federal district court quoted a statement asserting that '[S]egregation is a group phenomenon. Although the effects of discrimination are felt by each member of the group, any discriminatory practice is directed against the group as a unit and against individuals only as their connection with the group involves the anti-group sanction.'[27] In the 1960's, the terms 'identifiable minority' and 'cognizable group' began appearing in cases involving desegregation,[28] housing legislation,[29] jury selection,[30] and racial gerrymandering. With respect to the latter, one court pointed out that 'the gerrymander . . . does not directly or necessarily affect the individual right to vote. It is aimed at groups of citizens and is intended to diminish the likelihood that their candidate will be elected.' 'There is no principle,' the court held, 'which requires a minority racial or ethnic group to have any particular voting strength reflected in the council [of the City of Chicago]. The principle is that such strength must not be purposefully minimized on account of their race or ethnic origin.'[31] Earlier, the Supreme Court had declared that 'the Equal Protection Clause of the Fourteenth Amendment . . . protects voting rights and political groups . . ., as well as economic units, *racial communities*, and *other entities*.'[32] In the numerous ratio-hiring cases, the regular practice is to require that minority groups (perhaps including women) be represented in specified kinds of municipal or state employment in rough proportion to their numbers.[33]

These various judicial references to group rights are of course inconclusive. A Procrustean insistence that the evidence fits liberal individualist theory is possible. But the incongruities of that theory with respect to the equal protection of the law are receiving increased attention. Thus, Owen M. Fiss urges that, with respect to the interpretation of the equal protection clause, the 'antidiscrimination principle' (which focuses on the individual) ought to be abandoned, and that in its place a 'group-disadvantaging principle' ought to be adopted. 'The concern,' he says, 'should be with those laws or practices that particularly hurt a disadvantaged group.'[34] An individualist interpretation of equal protection provides a questionable basis for affirmative action—for example, when benefits go to persons who have not suffered discrimination themselves.

Rights for groups or communities are recognized not only at the domestic, but also at the international level. International action relating to Cyprus provides the clearest illustration of the assertion of irreducible community rights. The 1960 constitution of Cyprus, reflecting agreement among Britain, Greece, and Turkey, starts right out defining 'the Greek community' and 'the Turkish community'; numerous provisions treat these communities as corporate entities. Moreover, a resolution of the Consultative Assembly of the Council of Europe relating to Cyprus calls explicitly for the protection of two kinds of rights on the island: 'the human rights of all inhabitants,' and 'other rights belonging to the communities.'[35] Other actions at the international level, though clearly providing for group rights, are not so clear on the question of reducibility. A resolution of the U.N. Sub-Commission on Prevention of Discrimination and Protection of Minorities, for example, speaks of minorities that 'wish for a measure of differential treatment in order to preserve basic characteristics which they possess and which distinguish them from the majority of the population'; it says that 'differential treatment of such groups or of individuals belonging to such groups is justified. . . .'[36] And the U.N. Convention on the Elimination of All Forms of Racial Discrimination stipulates that parties 'shall, when the circumstances so warrant, take . . . special . . . measures to ensure the adequate development and protection of certain racial groups or individuals belonging to them for the purpose of guaranteeing them the full and equal enjoyment of human rights. . . .'

The second question is whether the legal rights that are accorded should be thought of as reflecting moral claims. Barker's negative answer, noted above, is surely inconclusive. His assumption that the authority of the state should be safeguarded against the claims of non-state groups is an assumption that those concerned with minorities may or may not share. And even he did not allege that *étatisme* necessarily follows an acceptance of the state as a moral person. Evils may flow, of course, from almost any kind of political arrangement, including the recognition of group rights. The parity arrangement in Tanganyika, for example, is not suggestive of moral sensitivity. But no reason is evident for rejecting out of hand the view that groups, considered as units, may have moral rights. On the contrary, the grant of legal status and rights to groups, as in Belgium, Cyprus, Fiji, and the United States, may well be in response to a moral claim. Why should the possibility be ruled out that the authority of the state should be limited not only by the moral rights of individuals ('inalienable' or human rights), but also by the moral rights of groups?

Self-Determination as the Moral Right of Dependent Peoples

As noted above, Mill and Barker speak of the desirability of making the state coextensive with the nation. The view is relevant to the idea of self-determination, which has been advanced since the time of the French Revolution, though more in the political than in the intellectual realm; and self-determination has often been described as a *right*. 'Every people,' Woodrow Wilson said, 'has a right to choose the sovereignty under which they shall live.'[37] The Charter of the United Nations speaks of the *principle* of self-determination, and the two human rights Covenants speak of the *right*. Speaking of it as a right, Wilson sometimes attributed it to *peoples* and sometimes to *nations*. The common reference in the interwar years was to *national* self-determination, but the U.N. Charter and the two human rights Covenants revert to the term *people*. 'All peoples,' the Covenants say, 'have the right of self-determination.' Who constitute a *people* is left vague.

Like the legal rights of communities, the right of nations or peoples to self-determination raises a question about the adequacy of the liberal focus on the individual and the state. Of course, it might be argued that the right of a nation or people is reducible to an individual right—that what is really recognized is the right of individuals to choose the sovereignty under which they will live, or the right to be governed (if they choose) along with others of their own kind. Such arguments, however, are not persuasive. Wilson's statement was not that every *person* but that every *people* has a right to choose the sovereignty under which to live. At most, the individual has a right to participate in the decision—and to leave the group if he does not like the outcome. Approximately the same rejoinder applies to the thought that individuals have a right to be governed together with their own kind. In contrast, a strong argument can be advanced that self-determination is the right of a group, of a corporate unit. The argument rests on words chosen when the right is asserted; on logic; and on an examination of practice.

The words chosen are sometimes ambiguous, as when Jefferson spoke of the right of 'one People'—especially since the pronoun that he associated with 'one People' was 'them.' At other times, the words chosen leave no doubt. Thus, in 1975 the General Assembly adopted a resolution calling for measures 'to enable the Palestinian people to exercise *its* inalienable national rights. . . .'[38] A just collective claim is here assumed.

Logic supports the point more strongly. Where an individual right is at stake, such as the right of free speech, violation is a possibility, and preventive or protective measures can be taken; and if a violation occurs, redress can be sought. If self-determination were an individual right, comparable statements could be made. But in fact, comparable statements cannot be made. There is never a thought that, when a people exercises its right of self-determination, the outcome might violate an individual right. No violation occurs even in the case of those who oppose the outcome. They retain the right to leave the group, but they have no right of protection against the group's decision, and no right of redress. The only individual right that might be violated is the right to participate in the decision. The foregoing suggests that it is the corporate unit that enjoys the right; the most that an individual can claim is a right to participate in the corporate choice.

That self-determination is the right of a corporate unit is also suggested by the way in which the right has been implemented. After World War I, it was simply assumed that certain components of the Russian and Austro-Hungarian Empires were nations entitled to independent statehood. Individual voters in Finland, Poland, Czechoslovakia, and so forth were not asked to choose. The victorious powers simply dealt with leaders of these entities whom they recognized, and arranged for independence. Even if there had been plebiscites giving individuals an opportunity to participate in the decision, they would have been within national units, and a majority vote would presumably have determined the fate of the entire unit, regardless of the wishes of the minority. In the few border areas where plebiscites in fact occurred, individuals voted not so much in their own right as to help in the settlement of conflicting claims between the adjacent nation-states. After World War II, the implementation of the right of self-determination has continued to be on a group basis. The dominant view in the United Nations is that a 'people' is to be defined as the population of a political dependency as a whole. In most cases, the imperial power endorsing self-determination and granting independence has dealt with whatever central authority it recognized in the dependency, though in some cases special votes or referenda have been held. Whatever the procedure, the 'self' that is 'determined' is always a group as a unit.

When we speak of a group's right of self-determination, what kind of a right is at issue? The question is important, especially in the light of Barker's view that moral rights should not be attributed to groups. In the light of that view, it is perhaps not surprising that Barker did not analyze the notion of a right of self-determination. Although self-determination might be a legal right (it is nominally a constitutional right in the U.S.S.R.), assertions of the right rarely give it this quality. When Jefferson asserted the right of 'one People,' he described it as a right 'to which the Laws of Nature and of Nature's God entitle them.' The right that he had in mind should thus be classified as natural or divine or moral. Similarly, when the General Assembly adopts a resolution speaking of 'the Palestinian people' and '*its* inalienable national rights,' it is not speaking of legal rights; rather, it is asserting that 'the Palestinian people' have a moral claim. Even when a state ratifies one of the Covenants, saying that 'all peoples have the right of self-determination,' it is not conferring a legal right on them. Rather, it is committing itself to the position that peoples have the moral right in question.

Assuming that self-determination is essentially the moral right of a group—of a collective entity, a unit, a corporate body—what is its basis? Several answers are possible. Those who believe that the individual's rights are natural or God-given can extend that belief to the rights of groups; they can say that the right comes into existence along with the group itself. Those who believe that the moral claims of individuals rest simply on a critical judgment about what ought to be can well say the same of the rights of groups. Both of these answers are compatible with a third possible answer, given earlier: that the existence of needs implies a right to act (within limits) to meet them, or that a conception of the good has a corresponding implication.

The Consent of the Governed: Can It Come from Groups?

The view that government derives its just power from the consent of the governed is noted above, along with the related tacit assumption that 'the governed' are individuals. The question now is whether that tacit assumption is justifiable.

The assumption is understandable if the population of the state is homogeneous, sharing a common culture. But if the population is divided into different communities, each cherishing and wanting to preserve its distinctive identity, why should it be assumed that the consent that counts comes from individuals? Cannot entire communities give or withhold consent as collective units?

The question calls for additional comment on the right of nations or peoples to self-determination. Although the usual outcome of an exercise of the right is independence (sovereign statehood), that is not the only possibility. Puerto Rico has chosen Commonwealth status, giving it a considerable measure of autonomy while remaining under the flag of the United States. The same kind of status is contemplated for the people of the Northern Marianas Islands. The people of the Cook Islands have obtained a similar status in relation to New Zealand; and the people of the island of Mayotte have voted to remain a part of France rather than join the other Comoros Islands in an independent state. Every minority that has any kind of special status might in principle have obtained it through an exercise of self-determination. Moreover, nothing prevents an exercise of self-determination from leading to a decision to drop all claim to distinctive status and to accept assimilation into, or fusion with, another society. Whatever the outcome, as already indicated, the decision is that of a collectivity. Even if the entity exercising self-determination is somehow split, with different parts choosing different futures for themselves, the decision is collective; it is the consent of the respective parts that is obtained. And if the group or part of it chooses to remain within an existing state, why should it not be said that the consent of the governed is the consent of a collectivity? Individuals may consent too, if only by submitting, but this does not gainsay the separate consent of the group. And if, in connection with self-determination, the consent of the group as a unit can be obtained by deliberate design, why cannot the consent of other groups be given in less formal ways? Individuals may, of course, protest the consent that the group gives, and may leave the group, but the group's decision stands.

The Question of Exceptions

In the light of the statement made at the outset—that modern liberal political theorists focus on relations between the individual and the state as if no groups count that are intermediate—let it be acknowledged that social classes and interest groups are commonly recognized. That fact, however, is beside the point, for the consideration given to social classes and interest groups has little to do with the consideration that ought to be given to ethnic communities. To be sure, social classes in Europe (as 'estates') were once differentially treated for political purposes, and in some countries a social class is at the same time an ethnic community. Moreover, an ethnic community may be an interest group. But liberal political theorists, apparently regarding selected aspects of the North Atlantic world as typical of the whole world, tend to ignore the possibilities suggested by these facts. Assuming that social and political arrangements within the state are arrangements for individuals, they treat social classes and interest groups as aggregations of individuals struggling with other such aggregations. They take it for granted that the various aggregations are integral parts of the society and polity, destined to remain so. They do not seem to think of the exceptional cases of aggregations that are culture groups with a corporate claim to differential political status and rights. Thus the consideration that they give to social classes and interest groups is not on a continuum with the consideration they give to states as corporate units, or to nations or 'peoples.' If one starts with the fact that states exist as corporate units, and goes on to a consideration of the claims of nations or 'peoples,' logical continuity is broken if the next step is to social classes and interest groups as they are usually considered. Logical continuity requires that the next step be a consideration of ethnic communities.

Are the theorists known as 'pluralists' exceptions to the generalization that an unjustifiable leap occurs from a consideration of the state, nation, or 'people' to a consideration of the individual?

In terms of the English pluralists (for example, Figgis, Laski, Cole, and Maitland) and of the German pluralist, Gierke, who influenced them, the answer might go either way. Of course, all of them intimate a framework, however vaguely, into which special status and rights for ethnic communities could perhaps be fitted. This is particularly true of Figgis, who concerned himself especially with the church and who spoke of the state as a *communitas communitatum*. Laski, too, made comments of an incidental sort suggesting some degree of autonomy for the countries of which the United Kingdom is composed, and for the Flemish and Walloons in Belgium. But it is abundantly clear that Laski and the other English pluralists, except Figgis, were thinking primarily if not exclusively of classes and interest groups that pursue individualistic values; they were not thinking of ethnic groups or culture groups that seek some kind of collective autonomy within a larger society or that seek to participate in the larger society as entities with status and rights. Their pluralism was the pluralism of economic associations and interests.

The principal steps beyond a recognition of the state and nation toward the recognition of status and rights for other comparable groups have been taken by scholars outside the mainstream of political theory—scholars whose orientation is predominantly empirical. Furnivall is credited with coining the term 'plural society,' and others influenced by him (notably M. G. Smith, Leo Kuper, and Leo A. Depres) are obviously concerned about the status and role (if not the status and rights) of ethnic groups. In the field of comparative politics, Arend Lijphart ('consociational democracy'), Val R. Lorwin ('segmented pluralism'), Hans Daalder, and others have similar concerns. Kenneth D. McRae, whose background is in political theory, belongs on the same list. A literature is growing that does not proceed on the assumption that once the state and nation have been recognized, the remaining questions concern relationships between the individual and the state.

What Difference Does It Make?

What difference does it make? Why is it important that, alongside the principle that individuals are right-and-duty-bearing units, a comparable principle should be accepted for the benefit of ethnic communities? The answer has a number of parts.

1. Whether communities as well as individuals are considered as potential right-and-duty-bearing units should make a difference in intellectual inquiry. The traditional and present stress on the individual leads to a failure even to think about groups in some contexts where the omission is obviously deplorable, or to a gross neglect of groups. According to prevailing norms, it is all right to think of differential treatment for the population of states and for nations, but not for other communities or groups with a distinctive identity. Put somewhat differently, a stress on the individual and on the principle of equal treatment tends to promote the view that it is improper even to think about differences of race, sex, language, and religion unless it be to combat discrimination based on these characteristics. It tends to promote blindness to group differences and a kind of unspoken assumption either that societies are homogeneous or that right-thinking persons will treat them as if they were.

Illustrations of these tendencies are not hard to find. They are present, for example, in John Rawls' *A Theory of Justice*. As noted earlier, Rawls is wholly preoccupied with the question of justice for individuals. He does not deal with the problem of ethnic communities. He takes no note at all of differences of language. He mentions race only to rule it out as a basis for discrimination, and he mentions religion out of concern for the individual believer rather than out of concern for religious communities. He mentions self-determination, not as the right of a group to choose whether or not to be a sovereign state, but as the right of a state to be free of external intervention. The society to which his theory of justice applies is a society of individuals; he assumes that all societies are alike in that they consist of individuals and not of groups.

Similar statements apply to Hanna Pitkin's *The Concept of Representation*. Pitkin seems to take into account only British and American experience—and only those aspects of that experience that other political philosophers and theorists have noted. The representation of which she speaks is the representation of individuals, of constituencies, of interests, and of the 'nation' as a whole. Of course, the 'persons' of whom she speaks might be artificial or corporate, but she does not seem to think of this possibility. She does not acknowledge that representation might go to racial communities (as it does in Fiji and New Zealand), or to religious communities (as it has in Lebanon), or to linguistic communities (as it does in the Belgian Cabinet), or to ethnic communities of any sort.

Carole Pateman's *Participation in Democratic Theory* also illustrates the point. Pateman assumes that the only participants are individuals. One can read her book without finding any reason why seats in the House of Commons are allocated on a quota basis to the English, the Scots, the Welsh, and the Irish, respectively, or even an acknowledgement that this happens.

J. P. Plamenatz's *Consent, Freedom, and Political Obligation* reinforces the point. Plamenatz does not even mention the possibility that consent might come from a group as a collective unit, that freedom (i.e., 'national liberation') might be desired by a group, or that political obligation might rest on a group.

In each of these cases, individualistic assumptions, combined with the dichotomy between the state and the individual, lead to inattention to practices that go counter to those assumptions. It is not that the practices are rejected; they are simply not considered. Vision is narrowed, and those studying the subjects treated are not reminded of and instructed on possibilities that they ought to take into account.

2. If, in principle, communities as well as individuals were accepted as right-and-duty-bearing units, the chance would be increased that a coherent and intellectually defensible doctrine or set of doctrines could be developed, which would respond to practical problems. Individuals want freedom and equality, to be sure, but there is also a 'quest for community.'[39] To focus only on the rights of individuals is to focus only on forces making for atomization and estrangement and to ignore primordial collective sentiment and group loyalties. Because of the failure to consider the appropriate role of communalism in the scheme of things, theory and doctrine go along one line and practice often goes along another; and individualism is assumed while anomie is bewailed. The thinking that occurs is compartmentalized—or cynical or naive.

3. If ethnic communities as well as individuals were explicitly accepted as right-and-duty-bearing units, it would probably make a difference in their representation in various activities. To be sure, individualism and even the principle of treatment according to merit are often modified in

practice in favor of group claims, as in affirmative action programs. Nevertheless, individualism gives an advantage to members of the dominant group. Their cultural characteristics permit them to establish rapport most easily with those who already have influence and power. They command the dominant language. These qualities are likely to make them seem most suitable for appointive and elective offices and for leadership positions in all walks of life. Thus they tend to obtain disproportionate representation in the various elites. Persons from the minorities who become members of an elite may or may not be representative of their own culture group; they are likely to be co-opted, perhaps because they have more or less abandoned the culture from which they sprang.

4. If ethnic communities as well as individuals were accepted as right-and-duty-bearing units, it should make a difference to the fate of communities that are nondominant and to the psychological health of their members. Individualism, combined with the usual stress on personal merit, is destructive of cultures other than the majority or dominant culture. The schools—at every level—are likely to promote the dominant culture and to undermine all others. The standards and the procedures for recruiting elites are likely, as indicated above, to favor persons who belong to the dominant culture or are willing to assimilate into it. The minority person who adheres to a minority culture is likely to be looked upon as second class and second rate, his culture disparaged as unworthy. The whole attitude is an attack on the existence of the group and the self-respect of its members. It means oppression, and perhaps exploitation as well.

5. It would facilitate affirmative action if ethnic communities were accepted as right-and-duty-bearing units. After all, the discrimination for which affirmative action is compensatory was directed against individuals because of their membership in certain communities, and through them against the community as such. The discrimination was in a sense impersonal; it was not that a given person was to be denied certain opportunities and thus be excluded or kept down; it was rather that the whole community was to be kept in its place. The reciprocal of this is to take compensatory action for the whole community and to let individual members benefit even if they have not personally suffered discrimination. Such action is hard to justify, however, if the focus is simply on the individual and the state. It is hard to justify especially if affirmative action includes the preferential treatment of some, and therefore the prejudicial treatment of others. The point is brought out in the DeFunis case—the case of a white who claimed that he was denied equal protection when the Law School of the University of Washington denied him admission while granting admis-

sion to apparently less qualified blacks. The case went into the courts, but the issue was never resolved because it had become moot by the time the Supreme Court was ready to act. The issue would be much easier to handle—in fact, it would probably not arise as an issue—if it were accepted that communities as well as individuals are entitled to certain kinds of status and rights.

6. As already indicated, to accept communities as right-and-duty-bearing units would provide a more satisfactory doctrinal basis for some actual practices; it would also open up the question of engaging in comparable additional practices. For example, as noted above, American courts are treating certain groups as 'cognizable'; in the name of the principle that the state shall not discriminate against individuals, the courts are ordering measures benefiting members of such groups, whether or not they have suffered discrimination. Moreover, corrective equity for a cognizable group may impair the interests, if not the rights, of a group that is noncognizable. For instance, a community of Hasidic Jews in the Williamsburgh district of New York could be divided against its will between two electoral districts so as to undo the effects of discrimination against blacks.[40] An exclusive emphasis on individualism thus leads to paradoxes that need to be resolved.

Soul City offers another paradox. It is being developed in North Carolina under black leadership, the idea being that it is to be mainly for blacks. But undiscriminating individualism makes it impossible to state this explicitly or officially. The merits of the project can scarcely even be debated in terms of the principle relevant to it—that communities as such (in this case the black community) deserve consideration and may have rights.

Still another paradox appears in the case of the Old Order Amish in Wisconsin.[41] The issue was whether the religious community had a right of survival that modified the right of the child to an education. The Amish were willing to send their children to public schools through the eighth grade, but feared that their community might be destroyed if the law requiring attendance to the sixteenth year were enforced against them. In this case, interestingly enough, the Supreme Court gave precedence to the right of the religious community. But the court acted on the basis of the first amendment guarantee of freedom of religion, leaving the presumption untouched that nonreligious ethnic communities do not have a comparable right.

7. A doctrine accepting both individuals and communities as right-and-duty-bearing units is susceptible to universal application, whereas a doctrine focusing on individuals is not. Even if the melting pot could produce homogeneity in the United States, it could not possibly do so in most countries of the world. Actually, it is out of the question in the United States too.

All countries of the world are in some degree heterogeneous. The tendency to think of states as if they were nation-states is highly misleading, for scarcely a state qualifies for the label.[42] Virtually all states are polyglot in the sense that they are multilingual, multiracial, multireligious, or multinational. If every culture group in the world were assumed to be a 'nation' entitled to be a state, it would mean the division of virtually every existing state and the creation of mini-states numbering in the thousands. To have a doctrine that responds to the heterogeneity of the world it is necessary to provide a place for (that is, to permit the grant of status and rights to) groups that are intermediate between the individual and the state. Choices can then be deliberately made concerning the relative emphasis on the two principles. Sometimes the emphasis will properly be on individual rights and therefore on equal treatment regardless of ethnic differences. Sometimes the emphasis will properly be on the rights of ethnic communities and therefore on the differential treatment of members and nonmembers. The implication is that the state should not be conceived as a monolithic unity but as an agency for recognizing groups, determining what legal status and rights they shall have, supervising and coordinating their interrelationships, and itself conducting certain kinds of functions in which all have a common interest.

8. If communities as well as individuals were accepted as right-and-duty-bearing units, there would be consequences for both justice and peace.

In principle, the granting of status and rights of ethnic communities on an intermediate basis should extend justice by giving minorities their due and reducing the discrimination and oppression to which they are commonly subjected. At the same time, this consequence cannot simply be assumed. After all, the concept of status and rights for communities does not mean simply status and rights for *minority* communities. Dominant or majority communities would necessarily also have status and rights and would have an opportunity to influence the decisions that are made. It is too much to expect that, as a rule, they would be magnanimous and benign. The problem would be to induce them to be fair. In a sense, dominant communities now commonly arrogate special privilege to themselves under the cover of individualism and the principle of treatment according to merit, and the temptation to do this might or might not be reduced if community rights as such were explicitly considered. The record of the whites of South Africa, who endorse the idea of rights for different ethnic communities, is appalling. It is at least arguable that even if justice calls for community rights in principle, it would be better strategy in practice for minority communities to forego their claims and to concentrate instead on the principle of nondiscrimination. But this would have to be a short-run strategy, for certain countries only; as already indicated, it would not provide a suitable universal basis for organizing mankind.

In principle, too, the grant of status and rights to communities on an intermediate basis should make for peace—on the assumption that justice is one of the conditions of peace. But it is unrealistic to expect the prompt achievement of justice even if just rules are accepted. Struggle is likely to be necessary. Hope for justice might actually increase violence, as surer and more rapid change is demanded by some and resisted by others. In the long run, however, it seems probable that the interests of peace as well as the interests of justice would be served.

Two Caveats

Two caveats are in order. No criticism is intended of the idea of individual human rights. They are precious. And defense of them might need to be even more vigilant where groups enjoy status and rights, for groups as well as the state might violate them. The point here is not that the problem of equal treatment for individuals should be ignored, but that the rule of equal treatment must be interpreted in the light of a counterpart: that ethnic communities—as well as states, nations, and 'peoples'—may also have just claims. Reasonable classification is accepted as compatible with equal treatment, and for certain purposes it should be regarded as reasonable to classify people into groups by language, race, or religion. In appropriate circumstances, the relevant claims should be interpreted and applied in the light of each other. Thus, as in the Old Order Amish case, the right of a child to an education and the right of the state to require school attendance until the sixteenth year would be considered in terms of the right of a community to preserve itself. And the right of an individual to freedom of expression might be interpreted in terms of the right of a linguistic community to preserve its language.

The second caveat is that the case made here is general in its terms and leaves many questions unresolved. The criteria for deciding whether a community should be recognized and what status and rights it should have are left virtually unexplored. It is obviously not the argument that just any combination of persons is entitled to call itself a group and to have whatever status and rights it wants. Present practices over the world are suggestive of what might be desirable, but much examining and appraising need to occur before generally applicable standards of judgment can be worked out.

Conclusion

The requirements of logic and the long-term requirements of universal justice commend the idea of accepting communities as right-and-duty-bearing units. It is quite illogical to take the view that only states, nations, and 'peoples' are entitled to be treated as entities and that lesser groups are not. It is illogical to jump from the state, nation, or 'people' on the one side, to the individual on the other, and to say that the ethnic communities that exist in-between do not deserve consideration. Not only is it illogical, it is also unjust. It is unjust to accept or assume status and rights for states, nations, and 'peoples,' but to reject them for ethnic communities that are also historically constituted. And it is even unjust to individuals to say that those who belong to dominant groups can enjoy the attendant advantages and satisfactions, whereas those who belong to nondominant and minority groups must either abandon their culture or accept second-class status. It is not enough for political theorists to contemplate simply the individual and society, or relationships between man and the state. It is time for them to contemplate mankind in its great variety.

Notes

1. Though not presuming to classify Dante Germino ideologically, I might cite his statement that 'the primary purpose of a political philosopher is to explore the individual's relationship to society. . . .' See his contribution, 'The Contemporary Relevance of the Classics of Political Philosophy,' in Fred I. Greenstein and Nelson W. Polsby, eds., *Political Science: Scope and Theory*, Vol. 1, *Handbook of Political Science* (Reading, Mass.: Addison-Wesley 1975), 259.
2. Cf. Morris Ginsberg, *On Justice in Society* (Ithaca: Cornell University Press 1965), 74–75; S. I. Benn and R. S. Peters, *The Principles of Political Thought* (New York: Free Press 1965), 107–16.
3. Cf. Otto Gierke, *Natural Law and the Theory of Society 1500 to 1800*, trans. with an introduction by Ernest Barker (Cambridge: Cambridge University Press 1934), I, lxiv, lxxxvii, 174, 175; Frederic William Maitland, *Collected Papers* (Cambridge: Cambridge University Press 1911), III, 304–20; Morris R. Cohen, *Reason and Nature: An Essay on the Meaning of Scientific Method* (2nd ed., Glencoe, Ill.: Free Press 1953), 388–97; Harold J. Laski, 'Morris Cohen's Approach to Legal Philosophy,' *University of Chicago Law Review*, xv (Spring 1948), 577–82; Leicester C. Webb, 'Corporate Personality and Political Pluralism,' in Webb, ed., *Legal Personality and Political Pluralism* (Melbourne: Melbourne University Press 1958), 45–65; Dirk Jellema, 'Abraham Kuyper's Attack on Liberalism,' *Review of Politics*, xix (October 1957), 482–85; Bernard

Zylstra, *From Pluralism to Collectivism: The Development of Harold Laski's Political Thought* (Assen, The Netherlands: Van Gorcum 1968), 25, 38–39, 50–53.

4. *Hobbes's Leviathan* (Oxford: Clarendon Press 1909), chap. xviii, 133.
5. George H. Sabine, *A History of Political Theory* (New York: Holt 1950), 475.
6. Ernest Barker, ed., *Social Contract: Essays by Locke, Hume, and Rousseau* (New York: Oxford University Press 1962), 56–57.
7. Ibid., 194.
8. Van Dyke, 'Justice as Fairness: For Groups?' *American Political Science Review*, Vol. 69 (June 1975), 607–14.
9. Barker (fn. 6), 272–73.
10. Ibid., xii.
11. John Stuart Mill, *Considerations on Representative Government* (Indianapolis: Bobbs-Merrill 1958), 230, 233.
12. Ernest Barker, *Principles of Social & Political Theory* (Oxford: Clarendon Press 1951), 3, 42.
13. Ibid., 55.
14. Ibid., 56.
15. Ibid., 139.
16. Ibid., 71.
17. Cf. the definition of a *right* offered by Plamenatz: 'A right is a power which a creature ought to possess, either because its exercise by him is itself good or else because it is a means to what is good, and in the exercise of which all rational beings ought to protect him.' J. P. Plamenatz, *Consent, Freedom, and Political Obligation* (London: Oxford University Press 1938), 82.
18. Van Dyke, 'Human Rights and the Rights of Groups,' *American Journal of Political Science*, xviii (November 1974), 725–41.
19. Great Britain. Parliamentary Papers. *Inter-territorial Organisation in East Africa*. Colonial No. 191 (December 1945), 8.
20. Cf. Tanganyika. *Report of the Committee on Constitutional Development 1951* (Dar es Salaam: Government Printer 1951), 2, 18–19; Cranford Pratt, 'Multi-Racialism and Local Government in Tanganyika,' *Race*, 11 (November 1960), 35–36; Yash Tandon, 'A Political Survey,' in Dharam P. Ghai, ed., *Portrait of a Minority: Asians in East Africa* (Nairobi: Oxford University Press 1965), 79.
21. Cf. Van Dyke, 'One Man One Vote and Majority Rule as Human Rights,' *Revue des Droits de l'Homme*, vi, Nos. 3–4 (1973), 456–58.
22. Great Britain. *Fiji Independence Order 1970*, 'The Constitution of Fiji,' Articles 45 and 68.
23. Robert Senelle, 'The Revision of the Constitution, 1967–1971,' *Memo From Belgium*, Nos. 144–145–146, January–February–March, 1972 (Ministry of Foreign Affairs, External Trade and Cooperation in Development), 130.
24. *Native American Church* v. *Navajo Tribal Council*, 272 F. 2d 131 (10th Cir. 1959). U.S. Department of the Interior, Office of the Solicitor, *Handbook of Federal Indian Law*, by Felix S. Cohen (Washington 1942), 122–23, 278.
25. *United States* v. *Carolene Products Co.*, 304 U.S. 144 (1938), at 153, fn. 4.

26. *Beauharnais* v. *Illinois*, 343 U.S. 250 (1951), at 262.
27. *United States* v. *Jefferson County Board of Education*, 372 F. 2d 836 (1966), at 866, quoting Note, *University of Chicago Law Review*, xx (1953), 577.
28. *Cisneros* v. *Corpus Christi Independent School Dist.*, 324 F. Supp. 599 (1970), at 606, 627; *United States* v. *State of Texas*, 342 F. Supp. 24 (1971), at 24.
29. *Hunter* v. *Erickson*, 393 U.S. 385 (1969), at 393.
30. *Hernandez* v. *Texas*, 347 U.S. 475 (1954) at 478. *United States* v. *Hunt*, 265 F. Supp. 178 (1967), at 188.
31. *Cousins* v. *City Council of City of Chicago*, 466 F. 2d 830 (1972), at 843, 851. Cf. *Sims* v. *Baggett*, 247 F. Supp. 103 (1965); *Howard* v. *Adams County Board of Supervisors*, 453 F. 2d 455 (1972), at 457; *Graves* v. *Barnes*, 343 F. Supp. 704 (1972), at 728, 730; *Klahr* v. *Williams*, 339 F. Supp. 922 (1972), at 927; *White* v. *Regester*, 412 U.S. 755 (1972), at 765; *Beer* v. *United States*, 374 F. Supp. 363 (1974), at 393.
32. *Williams* v. *Rhodes*, 393 U.S. 23 (1968), at 39; emphasis added.
33. See, for example, *Officers for Justice* v. *Civil S. Com'n, C. & C. San Francisco*, 371 F. Supp. 1328 (1973), at 1332.
34. Fiss, 'Groups and the Equal Protection Clause,' *Philosophy & Public Affairs*, v. (Winter 1976), 157.
35. Council of Europe, Consultative Assembly, Sixteenth Ordinary Session, Resolution 290 (1965).
36. E/CN.4/Sub.2/40/Rev.1 (June 1949), 2. Cf. E/CN.4/641 (25 October 1951).
37. Michla Pomerance, 'The United States and Self-Determination: Perspectives on the Wilsonian Conception,' *American Journal of International Law*, Vol. 70 (January 1976), 2.
38. A/Res/3375, XXX (13 November 1975); emphasis added.
39. Robert A. Nisbet, *The Quest for Community* (New York: Oxford University Press 1953).
40. *United Jewish Org. of Williamsburgh, Inc.* v. *Wilson*, 377 F. Supp. 1164 (1974); 500 F. 2d 434 (1974).
41. *Wisconsin* v. *Yoder*, 406 U.S. 205 (1972).
42. Walker Connor, 'Ethnic Nationalism as a Political Force,' *World Affairs*, Vol. 133 (September 1970), 91–98; Connor, 'Nation-Building or Nation-Destroying?' *World Politics*, xxiv (April 1972), 320; Connor, 'The Politics of Ethnonationalism,' *Journal of International Affairs*, xxvii, No. 1 (1973), 12.

2 Marx, Engels, and the National Question

EPHRAIM NIMNI

The writings of Marx and Engels on the national question reveal great differences in interpretation from one historical situation to another. In this paper I propose that there is an underlying paradigm which makes their seemingly divergent analyses part of a coherent whole. The main parameters of this paradigm are derived from three conceptions widely considered central to historical materialism: the theory of evolution; the theory of economic determination of the forces of production; and a derivative category of both, the Eurocentric bias in the analysis of concrete case studies.

The theory of *evolution* holds that social transformation can be grasped in universal laws of historical development. History is a progressive series of changes through universal and hierarchically defined stages. There are many variations of this theory, but in broad terms, it is accepted by the vast majority of schools that constitute the Marxist tradition.

The second parameter is the theory of economic determination of the forces of production. This theory is a form of *economic reductionism*, because it declares that all meaningful changes within the social arena take place in the sphere of economic (class) relations. Marx himself expressed this theory in terms of his metaphoric distinction between *base* and *superstructure*. The superstructure is shaped and determined, after various stages of more or less complex mediations, by the processes of change that occur at the level of the base.

The third parameter, the Eurocentric bias in concrete case studies is, strictly speaking, derived from the first two. It is not a separate analytical category, and cannot be understood without reference to economic reductionism or the theory of evolution. It warrants separate consideration, however, because of its important methodological consequences when the

I wish to thank Ivar Oxaal, Ernesto Laclau, Bob Jessop, Bill Brugger and Norman Wintrop for their comments and suggestions on an earlier version of this paper.

Ephraim Nimni, 'Marx, Engels and the National Question', *Science & Society* Vol. 53/3 (1989), pp. 297–326 (minus 316–25). Reprinted by permission of *Science & Society*.

Marxist analysis of national phenomena is applied to the non-European world. The Marxist tradition is trapped in the paradoxical situation of claiming to be a universal theory of social emancipation, while using an ethnocentric methodology to conceptualize social formations located outside the area of Western culture. *Eurocentrism*, then, refers to the construction of a model of development which universalizes empirically observed European categories of development: social transformation in different societies is understood in terms of a Western developmental rationale; 'the country that is more developed industrially shows, to the less developed, the image of its own future' (Marx, 1977, Vol. I, 19).

I will argue that the above-mentioned parameters give coherence and unity to the apparently contradictory positions of Marx and Engels on the national question.

The Problematic Heritage of Marx and Engels

An influential group of Marx-Engels scholars maintains, in a variety of works, that the latter had no theoretically coherent approach to the national question; that Marx and Engels related to every national movement on a purely '*ad hoc*' basis; and that their attitude was often dictated by circumstantial political events (Davis, 1967; Löwy, 1976, 81; Talmon, 1981, 38; Pelczynski, 1984, 262; Haupt, 1974, 13; for a different approach see Walicki, 1982, 375).

Contrary to this position, I argue that Marx and Engels had a coherent view of the national question, even if there is no single literature that directly presents their theories in an explicit way. The social-evolutionary and economic reductionist parameters provide the basis for a theory of the national question which is compatible with the apparently contradictory positions held by the founding fathers of historical materialism in relation to various movements of national emancipation. This largely unwritten, but no less real and influential, perception of the national question provided the intellectual basis for the way in which subsequent generations of Marxists have understood the burdensome problem of nationalism.

Two considerations were crucial in the formulation of Marx' and Engels' understanding of the national question: the first was their use of a universal, but at the same time, historically located model for national development. This is the model 'state—language—nation.' The second concerned the capacity or incapacity of concrete national communities to evolve from 'lower' to 'higher' stages of development. This is the theory of 'historical vs. non-historical' nations. It is necessary to evaluate these two considerations in some detail.

The Pattern 'State—Language—Nation"

For Marx and Engels, the 'modern nation' was the direct outcome of a process whereby the feudal mode of production was superseded by the capitalist mode of production, causing dramatic concomitant changes in the process of social organization. This event impelled most Western European social formations to evolve into linguistically cohesive and politically centralized units through the formation of 'modern states.' Thus, what Marx and Engels called 'modern nations' only came into existence through the embryonic capitalist economy in transition from feudalism to capitalism. As a direct result of this process, the feudal society was slowly united under the structure of the embryonic modern state. This caused the destruction of local peculiarities, initiating the process of uniformization of populations, which was considered an important condition for the formation of a market economy (Engels, 1977a, 1977b; Haupt and Weill, 1974, 281).

In Marx' view, one of the strongest indicators of uniformization was the emergence and development of Western European languages. A crucial characteristic of the capitalist mode of production is the intensification of the division of labor, coupled with a growing interdependence among units of production, holding together a mass of dispossessed free laborers capable of selling their labor-power in a free market. Capitalism breaks the isolation of feudal units, increasing the interaction of the various participants in the newly formed market. This in turn necessitates a 'medium' for efficient communication; thus according to Marx, Western European languages emerged to fulfill this role and to consolidate distinct and recognizable linguistic units based on the embryonic absolutist state (Haupt and Weill, 1974, 275). This is, in essence, Marx' and Engels' account of the emergence of 'modern nations.' From this argument it is possible to derive two important criteria that distinguish 'modern nations' from more 'ancient' national communities: 1) modern nations must hold a population large enough to allow for an internal division of labor which characterizes a capitalist system with its competing classes; and 2) modern nations must occupy a cohesive and 'sufficiently large' territorial space to provide for the existence of a 'viable state' (Bloom, 1975, 44).

This understanding of the formation of 'modern nations' is clearly derived from Marx' and Engels' observation of the process in Western Europe—particularly France, and to a limited extent, England. But above all, it adheres to the view of the French Revolution as the model for national development. The national consolidation that took place after the French Revolution was a model for national formation in other 'less developed' parts of the world. Given the importance of the 'French model' in Marx' and Engels' thought, it may be useful briefly to discuss the national process in that country, particularly at the time of the French Revolution.

The Jacobins and other French revolutionaries believed that the best way to establish a democratic state was to follow a path of tight centralization and linguistic standardization. They saw the existence of non Parisian-French speaking peoples within the boundaries of the French state as a considerable menace to this process of uniformization. The geographical area occupied by the French absolutist state, however, was in fact inhabited during the best part of the pre-revolutionary period by a conglomerate of linguistic communities, some of which spoke Romance languages (Langue D'Oc, Langue D'Oil, Catalan), others Celtic languages (Breton), and other ancient pre-Latin languages (Euzkera). In reality, the language of the court of Versailles, which subsequently became 'French,' was spoken by only a minority of the population. During the Middle Ages there were not one but several French languages. Each province spoke and wrote its own 'dialect' (Giraud, 1968, 27).

During the period preceding the Revolution the language of Paris began to exercise definitive supremacy, eventually converting itself into the official language of the state (Doujot, 1946). After the Revolution this process was greatly encouraged by the revolutionary government, anxious to create a 'national state' with a uniform language for all its citizens. But this task was not at all easy. According to Brunnot (1958, 44–49), of a total population of about 25 million, between six and seven million did not understand Parisian French; a similar number was capable only of holding a very basic conversation in this language; ten million were bilingual, using their respective 'dialects' as their mother tongue and Parisian French as the 'lingua franca.' Only three million inhabitants of Paris and surrounding areas spoke 'French' as their mother tongue, and an even smaller number were literate in this language.

This situation was reported to the 1791 constitutional convention, resulting in intensified efforts by the revolutionary government to spread the use of the French language as fast as possible. Two closely connected factors account for this: the revolutionaries' wish to create a democratic and tightly centralized state, and the need to ensure the hegemony of the Parisian bourgeoisie against pockets of feudal and aristocratic resistance in remote locations. Given the close association between Parisian French and revolutionary aims, it is hardly surprising that the counterrevolution was stronger in those areas where French was hardly spoken—Brittany, for example. A tightly centralized state was bound to destroy the administrative and cultural autonomy of the non-French national communities.

The combination of cultural imperialism and tight administrative centralization led to an almost complete destruction of the culture and language of the non-Parisian French national communities. As the animosity of the oppressed national communities towards the Parisian bourgeoisie grew, they became the rallying point for counterrevolutionary activities. In response the Jacobins equated the national identity of those unfortunate peoples with counterrevolution, without realizing that it was the Jacobins' own lack of sensitivity towards their cultural aspirations that was pushing these communities into the arms of the reaction. The Jacobin Deputies Barère and Grégoire presented a report to the constitutional assembly of 1794 with a revealing title: *Report on the Need and Means to Destroy Rural Dialects (Patois) and Universalize the Use of the French Language*. This work eloquently illustrates the ideas of the Jacobins in relation to what we may call today 'national minorities' (Rosdolsky, 1986, 31–32; Salvi, 1973, 477).[1] One year later, the deputies advanced the following revolutionary slogan: 'In the one and undivided Republic, the one and undivided use of the language of freedom"—a slogan which, as Rosdolsky argues, conveniently forgot that French was also the language of the court of Versailles and of prerevolutionary absolutism in general.

This tendency to use the French language as the cultural medium for the advancement of revolutionary goals was noted by Marx, in his famous refutation of Lafargue's attempt to pursue the abolition of all national differences:

> . . . the English laughed very much when I began my speech by saying that our friend Lafargue and others had spoken '*en français*' to us, i.e., a language that nine tenths of the audience did not understand. I also suggested that by the negation of nationalities, he appeared quite unconsciously to understand their absorption by the *model French nation*. (MECW, Vol. 21, 288–9.)

Marx, however, did not draw any theoretical conclusions from this incident, and continued to believe that the 'French model' was the universal path for national development. State centralization and national unification with the consequent assimilation of small national communities was the only viable path to social progress. The preference for large centralized states was not only a strategic consideration, but also the basis of Marx' and Engels' unwritten conceptualization of the national phenomenon. The framework for this position can be detected in their conceptualization of civil society, the national state, and what they called the 'historical nations.'

The concept of 'civil society' was taken by Marx from Hegel's political philosophy. Civil society, for Hegel, is the place where individual self-interest receives its legitimation and becomes emancipated from religious and other considerations, which until the formation of civil society limited the free play of individual interests (Avineri, 1972, 142). This definition of civil society should be not confused with Hegel's definition of the state.

Civil society is based on needs of a 'lower kind,' which are best defined in the concept of *Verstand* (knowledge, understanding in the concrete mechanical sense). The state is the expression of a 'higher level of reason' which Hegel calls *Vernunft* (an ethical principle that permits essential understanding or consciousness). For Hegel, the state is the consciousness of freedom, but in a way that permits one to enjoy that freedom 'in conjunction with others,' while in civil society people realized their freedom with disregard for the freedom of others (Avineri, 1972, 143).

Marx was certainly influenced by the Hegelian conceptualization of civil society and its relation to the state, but he located that relationship in the developmental historicity of both concepts within the process of production. Civil society emerges, for Marx, at a specific stage of development of the productive forces. Here he inherited the evolutionist-universal perspective developed by Hegel; but he explicitly rejected its idealistic base. This becomes clear when Marx argues that the modern state, by its very constitution, is unable to overcome the egoism of civil society, because 'mere political emancipation' (the 'bourgeois state') leaves intact the world of private interest (civil society). Marx (1974, 57) concludes that:

> Civil society embraces the whole material intercourse of individuals within a definite stage of development of productive forces. It embraces the whole commercial and industrial life of a given stage, and, insofar, transcends the state and the nation, though, on the other hand again, it must assert itself in its foreign relations as *nationality* and inwardly must organise itself as state. (Emphasis added.)

This is an important consideration. The *general* form of civil society is present in the more *specific* forms of 'state' and 'nation,' and given that civil society is only the reflection of the dominant forces within it, it follows that in the capitalist mode of production the dominant class (the bourgeoisie) determines the content of civil society, while civil society itself, as described by Marx, *can not* exist outside capitalist relations of production.

The implications of Marx' discussion of civil society are important for the national question. The 'modern nation' is a historical phenomenon that has to be located at a precise historical period; this is the era of the ascendancy of the bourgeoisie as a hegemonic class—the period of consolidation of the capitalist mode of production.

In this context the different treatment given by Marx and Engels to different national communities acquires meaning and coherence. The 'modern nation' is an epiphenomenal result of the development of the bourgeoisie as the hegemonic class, and the former must be evaluated on the merits of the latter. If it represents a higher stage of development of the productive forces in relation to a pre-determined process of historical change; if it abolishes the feudal system by building a 'national state'; then the nationalist movement deserves support as a 'tool' for progressive social change. If, however, the nationalist movement emerges among linguistic or cultural communities incapable of surviving the upheavals of capitalist transformation, because they are too small or have a weak or non-existent bourgeoisie, then the nationalist movement becomes a 'regressive' force—one which is incapable of overcoming the stage of 'peasant-feudal' social organization. Marx and Engels repeatedly argued that national communities incapable of constituting 'proper national states' should 'vanish' by being assimilated into more 'progressive' and 'vital' nations.

The conceptualization of the emergence and development of 'modern nations' presented in this social-evolutionary and epiphenomenal way may be seen in every analysis of concrete features of national movements in the works of Marx and Engels and constitutes their theory of national development, even though the general theoretical question is not specifically discussed in any single work. There is, however, a problem that must be addressed in order to understand the implications of Marx' and Engels' position on the national question: the terminological ambiguity that recurs in their works.

The Terminological Ambiguity

In different European languages the concepts of 'people,' 'nation' and 'nationality' have at times different and confusing meanings. This situation is further complicated by the no less confusing and indiscriminate use of this terminology in the specialist literature. The terms 'nation,' 'nationality,' 'people,' 'nation state,' are either taken as synonyms or to mean different things in different situations, creating a terminological confusion that is seldom clarified with clear-cut definitions (Vilar, 1962, 29). Marx and Engels were not an exception to this rule; the terms 'nation' and 'nationality' have different meanings in their work (Haupt, 1974, 21).

In English and French the word 'nation' usually refers to the population of a sovereign state, but it is sometimes taken to mean clearly identifiable national communities that lack a national state (for example, the Welsh nation or the Catalan nation). The word 'nationality' has two different and confusing meanings: 1) a synonym of citizenship, juridical definition of membership of a state usually defined by entitlement to a passport (British nationality, French nationality); and 2) a community of culture and/or descent, which also incorporates some of the meanings of the more contemporary term 'ethnicity' (English nationality, Welsh nationality).[2]

Marx and Engels generally used the word 'nation' in its English and French meaning to designate the permanent population of a nation-state.

The term 'nationality,' however, was used in its Central and Eastern European denotation, to designate an ethno-cultural community that had not achieved full national status because it lacked a state of its own (Rosdolsky, 1965, 337). In Marx' and Engels' works, 'nationalities' will either become 'nations' by acquiring a state of their own (Poland, Ireland), or alternatively they are said to be 'historyless peoples' (*Geschichtslosen Völker*), national communities that lack 'historical vitality' because of their inability to consolidate a national state. For Marx and Engels, these 'non-historical nationalities' are intrinsically reactionary because of their inability to adapt to the capitalist mode of production. This is because their survival is only guaranteed in the old order; so, by necessity, they have to be regressive to avoid extinction.

Consequently, modern nations are for Marx and Engels what we today call 'nation states': ethno-cultural and linguistic communities with their own state. Nationalities are ethno-cultural and linguistic groups not developed into full nations because they lack their own state. This model of national formation is greatly inspired by the historical development of the French and, to a lesser extent, the British case, which by nature of being 'the most advanced nations' must serve as a model for 'less developed' national communities.

There is however, another dimension to Marx' and Engels' discussion of national communities. *Nations*, as noted earlier, were for Marx one of the concrete forms of the general form 'civil society.' Civil society only comes into existence as a specific configuration of certain classes. Since the bourgeoisie is the universally dominant class, civil society gives legitimacy to bourgeois class domination by creating the impression that the class requirements of the bourgeoisie to reproduce its conditions of existence are the 'general' requirements of society as a whole. Thus, the state in its 'national' form must promote the best possible conditions for fulfillment of these 'general' requirements, which point toward the 'final goal' of abolishing capitalist relations of production. This has far-reaching consequences for the 'nation,' which can be schematized in the following way: Abolition of capitalism will cause the abolition of: a) civil society as an entity reproducing the conditions of existence of class societies; b) the bourgeoisie as the hegemonic class of civil society and the proletariat as the subordinated oppressed class; c) the state as the instrument through which the bourgeoisie controls civil society; and d) the nation as the framework for the existence of the bourgeois state.

The nation, as the framework for the existence of the capitalist (national) state, creates a 'linguistic unit' that is essential in consolidating the conditions of existence of capitalism, by generating a medium of communication (language) and a focus of identity which gives a general appearance to the sectarian interests of the bourgeoisie (nationalism). Thus, in terms of this unilinear and Eurocentric process of development, the nation is crucially linked to the capitalist state, because *both* are concrete epiphenomenal expressions of 'civil society'—the mechanism which created them in the first place. Once the state is abolished (or withers away), a similar fate awaits the nation. Consider the statement in the *Communist Manifesto*:

> . . . the proletariat must first of all acquire political supremacy, must rise to be the leading class of the nation, it is, so far, itself national, though not in the bourgeois sense of the word.

This is a tactical ploy to gain power from the bourgeoisie on its own terrain, since the nation will be abolished by the advancing tide of history:

> National differences and antagonisms between peoples are daily more and more vanishing owing to the development of the bourgeoisie, to freedom of commerce, to the world market, to uniformity in the mode of production and in the conditions of life corresponding thereto. The supremacy of the proletariat will cause them to vanish still faster.

Marx and Engels expected the proletariat to become the 'national class' for a short period, believing that this is a transitional but historically necessary step in order to advance to a 'higher' stage, the abolition of the national state. In this sense Marx' ironic remarks on Lafargue's speech do not indicate that he rejected the abolition of nations as such, but merely that he rejected the idea that this stage of development had come to pass at the time of the meetings of the First International.

The parameters of analysis outlined in the introduction help to give coherence to the apparently contradictory formulations of Marx and Engels on the national question. Their support for the right to self-determination in the Irish and Polish case, as well as their opposition to self-determination for the so-called 'South Slavs,' can be explained in terms of the rigid evolutionary model, the epiphenomenal economism, and the Western Eurocentric approach that permeated their interpretations. These parameters of analysis, concerned as they were with the universal effect of the transformation of the productive forces, are insensitive to the specific circumstances that generate the emergence of concrete national movements. Classical Marxist epistemology is concerned only with the impact of universal processes of social transformation, and is therefore blind to all those aspects that cannot be directly derived from the laws of political economy. The nation is understood as a residual creation of the productive forces to secure the conditions of domination of the bourgeoisie during the transition to, and consolidation of, the capitalist mode of production. A clear effect of this understanding is the most unfortunate aspect of Marx' and Engels' conceptualization of the national question: the theory of nations 'without history.'

The Theory of Nations 'Without History'

Bozě! . . ., Ach nikdo není na zemi Kdoby Slavům (sic) spravedlivost činil?[3]

The way in which Marx and Engels related to a number of stateless or numerically small national communities has been a source of both embarrassment and amazement for a considerable number of commentators within the Marxist tradition, from the second international right up to recent works on the subject (Kautsky, 1978; Davis, 1967, 73; Haupt, 1974, 22; Löwy, 1976, 83). However the most detailed and illuminating discussion can be found in R. Rosdolsky's seminal work. With the exception of Rosdolsky's thorough and illuminating research, there have been few attempts to understand Marx' and Engels' position on the subject, and no attempt to locate it in the context of their overall theoretical positions. The following discussion will try to provide a link between the theory of non-historical nations and the general Marxist views on the national question.

As has been noted, the idea of progressive centralization as the economy develops from a lower to a higher stage is at the heart of Marx' and Engels' analysis of the national question. It is therefore hardly surprising to find that Marx and Engels regarded every form of nationalist ideology and activity as aimed towards the formation and consolidation of national states. Nationalist ideology is for Marx a mere epiphenomenon of the growth of the nation (Smith, 1973, 21). One of the main problems with this pattern of analysis is that it leads on the one hand to a gross overestimation of the structural need of the bourgeoisie to build a national state, and on the other hand to a parallel underestimation of cultural and ethnic factors (insofar as they are not explained as epiphenomena of the economy) in the formation of national communities. The problem here is not only the use of Western European modes of development, but also a 'capital-centred' emphasis in the discussion of all aspects of national phenomena. Nationalist movements and national communities are always defined in terms of their functionality within the capitalist system (Gallisot, 1979, 809). Once the goal of national communities is defined to be the formation of national states, the resultant problem in this over-simplified analysis is how to explain the existence and behavior of nationalist movements that are neither capable of forming, nor willing to form, a national state.

If, in accordance with the Marxian interpretation, the growth of the nation only heralds the formation of national states so that the bourgeoisie can secure its hegemonic position, then national communities incapable of constituting national states are acting against 'the tide of history.' They perform a 'reactionary function,' since they cannot develop a 'healthy' and hegemonic bourgeoisie, a condition '*sine qua non*' for the subsequent proletarian revolution. This analysis, however, leads to an even more serious and disturbing conclusion: these usually small national communities are not only 'functionally' reactionary, but *intrinsically* reactionary relics of the past, which must disappear to pave the way for social progress. Since the only purpose of national agitation is the drive to build a national state, national communities that because of their size are not viable independent economic units have no '*raison d'être*.' If these national communities wish to follow a path of national revival, they will become 'socially regressive,' since they cannot adapt to the capitalist mode of production and therefore have to remain 'feudal enclaves' in order to subsist as independent entities. Furthermore, these 'feudal enclaves' have no other choice but to 'closely associate' with those reactionary forces that oppose the 'progressive' unifying role of the bourgeoisie. These unfortunate national communities ('ethnographic monuments' in Engels' words) must culturally and politically perish in order to make way for the unifying role of the bourgeoisie.

The central idea behind this dubious concept of 'non-historical nations' is that peoples (*Völker*) who had proven to be unable to build a state over a period of time will never be able to do so (Davis, 1967, 2). Hegel makes a sharp distinction between 'nations' and 'states.' For Hegel, a group of people may exist as a nation, but in such a condition the nation is unable to contribute to the unfolding of world history. A nation, according to Hegel, will only fulfill its 'historical mission' if it is capable of building a stable state. Therefore it is not an accident that what Hegel calls 'uncivilized peoples' have no history, because they have been proven 'incapable of having a state.'

These idealistic speculations are perhaps one of the weakest features of Hegel's political philosophy and are certainly in direct opposition to a historical materialist conception of history. It is indeed strange to find this conceptualization echoed in the works of the founders of historical materialism. The revival of Hegelian terminology, particularly in the context of the 1848 revolutions, was coupled with increasing usage of abusive language *vis-à-vis* communities that did not conform to the path to national development discussed above. The intense hostility of Marx and Engels towards these national communities can be ascertained from the following quotations.

Spaniards and Mexicans

The Spaniards are indeed degenerate. But a degenerate Spaniard, a Mexican that is the ideal. All vices of the Spaniards—Boastfulness, Grandiloquence, and

Quixoticism—are found in the Mexicans raised to the third power. (Marx, corresp., December 1847, in Aguilar, 1969, 67.)

Scandinavians

Scandinavism is enthusiasm for the brutal, sordid, piratical old norse national traits, for the deep inner life which is unable to express its exuberant ideas and sentiments in words, but can express them in deeds, namely in rudeness towards women, perpetual drunkenness and wild berserk frenzy alternating with tearful sentimentality . . . Obviously, the more primitive a nation is, the more closely its customs and way of life resemble those of the old norse people, the more 'scandinavian' it must be. (MECW, Vol. 7, 422.)

Chinese

It is almost needless to observe that, in the same measure in which opium has obtained the sovereignty over the Chinese, the Emperor and his staff of pedantic mandarins have become dispossessed of their own sovereignty. It would seem as though history had first to make this whole people drunk before it could rise them out of their hereditary stupidity. (Marx, 'Revolution in China and in Europe,' *New York Daily Tribune*, 14 June 1853, in Avineri, ed., 1969, 68.)

North African Bedouins

The struggle of the Bedouins was a hopeless one, and though the manner in which brutal soldiers like Bugeaud have carried on the war is highly blameworthy, the conquest of Algeria is an important and fortunate fact for the progress of civilisation . . . and even if we may regret that the liberty of the Bedouins of the desert has been destroyed, we must not forget that these same Bedouins were a nation of robbers, whose principal means of living consisted in making excursions upon each other. . . . (Engels, in Avineri, ed., 1969, 47.)

This is only a sample; Marx and Engels were, to put it mildly, impatient with and intolerant of ethnic minorities. It is possible to ascertain this from their private correspondence, in which the most infamous example is the characterization of Lasalle as a 'Jewish Nigger.'[4] But the dichotomy 'historical/non-historical nations' was revived by Marx and Engels in the context of the 1848 revolution while discussing the revival to national life of the Czechs, Slovaks, Ukrainians (Ruthenians), and Serbs, all of which were Eastern European national communities that spoke Slavonic-related languages. These diverse national communities were constituted into a fictitious unit called the 'Southern Slavs.'

If the conditions of a national community do not allow for the formation of a 'viable' state, the national community has to assimilate to a larger state and a more viable national community, with 'democracy as compensation' (MECW, 227, 362–8). But not only is this process of national assimilation highly desirable in Marx' and Engels' view; it also cannot be opposed. Nations that are incapable of forming national states and still persist in their claim to nationhood oppose the inexorable process of capitalist development. The conclusion was that, if national survival is to occur, the national community in question must seek to return to the state of affairs that preceded capitalist transformation, a retrograde step in the evolution of humanity.

In this context, as Rosdolsky rightly argues, the old Hegelian terminology served a very useful purpose in the analysis of the Slavonic national communities. These unfortunate peoples were defined as 'non-historical,' in much the same way as Hegel used the term for the same peoples a century before. These national communities were understood as incapable of having national states of their own because they were either 'too small' or they lived in areas of mixed population, in the midst of a 'more energetic stock' (usually German, but also Magyar), in a situation in which the other national community was considered 'more advanced' and 'better equipped' in terms of its ability to build a national state.

> Bohemia and Croatia (another disjected member of the Slavonic family, acted upon by the Hungarian, as Bohemia by the German) were the homes of what is called on the European continent 'Panslavism.' Neither Bohemia nor Croatia was strong enough to exist as a nation by herself. Their respective nationalities, gradually undermined by the action of historical causes that inevitably absorbs into *a more energetic stock*, could only hope to be restored to anything like independence by an alliance with other Slavonic nations. (Marx, 'Panslavism—The Schleswig Holstein War,' in Aveling, ed., 1971, 48, emphasis added.)

Thus, if the Slavonic East European nationalities cannot constitute national states, their only hope for survival was to constitute a federation of 'Slavonic Nations,' under the leadership of the Czar of all Russia, the 'bulwark of European reaction.' The democratic movement in the Austro-Hungarian Monarchy will assimilate these 'remnants of peoples,' transforming their culture and national identity into the 'superior' German and Magyar culture, granting to them a democratic way of life as compensation. But given that national communities persisted in preserving their 'backward' national identities and culture, they could only subsist on condition that they locate themselves within the sphere of influence of the equally 'backward' semi-feudal Russian absolutism.

Engels (MECW, Vol. 8, 234–5) provided the theoretical justification for this view:

> There is no country in Europe which does not have in some corner or other one or several fragments of peoples, the remnant of a former population that was suppressed and held in bondage by the nation which later became the main vehicle for historical development. These relics of a nation, mercilessly trampled under the

course of history . . . always become fanatical standard bearers of counter revolution and remain so until their *complete extirpation* or loss of their national character, just as their whole existence in general is itself a protest against a great historical revolution.

Such in Scotland are the Gaels, the supporters of the Stuarts from 1640 to 1745.

Such in France are the Bretons, the supporters of the Bourbons from 1742 to 1800.

Such in Spain are the Basques, the supporters of Don Carlos.

Such in Austria are the panslavist Southern Slavs, who are nothing but residual fragments of peoples, resulting from an extremely confused thousand years development. This residual fragment, which is likewise extremely confused, sees its salvation only in the reversal of the whole European movement, which in its view ought to go not from west to east, but from east to west . . .

Here we find with unusual clarity the repetition of the eurocentric pattern which first emerged with the French revolution. The revolution will destroy the particularism of small nationalities, incorporating them into the 'higher' and more 'developed' nations, becoming in this way the vehicle for emancipation from feudalism and superstition. German is the 'language of liberty' for the Czechs in Bohemia, in the same way as French is the 'language of liberty' for the Occitans and Bretons in the French State. In the same way as the Jacobins perceived the non-French nationalities as intrinsically reactionary, Marx and Engels so perceived the 'South Slavs' in the Austro-Hungarian Empire (Rosdolsky, 1964, 100; 1980, 24; 1986, 34).

The same argument that so strongly denies the right to self-determination and historical continuity of the 'non-historical' nations also sustains a strong justification for the emancipation and state independence of the so-called 'historical nations.' These are national communities capable of being agents of historical transformation, that will further the formation of a strong capitalist economy. Marx and Engels strongly supported the right to state independence of the Irish and Poles, since they were considered historical nations that did not have a national state. In this sense, the right to self-determination (meaning state independence) is not an absolute right; it is the right of 'some' nations—those which are capable of being 'agents' or 'vehicles' of social transformation, for themselves and for the nations that oppress them. The most important example was Poland (MECW, Vol. 7, 250–351).

Similar observations were made by Marx and Engels on the Irish question. They reasoned that England cannot embark on a true revolutionary path until it 'got rid' of the Irish problem. Marx conclusively shows how the occupation of Ireland 'underdeveloped' the country by making it an appendix of the British economy (Marx, 1977, Vol. I, 652–666). The separation and independence of Ireland from England was not only a vital step for Irish development, but also was essential for the British people since 'a nation that oppresses another forges its own chains, because the average English worker hates the Irish worker as a competitor who lowers wages and standard of life,' and this proletarian antagonism is nourished by the bourgeoisie in its goal to divide the workers (Marx and Engels, 1974, 258–60).

But this analysis is not applicable to the 'non-historical nations,' and there is no *contradiction* or *incoherence*. The Irish and Polish national movements are perceived to advance the course of 'progress' by constituting national states capable of developing a 'healthy' contradiction between the proletariat and the bourgeoisie. Furthermore, their state independence will be a considerable help for the proletarian struggles within the nations that subjugate them. The 'non-historical' nations, by contrast, cannot develop a bourgeoisie, because they either are 'peasant nations,' or cannot develop a state of their own, or live in a mixed area of residence, or are too small to create an internal market. In these conditions, the 'non-historical' nations must seek alliances with the defenders of 'the old order,' since this is the only way to secure their survival. The 'irresistible flow of progress' requires the voluntary assimilation or the annihilation of these national communities. If they persist in maintaining their national identity in alliance with reactionary forces, they will be simply 'trampled over' by the forces of progress.

The contrast between Marx' and Engels' perceptive discussion of the Irish question and their ethnocentric attitude towards the 'South Slavs' puzzled and surprised many observers and commentators. The most common explanation is that they had 'no theory' on the national question, and the inconsistencies are the direct result of their 'ad hoc' positions. Marx' and Engels' discussions of concrete national situations are considered to be connected to circumstantial political events and are seen to be devoid of any theoretical significance. This is the position of, among others, Löwy (1976, 81) and Davis (1967, 79–82).

I argue, however, that the presence of important traces of Hegelian historicism in their universal evolutionary theory, and the related understanding of the national state as a historical construct to secure the conditions of existence of the bourgeoisie, make an '*ad hoc*' discussion of the national question unthinkable. . . .

Conclusion

The analytical parameters outlined in the introduction inform the conceptual requirement that every 'modern nation' must form a national state to further the development of the bourgeoisie. Furthermore, the formation of a national state is a *sine qua non* functional requirement for the survival of a national community in a capitalist mode of production. National communities incapable of forming national states are hindering the development of the progressive centralization and uniformation of humanity, and must therefore assimilate to more 'vital' and 'energetic' nations capable of forming national states with democracy 'as compensation.' The national state is the condition for a mature bourgeoisie and the requisite for the final contradiction that will render both the nation and the state historically obsolete. The 'model' for national development is that of the 'large' Western European nations, particularly France, but also British England, which is considered a 'successful case' of assimilation of the Celtic fringe, with the important exception of Ireland—a 'historical' nation.

This perception of the national community is the nucleus of the misleading heritage of European Marxism. It informed the main debates in the Second and Third Internationals, and formed the framework in which subsequent generations of Marxists thought the national question. The epistemological requirement locating the national phenomenon within a hierarchical, universal and developmental continuum must be seriously challenged, if the Marxist tradition is to provide a more sensitive discussion of the multi-dimensionality of the national arena. Only those Marxist theories capable of breaking with the abortive rigidities of the above-mentioned parameters managed to provide a more sensitive analysis of the national phenomenon. The work of Otto Bauer is perhaps the single most important exception to the misleading analytical stance.

Notes

1. Rosdolsky (1964, 100; 1980, 24; 1986, 31) quotes a revealing passage: 'Federalism and superstition speak low Breton . . . the emigration and hatred to the republic speak German, the counter-revolution speaks Italian and fanaticism speaks Basque (Euzkera). . . . It is necessary to popularise the (French) language; it is necessary to stop *this linguistic aristocracy* that seems to have established a civilised nation in the midst of barbaric ones' ('Séance du 8 Pluviôse,' *Gazette Nationale, ou le Moniteur Universel*).
2. In other Western European languages, the term has a more restricted meaning because the term 'people' (*peuple, pueblo, volk* in French, Spanish and German) has a wider ethno-political denotation. In German the term *Nationalität* acquires almost exclusively the denotation (2), since the denotation (1) is covered by the word *Staatsangehörigkeit*. Also the term *Volkszugehörigkeit* defines people of the same (normally German) ancestral ethnic origin, and it is enshrined in the 'Transitional Provisions of the Basic Law of the Federal Republic of Germany,'

article 116 (1), 'Definition of German Citizenship.' The other well-known case of an ethnic criterion enshrined in Basic Laws of a state is the State of Israel; see sections (1) and (4) of the 'Law of Return.' In Slavic languages, the term *narod* and related forms has also an ethno-political denotation. For a recent discussion of the lack of an English equivalent for the Russian *narod'nost*, see the illuminating article by T. Shanin (1986, 113ff).

3. 'God!, is there anybody in this earth that will do justice to the Slavs?'; the desperate plight of the Czechs, disdainfully quoted by Engels in a letter to Kautsky on February 1882 (*MEW*, Vol. 35, 272; quoted by Rosdolsky, 1964, 197; 1980, 136; 1986, 137).
4. 'It is now perfectly clear to me that, as testified by his cranial formation and hair growth, he is descended from the negroes who joined Moses' exodus from Egypt (unless his paternal mother or grandmother was crossed with a nigger). Well this combination of Jewish and Germanic stock with the negroid basic substance is bound to yield a strange product' (Marx to Engels on 30 July 1862; *MEW*, Vol. 30, 259, English translation in Raddatz, ed., 1981).

References

Aguilar, L. 1969. *Marxism in Latin America*, New York: W. Knopf.

Aveling, E. M., ed. 1971. *Revolution and Counterrevolution*. London: Unwin Books.

Avineri, S., ed. 1969. *Karl Marx on Colonialism and Modernisation*. New York: Anchor Books.

Avineri, S. 1972. *Hegel's Theory of the Modern State*. New York: Cambridge University Press.

Bauer, O. 1975 (1907). 'Die Nationalitätenfrage un die Sozialdemokratie.' In *Otto Bauer Werkausgabe*, Vol. I. Vienna: Europaverlag.

Bloom, S. 1975. *El Mundo de las Naciones*. Spanish translation of *The World of Nations*. Buenos Aires: Siglo Veintiuno Editores.

Brunnot, C. F. 1958. *Histoire de la Langue Française*. Paris.

Cummings, I. 1980. *Marx, Engels and National Movements*. London: Croom Helm.

Cutler, A., B. Hindess, P. Hirst, and A. Hussain. 1978. *Marx's 'Capital' and Capitalism Today*. Two volumes. London: Routledge & Kegan Paul.

Davis, H. B. 1967. *Socialism and Nationalism*. New York: Monthly Review Press.

Doujot, A. 1946. *Le Patois*. Paris: Librairie Delagrave.

Engels, F. 1977a. 'Über den Verfall des Feudalismus un das Aufkommen der Bourgeoisie.' *MEW*, Vol. 21, 395ff. Berlin: Dietz Verlag.

Engels, F. 1977b. 'Decay of Feudalism and Rise of Nation States.' In F. Engels, *The Peasant War in Germany*. Moscow: Progress Publishers, 178ff.

Gallisot, R. 1979. 'Nazione e Nazionalitá nei Dibattiti del Movimento Operaio.' In *Storia del Marxismo*, Vol. 2, eds. E. Hobsbawn, G. Haupt, F. Marek, and E. Ragionieri. Turin: Einaudi Editore.

García, Pelayo, M. 1979. *El Tema de las Nacionalidades en la Teoría de la Nación en Otto Bauer*. Madrid: Fundación Pablo Iglesias.

Giraud, P. 1968. *Patois et les Dialectes Français*. Paris: Presses Universitaires de France.

Herod, C. 1976. *The Nation in the History of Marxian Thought*. The Hague: Martinus Nijhoff.

Kaustky, K. 1978 (1887). 'La nacionalidad moderna' ('Die Moderne Nationalität'). In *La Segunda Internacional y el Problema Nacional y Colonial*, part 1. *Cuadernos de pasado y presente*, 73. Mexico: Siglo Veintiuno Editores.

Haupt, G. 1974. 'Les Marxistes face à la question nationale: l'histoire du problème.' In *Les Marxistes et la Question Nationale,* eds. G. Haupt, M. Löwy, and C. Weill. Paris: Maspero.

Haupt, G. and C. Weill. 1974. 'L'Eredità di Marx ed Engels e la Questione Nazionale.' *Studi Storici*, 15:2. Rome: Istituto Gramsci Editore.

Hegel, G. 1953. *Philosophy of Right*. Translated with notes by T. M. Knox. Oxford: Clarendon Press.

Kogan, A. G. 1949. 'The Social Democrats and the Conflict of Nationalities in the Habsburg Monarchy.' *Journal of Modern History*, 21, 204–217.

Löwy, M. 1976. 'Marxists and the National Question.' *New Left Review*, 96.

Marcuse, H. 1969. *Reason and Revolution*. Boston: Beacon Press.

Marx, K. 1974. *The German Ideology*. Students' edition. London: Lawrence & Wishart.

Marx, K. 1977 (1887). *Capital*. 3 volumes. London: Lawrence & Wishart.

Marx, K., and F. Engels. 1974. *On Colonialism*. Moscow: Progress Publishers.

Marx, K., and F. Engels. 1976. *Marx and Engels Collected Works* (MECW). London: Lawrence & Wishart.

Marx, K., and F. Engels. 1977. *Marx Engels Werke* (MEW). Berlin: Dietz Verlag.

Pelczynski, Z. A. 1984. 'Nation, Civil Society, State: Hegelian Sources of the Marxian Non-Theory of Nationality.' In *The State and Civil Society,* ed. Z. A. Pelczynski. London: Cambridge University Press.

Raddatz, F. J., ed. 1981. *Marx and Engels Personal Letters*. London: Weidenfeld and Nicolson.

Reyburn, H. A. 1967. *The Ethical Theory of Hegel*. Oxford: Clarendon Press.

Rosdolsky, Roman. 1964. 'Friedrich Engels und das Problem der 'geschichtslosen' Völker (Die Nationalitätenfrage in der Revolution 1848–1849 im lichte der "Neuen Rheinischen Zeitung").' *Archiv für Sozialgeschichte*, Vol. 4. Hannover.

Rosdolsky, Roman. 1965. 'Workers and Fatherland.' *Science & Society*, 29.

Rosdolsky, Roman. 1980 (1964). 'Friedrich Engels y el problema de los pueblos "sin historia".' *Cuadernos de pasado y presente*, 88. Mexico: Siglo Veintiuno Editores.

Rosdolsky, Roman. 1986 (1979). *Engels and the 'Nonhistoric' Peoples: The National Question in the Revolution of 1848*. Glasgow: Critique Books.

Salvi, S. 1973. *Le Nazione Proibite: Guida a Dieci Colonie 'Interne' Dell'a Europa Occidentale*. Florence: Vallechi Editore.

Shanin, T. 1986. 'Soviet Theories of Ethnicity: The Case of The Missing Term.' *New Left Review*, 158.

Smith, A. D. 1973. '"Ideas" and "Structure" in the Formation of Independence Ideas.' *Philosophy of Social Sciences*, Vol. 3.

Talmon, J. L. 1981. *The Myth of the Nation and the Vision of the Revolution*. Berkeley: University of California Press.

Vilar, P. 1962. *La Catalogne dans L'Espagne Moderne*. Paris: Bibliothèque Générale de L'Ecole Pratique des Hautes Etudes.

Walicki, A. 1982. *Philosophic and Romantic Nationalism: The Case of Poland*. Oxford: Clarendon Press.

II Cultural Membership

3 National Self-Determination

AVISHAI MARGALIT AND JOSEPH RAZ

In the controversy-ridden fields of international law and international relations, the widespread recognition of the existence of national rights to self-determination provides a welcome point of agreement. Needless to say, the core consensus is but the eye of a raging storm concerning the precise definition of the right, its content, its bearers, and the proper means for its implementation. This paper will not address such questions, though indirectly it may help with their investigation. Its concern is with the moral justification of the case for national self-determination. Its purpose is critical and evaluative, its subject lies within the morality of international relations rather than within international law and international relations proper.

It is assumed throughout that states and international law should recognize such a right only if there is a sound moral case for it. This does not mean that international law should mirror morality. Its concern is with setting standards that enjoy the sort of clarity required to make them the foundations of international relations between states and fit for recognition and enforcement through international organs. These concerns give rise to special considerations that should be fully recognized in the subtle process of applying moral principles to the law. The derivation of legal principles from moral premises is never a matter of copying morality into law. Still, the justification of the law rests ultimately on moral considerations, and therefore those considerations should also help shape the contours of legal principles. That is why the conclusions of this paper bear on controversies concerning the proper way in which the law on this subject should develop, even though such issues are not here discussed directly.

We are grateful to Lea Brilmayer, Moshe Halbertal, David Heyd, and the editors of the Journal for helpful comments on an earlier draft.

Avishai Margalit and Joseph Raz, 'National Self-Determination', *Journal of Philosophy*, Vol. 87/9 (1990), pp. 439–61 (minus 441–2, 454–61). Reprinted by permission of the *Journal of Philosophy*. The excerpt here reprinted is part of an article exploring the conditions under which groups enjoy a right to national self-determination. However, given the purpose of the present volume, only the part of the paper examining the value of membership in what the authors call 'encompassing groups' is reproduced here. The article is reprinted in full in J. Raz, *Ethics in the Public Domain* (Oxford University Press, 1994).

Moral inquiry is sometimes understood in a utopian manner, i.e., as an inquiry into the principles that should prevail in an ideal world. It is doubtful whether this is a meaningful enterprise, but it is certainly not the one we are engaged in here. We assume that things are roughly as they are, especially that our world is a world of states and of a variety of ethnic, national, tribal, and other groups.[1] We do not question the justification for this state of affairs. Rather, we ask whether, given that this is how things are and for as long as they remain the same, a moral case can be made in support of national self-determination.

1. Isolating the Issue

The core content of the claim to be examined is that there is a right to determine whether a certain territory shall become, or remain, a separate state (and possibly also whether it should enjoy autonomy within a large state). The idea of national self-determination or (as we shall refer to it in order to avoid confusion) the idea of self-government encompasses much more. The value of national self-government is the value of entrusting the general political power over a group and its members to the group. If self-government is valuable then it is valuable that whatever is a proper matter for political decision should be subject to the political decision of the group in all matters concerning the group and its members. The idea of national self-government, in other words, speaks of groups determining the character of their social and economic environment, their fortunes, the course of their development, and the fortunes of their members by their own actions, i.e., by the action of those groups, in as much as these are matters which are properly within the realm of political action.[2] Given the current international state system, in which political power rests, in the main, with sovereign states,[3] the right to determine whether a territory should be an independent state is quite naturally regarded as the main instrument for realizing the ideal of self-determination. Consideration of this right usually dominates all discussions of national self-determination. To examine the justification of the right is the ultimate purpose of this article. But we shall continuously draw attention to the fact that, as we shall try to show, the right of self-determination so understood is not ultimate, but is grounded in the wider value of national self-government, which is itself to be only instrumentally justified.

The next section deals with the nature of the groups that might be the subject of such a right. Section III considers what value, if any, is served by the enjoyment of political independence by such groups. Section IV examines the case for conceding that there is a moral right to self-determination.

This examination may lead to revising our understanding of the content of the right. It may reveal that moral considerations justify only a narrower right, or that the argument that justifies the right warrants giving it a wider scope. But the core as identified here will provide the working base from which to launch the inquiry. . . .

2. Groups

Assuming that self-determination is enjoyed by groups, what groups qualify? Given that the right is normally attributed to peoples or nations, it is tempting to give that as the answer and concentrate on characterizing 'peoples' or 'nations.' The drawbacks of this approach are two: it assumes too much and it poses problems that may not require a solution.

It is far from clear that peoples or nations rather than tribes, ethnic groups, linguistic, religious, or geographical groups are the relevant reference group. What is it that makes peoples particularly suited to self-determination? The right concerns determination whether a certain territory shall be self-governing or not. It appears to affect most directly the residents of a territory, and their neighbors. If anyone, then residents of geographical regions seem intuitively to be the proper bearers of the right. Saying this does not get us very far. It does not help in identifying the residents of which regions should qualify. To be sure, this is the crucial question. But even posing it in this way shows that the answer, 'the largest regions inhabited by one people or nation,' is far from being the obvious answer.

We have some understanding of the benefits self-government might bring. We need to rely on this in looking for the characteristics that make groups suitable recipients of those benefits. We want, in other words, to identify groups by those characteristics which are relevant to the justification of the right. If it turns out that those do not apply to peoples or nations, we shall have shown that the right to self-determination is misconceived and, as recognized in international law, unjustified. Alternatively, the groups identified may encompass peoples (or some peoples) as well as other groups. This will provide a powerful case for redrawing the boundaries of the right. Either way we shall be saved much argument concerning the characterization of nations which, interesting as it is in itself, is irrelevant to our purpose.

Having said that, it may be useful to take nations and peoples as the obvious candidates for the right. We need not worry about their defining characteristics. But we may gain insight by comparing them with groups, e.g., the fiction-reading public, or Tottenham Football Club supporters, which obviously do not enjoy such a right. Reflection on such examples suggests six characteristics that in combination are relevant to a case for self-determination.

1. The group has a common character and a common culture that encompass many, varied and important aspects of life, a culture that defines or marks a variety of forms or styles of life, types of activities, occupations, pursuits, and relationships. With national groups we expect to find national cuisines, distinctive architectural styles, a common language, distinctive literary and artistic traditions, national music, customs, dress, ceremonies and holidays, etc. None of these is necessary. They are but typical examples of the features that characterize peoples and other groups that are serious candidates for the right to self-determination. They have pervasive cultures, and their identity is determined at least in part by their culture. They possess cultural traditions that penetrate beyond a single or a few areas of human life, and display themselves in a whole range of areas, including many which are of great importance for the well-being of individuals.

2. The correlative of the first feature is that people growing up among members of the group will acquire the group culture, will be marked by its character. Their tastes and their options will be affected by that culture to a significant degree. The types of careers open to one, the leisure activities one learned to appreciate and is therefore able to choose from, the customs and habits that define and color relations with strangers and with friends, patterns of expectations and attitudes between spouses and among other members of the family, features of lifestyles with which one is capable of empathizing and for which one may therefore develop a taste—all these will be marked by the group culture.

They need not be indelibly marked. People may migrate to other environments, shed their previous culture, and acquire a new one. It is a painful and slow process, success in which is rarely complete. But it is possible, just as it is possible that socialization will fail and one will fail to be marked by the culture of one's environment, except negatively, to reject it. The point made is merely the modest one that, given the pervasive nature of the culture of the groups we are seeking to identify, their influence on individuals who grow up in their midst is profound and far-reaching. The point needs to be made in order to connect concern with the prosperity of the group with concern for the well-being of individuals. This tie between the individual and the collective is at the heart of the case for self-determination.

As one would expect, the tie does not necessarily extend to all members of the group, the failure of socialization is not the only reason. The group culture affects those who grow up among its members, be they members or not. But to say this is no more than to point to various anomalies and dilemmas that may arise. Most people live in groups of these kinds, so that those who belong to none are denied full access to the opportunities that are shaped in part by the group's culture. They are made to feel estranged and their chances to have a rewarding life are seriously damaged. The same is true of people who grow up among members of a group so that they absorb its culture, but are then denied access to it because they are denied full membership of the group.

Nothing in the above presupposes that groups of the kind we are exploring are geographically concentrated, let alone that their members are the only inhabitants of any region. Rather, by drawing on the transmission of the group culture through the socialization of the young, these comments emphasize the historical nature of the groups with which we are concerned. Given that they are identified by a common culture, at least in part, they also share a history, for it is through a shared history that cultures develop and are transmitted.

3. Membership in the group is, in part, a matter of mutual recognition. Typically, one belongs to such groups if, among other conditions, one is recognized by other members of the group as belonging to it. The other conditions (which may be the accident of birth or the sharing of the group culture, etc.) are normally the grounds cited as reasons for such recognition. But those who meet those other conditions and are yet rejected by the group are at best marginal or problematic members of it. The groups concerned are not formal institutionalized groups, with formal procedures of admission. Membership in them is a matter of informal acknowledgment of belonging by others generally, and by other members specifically. The fiction-reading public fails our previous tests. It is not identified by its sharing a wide-ranging pervasive culture. It also fails the third test. To belong to the fiction-reading public all we have to do is to read fiction. It does not matter whether others recognize us as fiction-reading.[4]

4. The third feature prepares the way for, and usually goes hand in hand with, the importance of membership for one's self-identification. Consider the fiction-reading public again. It is a historically significant group. Historians may study the evolution of the fiction-reading public, how it spread from women to men, from one class to others, from reading aloud in small groups to silent reading, from reliance on libraries to book buying, etc.; how it is regarded as important to one's qualification as a cultured person in one country, but not in another; how it furnishes a common topic of conversation in some classes but not in others; how belonging to the group is a mark of political awareness in some countries, while being a sign of escapist retreat from social concerns in another.

Such studies will show, however, that it is only in some societies that the existence of these features of the fiction-reading public is widely known.

For the most part, one can belong to the group without being aware that one is a typical reader, that one's profile is that of most readers. Sometimes this is a result of a mistaken group image's being current in that society. Our concern is rather with those cases where the society lacks any very distinct image of that group. This indicates that, in such societies, membership of that group does not have a highly visible social profile. It is not one of the facts by which people pigeonhole each other. One need not be aware who, among people one knows, friends, acquaintances, shopkeepers one patronizes, one's doctor, etc., shares the habit. In such societies, membership of the fiction-reading public is not highly visible, that is, it is not one of the things one will normally know about people one has contact with, one of the things that identify 'who they are.' But it happens in some countries that membership of the reading public becomes a highly visible mark of belonging to a social group, to the intelligentsia, etc. In such countries, talk of the recently published novel becomes a means of mutual recognition.

One of the most significant facts differentiating various football cultures is whether they are cultures of self-recognition: whether identification as a fan or supporter of this club or that is one of the features that are among the main markers of people in the society. The same is true of occupational groups. In some countries, membership is highly visible and is among the primary means of pigeon-holing people, of establishing 'who they are'; in others, it is not.

Our concern is with groups, membership of which has a high social profile, that is, groups, membership of which is one of the primary facts by which people are identified, and which form expectations as to what they are like, groups, membership of which is one of the primary clues for people generally in interpreting the conduct of others. Since our perceptions of ourselves are in large measure determined by how we expect others to perceive us, it follows that membership of such groups is an important identifying feature for each about himself. These are groups, members of which are aware of their membership and typically regard it as an important clue in understanding who they are, in interpreting their actions and reactions, in understanding their tastes and their manner.

5. Membership is a matter of belonging, not of achievement. One does not have to prove oneself, or to excel in anything, in order to belong and to be accepted as a full member. To the extent that membership normally involves recognition by others as a member, that recognition is not conditional on meeting qualifications that indicate any accomplishment. To be a good Irishman, it is true, is an achievement. But to be an Irishman is not. Qualification for membership is usually determined by nonvoluntary criteria. One cannot choose to belong. One belongs because of who one is. One can come to belong to such groups, but only by changing, e.g., by adopting

their culture, changing one's tastes and habits accordingly—a very slow process indeed. The fact that these are groups, membership of which is a matter of belonging and not of accomplishment, makes them suitable for their role as primary foci of identification. Identification is more secure, less liable to be threatened, if it does not depend on accomplishment. Although accomplishments play their role in people's sense of their own identity, it would seem that at the most fundamental level our sense of our own identity depends on criteria of belonging rather than on those of accomplishment. Secure identification at that level is particularly important to one's well-being.

6. The groups concerned are not small face-to-face groups, members of which are generally known to all other members. They are anonymous groups where mutual recognition is secured by the possession of general characteristics. The exclusion of small groups from consideration is not merely *ad hoc*. Small groups that are based on personal familiarity of all with all are markedly different in the character of their relationships and interactions from anonymous groups. For example, given the importance of mutual recognition to members of these groups, they tend to develop conventional means of identification, such as the use of symbolic objects, participation in group ceremonies, special group manners, or special vocabulary, which help quickly to identify who is 'one of us' and who is not.

The various features we listed do not entail each other but they tend to go together. It is not surprising that groups with pervasive cultures will be important in determining the main options and opportunities of their members, or that they will become focal points of identification, etc. The way things are in our world, just about everyone belongs to such a group, and not necessarily to one only. Membership is not exclusive and many people belong to several groups that answer to our description. Some of them are rather like national groups, e.g., tribes or ethnic groups. Others are very different. Some religious groups meet our conditions, as do social classes, and some racial groups. Not all religious or racial groups did develop rich and pervasive cultures. But some did and those qualify.

3. The Value of Self-Government

(A) *The Value of Encompassing Groups*. The description of the relevant groups in the preceding section may well disappoint the reader. Some will be disappointed by the imprecise nature of the criteria provided. This would be unjustified. The criteria are not meant to provide operational legal definitions. As such they clearly would not do. Their purpose is to pick on the features of groups which may explain the value of self-determination. As already mentioned, the key to the explanation is in the importance of these groups to the well-being of their members. This thought guided the selection of the features. They are meant to assist in identifying that link. It is not really surprising that they are all vague matters of degree, admitting of many variants and many nuances. One is tempted to say 'that's life.' It does not come in neatly parceled parts. While striving to identify the features that matter, we have to recognize that they come in many shapes, in many shades, and in many degrees rife with impurities in their concrete mixing.

A more justified source of disappointment is the suspicion that we have cast the net too wide. Social classes clearly do not have a right to self-determination. If they meet the above conditions then those conditions are at best incomplete. Here we can only crave the reader's patience. We tried to identify the features of groups which help explain the value of self-determination. These may apply not only beyond the sphere in which the right is commonly recognized. They may apply to groups that really should not possess it for other reasons yet to be explored.

The defining properties of the groups we identified are of two kinds. On the one hand, they pick out groups with pervasive cultures; on the other, they focus on groups, membership of which is important to one's self-identity. This combination makes such groups suitable candidates for self-rule. Let us call groups manifesting the six features *encompassing groups*. Individuals find in them a culture which shapes to a large degree their tastes and opportunities, and which provides an anchor for their self-identification and the safety of effortless secure belonging.

Individual well-being depends on the successful pursuit of worthwhile goals and relationships. Goals and relationships are culturally determined. Being social animals means not merely that the means for the satisfaction of people's goals are more readily available within society. More crucially it means that those goals themselves are (when one reaches beyond what is strictly necessary for biological survival) the creatures of society, the products of culture. Family relations, all other social relations between people, careers, leisure activities, the arts, sciences, and other obvious products of 'high culture' are the fruits of society. They all depend for their existence on the sharing of patterns of expectations, on traditions preserving implicit knowledge of how to do what, of tacit conventions regarding what is part of this or that enterprise and what is not, what is appropriate and what is not, what is valuable and what is not. Familiarity with a culture determines the boundaries of the imaginable. Sharing in a culture, being part of it, determines the limits of the feasible.

It may be no more than a brute fact that our world is organized in a large measure around groups with pervasive cultures. But it is a fact with far-reaching consequences. It means, in the first place, that membership of such groups is of great importance to individual well-being, for it greatly affects one's opportunities, one's ability to engage in the relationships and pursuits marked by the culture. Secondly, it means that the prosperity of the culture is important to the well-being of its members. If the culture is decaying, or if it is persecuted or discriminated against, the options and opportunities open to its members will shrink, become less attractive, and their pursuit less likely to be successful.

It may be no more than a brute fact that people's sense of their own identity is bound up with their sense of belonging to encompassing groups and that their self-respect is affected by the esteem in which these groups are held. But these facts, too, have important consequences. They mean that individual dignity and self-respect require that the groups, membership of which contributes to one's sense of identity, be generally respected and not be made a subject of ridicule, hatred, discrimination, or persecution.

All this is mere common sense, and is meant to be hedged and qualified in the way our common understanding of these matters is. Of course, strangers can participate in activities marked by a culture. They are handicapped, but not always very seriously. Of course, there are other determinants of one's opportunities, and of one's sense of self-respect. Membership of an encompassing group is but one factor. Finally, one should mention that groups and their culture may be pernicious, based on exploitation of people, be they their members or not, or on the denigration and persecution of other groups. If so, then the case for their protection and flourishing is weakened, and may disappear altogether.

Having regard for this reservation, the case for holding the prosperity of encompassing groups as vital for the prosperity of their members is a powerful one. Group interests cannot be reduced to individual interests. It makes sense to talk of a group's prospering or declining, of actions and policies as serving the group's interest or of harming it, without having to cash this in terms of individual interests. The group may flourish if its culture prospers, but this need not mean that the lot of its members or of anyone else has improved. It is in the interest of the group to be held in high regard by others, but it does not follow that, if an American moon landing increases the world's admiration for the United States, Americans necessarily benefit from this. Group interests are conceptually connected to the interests of their members but such connections are nonreductive and generally indirect. For example, it is possible that what enhances the interest of the group provides opportunities for improvement for its members, or that it increases the chance that they will benefit.

This relative independence of group interest is compatible with the view that informs this article: that the moral importance of the group's interest depends on its value to individuals. A large decline in the fortunes of the group may, e.g., be of little consequence to its members. There is no a priori way of correlating group interest with that of its members or of other individuals. It depends on the circumstances of different groups at different times. One clear consequence of the fact that the moral significance of a group's interest is in its service to individuals is the fact that it will depend, in part, on the size of the group. The fortunes of a larger group may be material to the well-being of a larger number of people. Other things being equal, numbers matter.

(B) *The Instrumental Case.* Does the interest of members in the prosperity of the group establish a right to self-determination? Certainly not, at least not yet, not without further argument. For one thing we have yet to see any connection between the prosperity of encompassing groups and their political independence. The easiest connection to establish under certain conditions is an instrumental one. Sometimes the prosperity of the group and its self-respect are aided by, sometimes they may be impossible to secure without, the group's enjoying political sovereignty over its own affairs. Sovereignty enables the group to conduct its own affairs in a way conducive to its prosperity.[5] There is no need to elaborate the point. It depends on historical conditions. Hence the prominence of a history of persecution in most debates concerning self-determination. But a history of persecution is neither a necessary nor a sufficient condition for the instrumental case for self-government. It is not a necessary condition, because persecution is not the only reason why the groups may suffer without independence. Suffering can be the result of neglect or ignorance of or indifference to the prosperity of a minority group by the majority. Such attitudes may be so well entrenched that there is no realistic prospect of changing them.

Persecution is not a sufficient condition, for there may be other ways to fight and overcome persecution and because whatever the advantages of independence it may, in the circumstances, lead to economic decline, cultural decay, or social disorder, which only make their members worse off. Besides, as mentioned above, pernicious groups may not deserve protection, especially if it will help them to pursue repressive practices with impunity. Finally, there are the interests of nonmembers to be considered. In short, the instrumental argument (as well as others) for self-government is sensitive to counterarguments pointing to its drawbacks, its cost in terms of human well-being, possible violations of human rights, etc.

We shall return to these issues below. First, let us consider the claim that the instrumental argument trivializes the case for self-government by overlooking its intrinsic value. Of the various arguments for the intrinsic value of self-government which have been and can be advanced, we examine one which seems the most promising.

(C) *An Argument for the Intrinsic Value of Self-government.* The argument is based on an extension of individual autonomy or of self-expression (if that is regarded as independently valuable). The argument unravels in stages: (1) people's membership of encompassing groups is an important aspect of their personality, and their well-being depends on giving it full expression; (2) expression of membership essentially includes manifestation of membership in the open, public life of the community; (3) this requires expressing one's membership in political activities within the community. The political is an essential arena of community life, and consequently of individual well-being; (4) therefore, self-government is inherently valuable, it is required to provide the group with a political dimension.

The first premise is unexceptionable. So is the second, though an ambiguity might be detected in the way it is often understood. Two elements need separating. First, given the importance of membership to one's well-being, it is vital that the dignity of the group be preserved. This depends, in part, on public manifestations of respect for the group and its culture, and on the absence of ridicule of the group, etc., from the public life of the society of which one is a member. One should not have to identify with or feel loyalty to a group that denigrates an encompassing group to which one belongs. Indeed, one should not have to live in an environment in which such attitudes are part of the common culture. Second, an aspect of well-being is an ability to express publicly one's identification with the group and to participate openly in its public culture. An encompassing group is centered on mutual recognition and is inevitably a group with a public culture. One cannot enjoy the benefits of membership without participation in its public culture, without public participation in its culture.

Both elements are of great importance. Both indicate the vital role played by public manifestations of group culture and group membership among the conditions of individual well-being. To the extent that a person's well-being is bound up with his identity as a member of an encompassing group it has an important public dimension. But that dimension is not necessarily political in the conventional narrow sense of the term. Even where it is, its political expression does not require a political organization whose boundaries coincide with those of the group. One may be politically active in a multinational, multicultural polity.

Here supporters of the argument for the intrinsic value of self-government may protest. The expression of membership in the political life of the community, they will say, involves more than its public expression. It involves the possibility of members of an encompassing group participating in the political life of their state, and fighting in the name of group interests in the political arena. Such actions, they will insist, may be not only instrumentally valuable to the group, but intrinsically important to its politically active members. They are valuable avenues of self-fullfilment. These points, too, have to be readily admitted. There is no reason to think that everyone must take part in politics, or else his or her development is stunted and personality or life are deficient. In normal times, politics is but an option that people may choose to take or to leave alone. Although its availability is important, for its absence deprives people of valuable opportunities, its use is strictly optional. Even if it is possible to argue that one's personal well-being requires some involvement with larger groups, and the avoidance of exclusive preoccupation with one's own affairs and those of one's close relations or friends, that involvement can take nonpolitical forms, such as activity in a social club, interest in the fortunes of the arts in one's region, etc.

Politics is no more than an option, though this is true in normal times only. In times of political crises that have moral dimensions, it may well be the duty of everyone to stand up and be counted. In Weimar, Germans had a moral duty to become politically involved to oppose Nazism. There are many other situations where an apolitical attitude is not morally acceptable. But all of them are marked by moral crises. In the absence of crisis there is nothing wrong in being nonpolitical.

Having said this, we must repeat that the option of politics must remain open, and with it the option of fighting politically for causes to do with the interests of one's encompassing groups. But there is nothing here to suggest that this should be done in a political framework exclusive to one's group or dominated by it. There is nothing wrong with multinational states, in which members of the different communities compete in the political arena for public resources for their communities. Admittedly, prejudice, national fanaticism, etc., sometimes make such peaceful and equitable sharing of the political arena impossible. They may lead to friction and persecution. This may constitute a good argument for the value of self-government, but it is an instrumental argument of the kind canvassed above. There is nothing in the need for a public or even a political expression of one's membership of an encompassing group which points to an intrinsic value of self-government.

(D) *The Subjective Element.* In an indirect way, the attempt to argue for the intrinsic value of self-government does point to the danger of misinterpreting the instrumental approach to the question. First, the argument does not deny the intrinsic value of the existence of the political option as a venue for activity and self-expression to all (adult) members of society. We are not advocating a purely instrumentalist view of politics generally. The intrinsic value to individuals of the political option does not require expression in polities whose boundaries coincide with those of encompassing groups. That is the only point argued for above.

Second, the pragmatic, instrumentalist character of the approach advocated here should not be identified with an aggregating impersonal consequentialism. Some people tend to associate any instrumentalist approach with images of a bureaucracy trading off the interest of one person against that of another on the basis of some cost-benefit analysis designed to maximize overall satisfaction; a bureaucracy, moreover, in charge of determining for people what is really good for them, regardless of their own views of the matter. Nothing of the kind should be countenanced. Of course, conflicts among people's interests do arise, and call for rational resolution that is likely to involve sacrificing some interests of some people for the sake of others. Such conflicts, however, admit of a large degree of indeterminacy, and many alternative resolutions may be plausible or rational. In such contexts, talking of maximization, with its connotations of comparability of all options, is entirely out of place.

Furthermore, nothing in the instrumentalist and pragmatic nature of our approach should be allowed to disguise its sensitivity to subjective elements, its responsiveness to the perceptions and sensibilities of the people concerned. To a considerable extent, what matters is how well people feel in their environment: Do they feel at home in it or are they alienated from it? Do they feel respected or humiliated? etc. This leads to a delicate balance between 'objective' factors and subjective perceptions. On the one hand, when prospects for the future are concerned, subjective perceptions of danger and likely persecution, etc., are not necessarily to be trusted. These are objective issues on which the opinion of independent spectators may be more reliable than that of those directly involved. On the other hand, the actual issue facing the independent spectators is how people will respond to their conditions, what will be their perceptions, their attitudes to their environment, to their neighbors, etc. Even a group that is not persecuted may suffer many of the ills of real persecution if it feels persecuted. That its perceptions are mistaken or exaggerated is important in pointing to the possibility of a different cure: removing the mistaken perception. But that is not always possible, and up to a point in matters of respect, identification, and dignity, subjective responses, justified or not, are the ultimate reality so far as the well-being of those who have them is concerned. . . .

Notes

1. This fact is doubly relevant. It is a natural fact about our world that it is a populated world with no unappropriated lands. It is a social and a moral fact that it is a world of nations, tribes, peoples, etc., that is, that people's perception of

themselves and of others and their judgments of the opportunities and the responsibilities of life are shaped, to an extent, by the existence of such groups and their membership of them. It may be meaningful to claim that our views regarding national self-determination apply only to a populated world like ours. One may point to different principles that would prevail in a world with vast unoccupied fertile lands. Such speculation is utopian but it may serve to highlight some of the reasons for the principles that apply in our condition. To speculate concerning a reality different from ours in its basic social and moral constitution is pointless in a deeper way. Such social facts are constitutive of morality. Their absence undercuts morality's very foundations. We could say that under such changed conditions people will have normative beliefs and will be guided by some values. But they are not ones for which we can claim any validity.

2. This qualification is to take account of the fact that, according to doctrines of limited government, certain matters are outside the realm of politics, and no political action regarding them may be undertaken.
3. Among the exceptions to this rule are the slowly growing importance of supernational, especially regional, associations such as the European Community, the growth of a doctrine of sovereignty limited by respect for fundamental human rights, and the continuing (usually thinly veiled) claims of some states that they are not bound by the international law regarding the sovereignty of states.
4. The fiction-reading public can take the character of a literary elite with mutual recognition as part of its identity. The importance of 'acceptability' in such groups has often been noted and analyzed.
5. This is not meant to suggest that there are not often drawbacks to self-rule. They will be considered below.

4 Minority Cultures and the Cosmopolitan Alternative

JEREMY WALDRON

If it were appropriate to make dedications, this Article would be for Salman Rushdie, who a few months ago celebrated his one-thousandth day in hiding in Britain under police protection from the sentence of death passed upon him in Tehran in 1988. I want to begin with an extended quotation from an essay entitled *In Good Faith*, which Rushdie wrote in 1990 in defense of his execrated book *The Satanic Verses*:

If *The Satanic Verses* is anything, it is a migrant's-eye view of the world. It is written from the very experience of uprooting, disjuncture and metamorphosis (slow or rapid, painful or pleasurable) that is the migrant condition, and from which, I believe, can be derived a metaphor for all humanity.

Standing at the centre of the novel is a group of characters most of whom are British Muslims, or not particularly religious persons of Muslim background, struggling with just the sort of great problems that have arisen to surround the book, problems of hybridization and ghettoization, of reconciling the old and the new. Those who oppose the novel most vociferously today are of the opinion that intermingling with a different culture will inevitably weaken and ruin their own. I am of the opposite opinion. *The Satanic Verses* celebrates hybridity, impurity, intermingling, the transformation that comes of new and unexpected combinations of human beings, cultures, ideas, politics, movies, songs. It rejoices in mongrelization and fears the absolutism of the Pure. *Mélange*, hotchpotch, a bit of this and a bit of that is *how newness enters the world*. It is the great possibility that mass migration gives the world, and I have tried to embrace it. *The Satanic Verses* is for change-by-fusion, change-by-conjoining. It is a love-song to our mongrel selves . . .

I was born an Indian, and not only an Indian, but a Bombayite—Bombay, most cosmopolitan, most hybrid, most hotchpotch of Indian cities. My writing and thought have therefore been as deeply influenced by Hindu myths and attitudes as

Earlier versions of this paper were presented at a workshop at Boalt Hall and at a meeting of the Bay Area Conference on Political Thought in November 1991. I am grateful to all who participated in those discussions for their suggestions and comments.

Jeremy Waldron, 'Minority Cultures and the Cosmopolitan Alternative', *University of Michigan Journal of Law Reform*, Vol. 25 (1992), pp. 751–93 (minus 766–77). Reprinted by permission of the *University of Michigan Journal of Law Reform*.

Muslim ones. . . . Nor is the West absent from Bombay. I was already a mongrel self, history's bastard, before London aggravated the condition.[1]

It is not my intention here to contribute further to the discussion of *The Satanic Verses* or of the price its author has paid for its publication.[2] Instead, I want to take the comments that I have just quoted as a point of departure to explore the vision of life, agency, and responsibility that is implicit in this affirmation of cosmopolitanism. I want to explore the tension between that vision and the more familiar views with which we are concerned in this Symposium—views that locate the coherence and meaning of human life in each person's immersion in the culture and ethnicity of a particular community.

1. Communitarianism

What follows is in part a contribution to the debate between liberals and communitarians, though those labels are becoming rather tattered in the modern discussion.[3]

Although there is a rough correlation between the liberty claimed by Rushdie and the ideal of liberal freedom, the life sketched out by Rushdie really does not answer to the more earnest or high-minded characterizations of the liberal individual in modern political philosophy. Modern liberal theorists place great stress on the importance of an autonomous individual leading his life according to a chosen plan; his autonomy is evinced in the formulation and execution of a life-plan and the adoption of ground-projects, and his rights are the liberties and protections that he needs in order to do this.[4] Liberals stress the importance of each individual's adoption of a particular conception of the good, a view about what makes life worth living, and again a person's rights are the protections he needs in order to be able to choose and follow such values on equal terms with others who are engaged in a similar enterprise.[5] The approach to life sketched out by Rushdie has little in common with this, apart from the elements of freedom and decision. It has none of the ethical unity that the autonomous Kantian individual is supposed to confer on his life;[6] it is a life of kaleidoscopic tension and variety. It is not the pursuit of a chosen conception of goodness along lines indicated by Ronald Dworkin;[7] nor does its individuality consist, in Rawls's words, in 'a human life lived according to a plan.'[8] Instead, it rightly challenges the rather compulsive rigidity of the traditional liberal picture.[9] If there is liberal autonomy in Rushdie's vision, it is choice running rampant, and pluralism internalized from the relations *between* individuals to the chaotic coexistence of projects, pursuits, ideas, images, and snatches of culture *within* an individual.[10]

If I knew what the term meant, I would say it was a 'postmodern' vision of the self. But, as I do not, let me just call it 'cosmopolitan,' although this term is not supposed to indicate that the practitioner of the ethos in question is necessarily a migrant (like Rushdie), a perpetual refugee (like, for example, Jean-Jacques Rousseau), or a frequent flyer (like myself). The cosmopolitan may live all his life in one city and maintain the same citizenship throughout. But he refuses to think of himself as *defined* by his location or his ancestry or his citizenship or his language. Though he may live in San Francisco and be of Irish ancestry, he does not take his identity to be compromised when he learns Spanish, eats Chinese, wears clothes made in Korea, listens to arias by Verdi sung by a Maori princess on Japanese equipment, follows Ukrainian politics, and practices Buddhist meditation techniques. He is a creature of modernity, conscious of living in a mixed-up world and having a mixed-up self.

I want to use the opportunity provided by Rushdie's sketch of such a life to challenge the claims that are made by modern communitarians about the need people have for involvement in the substantive life of a particular community as a source of meaning, integrity, and character.[11] One of the things that we are going to find, as we proceed with this exploration, is the importance of pressing the communitarian on the meaning of the term 'community.' Many of us have been puzzled and frustrated by the absence of a clear understanding of this concept in some of the assertions made by communitarians like Alasdair Macintyre, Michael Sandel, Charles Taylor, and Michael Walzer.[12] I do not mean the absence of a precise definition. I mean the absence of any settled sense about the *scope* and *scale* of the social entity that they have in mind.

When they say that the modern individual is a creation of community,[13] or that each of us owes her identity to the community in which she is brought up,[14] or that our choices necessarily are framed in the context of a community,[15] or that we must not think of ourselves as holding rights against the community,[16] or that communities must have boundaries,[17] or that justice is fidelity to shared understandings within a community,[18] what *scale* of entity are we talking about? Is 'community' supposed to denote things as small as villages and neighborhoods, social relations that can sustain *gemeinschaft*-type solidarity and face-to-face friendships? What is the relation between the community and the political system? Is 'community' supposed to do work comparable to 'civil society,' picking out the social infrastructure of whatever state or political entity we are talking about? If, as John Dunn recently has argued,[19] the concept of *the state* no longer picks out a natural kind, denoting as it does political entities as small as Fiji and as large as the United States, as tight as Singapore and as loose as the Commonwealth of Independent States (C.I.S.), is there any sense in supposing that for every state there is just one community or society to which individuals owe their being and allegiance?

Should we even suppose that communities are no bigger than states? If each of us is a product of a community, is that heritage limited to national boundaries, or is it as wide (as *world*wide) as the language, literature, and civilization that sustain us? Are we talking about particular communities, at the level of self-contained ethnic groups, or are we talking about the common culture and civilization that makes it possible for a New Zealander trained at Oxford to write for a symposium in the *University of Michigan Journal of Law Reform*?[20]

I suspect that the popularity of modern communitarianism has depended on *not* giving unequivocal answers to these questions. I suspect that it depends on using premises that evoke community on one scale (usually large) to support conclusions requiring allegiance to community on quite a different scale (usually small).

For the purposes of this Article, I want to single out one meaning of the term as worthy of special attention. It is 'community' in the sense of *ethnic* community: a particular people sharing a heritage of custom, ritual, and way of life that is in some real or imagined[21] sense immemorial, being referred back to a shared history and shared provenance or homeland. This is the sense of 'community' implicated in nineteenth- and twentieth-century nationalism. I shall use community in this sense as a sort of counterpoint to my exploration of Rushdie's cosmopolitan ideal. I want to pin down the communitarian critique of the cosmopolitan style of life to something like the claim, made by the German historian Johann Gottfried Von Herder, that (in Isaiah Berlin's paraphrase) 'among elementary human needs—as basic as those for food, shelter, security, procreation, communication—is the need to belong to a particular group, united by some common links—especially language, collective memories, continuous life upon the same soil,' and perhaps 'race, blood, religion, a sense of common mission, and the like.'[22]

Some will protest that it is unfair to pin matters down in this way. Michael Sandel, they will say, is not Johann Gottfried Von Herder. But the aim is not to underestimate the subtlety of any particular philosopher's position. From time to time, it is important for us not only to read the ordinary ambiguous literature of communitarianism, but also to see how much substance there would be if various *determinate* communitarian claims were taken one by one, and their proponents were forced to abandon any reliance on vagueness and equivocation. In the end, that is the best way to evaluate the array of different meanings that are evoked in this literature. This Article is certainly not a complete execution of that task, but it is intended as a substantial beginning.

2. Minority Culture as a Human Right

There is an additional reason for being interested in social entities on this scale. In modern discussions of human rights, we are presented with the claim that particular cultures, communities, and ethnic traditions have a right to exist and a right to be protected from decay, assimilation, and desuetude. The claim is presented, in a rather modest form, in Article 27 of the International Covenant on Civil and Political Rights:

> In those States in which ethnic, religious or linguistic minorities exist, persons belonging to such minorities shall not be denied the right, in community with the other members of their group, to enjoy their own culture, to profess and practise their own religion, or to use their own language.[23]

Now, as it stands, this provision leaves quite unclear what is to count as the enjoyment of one's culture, the profession of one's religion, and the use of one's language. Are these goods secured when a dwindling band of demoralized individuals continues, against all odds, to meet occasionally to wear their national costume, recall snatches of their common history, practice their religious and ethnic rituals, and speak what they can remember of what was once a flourishing tongue? Is that the *enjoyment* of their culture? Or does enjoyment require more along the lines of the active flourishing of the culture on its own terms, in something approximating the conditions under which it originally developed?

Many have thought that respect for minority cultures does require more. A recent United Nations report rejected the view that Article 27 is nothing but a nondiscrimination provision: it insisted that special measures for minority cultures (such as some form of affirmative action) are required and that such measures are as important as nondiscrimination in defending fundamental human rights in this area.[24] Such affirmative measures may include subsidies from the wider society.[25] But they also may involve the recognition that minority cultures are entitled to protect themselves by placing limits on the incursion of outsiders and limits on their own members' choices about career, family, lifestyle, loyalty, and exit—limits that might be unpalatable in the wider liberal context.[26]

It is not my intention to get involved in a detailed debate about the interpretation of Article 27. Instead, I want to examine the implicit claim about human life that lies behind provisions like this. For, once again, we are dealing with the Herderian claim[27] that there is a human yearning or need to *belong*: a need that is in danger of being miserably frustrated—for example in the case of North American aboriginal groups. This is the need that scholars appeal to when they criticize or defend various interpretations of the right of cultural preservation.

3. A Thin Theory of the Good

So there are two visions to be considered—the cosmopolitan vision intimated by Salman Rushdie and the vision of belonging and immersion in the life and culture of a particular community espoused by the proponents of Article 27.

It is important to see that these are not merely different lifestyles of the sort that old-fashioned liberalism could comfortably accommodate in a pluralistic world—some like campfires, some like opera; some are Catholics, some are Methodists—that sort of thing. Instead, we are talking, as I indicated earlier, about the background view of life, agency, and responsibility that is presupposed already by any account of what it is for lifestyles to be diverse or for diversity to be tolerated.

This contrast between lifestyle and background assumptions is worth explaining a little further. Any political theory, *including* a theory of toleration or liberal neutrality, must be predicated on some view of what human life is like. This is true even if it is only what philosophers call a 'thin' theory[28]—that is, a theory giving us the bare framework for conceptualizing choice and agency but leaving the specific content of choices to be filled in by individuals. We need a thin theory to tell us what goods should be at stake in a theory of justice, what liberties and rights are going to be called for, and, more broadly, what the skeletal outlines of human lives can be expected to be so that we can have some sense of how everything will fit together. For example, a liberal theory of rights needs to be able to say that religious choices and matters of conscience are very important to people (and so worthy of special protection) without begging any questions about what the content of those choices should be. A thin theory is also necessary in order to work out a subject-matter for a theory of justice: What is a just distribution ultimately a distribution of? Should we be interested in the just distribution of happiness, the just distribution of material resources, or the just distribution of human abilities and capacities?[29] Each society must share some consensus at this level, no matter what plurality it envisages on some other level.

Above all, we need a thin theory of choice, agency, and responsibility so that we can say something about the shape of individual lives in relation to matters like society, community, politics, and justice. We need to have some skeletal sense of how things are to fit together. Are we envisaging a society of *individuals* in some strong sense, or a community of persons bound together in some organic common life? Are we envisaging a society of equals, so that each person's claims against others are to be matched by others' reciprocal claims against him? Or are we envisaging a hierarchy, oriented functionally towards some nonegalitarian end?

We cannot make any progress at all in political philosophy unless we tie ourselves down to some extent here; certainly a liberal theory of neutrality that purports to be neutral about *everything* in this area quickly falls apart into fatuous incoherence. Critics of liberalism are fond of uncovering the assumptions made at this level, as if that were a way of discrediting the neutrality of the liberal ideal.[30] But every political theory must take some stand on what authentic human agency is like and how that relates to the fact of our location in society. The tensions that I intend to explore—between the cosmopolitan and communitarian account of human life and activities—are not merely disagreements at the level of comfortably competing lifestyles. They are not to be thought of as liberal bedfellows who have already settled the basic terms and conceptions of their association. They are tensions at a deep philosophical level.

4. Opposition and Authenticity

But are the two visions of human life that we are discussing really antagonists? It may seem odd to oppose them this starkly. Salman Rushdie is not noted as an opponent of aboriginal rights, nor are the Native American tribes particularly interested in *The Satanic Verses*. The defenders of Article 27 may frown on cultural impurity, but they are not proposing exactly to limit the freedom of those who, like Rushdie, choose to entangle their roots with foreign grafts. Not *exactly*; but the fact that one of the charges for which Rushdie was sentenced to death was apostasy is a sobering reminder of what it really may mean to insist that people must keep faith with their roots.[31]

Nor are the citizens of the world, the modernist dreamers of cosmopolis, proposing exactly to destroy minority cultures. Their apartments are quite likely to be decorated with Inuit artifacts or Maori carvings. Still, we know that a world in which deracinated cosmopolitanism flourishes is not a safe place for minority communities. Our experience has been that they wither and die in the harsh glare of modern life, and that the custodians of these dying traditions live out their lives in misery and demoralization.

We are dealing, in other words, with conceptions of man and society which, if not actually inconsistent, certainly are opposed in some important sense. Each envisions an environment in which the other is, to a certain extent, in danger.

It is also true that, although these two conceptions are not formally inconsistent, still the best case that can be made in favor of each of them tends to cast doubt upon the best case that can be made for the other.

Suppose first, that a freewheeling cosmopolitan life, lived in a kaleidoscope of cultures, is both possible and fulfilling. Suppose such a life turns out to be rich and creative, and with no more unhappiness than one expects to find anywhere in human existence. Immediately, one argument for the protection of minority cultures is undercut. It can no longer be said that all people *need* their rootedness in the particular culture in which they and their ancestors were reared in the way that they need food, clothing, and shelter.[32] People used to think they *needed* red meat in their diet. It turns out not to be true: vegetarian alternatives are available. Now some still may prefer and enjoy a carnivorous diet, but it is no longer a matter of necessity. The same—if the cosmopolitan alternative can be sustained—is true for immersion in the culture of a particular community. Such immersion may be something that particular people like and enjoy. But they no longer can claim that it is something that they need.

Of course, it does not follow from this that we are entitled to crush and destroy minority cultures. But the collapse of the Herderian argument based on distinctively human *need* seriously undercuts any claim that minority cultures might have to special support or assistance or to extraordinary provision or forbearance. At best, it leaves the right to culture roughly on the same footing as the right to religious freedom. We no longer think it true that everyone needs some religious faith or that everyone must be sustained in the faith in which be was brought up. A secular lifestyle is evidently viable, as is conversion from one church to another. Few would think it right to try to extirpate religious belief in consequence of these possibilities. But equally, few would think it right to subsidize religious sects merely in order to preserve them. If a particular church is dying out because its members are drifting away, no longer convinced by its theology or attracted by its ceremonies, that is just the way of the world. It is like the death of a fashion or a hobby, not the demise of anything that people really need.

So the sheer existence and vitality of the cosmopolitan alternative is enough to undercut an important part of the case for the preservation of minority cultures. Sometimes the cosmopolitan argument goes further. The stronger claim that Salman Rushdie suggests, in the passage we began with, is that the hybrid lifestyle of the true cosmopolitan is in fact the only appropriate response to the modern world in which we live.[33] We live in a world formed by technology and trade; by economic, religious, and political imperialism and their offspring; by mass migration and the dispersion of cultural influences. In this context, to immerse oneself in the traditional practices of, say, an aboriginal culture might be a fascinating anthropological experiment, but it involves an artificial dislocation from what actually is going on in the world. That it is an artifice is evidenced by the fact that such immersion often requires special subsidization and extraordinary provision by those who live in the real world, where cultures and practices are not so sealed off from one another. The charge, in other words, is one of *inauthenticity*.

Let me state it provocatively. From a cosmopolitan point of view, immersion in the traditions of a particular community in the modern world is like living in Disneyland and thinking that one's surroundings epitomize what it is for a culture really to exist. Worse still, it is like demanding the funds to live in Disneyland and the protection of modern society for the boundaries of Disneyland, while still managing to convince oneself that what happens inside Disneyland is all there is to an adequate and fulfilling life. It is like thinking that what every person most deeply needs is for one of the Magic Kingdoms to provide a framework for her choices and her beliefs, completely neglecting the fact that the framework of Disneyland depends on commitments, structures, and infrastructures that far outstrip the character of any particular facade. It is to imagine that one could belong to Disneyland while professing complete indifference towards, or even disdain for, Los Angeles.

That is the case from one side. Suppose, on the other hand, that we accept what defenders of minority culture often say—that there *is* a universal human need for rootedness in the life of a particular community and that this communal belonging confers character and depth on our choices and our actions.[34] Then the freedom that Rushdie claims looks deviant and marginal, an odd or eccentric exercise of license rather than a consummation of human liberty. It sometimes is said that claims of freedom must be made with respect to actions that make sense and that unintelligibility rather than hostility is the first obstacle to toleration.[35] If anything like this is correct, then the more credence that we give to the communitarian thesis, the less intelligible the claim to cosmopolitan freedom becomes.

From the point of view of community, the cosmopolitan freedom that Rushdie extols—the freedom to renounce his heritage and just play with it, mixing it with imagery and movies and jokes and obscenities—is like the freedom claimed by any other oddball: the freedom to sail the Atlantic in a bathtub or the freedom to steer one's way through a bewildering series of marriages and divorces. Those who hop from one community to another, merging their roots and never settling down into any stable practices and traditions may, like the bathtub sailor or the matrimonial athlete, excite our sneaking admiration. But when things go wrong for them, our pitying response will be, 'Well, what did you expect?'

A moment ago, we considered the view that immersion in the life of a minority culture is like hiding in Disneyland and that it is an inauthentic way of evading the complex actualities of the world as it is. But the charge of inauthenticity is likely to be returned with interest by the proponents of minority culture. From their point of view, it is the Rushdian life of shifting and tangled attachments that is the shallow and inauthentic way of living in the world. The cosmopolitan ideal, they will say, embodies all the worst aspects of classic liberalism—atomism, abstraction, alienation from one's roots, vacuity of commitment, indeterminacy of character, and ambivalence towards the good. The accusation is implicit in the undertones of words like 'deracinated' and 'alienated' or in the terminology that Rushdie turns bravely to his own purposes in the passage quoted earlier: 'hybrid,' 'impurity,' 'hotchpotch,' '*mélange*,' and 'mongrelization.'[36] It is no accident that these terms, which so accurately describe the cosmopolitan ideal, are fraught with negative and cautionary connotations. This is the case that must be answered if the cosmopolitan vision is to be sustained. . . .

7. Our Debt to Global Community

One advantage of our focus on the cosmopolitan vision is that it forces us to think a little more grandly about the scale on which community and friendship are available for the constitution of the individual and the sustenance of friendship and interdependence. Talk of community in the nostalgic first-person plural of belonging, is, as I have said, apt to evoke images of small-scale community, neighborhood, or intimacy—the aboriginal hunting band, the Athenian city-state, or the misty dawn in a Germanic village.

Think honestly, however, of the real communities to which many of us owe our allegiance and in which we pursue our values and live large parts of our lives: the international community of scholars (defined in terms of some shared specialization), the scientific community, the human rights community, the artistic community, the feminist movement, what's left of international socialism, and so on. These structures of action and interaction, dependence and interdependence, effortlessly transcend national and ethnic boundaries and allow men and women the opportunity to pursue common and important projects under conditions of goodwill, cooperation, and exchange throughout the world. Of course, one should not paint too rosy a picture of this interaction. Such groupings exhibit rivalry, suspicion, and divisive controversy as well; but no more than any common enterprise and certainly no more than the gossip or backbiting one finds in smaller, more localized entities. It is community on this global scale which is the modern realization of Aristotelean friendship: equals who are good at orienting themselves in common to the pursuit of virtue.[37] This form of community is quite missed by those who lament the loss of true friendship in modern life.[38]

Once we recognize this, the simple Herderian picture of the constitution of an individual through his belonging to a homogenous group begins to fall apart. Think how much we owe in history and heritage—in the culture, or the cultures that have formed us—to the international communities that have existed among merchants, clerics, lawyers, agitators, scholars, scientists, writers, and diplomats. We are not the self-made atoms of liberal fantasy, certainly, but neither are we exclusively products or artifacts of single national or ethnic communities. We are made by our languages, our literature, our cultures, our science, our religions, our civilization—and these are human entities that go far beyond national boundaries and exist, if they exist anywhere, simply *in the world*. If, as the communitarians insist, we owe a debt of provenance to the social structures that have formed us, then we owe a debt to the world and to the global community and civilization, as well as whatever we owe to any particular region, country, nation, or tribe.

The argument that we must not think of our individuality as self-made, but that we must own up to the role that society has played in the constitution of our selves and cultivate a sense of allegiance and obligation that is appropriate to that social provenance has been a staple of modern communitarian thought. It finds its most eloquent recent expression in a paper by Charles Taylor, entitled *Atomism*,[39] though I fear that in that article Taylor is guilty of exactly the equivocation I mentioned earlier: tracing our debt to society, in the sense of a whole civilization, and inferring an obligation to society, in the sense of a particular nation-state.[40]

Be that as it may, Taylor's argument is one that can be turned as easily against the partisans of small-scale community as against the advocates of atomistic individualism. For just as the allegedly self-made individual needs to be brought to a proper awareness of her dependence on social, communal, and cultural structures, so too in the modern world particular cultures and national communities have an obligation to recognize their dependence on the wider social, political, international, and civilizational structures that sustain *them*.

This is obvious in the case of indigenous communities in countries like the United States, Canada, Australia, and New Zealand. Indigenous communities make their claims for special provision and for the autonomous direction of their own affairs in the context of the wider political life of the countries where they are situated, and by the logic of Taylor's argument they must accept some responsibility to participate in and sustain this wider life. They are not entitled to accept the benefits of its protection and subsidization and at the same time disparage and neglect the structures, institutions, and activities that make it possible for indigenous communities to secure the aid, toleration, and forbearance of the large numbers of other citizens and other small communities by which they are surrounded.

Indigenous communities of course will lament that they are thus at the mercy of larger polities and that they have to make a case for the existence of their culture to fellow citizens who do not necessarily share their ethnic allegiance. They may yearn for the days of their own self-sufficiency, the days when the question of sharing their lands with anyone else simply did not arise.[41] They have that in common, I think, with Nozickian individualists who yearn for the days when the individual person was not so much at the mercy of the community and did not owe so much to the state, and who resent the processes that have brought them to this point.[42] Yet here we all are. Our lives or practices, whether individual or communal, are in fact no longer self-sufficient. We may pretend to be self-sufficient atoms, and behave as we are supposed to behave in the fantasies of individualistic economics; but the pretense easily is exposed by the reality of our communal life. And similarly—though we may drape ourselves in the distinctive costumes of our ethnic heritage and immure ourselves in an environment designed to minimize our sense of relation to the outside world—no honest account of our being will be complete without an account of our dependence on larger social and political structures that goes far beyond the particular community with which we pretend to identify ourselves.

If this is true of the relation of indigenous minorities to the larger state, it applies also to the relation of particular cultures and nations to the world order as a whole. The point is evident enough from the ironies of Article 27 of the International Covenant on Civil and Political Rights, quoted earlier, which claims the integrity of indigenous cultures as a matter of human rights.[43] One hardly can maintain that immersion in a particular community is all that people need in the way of connection with others when the very form in which that claim is couched—the twenty-seventh article of one of a succession of human rights charters administered and scrutinized by international agencies from Ottawa to Geneva—indicates an organized social context that already takes us far beyond a specific nation, community, or ethnicity. The point is not that we should all therefore abandon our tribal allegiances and realign ourselves under the flag of the United Nations. The theoretical point is simply that it ill behoves the partisans of a particular community to sneer at and to disparage those whose cosmopolitan commitments make possible the lives that they are seeking to lead. The activity of these international organizations does not happen by magic; it presupposes large numbers of men and women who are prepared to devote themselves to issues of human and communal values *in general* and who are prepared to pursue that commitment in abstraction from the details of their own particular heritage.

So far I have developed the *instrumental* side of Taylor's argument: just as individuals need communal structures in order to develop and exercise the capacities that their rights protect, so minority communities need larger political and international structures to protect and to sustain the cultural goods that they pursue. But Taylor's critique of individualist atomism also goes deeper than this. The very idea of individuality and autonomy, he argues, is a social artifact, a way of thinking about and managing the self that is sustained in a particular social and historical context.[44] I am sure that he is right about that. But we must not assume, simply because individuality is an artifact, that the social structures that are said to produce it are necessarily natural. Certainly there is nothing natural about communitarian, ethnic, or nationalist ideas. The idea of a small-scale national community is as much a product (and indeed a quite recent product) of civilization, growing and flourishing as the convergence of a number of disparate currents under particular conditions in a particular era, as is the idea of the autonomous individual.[45] Certainly, ethnic nationality is an idea which postulates or dreams its own naturalness, its own antiquity, its immemorial cultivation of a certain path of soil. Each national community, in Benedict Anderson's phrase, *imagines* itself as something that can be traced to the misty dawn of time.[46] But so did *individuals* dream themselves, as the natural units of mankind, in the heyday of atomistic philosophy.[47] The claim that we always have belonged to specific, defined, and culturally homogeneous peoples—the staple claim of modern nationalism—needs to be treated with the same caution as individualist fantasies about the state of nature: useful, perhaps, as a hypothesis for some theoretical purpose, but entirely misleading for others.

8. Kymlicka's View of the Social World

A. *The Importance of Cultural Membership*

In all of this, the cosmopolitan strategy is not to deny the role of culture in the constitution of human life, but to question, first, the assumption that the social world divides up neatly into particular distinct cultures, one to every community, and, secondly, the assumption that what everyone needs is just *one* of these entities—a single, coherent culture—to give shape and meaning to his life.

That assumption, I am afraid, pervades Will Kymlicka's recent book on community and culture,[48] and it is to his argument that I now want to turn. Kymlicka's aim is to show that liberal theorists, such as John Rawls and Ronald Dworkin, have underestimated radically the importance of culture as a primary good for the self-constitution of individual lives.[49] He wants to fill that gap and to enlist liberal theories in the cause of the preservation of minority cultures.[50]

Thus, Kymlicka's starting point is not so much the Herderian urge to belong, but a Rawlsian conviction about the importance to people of the freedom to form, reform, and revise their individual beliefs about what makes life worth living.[51] To sustain that freedom, one needs a certain amount of self-respect, and one needs the familiar protections, guarantees, opportunities, and access to the means of life—all the things that figure already on Rawls's list of the primary goods to be governed by a theory of justice.[52] In order to make the case that culture is also one of these primary goods, Kymlicka argues that people cannot choose a conception of the good for themselves in isolation, but that they need a clear sense of an established range of options to choose from.

> In deciding how to lead our lives, we do not start *de novo*, but rather we examine 'definite ideals and forms of life that have been developed and tested by innumerable individuals, sometimes for generations.' The decision about how to lead our lives must ultimately be ours alone, but this decision is always a matter of selecting what we believe to be most valuable from the various options available, selecting from a context of choice which provides us with different ways of life.[53]

Kymlicka elaborates the point by insisting that what we choose among are not ways of life understood simply as different physical patterns of behavior.

> The physical movements only have meaning to us because they are identified as having significance by our *culture*, because they fit into some pattern of activities which is culturally recognized as a way of leading one's life. We learn about these patterns of activity through their presence in stories we've heard about the lives, real or imaginary, of others. . . . We decide how to lead our lives by situating ourselves in these cultural narratives, by adopting roles that have struck us as worthwhile ones, as ones worth living (which may, of course, include the roles we were brought up to occupy).[54]

'What follows from this?' Kymlicka asks.

> Liberals should be concerned with the fate of cultural structures, not because they have some moral status of their own, but because it's only through having a rich and secure cultural structure that people can become aware, in a vivid way, of the options available to them, and intelligently examine their value.[55]

On the face of it, the argument is a convincing one. Of course, choice takes place in a cultural context, among options that have culturally defined meanings. But in developing his case, Kymlicka is guilty of something like the fallacy of composition. From the fact that each option must have a cultural meaning, it does not follow that there must be one cultural framework in which each available option is assigned a meaning. Meaningful options may come to us as items or fragments from a variety of cultural sources. Kymlicka is moving too quickly when he says that each item is given its significance by some entity called 'our culture,' and he is not entitled to infer from that that there are things called 'cultural structures' whose integrity must be guaranteed in order for people to have meaningful choices. His argument shows that people need cultural materials; it does not show that what people need is 'a rich and secure cultural structure.' It shows the importance of access to a variety of stories and roles; but it does not, as he claims, show the importance of something called *membership* in a culture.

Kymlicka's claim about the difference between physically and culturally defined options was an echo of an argument made earlier by Alasdair MacIntyre, and it may reinforce my point to discuss that argument as well. According to MacIntyre:

> We enter human society . . . with one or more imputed characters—roles into which we have been drafted—and we have to learn what they are in order to be able to understand how others respond to us and how our responses to them are apt to be construed. It is through hearing stories about wicked stepmothers, lost children, good but misguided kings, wolves that suckle twin boys, youngest sons who receive no inheritance but must make their own way in the world and eldest sons who waste their inheritance on riotous living and go into exile to live with the swine, that children learn or mislearn both what a child and what a parent is, what the cast of characters may be in the drama into which they have been born and what the ways of the world are. Deprive children of stories and you leave them unscripted, anxious stutterers in their actions as in their words.[56]

Again, it is important to see that these are heterogenous characters drawn from a variety of disparate cultural sources: from first-century Palestine, from the heritage of Germanic folklore, and from the mythology of the Roman Republic. They do not come from some *thing* called 'the structure of our culture.' They are familiar to us because of the immense variety of cultural materials, various in their provenance as well as their character, that are in fact available to us. But neither their familiarity nor their availability constitute them as part of a single cultural matrix. Indeed, if we were to insist that they are all part of the same matrix because they are all available to us, we would trivialize the individuation of cultures beyond any sociological interest. Any array of materials would count as part of a single culture whenever they were familiar to one and the same person. It would then be *logically* impossible for an individual to have access to more than one cultural framework.

Someone may object to the picture of cultural heterogeneity I am painting: 'Doesn't each item take its full character from the integrity of the surrounding cultural context, so that it is a distortion to isolate it from that context and juxtapose it with disparate materials?' Maybe that is true, for certain purposes. If we were making an anthropological study of each item, we *would* want to explore the detail of its context and provenance; we would look at the tale of the prodigal son in the context of Aramaic storytelling, and we would confine the children lost in the wood to the Germanic villages from which the Grimm brothers drew their collection of folklore. But that is absurd as an account of how cultural materials enter into the lives and choices of ordinary people. For that purpose, the materials are simply *available*, from all corners of the world, as more or less meaningful fragments, images, and snatches of stories. Their significance for each person consists in large part in the countless occasions on which they have been (from the anthropological purist's point of view) misread and misinterpreted, wrenched from a wider context and juxtaposed to other fragments with which they may have very little in common. Since this in fact is the way in which cultural meanings enter people's lives, Salman Rushdie's description of a life lived in the shadow of Hindu gods, Muslim film stars, Kipling, Christ, Nabokov, and the *Mabharata*[57] is at least as authentic as Kymlicka's insistence on the purity of a particular cultural heritage.[58]

If all this is correct, then membership in a particular community, defined by its identification with a single cultural frame or matrix, has none of the importance that Kymlicka claims it does. We need cultural meanings, but we do not need homogenous cultural frameworks. We need to understand our choices in the contexts in which they make sense, but we do not need any single context to structure all our choices. To put it crudely, we need culture, but we do not need cultural integrity. Since none of us needs a homogenous cultural framework or the integrity of a particular set of meanings, none of us needs to be immersed in one of the small-scale communities which, according to Kymlicka and others, are alone capable of securing this integrity and homogeneity. Some, of course, still may prefer such immersion, and welcome the social subsidization of their preference. But it is not, as Kymlicka maintained, a necessary presupposition of rational and meaningful choice.

B. Evaluation and Cultural Security

In addition to the claim (which I have just criticized) that each person needs to be a member of a particular cultural community, Kymlicka also argues that each person needs some assurance of the *security* of the cultural framework or frameworks from which she makes her choices.[59] This seems to me a self-defeating claim.

Kymlicka's liberal individual is supposed to be making not just a choice, but an evaluation: 'Which of the roles presented to me by the cultural materials at hand is a good role or an attractive one (for me)?' Now evaluation is a practical and, in part, a comparative matter. I choose role A because it seems a better way of living and relating to others than role B. It is difficult to see how one can make these comparisons without the ability to take a role, defined by a given culture, and compare it with what one might term loosely other ways of doing roughly the same sort of thing. For example, a traditional culture may define the role of *male elder*, a patriarchal position of tribal power, as a source of authority and the embodiment of tradition. Is this something for a young man to aspire to? One thing he may want to know is that the politics of patriarchal authority have, in almost all other social contexts, come under fierce challenge, and that people have developed other means of authoritative governance that do not embody male power and fatherhood in the same way. But to the extent that our young man can know this, he is not choosing from a cultural framework which is secure, in Kymlicka's sense. He only can make his choice a genuine *evaluation* to the extent that the culture he is scrutinizing is vulnerable to challenge and comparison from the outside. Unless the culture is vulnerable to his evaluation (and other evaluations like it), his evaluation will have no practical effect; and unless it has been vulnerable in this way in the past, he will have no basis for an informed and sensible choice.

To preserve a culture—to insist that it must be *secure*, come what may—is to insulate it from the very forces and tendencies that allow it to operate in a context of genuine choice. How does one tell, for example, whether the gender roles defined in a given culture structure have value? One way is to see whether the culture erodes and collapses as a way of life in a world once different ways of doing things are perceived. The possibility of the erosion of allegiance, or of the need to compromise a culture beyond all recognition in order to retain allegiance and prevent mass exodus, is the key to cultural evaluation. It is what cultures do, under pressure, as contexts of genuine choice. But if that is so, we cannot *guarantee* at the same time the integrity of a given community and say that its culture (or the fate of its culture) can *tell* people about the value and viability of this particular way of life. Either people learn about value from the dynamics of their culture and its interactions with others or their culture can operate for them at most as a museum display on which they can pride themselves. There is, I suppose, nothing wrong with such fierce nostalgic pride, but it certainly should not be confused with genuine choice and evaluation. To confer meaning on one's life is to take risks with one's culture, and these are risks that dismay those whose interest is the preservation of some sort of cultural purity.[60]

In general, there is something artificial about a commitment to *preserve* minority cultures. Cultures live and grow, change and sometimes wither away; they amalgamate with other cultures, or they adapt themselves to geographical or demographic necessity. To *preserve* a culture is often to take a favored 'snapshot' version of it, and insist that this version must persist at all costs, in its defined purity, irrespective of the surrounding social, economic, and political circumstances. But the *stasis* envisaged by such preservation is seldom itself a feature of the society in question, or if it is, it is itself a circumstantial feature. A society may have remained static for centuries precisely because it did not come into contact with the influence from which now people are proposing to protect it. If stasis is not an inherent feature, it may be important to consider, as part of *that very culture*, the ability it has to adapt to changes in circumstances. To preserve or protect it, or some favored version of it, artificially, in the face of that change, is precisely to cripple the mechanisms of adaptation and compromise (from warfare to commerce to amalgamation) with which all societies confront the outside world. It is to preserve part of the culture, but not what many would regard as its most fascinating feature: its ability to generate *a history*.

9. The Cosmopolitan Self

I have argued that the 'mongrelization' of identity that Salman Rushdie celebrated in the passage with which we began has none of the inauthenticity that the communitarian critique tends to suggest. I think it may well be a richer, more honest, and more authentic response to the world in which we live than a retreat into the confined sphere of a particular community.

But what becomes of *the self* in the cosmopolitan picture? This is the final question that I want to consider. If we live the cosmopolitan life, we draw our allegiances from here, there, and everywhere. Bits of cultures come into our lives from different sources, and there is no guarantee that they will all fit together. At least if a person draws his identity, as Kymlicka suggests, from a single culture, he will obtain for himself a certain degree of coherence or integrity. The coherence which makes his particular community a single cultural entity will confer a corresponding degree of integrity on the individual self that is constituted under its auspices.[61] By contrast, the self constituted under the auspices of a multiplicity of cultures might strike us as chaotic, confused, even schizophrenic.

The point is an important one. The cosmopolitan, as we have seen, is not in the business of disputing that people are formed by attachments and involvements, by culture and community. She acknowledges it, but acknowledges it—as it were—*too much* for the communitarian's comfort. For she shows how each person has or can have a variety, a multiplicity of different and perhaps disparate communal allegiances. Such integrity as the cosmopolitan individual has therefore requires *management*. Cultural structures cannot provide that management for her because too many of them are implicated in her identity, and they are too differently shaped.

The trouble is, if we talk too much about management, we fall into the trap of postulating the existence of a managerial entity, an agent existing in distinction from each of the disparate elements that together constitute the person in question. We have to postulate the 'I,' the true self who contrives somehow to keep the whole house in order. But who or what is this entity? How does it make its decisions? How does it know what sort of order to maintain?

One dominant theme in recent communitarian writing has been a critique of this picture of the independent self—the cosmopolitan manager, standing back a little from each of the items on the smorgasbord of its personality. In order to manage the disparate commitments, to see that they fit with one another, and to evaluate each item and compare it with others on the cultural menu, the self would have to be an ethereal sort of entity, without any content or commitments of its own. Michael Sandel quite properly has raised the question whether this is really the way that we want to view our personality and our character:

> [W]e cannot regard ourselves as independent in this way without great cost to those loyalties and convictions whose moral force consists partly in the fact that living by them is inseparable from understanding ourselves as the particular persons we are—as members of this family or community or nation or people, as bearers of this history, as sons and daughters of that revolution, as citizens of this republic. Allegiances such as these are more than values I happen to have or aims I 'espouse at any given time'. . . .
>
> To imagine a person incapable of constitutive attachments such as these is not to conceive an ideally free and rational agent, but to imagine a person wholly without character, without moral depth. For to have character is to know that I move in a history I neither summon nor command, which carries consequences none the less for my choices and conduct.[62]

Sandel's critique seems to present the defender of cosmopolitanism with an unhappy dilemma. Either he must embrace the ethereal self of liberal deontology—the self that chooses but is not identified with any of its choices: or he must admit that the self can have a substantial character of its own, a character essential to its identity. If he chooses the former, he gives a wholly unrealistic account of choice; for on what basis can this ghost choose if it is has no values, commitments, or projects of its own? If, on the other hand, he opts for the picture of a self with a substantial essence in order to avoid the imputed shallowness of the former conception, then cosmopolitanism begins to look unsatisfactory. For now the self must have not just cultural characteristics in all their plurality and variety, but *a distinct character*, and it has not been proven that the cosmopolitan mode of engaging with the world can provide that.[63]

To avoid the dilemma, we should go back and question the image of *management* and the assumptions about *identity* that are presupposed in this critique. So long as we think that the management of the self is like the personal governance of a community or a corporation, we will be driven to ask embarassing questions about the specific character of the 'I' in its capacity as manager. But suppose we think instead about personal identity, not in terms of hierarchical management, but in terms of the democratic self-government of a pluralistic population. Maybe the person is nothing but a set of commitments and involvements, and maybe the governance of the self is just the more or less comfortable (or at times more or less chaotic) coexistence of these elements. The threat, of course, is what we vulgarly call schizophrenia; but that may be better understood as radical conflict or dissonance rather than mere unregulated plurality. An image that may help to dispel this threat is that of the self-governance of a group of friends living and working together. Each friend has a character of her own and strengths and weaknesses of her own; they are quite different, but their variety and their frictions may be the key to their association and to their ability to undertake different projects and enterprises. No one, I hope, thinks that a friendship can be sustained only if one or the other friend is recognized as being *in charge* or only to the extent that all parties are agreed on some specific common purpose or charter. Friendship does not work like that, nor I think do the internal politics of the self. There may be, on occasions, antagonisms within the self (as indeed there are among friends); all of us, even the most culturally and psychologically secure, have the experience of inner conflict. But far from detracting from the self's integrity, the possibility of such conflict, and the variety and open texture of character that make it possible, seem indispensable to a healthy personality. It may be this limitless diversity of character—Rushdie's *mélange* or hotchpotch—that makes it possible for each of us to respond to a multifaceted world in new and creative ways.

These are mere speculations, and they need to be matched more closely to the empirical psychology of personality. However, I hope that they indicate how misleading it may be to indict a picture of human life or action, such as the cosmopolitan vision that I have outlined, on the basis of simplistic and rigid assumptions about what the self *must* be like. Human identity is not a simple thing. The openness and diversity of the cosmopolitan way of life may well hold more of a key to understanding the role of character and creativity in a changing world than the assumption of Sandel's critique that character is to be identified compulsively with a single preestablished cultural role.

Conclusion

At the beginning of this paper, I set out a quotation from Salman Rushdie's defence of *The Satanic Verses* in his collection *Imaginary Homelands*.[64] Let me conclude with another passage from *In Good Faith*, the essay in which Rushdie reflects on the politics of his own cultural roots:

> To be an Indian of my generation was also to be convinced of the vital importance of Jawaharlal Nehru's vision of a secular India. Secularism, for India, is not simply a point of view; it is a question of survival. If what Indians call 'communalism', sectarian religious politics, were to be allowed to take control of the polity, the results would be too horrifying to imagine. Many Indians fear that that moment may now be very near. I have fought against communal politics all my adult life. The Labour Party in Britain would do well to look at the consequences of Indian politicians' willingness to play the communalist card, and consider whether some Labour politicians' apparent willingness to do the same in Britain, for the same reason (votes), is entirely wise.[65]

I have chosen not to talk in this Article about the warning that Rushdie is sounding here, but to discuss more affirmatively the image of the modern self that he conveys. Still, I hope that we do not lose sight of the warning. The communitarianism that can sound cozy and attractive in a book by Robert Bellah or Michael Sandel can be blinding, dangerous, and disruptive in the real world, where communities do not come ready-packaged and where communal allegiances are as much ancient hatreds of one's neighbors as immemorial traditions of culture.

Rushdie wrote his piece originally for an English newspaper (hence his reference to the Labour Party). He said in effect that the British people, in the tensions of their new pluralism, had a right to expect something more from politicians, particularly on the Left, than a return to ethnic sectarianism. Something similar, I think, is true of legal and political philosophy. It is no secret that the old individualist paradigms are in crisis and that something must be done to repair or replace the tattered remnants of liberalism. But as shells rain down on Sarajevo,[66] as Georgia announces that it will withhold citizenship rights from inhabitants who cannot prove that their ancestors were Georgian speakers and lived in the territory before 1801,[67] as the long lines of refugees, in consequence, begin their fearful trudge toward the only homelands where they can expect to be welcomed or tolerated, as 'community' even in North America becomes increasingly a code word for the class and ethnic exclusivity of wealthy home-owner's associations[68]—in the midst of all that, I suggest that people have a right to expect something better from their political philosophers than a turn away from the real world into the cultural exclusiveness of the identity politics of community. I hope that, at any rate, the vision of cosmopolitanism developed here can provide the basis of an alternative way of thinking—one that embraces the aspects of modernity with which we all have to live and welcomes the diversity and mixture that for most people is their destiny, whatever the communitarians say.

Notes

1. Salman Rushdie, 'In Good Faith', in *Imaginary Homelands* 393, 394, 404 (1991).
2. *See* Jeremy Waldron, 'Religion and the Imagination in a Global Community', *The Times Literary Supplement*, London, 10–16 Mar. 1989: 248 (discussing the Salman Rushdie affair).
3. *See, e.g.*, Charles Taylor, 'Cross-Purposes: The Liberal-Communitarian Debate', in *Liberalism and the Moral Life*, 159 (Nancy L. Rosenblum ed., 1989) (discussing both the independence and interdependence between ontological issues and advocacy issues which confuse the debate between communitarianism and liberalism in social theory).
4. *E.g.*, John Rawls, *A Theory of Justice*, 395–439 (1971).
5. *See* Loren E. Lomasky, *Persons, Rights, and the Moral Community*, 37–83 (1987).
6. *See* ibid. at 42.
7. *See* Ronald Dworkin, *A Matter of Principle*, 191 (1985) (referring to a theory of equality in which government is neutral as to 'goodness' since each person's conception of what gives value to life differs).
8. Rawls, *supra* note 4, at 408.
9. Mackie presents a less rigid conception of a liberal life:

   > People differ radically about the kinds of life that they choose to pursue. Even this way of putting it is misleading: in general people do not and cannot make an overall choice of a total plan of life. They choose successively to pursue various activities from time to time, not once and for all.

   J.L. Mackie, 'Can There Be a Right-Based Moral Theory?', in *Theories of Rights*, 168, 175 (Jeremy Waldron ed., 1984). Raz expresses a similar idea:

   > The autonomous person is part author of his life. The image this metaphor is meant to conjure up is not that of the regimented, compulsive person who decides when young what life to have and spends the rest of it living it out according to plan. . . . [Autonomy] does not require an attempt to impose any special unity on one's life. The autonomous life may consist of diverse and heterogeneous pursuits. And a person who frequently changes his tastes can be as autonomous as one who never shakes off his adolescent preferences.

   Joseph Raz, *The Morality of Freedom*, 370–71 (1986). There is a strong temptation in traditional liberalism to take the form of an Aristotelean theory of ethical well-being and convert it to the purposes of liberalism. Instead of a single conception of the good life, authoritatively enunciated by Aristotle in

Nicomachean Ethics, 283 (bk. X, ch. 7) (David Ross trans., 1954), there are many such conceptions, and each person should be free to choose *one*. With Raz and Mackie, I think that the freedom of the modern self is less constrained than that: it is the freedom to make a variety of choices, not the freedom to choose just one out of a number of ethical conceptions.

10. Nietzsche too embraces this pluralistic view:

> But for the enrichment of knowledge it may be of more value not to reduce oneself to uniformity in this way, but to listen instead to the gentle voice of each of life's different situations; these will suggest the attitude of mind appropriate to them. Through thus ceasing to treat oneself as a *single* rigid and unchanging individuum one takes an intelligent interest in the life and being of many others.

Friedrich Nietzsche, *Human, All Too Human: A Book for Free Spirits*, 196 (R.J. Hollingdale trans., 1986).

11. The communitarian works I have in mind include, most prominently, Alasdair MacIntyre, *After Virtue: A Study in Moral Theory* (2d edn. 1984); Michael J. Sandel, *Liberalism and the Limits of Justice* (1982); Charles Taylor, 'Atomism', in *2 Philosophical Papers: Philosophy and the Human Sciences*, 187 (1985); and Michael Walzer, *Spheres of Justice* (1983); see also the extracts collected in *Liberalism and Its Critics* (Michael J. Sandel ed., 1984).
12. *See supra* note 11.
13. Karl Marx, 'Grundrisse', in *Selected Writings*, 345, 346 (David McLellan ed., 1977).
14. Sandel, *supra* note 11, at 179–80.
15. Will Kymlicka, *Liberalism, Community, and Culture*, 165 (1989).
16. Taylor, *supra* note 11, at 198.
17. Robert C. Post, 'The Social Foundations of Defamation Law', 74 *Cal. L. Rev.* 691, 736 (1986).
18. Walzer, *supra* note 11, at 313.
19. John Dunn, *Interpreting Political Responsibility*, 124 (1990).
20. Jeremy Waldron, 'Particular Values and Critical Morality', 77 *Cal. L. Rev.* 561, 582 (1989); *see also* Michael Ignatieff, *The Needs of Strangers*, 139–40 (1985) ('Our political images of civic belonging remain haunted by the classical *polis*, by Athens, Rome and Florence. Is there a language of belonging adequate to Los Angeles?').
21. For 'imagined', see the excellent discussion in Benedict Anderson, *Imagined Communities: Reflections on the Origin and Spread of Nationalism*, 15–16 (1983). Anderson stresses, quite rightly, that 'imagined' does not imply 'fabricated'. ibid., at 15.
22. Isaiah Berlin, 'Benjamin Disraeli, Karl Marx and the Search for Identity', in *Against the Current*, 252, 257 (Henry Hardy ed., 1980).
23. International Covenant on Civil and Political Rights, *adopted* Dec. 19, 1966, art. 27, 999 U.N.T.S. 172, 179.
24. Francesco Capotorti, *Study on the Rights of Persons Belonging to Ethnic, Religious and Linguistic Minorities*, 40–41, 98–99, U.N. Doc. E/CN.4/Sub. 2/384/Rev. 1 (1979).

25. Ibid. at 98–99.
26. For example, Canadian legislation places restrictions on the ability of non-Indians to reside on or use Indian lands:

    [A] deed, lease, contract, instrument, document or agreement of any kind, whether written or oral, by which a band or a member of a band purports to permit a person other than a member of that band to occupy or use a reserve or to reside or otherwise exercise any rights on a reserve is void.

    Indian Act, R.S.C., ch. 1-5, – 28(1) (1985) (Can.). Some aboriginal leaders in Canada have proposed a variety of changes in local electoral requirements to assure recognition of the political rights of aboriginal peoples, regardless of the ethnic composition of the majority in a given region. See Michael Asch, *Home and Native Land: Aboriginal Rights and the Canadian Constitution*, 102–04 (1984); *see also* Kymlicka, *supra* note 15, at 146–47. Proposed changes include the imposition of residency requirements of between three and ten years before newcomers can vote for or hold public office in aboriginal communities. Asch, *supra* at 103. In both the United States and Canada, participants in mixed marriages may suffer certain disabilities even when they reside on reservations or in aboriginal territories. For a general discussion, see Kymlicka, *supra* note 15, at 148–49. The United States Supreme Court has recognized the jurisdiction of tribal authorities over Native American children born off the reservation in a case where a Native American mother had purposely given birth off the reservation in order to be able to relinquish her children to non-Native American adoptive parents. *See* Mississippi Band of Choctaw Indians v. Holyfield, 490 U.S. 30, 51–53 (1989). This is about as far as the claims have gone in the context of aboriginal cultural rights in the United States. But of course it would be irresponsible to advance general theses about minority cultures without also recognizing their tendency to shade into nationalist claims for regional autonomy and self-determination, claims that throw boundaries and general political stability seriously into question. *See infra* text accompanying note 92.
27. *See supra* note 22 and accompanying text.
28. For a general discussion of a 'thin theory' of human good, see Rawls, *supra* note 4, a: 396.
29. *See ibid.* at 90–95 (discussing 'primary goods'); *see also* Ronald Dworkin, 'What Is Equality?' (pts. 1 & 2) 10 *Phil. & Pub. Aff.* 185, 283 (1981) (discussing 'equality of welfare' and 'equality of resources'); Amartya Sen, 'Equality of What?', in *Liberty, Equality, and Law*, 137 (Sterling M. McMurrin ed., 1987).
30. Thomas Nagel, for example, says the following about Rawls's construction:

    The model contains a strong individualistic bias, which is further strengthened by the motivational assumptions of mutual disinterest and absence of envy. These assumptions have the effect of discounting the claims of conceptions of the good that depend heavily on the realtion between one's own position and that of others. . . . The original position seems to presuppose not just a neutral theory of the good, but a liberal, individualistic conception according to which the best that can be wished for someone is the unimpeded pursuit of his own path, provided it does not interfere with the rights of others.

Thomas Nagel, 'Rawls on Justice', in *Reading Rawls: Critical Studies on Rawls' A Theory of Justice*, 1, 9–10 (Norman Daniels ed., 1975). Nagel is right that Rawls makes these assumptions. They constitute his thin theory of human choice and agency. They *are* controversial; but the existence of that controversy no more undermines the claim to liberal neutrality than the existence of a controversy about what counts as a hostile act undermines a claim to neutrality in international law. *See* Jeremy Waldron, 'Legislation and Moral Neutrality', in *Liberal Neutrality*, 61, 78–81 (Robert E. Goodin & Andrew Reeve eds., 1989).

31. Rushdie, *supra* note 1, at 405 ('I do not accept the charge of apostasy, because I have never in my adult life affirmed any belief, and what one has not affirmed one cannot be said to have apostasized [sic] from.').
32. *Cf. supra* note 22 and accompanying text.
33. *See supra* note 1 and accompanying text.
34. *See supra* notes 11, 22 and accompanying text.
35. For example, Benn and Weinstein argue that 'it is apposite to discuss' whether an action is free

> only if [the end it pursues] is a possible object of reasonable choice; cutting off one's ears is not the sort of thing anyone, in a standard range of conditions, would reasonably do, *i.e.* 'no one in his senses would think of doing such a thing' (even though some people have, in fact, done it). It is not a question of logical absurdity; rather, to see the point of saying that one is (or is not) free to do X, we must be able to see that there might be some point in doing it.

S.I. Benn & W.L. Weinstein, 'Being Free to Act, and Being a Free Man', 80 *Mind*, 194, 195 (1971).

36. *See supra* text accompanying note 1.
37. Aristotle, *supra* note 9, at 196 (bk. VIII, ch. 3).
38. *Cf.* Robert N. Bellah et al., *Habits of the Heart*, 115–16 (1985) ('The conception of friendship put forward by Aristotle . . . had three essential components. Friends must enjoy one another's company, they must be useful to one another, and they must share a common commitment to the good.').
39. Taylor, *supra* note 11.
40. Ibid. at 197–98 ('[P]roof that [our distinctively human] capacities can only develop in society . . . is a proof that we ought to belong to or sustain society . . .').
41. For the dangers of taking this yearning as a basis for rectificatory justice, see Jeremy Waldron, 'Superseding Historic Injustice', 103 *Ethics* 4 (1992); *see also* Jeremy Waldron, 'Historic Injustice: Its Remembrance and Supersession', in *Justice, Ethics and New Zealand Society*, 139 (Graham Oddie & Roy W. Perrett eds., 1992).
42. *See generally* Robert Nozick, *Anarchy, State, and Utopia* (1974).
43. *See supra* note 23 and accompanying text.
44. *See* Charles Taylor, *Sources of the Self* (1989). Taylor has traced the provenance of these individualist ways of thinking in this massive and important book.
45. *See* Anderson, *supra* note 21, at 50–65, 80–103 (describing the role of imperialist administration in creating not only national entities but also national consciousness in what used to be imperial colonies).

46. *See* ibid. at 129–40.
47. *Cf.* John Locke, *Two Treatises of Government*, 269 (Peter Laslett ed., student edn. 1988) (3d edn. 1698) ('To understand Political Power right, and derive it from its Original, we must consider what State all Men are naturally in, and that is, a *State of perfect Freedom* to order their Actions, and dispose of their Possessions, and Persons as they think fit, within the bounds of the Law of Nature, without asking leave, or depending upon the Will of any other Man.').
48. Kymlicka, *supra* note 15.
49. Ibid. at 162–66.
50. Ibid.
51. *See* Rawls, *supra* note 4, at 407–24; *see also* John Rawls, *Reply to Alexander and Musgrave*, 88 Q.J. Econ. 633, 641 (1974) ('[F]ree persons conceive of themselves as beings who can revise and alter their final ends and who give first priority to preserving their liberty in these matters.').
52. Rawls, *supra* note 4, at 90–95.
53. Kymlicka, *supra* note 15, at 164 (quoting Rawls, *supra* note 4, at 563–64) (citation omitted).
54. Ibid. at 165.
55. Ibid.
56. MacIntyre, *supra* note 11, at 216; *but cf.* Susan M. Okin, 'Humanist Liberalism', in *Liberalism and the Moral Life*, 39, 48 (Nancy L. Rosenblum ed., 1989) ('MacIntyre gives, with no apparent consciousness of its sexism, a list of the characters "we" need as the models around which to shape our lives as narratives. The only female characters in the list are a wicked stepmother and a suckling wolf.').
57. *See* Rushdie, *supra* note 1, at 404.
58. *But cf.* Post, *supra* note 17, at 736 ('A community without boundaries is without shape or identity . . .').
59. Kymlicka, *supra* note 15, at 169.
60. I think what this shows, by the way, is that Kymlicka's strategy (arguing from liberal premises) is simply a dangerous one for the proponents of cultural preservation to adopt. The liberal conception of autonomous choice evokes a spirit of discernment, restlessness, and comparison. It is, I think, simply antithetical to the idea that certain structures of community are to be *preserved* in their integral character. As long as cultures depend for their existence on people's allegiance and support, their use as frameworks of choice for individual lives is always liable to cut across the interest we have in preserving them.
61. But this can be exaggerated. However we define and individuate cultures, can we simply assume that each culture is coherent in this sense? Aren't some cultures, even some traditional ones, riven by contradictions? And isn't the artifice of 'preservation' likely to heighten any contradictions that exist as well as to introduce new ones? Moreover, are we really in a position to assume that coherence means the same in the context of a social entity, like a cultural framework, and an individual entity, like a person constituting a life? I leave these challenging questions for another occasion, noting only that they seldom are addressed by those who insist on the communitarian provenance of the self.

62. Sandel, *supra* note 11, at 179; *see also* Charles Taylor, *Hegel and Modern Society*, 157 (1979) ('The self which has arrived at freedom by setting aside all external obstacles and impingements is characterless, and hence without defined purpose, however much this is hidden by such seemingly positive terms as "rationality" or "creativity".').
63. MacIntyre makes a similar suggestion:

> [W]e all approach our own circumstances as bearers of a particular social identity. I am someone's son or daughter, someone else's cousin or uncle; I am a citizen of this or that city, a member of this or that guild or profession; I belong to this clan, that tribe, this nation. Hence what is good for me has to be the good for one who inhabits these roles. As such, I inherit from the past of my family, my city, my tribe, my nation, a variety of debts, inheritances, rightful expectations and obligations. These constitute the given of my life, my moral starting point. This is in part what gives my life its own moral particularity.
>
> This thought is likely to appear alien . . . from the standpoint of modern individualism. From the standpoint of individualism I am what I myself choose to be. I can always, if I wish to, put in question what are taken to be the merely contingent social features of my existence.

MacIntyre, *supra* note 11, at 220.
64. *See supra* note 1 and accompanying text.
65. Ibid. at 404.
66. *See* 'Serbs Step Up Fighting for Piece of Bosnia Capital', *N.Y. Times*, 23 Apr. 1992, at A10.
67. *See* Eric Hobsbawm, 'Grand Illusions: The Perils of the New Nationalism', 253 *Nation* 537, 555 (4 Nov. 1991).
68. *See* Mike Davis, *City of Quartz: Excavating the Future in Los Angeles*, 153–56 (1990).

III Forms of Cultural Pluralism

5 Individual Rights against Group Rights

NATHAN GLAZER

The United States today is in the midst of a great national debate which must have bearing, in time, for any nation that is composed of many ethnic and racial strands—and that means the great majority of the nations of the world. The debate, which takes place in the executive, legislative, and judicial branches of government, in the scholarly periodicals and the mass media, among unions and employers, in schools and universities, centers on the meaning of justice for minorities that have previously been treated unjustly. What it has done for us is to underline how simple were our understandings of the problems of racial and group discrimination in 1964, when one of the major pieces of legislation in American history, the Civil Rights Act of 1964, was passed.

In 1964, in the United States, ending discrimination seemed a simple matter. Presumably one could recognize a discriminatory act—not hiring blacks, or not promoting them, not paying them more than X dollars, or not allowing them into this college or hospital. And one could devise penalties to punish such acts. Many cases are brought every day under the Civil Rights Act of 1964 and other pieces of legislation, federal and state, that ban discrimination, and many people who have been discriminated against find relief under these acts. The penalties are sufficiently severe—in particular, the granting of back pay for a period of years to individuals who have been discriminated against in employment—to make employers careful to avoid discrimination. The effects of the act, it has been argued, were evident in a marked improvement in the numbers of blacks employed in better jobs after 1964.

Individuals take these actions to complain against discrimination, in order to vindicate rights that have been denied because of a group characteristic. Can we, however, solve the problems of group discrimination by using the language, and the law, of individual rights?

Nathan Glazer, 'Individual Rights against Group Rights', in Nathan Glazer, *Ethnic Dilemmas: 1964–1982* (Harvard University Press, Cambridge MA, 1983), pp. 254–73.

In that question is encapsulated the dilemma of justice for discriminated-against minorities. The individual has received discriminatory treatment because of a group characteristic. The law is written so as to vindicate the rights of individuals. But can the rights of individuals be vindicated, can the effects of past discrimination on the groups be overcome, if only that individual who takes action on the basis of discrimination receives satisfaction and compensation as the result of his individual charge of discrimination? Does not every other individual who is a member of the group also require satisfaction and compensation? But if the whole concept of legal rights has been developed in individual terms, how do we provide justice for the group? And if we provide justice for the group—let us say, a quota which determines that so many jobs must go to members of the group—then do we not, by that token, deprive individuals of other groups, not included among the discriminated-against groups, of the right to be treated and considered as individuals, independently of any group characteristic?

These are the issues that have arisen in the United States. I would like to break them down into a number of questions:

1. Why are our laws written as if the problem of discrimination is one affecting individuals; why do we in effect assert that justice in the face of discrimination is justice for the individual, rather than a new and equal status for the group?

2. Can laws and practices written as if the grievance is borne by individuals overcome the effects of group discrimination and provide satisfaction to groups?

3. If, alternatively, we provide compensation to individuals on the basis of minority-group membership, have we deprived individuals of majority groups of rights?

4. Is there any general principle that can guide us as to when we should try to overcome discrimination by concentrating on the rights of individuals, and when we should try to overcome it by concentrating on the rights of groups?

Let me explain the perspective from which I will approach these questions. I am a sociologist, not a political philosopher or a lawyer. As a political philosopher or a lawyer, I would try to find basic principles of justice that can be defended and argued against all other principles. As a sociologist, I look at the concrete consequences, for concrete societies, of different policies. And here one major principle guides me. It is whether those practices lead to a general acceptance of the policies meant to overcome discrimination as good and decent policies, and lead to the widest measure of acceptance, among minorities as well as majorities. That may be denounced as a purely pragmatic or 'functionalist' principle, which leaves aside the great objectives of equality and justice. But these objectives are incorporated in that principle, too, because people today will not accept arrangements that maintain great inequalities and that offend strongly their sense of justice. These are key realities to be taken into account in using the pragmatic principle I have proposed: what policies to overcome discrimination give us the opportunity to best satisfy all the groups of a multiethnic society so they can live in some reasonable degree of harmony?

It is an interesting problem to ponder why it is that the deprivation of individual rights on the basis of some group characteristic—race, religion, national origin—is nevertheless treated in law, at least in American law, as a problem of protecting the rights of an individual. The Fifth Amendment to the constitution, which limits the federal government and provides the language used in the Fourteenth Amendment, the foundation of constitutional protection for blacks and other minorities, reads: 'No *person* shall . . . be deprived of life, liberty, or property, without due process of law' (my italics). And the Fourteenth Amendment, adopted to protect the rights of the newly freed slaves, reads: 'No State shall make or enforce any law which shall abridge the privileges or immunities of *citizens* of the United States; nor shall any State deprive any *person* of life, liberty, or property, without due process of law; nor deny to any person within its jurisdiction the equal protection of the laws' (my italics). Citizens, persons—this is the language designed to defend a group, blacks, and which by extension of activist Supreme Courts defends the rights of Chinese, Japanese, Indians, Mexican Americans, Puerto Ricans, aliens, women, and many other groups defined in various ways. The same kind of language is to be found in the Civil Rights Act of 1964 and the Voting Rights Act of 1965; they refer to no single group. The legislation, just like the constitution, attempts to be colorblind in a society where color and national origin are key realities determining in some measure the fate of the individuals of any group.

It is not only the constitutional and legal language that attempts to overcome the problems of group prejudice by guaranteeing the rights of individuals; the most important American philosophical contribution to the problem of justice in recent times, John Rawls's *A Theory of Justice*, also ignores the problem of justice for groups, as Vernon Van Dyke points out in a perceptive essay:

> [Rawls] stipulates that those in the original situation 'should care about the well-being of some of those in the next generation' . . . but he does not make a comparable stipulation about racial, linguistic, religious or national groups that are weak or disadvantaged or that cherish or want to preserve their distinctive characteristics and identity . . . I do not see in the book a single reference to differences of language. Race is mentioned mainly to be ruled out as a ground of discrimination. Religion is

mentioned at a number of points, but almost always with the individual believer in mind rather than the collective body of the faithful.[1]

It is an intriguing problem, and undoubtedly the answer is that the language and theory of the protection of human rights developed in a time and place (England in the seventeenth century) when the issue was seen as one of deprivation because of conscience, because of individual decision and action, rather than one of deprivation because of race, color, or national origin. England was relatively homogeneous, *except* for religion and political attitudes which largely flowed from religious conviction. These were seen as individual decisions, and protecting diversity was seen as an issue of protecting the diversity that flowed from individual decisions.

But what of that diversity that flows from the accidents of birth into a preexisting community—defined by race, national origin, or religion? As Van Dyke reminds us by pointing out that Rawls in speaking of religion has 'the individual believer in mind, rather than the collective body of the faithful,' religion involves not only individual choice, but in the great majority of cases faith determined by birth, just as much as color or mother tongue is determined by birth. This makes it very different from an act of individual conscience, as one can well see when one considers the meaning of Catholicism and Protestantism in Northern Ireland, of Islam and non-Islam in Malaysia. It would be play-acting in these countries to try to solve the serious problems of group conflict by legislating the freedom of the practice of religion, for that is not the issue. The issue in these countries, and in other countries where religious conflicts take on what I would call an ethnic character—that is, conflicts of groups of contrasting cultures defined by birth—is the relative economic and social positions of the two religious communities, not the free practice of religion.

Is there an alternative legal and constitutional language to protect individuals who are penalized because of a group affiliation? Of course there is. It is the language that specifically guarantees the rights of groups, by name, that specifically reserves for groups a certain proportion of posts in government, in the civil services, in the universities, in business. This kind of approach to group rights is clearly just as compatible with a regime committed to human rights as the approach that focuses only on the individual. In one measure or another, we see this kind of approach in Canada, Belgium, Indian, Malaysia. Yet in the United States the attempt to reserve places, by number, in key areas of political life and economy is strongly resisted as a subversion of individual rights. And indeed, the revolutionary effort in the middle 1960s to establish a firm legislative basis for overcoming discrimination against blacks and other minorities expressly used language that protected the individual, carefully avoided specifying in any legislation what groups were to be protected, and specifically banned any approach that emphasized reserving places for different groups. This was the clear intention of Congress, and the American people, majority and minority, when the Civil Rights Act of 1964 was passed. To protect against the possibility that the act might make possible a group remedy—let us say, quotas for employment for some groups that had been discriminated against—this was specifically forbidden in the act. Perhaps that demonstrated the general naïveté that prevailed as to what would be necessary to raise a whole group that had faced discrimination over a long period of time. I have already pointed out that in other nations a different approach has been taken to the problem of raising a group—an approach that has straightforwardly adopted numerical quotas to ensure that appropriate numbers of the group received the benefits of education or employment. And so we have 'reservations' for scheduled castes and tribes in India, and special programs to increase the number of Malays in higher education and business employment in Malaysia.

As against this group-based approach, the American approach, both in legislation and in the important Supreme Court decisions that preceded and succeeded it, used the language of individual rights. It was in each case an individual that brought suit—*Brown* v. *the Board of Education, Griggs* v. *Duke Power*. One must neither overestimate nor underestimate the significance of the language and law that emphasize the vindication of an individual's rights. One must not overestimate it: it was organizations representing group interests that were sought out by individual plaintiffs, or that alternatively sought them out. It was the resources of groups that were required to argue cases up to the Supreme Court. It was the position of the entire group that one hoped to raise by individual test cases. If Brown could not be segregated on the basis of race, neither could White or Wilkins or any other black. If Griggs could not be denied a job because the test he took for employment did not properly test his aptitude or capacities for the job in question, neither could any other black be denied employment on that basis.

But we should not underestimate, either, the significance of the individual aspect of these rights. Each case goes into the individual's account of discrimination, the damage to the individual. And even if the justices know well that by acting against an individual complaint of discrimination they are raising the status and enhancing the rights of an entire group, it was expected—certainly in 1964—that these rights would become effective because *individuals* would claim them, and because they would now be treated as individuals, without distinctions of color or national origin.

Could such an approach to overcoming group discrimination—the approach that assumed that individuals would act to vindicate their rights, and that actions of individuals would overcome the deprived status of groups—really be effective? One of the main charges against the enforcement provisions of the Civil Rights Act of 1964, as written and intended by Congress, is that it is unreasonable to expect that a group would overcome a heritage of generations of discrimination by the actions of *individuals* to acquire, on their own initiative, education, jobs, political representation. It was for this reason that the agencies involved began to take actions that aroused a good deal of dissent in Congress.

To begin with, they began to require that large employers take censuses of their employees on the basis of race and ethnic group, in order to make a preliminary assessment of whether certain groups were absent or under-represented in certain levels of employment. Note that the first step in requiring these reports was to decide which groups an employer would have to report upon. The legislation was silent on which particular groups were protected from discrimination—all individuals were protected from discrimination on the basis of race, color, national origin, religion. But in order to set up a system for employer reporting, some groups had to be selected, by administrative regulations, as being the particular focus of Congressional attention. It was a rather strange categorization of groups that the enforcing agency adopted for reporting. There was no question that Negro Americans were the major concern of the Congress, as they were the major target of discrimination. Thus employers were required to report on the number of Negro employees. Mexican Americans and Puerto Ricans, two large groups of lower than average educational and occupational achievement, were incorporated into a new category of 'Spanish Surnamed' or 'Hispanics,' which also included anyone with a Spanish name, whether his or her origin was Spain or Cuba or some other place. Finally, a fourth category was defined, 'Oriental' or 'Asian American,' which consisted principally of Chinese and Japanese. All the rest were 'others' or 'white.' Educational agencies required reporting on the same categories from colleges and universities and schools.

The problem of the reporting system was, first, that it created amalgams by including groups that had presumably faced discrimination and those that had not (for example Mexican Americans and Cubans); secondly, that it set up a category composed of groups (Chinese and Japanese) that had faced discrimination but had nevertheless already overcome the handicaps of discrimination to score higher in education and occupational achievement than the 'others' who were to serve as a benchmark by which to determine statistically the elimination of discrimination; thirdly, that it excluded some groups that felt they too, whether in the past or the present, had faced discrimination. Thus Americans of Italian and Polish and other Slavic origin have often felt they have faced discrimination; but they were lumped with the 'others.' Jews have certainly faced discrimination but were also included among 'others.' In effect, the enforcing agencies had created two kinds of groups by this system of reporting—those which were its peculiar concern as objects of possible discrimination, and those which were of no concern at all and received no recognition as facing possible discrimination. A new form of the famous Orwellian principle was introduced: all groups were protected against discrimination according to the law, but some groups according to the enforcing agencies were more protected than others. Drawing a line between the first and the second was no easy matter in a complex multiethnic society where group prejudice has a long history and where it would be a foolhardy social analyst who would claim that only the four affected categories defined by the enforcing agencies were even today subject to discrimination.

A second problem arose with the reporting system: it was used to make presumptions of discrimination. While the law rejects the notion that statistical disparities alone are evidence of discrimination, this in effect is how the agencies enforcing civil rights laws acted. They took statistical disparities as evidence of discrimination, and tried to pressure employers, public and private, into overcoming them by hiring on the basis of race, color, and national origin—exactly what the original Civil Rights Act of 1964 had forbidden.

But was there any alternative to censuses of given groups and presumptions of discrimination on the basis of disparity? The defenders of this approach pointed out that to attack discrimination in any other way was costly to the individual who had faced discrimination and uncertain of satisfactory results. The individual would have to complain of discrimination to the enforcing agency, wait for investigation, conciliation, a final decision of whether his case was found, possibly subsequent court proceedings. Or alternatively he would have to begin litigation on his own. And once having initiated a case, how was an enforcing agency or a court to settle the question of discrimination? Discriminatory acts could be rationalized away, concealed behind other ostensible bases of action, dissembled, would be difficult to determine precisely. It was easier to go to the numbers.

Was then the Congress simply naïve in its assumption in 1964 that discrimination was not to be overcome by seeking disparities and imposing quotas? I think not. There were two important reasons why such an approach could be defended. The first was that in a democracy each group wields political power. That political power would in many cases prevent the bland hiding of discrimination behind rationalizations. With political power would come political representation and representation in the government service (where political considerations directly dictate appointments at the highest levels, and are influential at lower levels). Even without the warrant of specific law, political representation would lead to some rough justice in the distribution of government jobs, contracts and favors so that each group would get a share. Thus, in determining candidates for public office, parties often use as one principle the 'balanced ticket'—each major group is represented on the party list of candidates—for in a two-party system each party must appeal to almost every group. Representation in elected office means influence in making political appointments to government service. Political appointees in government service hand out contracts, place government money in banks, provide benefits of various types to businesses, universities, schools. In effect, political representation is seen as a key to more general representation of all the major segments of a society. And the Civil Rights Act of 1964, supplemented by an extremely severe Voting Rights Act of 1965, ensured that all obstacles to the registration and voting of minority groups would be swept away, as indeed they have been.

The second reason why Congress might well have believed that a purely individual approach to overcoming discrimination was not utopian was that other groups that had faced discrimination in the past—Jews, Chinese, Japanese—had, even without the powerful assistance of federal rights legislation, risen on the basis of individual initiative. If discrimination was illegal, if penalties for discrimination were, even if at only the margin, severe, would one not expect that the initiative of blacks, Mexican Americans, and Puerto Ricans would also operate to raise them politically, educationally, and economically?

Was this faith justified? It would be possible to answer that by studying intensively progress made by minorities in the six years between 1964, when the Civil Rights Act was passed, and 1970 and 1971, when policies based on requiring employment to reach statistical goals or quotas became increasingly common in the United States owing to the regulations of executive agencies and the rulings of federal courts. This is not the place for such an examination. Nor do we have fully satisfactory techniques to separate out, in any social change, one cause from a variety of others that are operating. It was after all also during those years that black demands were most militant and the fear of urban riots and possible urban insurrections greatest. Nevertheless, it is my judgment that great progress was made in those years, and that the point of view of Congress on minority progress was vindicated by that progress: black political representation did rapidly increase (it has continued to increase), black movement into colleges and universities leapt upward, black progress in closing the gap in earnings between whites and blacks was substantial.[2]

Of course this judgment is disputed; there is a great battle of the statistics and their interpretation which I cannot go into here. But behind the battle of the statistics lie ideological orientations. Those who feel that

American society is irredeemably racist, that the public opinion polls showing a decline in prejudice are simply deceptive, that progress for blacks and other minorities is impossible except through governmental intervention, try to find in the statistics the evidence that supports their judgment of no or little progress. Those who believe that prejudice and discrimination have declined in the United States, that the United States is still basically an open society in which deprived groups and immigrants can achieve equality with older settlers and groups, see in the statistics the evidence that vindicates their faith.

Aside from this basic orientation, there is another difference in view that separates pessimists and optimists. Those who believe that blacks have been severely damaged by centuries of slavery and discrimination and prejudice do not see how simply opening up nondiscriminatory opportunity can raise blacks (and one may, in lesser measure, make the same argument for other groups). Too many blacks are too crippled, the argument goes, to act individually to take advantage of new non-discriminatory opportunity. And therefore one cannot count on individual initiative, one must assure by goal and quota that given numbers of blacks are employed, promoted, taken into colleges and professional schools.

This brings us to my third question. If we set a number, if we say one must employ one black teacher for one white teacher until the number of blacks reaches 20 percent of the teaching force—as a judge in Boston requires—or if we say that 16 percent of all places to a medical school must be reserved for certain specified minorities—as the Medical School of the University of California at Davis did—are we depriving the majority, the nonminority group, of any rights? The kind of action I have described is now widespread in the United States. Many police and fire departments must hire today on the basis of racial quotas, many teaching and supervisory appointments must be filled on this basis, many medical and other professional schools have goals for minority admissions. A major constitutional case, decided by the Supreme Court in 1978, dealt with this issue. This was the case of Allan Bakke, who applied for admission to the University of California Medical School, was denied admission twice, and claimed that his individual right to admission on a nondiscriminatory basis was denied because the school reserved 16 percent of its places for minorities.

Was it a fair claim he made? One could answer Bakke—and he was so answered, in many *amicus* briefs filed with the Supreme Court—that very few of the many applicants to medical schools are accepted in any case; that blacks, who form 11 percent of the population, have only 2 percent of the doctors; that these numbers will not increase unless a specific effort to reach a certain number of black admissions is made; that one cannot argue that there is a discrimination against the majority when they have 84 percent of the places.

But on the other hand, it can be argued that the black proportion in medical schools has increased greatly in recent years; that there are other ways of recruiting blacks to medical schools than by setting a fixed numerical quota; and that the constitution and the civil rights laws forbid discrimination against any *person* on account of race, color, or national origin, and this applies to whites, as well as blacks. Blacks were given the opportunity to enter the medical school both by means of the regular admission process, and by means of the special admission process for minorities, for which 16 percent of places were reserved. Whites were given the opportunity to enter the medical school only by means of the regular admission procedure. As a result, less-qualified minority applicants were accepted in place of majority applicants.

If one thinks of a rough justice proportioned according to the size of groups, then Bakke should have lost. There are very few black doctors; there should be more. But if one thinks of individual rights, the right to be considered in one's own person independently of race, color, or national origin, Bakke should have won—as, in a very narrow decision, he ultimately did.[3]

There are two notions of justice in conflict here, one which says justice is apportioning rewards to groups on the basis of proportionality, the other which says justice is to be color-blind, to consider only the individual. Bakke can say, 'I don't care how many black and white doctors there are, I want to be considered for admission on my individual merits, independently of race, *I* want to be a doctor; it is not the white race that wants to be a doctor.'

While it was an issue of admission to medical schools that has reached the Supreme Court, it is generally accepted that the principles governing employment and promotions are not very different. Here, too, one faces the same conflict: justice as proportionality by group or justice as the consideration of the isolated individual regardless of race, color, national origin, religion.

The American people, raised on the language of individual rights, are remarkably uniform in their views. The Gallup poll has shown that huge majorities of whites and substantial majorities of blacks are against preferential treatment on the basis of race (see Chapter 9). Individualism, one may say, is still strong in America.

It would be nice if we could avoid the dilemma, if individual choice in a multiethnic society, in the absence of discrimination, aggregated into a rough proportionality that meant justice satisfying both the individual and the group standard. But it doesn't—or it hasn't yet. That is the problem. Can we rest on principle when there are these substantial differences of representation between racial and ethnic groups? Or is it the task of a just society to make representation equal, even if this means the individual is not treated as an individual, but must be considered as a member of a group?

Is there a principle that suggests which course of multiethnic society will or should follow: whether to deal with discrimination and group difference by establishing defined places in government and economy for each group, or whether, alternatively, to emphasize the right of the individual to be considered without regard to group characteristics for election to office, for appointment to government posts, for employment, for admission to educational institutions? I have already placed in opposition to the dominant individual-rights approach that we see in the United States and, I believe, in the United Kingdom, in France, and in Australia, the approach in terms of rights for groups that we see, in different degrees, in Canada and Belgium, in Lebanon before its tragic civil war, in Malaysia and India. Undoubtedly if I knew more about other multiethnic states (for example Czechoslavakia and Yugoslavia) I could add more to the group approach. One may also add South Africa as a state committed to group rights—though the use of the term will certainly sound ironic here. The legitimation in South Africa for the removal from politics and the higher reaches of the economy of blacks, coloured, Indians, is that each group is distinct and to be kept separate. This rationalization can be seized on by the subordinate groups to demand group representation at the center.

Whether a nation elects to handle multiethnic diversity by formally ignoring it or by formally recognizing it has no bearing on whether it is a democracy or not: whether it be a democracy, a 'people's democracy,' a dictatorship, or an autocracy, either approach to multiethnic diversity is possible. What this suggests is that the *form* of a nation's response to diversity—individual rights or group rights—should have no bearing on whether we consider that nation responsive to human rights and to civil rights. Rather, we should realize, there are two quite distinct forms of response. In the United States, divided as we are by this issue, we seem to believe that one course upholds the Constitution while the other betrays it, and thus that one course enhances democracy and equality in the United States but that the other course reduces it. I am a partisan of the individual-rights approach for the United States but given the diversity of handling these kinds of issues in other equally democratic countries of the world, I do not believe the issue can be decided in these terms.

I believe the key principle that does in fact and should determine for a multiethnic state—including the United States—whether it elects the path of group rights or individual rights, is whether it sees the different groups as remaining permanent and distinct constituents of a federated society or whether it sees these groups as ideally integrating into, eventually assimilating into, a common society. If the state sets before itself the model that group membership is purely private, a shifting matter of personal choice and degree, something that may be weakened and dissolved in time as other identities take over, then to place an emphasis on group rights is to hamper this development, to change the course of the society, to make a statement to all its individuals and groups that people derive rights not only from a general citizenship but from another kind of citizenship within a group. And just as laws and regulations are required to determine who is a citizen of the state and may exercise the rights of a citizen, so would laws and regulations be required to determine who is a citizen of a subsidiary group, and who may exercise the rights of such a citizenship.

If, on the other hand, the model a society has for itself, today and in the future, is that it is a confederation of groups, that group membership is central and permanent, and that the divisions among groups are such that it is unrealistic or unjust to envisage these group identities weakening in time to be replaced by a common citizenship, then it must take the path of determining what the rights of each group shall be. Thus, Canada sees itself a federation of two founding peoples, English and French; Malaysia cannot conceive of the dividing line between Malay and Chinese disappearing; Belgium tried to work as a unitary state, with the dominance of the French-speaking element, but once the Flemish-speaking element asserted its claim to equal rights, its constitution had to accept these two central elements in the state as permanent.

There are of course other important differences among multiethnic states: there are those in which one group was clearly subordinate, a minority facing discrimination; and there are those in which different groups did not see each other as arranged in a hierarchy of higher and lower. But in almost all multiethnic situations groups do rank each other. While the hierarchy may not be as absolute as it is in South Africa, or as it was in the southern United States, that is, a strict caste-like situation fixed in law, there is generally some sense of grievance by one group against another. But this issue does not affect the principle I have proposed. Groups that are roughly parallel in political and economic strength may nevertheless be so diverse, or consider themselves so different, that the idea of integration or assimilation to a common norm is inconceivable. This is certainly the case for Anglophones and Francophones in Canada, Flemish-speakers or French-speakers in Belgium. On the other hand, groups that are ordered in a hierarchy, that are considered 'higher' or 'lower,' reflecting real and substantial economic and political inferiority, may nevertheless set as their ideal and ultimately expect integration into the common society. This was certainly the objective of the American Negro civil rights movements until the late 1960s—black leaders wanted nothing more than to be Americans, full Americans, with the rights of all other Americans. And this was also the objective of European immigrant groups to the United States, many of whom as immigrant and second-generation communities faced discrimination. Similarly, West Indian immigrants to Britain viewed themselves and, I believe, still view themselves as black Britons, wanting nothing more than full acceptance, the same rights in all spheres that all other citizens hold.

There is thus such a thing as a state ideology or a national consensus that shapes and determines what attitude immigrant and minority groups will take toward the alternative possibilities of group maintenance and group rights on the one hand, or individual integration and individual rights on the other. It is interesting to contrast immigrant groups, from the same background, in Canada and the United States. Canada, because it was already based on two founding, distinct national elements, gave more opportunity for incoming minority groups to select group maintenance as a possibility. Thus it appears there is somewhat less integration, somewhat greater commitment to group maintenance, among Slavic groups and Jews who went to Canada, compared with groups of the same origins that went to the United States. The United States, whatever the realities of discrimination and segregation, had as a national idea a unitary and new ethnic identity, that of American. The United States was a federation of states which were defined politically, not ethnically; Canada was a federation of peoples, organized into different provinces. The impact of this originating frame for ethnic self-image can be seen on subsequent immigrants into the two countries. And, I would hazard, one can see the same difference in legal institutions, with a greater willingness in Canada formally and legally to accept the existence of ethnic groups, I would not exaggerate the difference, but it is there.

But what I would emphasize is that for some societies a choice is possible. There are facts and ideals that point both ways. And now I return to the United States. The society can go one way or the other, toward individual rights or group rights—which is why the division over the Bakke case was so intense, even among those elite, educated elements of the society that in the 1960s, during the civil rights struggle, formed a solid phalanx of one opinion in favor of individual rights. In the United States, coexisting with the facts of eager immigrant groups entering the country, becoming Americanized, rising economically, socially, politically, were the equally powerful facts that the status of blacks, of Chinese, of Japanese, of Indians was defined in law, in racial terms, for purposes of discrimination and segregation. And coexisting with the overarching national goal or image of one nation, of individuals endowed with equal rights, was a minority sentiment—encouraged undoubtedly in part by discrimination—in favor of cultural pluralism, the maintenance of group identity. A large body of opinion in the United States always fought discrimination and segregation as a betrayal of the American ideals of individual rights and equality. In the middle 1960s, with the passage of the Civil Rights Act of 1964 and the Immigration Act of 1965, which eliminated all references to race and all quotas on the basis of nationality, it seemed as if the individual-rights ideal had triumphed. But then, as we saw, the question came up of how to achieve practical equality, and we began to slide again toward group definition, this time for purposes of correction and benefit, rather than for purposes of discrimination and segregation.

Clearly one key issue is whether previously subordinated or separate groups can envisage progress under a course of individual rights. Gordon P. Means puts the issue well:

> A good case can be made both for and against special privileges. Such a system can be an effective strategy for inducing rapid social change, in settings where cultural variables need to be taken into account. Without preferential privileges, there may be no inducement for improving the opportunity structures of deprived or encapsulated cultural and ethnic groups. Where group identity and communal and ethnic prejudices permeate a society, it is naive, if not hypocritical to talk about the equality of opportunity based upon individual achievement and universalistic norms.[4]

I would emphasize the words 'where group identity and communal and ethnic prejudices permeate a society.' If in a society the groups are sharply divided from one another, so that their boundaries are clear, are firmly set by law or custom, are not expected to become permeable; and if they live in a long historical tradition in which group identification has been used and is used for purposes of discrimination and separation, there may be no alternative: special preferences may be necessary to protect the inferior group and to foster intergroup harmony. Thus we must determine an issue of fact. But we must also determine an issue of direction. Because if inferiority and difference are being overcome, we must consider the negative consequences of selecting the path of group rights and preferences, and we would wish to avoid them if possible. As Means continues, 'Yet, when all has been said, it must also be acknowledged that the system of group special rights does involve considerable social costs and is a rather crude strategy for inducing social transformation.'

An Indian Supreme Court justice has also suggested language helpful in confronting the dilemma. The case before him dealt with special preferences which were originally granted to the most backward castes, but which—a tendency one might expect in the case of special preferences—

have become more expansive to include other less backward castes and classes. Justice Krishna Iyer wrote:

> The social disparity must be so grim and substantial as to serve as a basis for benign discrimination. If we search for such a class, we cannot find any large segment other than the scheduled castes and scheduled tribes.[5]

This is a test we can apply. Is the social disparity so grim and substantial that there is no alternative to benign discrimination?

We now understand the basis, in facts and ideals, that will move a multiethnic society in one direction or another. But what are the implications of choosing one path or another? If we choose the group-rights approach we say that the differences between some groups are so great that they cannot achieve satisfaction on the basis of individual rights. We say, too, that—whether we want to or not—we will permanently section the society into ethnic groups by law. Even if advocates of group rights claim this is a temporary solution to problems of inequality, as they do in India and in the United States, it is inconceivable to me that benefits given in law on the basis of group membership will not strengthen groups, will not make necessary the policing of their boundaries, and will not become permanent in a democratic society, where benefits once given cannot be withdrawn. In effect, American society, which was moving toward an emphasis on individual rights in which group affiliation and difference were to become a matter of indifference to the state, in which the state was to be concerned only that such affiliation did not affect the fate of individuals, will become something very different if it continues to move along the path of group rights. More groups will join the four already selected as special beneficiaries. And with every movement in the direction of group rights, the individual's claim to be considered only as an individual, regardless of race, color or national origin, will be reduced, as more and more places are reserved to be filled on the basis of group affiliation.

When a society, such as American society, faces both ways, with one tradition insisting on a unitary identity, and another—a minority tradition—arguing for cultural pluralism, with many groups barely differentiated from each other in wealth and power, but others lagging much further behind, there is no escape from difficult choices. Are the differences among groups in American society 'so grim and substantial' that there is no other course but special privilege? To me, and to other analysts of the American scene, the speed with which gaps between blacks and whites—and gaps between most minority groups and the rest of the society—are being closed in political representation, in income, in education, is rapid and satisfactory. To others, these changes are paltry and insignificant. To me, too, the overall direction of American society has been toward a society with a common identity, based on common ideals, one in which group identities are respected as private and individual choices but in which these identities are strictly excluded from a formal, legal, constitutional role in the polity. To others, the fact that groups were in the past legally defined for purposes of discrimination and segregation and exclusion is sufficient reason why we should resurrect legal group definitions for purposes of reparation and compensation.

The choices we are now making on the difficult issue of individual rights versus group rights will tell us which view of American society will prevail, and what, in consequence, the fate of individual rights in American society is to be.

Notes

1. Vernon Van Dyke, 'Justice as Fairness: For Groups,' *American Political Science Review* 69 (1975): 607.
2. See Glazer, *Affirmative Discrimination*, pp. 40–43.
3. See Nathan Glazer, 'Why Bakke Won't End Reverse Discrimination,' *Commentary*, September 1978, pp. 36–41.
4. Gordon, P. Means, 'Human Rights and the Rights of Ethnic Groups—A Commentary,' *International Studies Notes* (1974): 17.
5. Robert L. Hardgrave, Jr., 'DeFunis and Dorairajan: 'Protective Discrimination' in the United States and India,' paper delivered at the 1976 annual meeting of the American Political Science Association, Chicago, Illinois, September 2–5, 1976.

6 Pluralism: A Political Perspective

MICHAEL WALZER

Democracy and Nationalism

Most political theorists, from the time of the Greeks onward, have assumed the national or ethnic homogeneity of the communities about which they wrote. Prior to the work of Rousseau, theory was never explicitly nationalist, but the assumption of a common language, history, or religion underlay most of what was said about political practices and institutions. Hence, the only empire systematically defended in the great tradition of political theory was the Christian empire of the Middle Ages: one religious communion, it was argued, made one political community. The religiously mixed empires of ancient and modern times, by contrast, had no theoretical defenders, only publicists and apologists. Political thinking has been dominated by the Greece of Pericles, not of Alexander; by republican Rome, not the Roman empire; by Venice and Holland, not the Europe of the Hapsburgs. Even liberal writers, ready enough to acknowledge a plurality of interests, were strikingly unready for a plurality of cultures. One people made one state. the argument of the authors of *The Federalist Papers* (1787–1788) may be taken here to sum up a long tradition of thought. The Americans, John Jay wrote, were a people 'descended from the same ancestors, speaking the same language, professing the same religion, attached to the same principles of government, very similar in their manners and customs.' Surely a 'band of brethren' so united 'should never be split into a number of unsocial, jealous, and alien sovereignties.'

Jay's description was only very roughly true of America in 1787, and clearly the maxim *One people, one state* has, throughout human history, been honored most often in the breach. Most often, brethren have been divided among alien sovereignties and forced to coexist with strangers under an alien sovereign. National and ethnic pluralism has been the rule, not

---

Michael Walzer, 'Pluralism: A Political Perspective'. Reprinted by permission of the publishers, from *The Harvard Encyclopedia of American Ethnic Groups*, ed. Stephen A. Thernstrom (Harvard University Press, Cambridge MA, 1980), pp. 781–87.

the exception. The theoretical preference for cultural unity existed for centuries alongside dynastic and imperial institutions that made for disunity. Only in the late 18th and 19th centuries was the old assumption of homogeneity, reinforced by new democratic commitments, transformed into a practical demand for separation and independence. Underlying that demand were two powerful ideas: first, that free government was only possible under conditions of cultural unity; second, that free individuals would choose if they could to live with their own kind, that is, to join political sovereignty to national or ethnic community. No doubt these ideas could be challenged. Marx and his followers emphatically denied that they were true, arguing that conceptions of 'kind' were ultimately based on class rather than ethnic distinctions. But the two ideas had the support of a long intellectual tradition, and they happily supported one another. They suggested that democracy and self-determination led to the same political arrangements that their effective exercise required: the replacement of empires by national states.

In practice, this replacement took two very different forms. The new nationalist politics was first of all expressed in the demand for the unification of peoples divided—as were the Germans, Italians, and Slavs—among the old empires and a variety of petty principalities. Nationalist leaders aimed initially at large states and at a broad (pan-German or pan-Slavic) definition of cultural homogeneity. Yugoslavia and Czechoslovakia are products of this first nationalism which, though it entailed the breakup of empires, was still a politics of composition, not of division. The Zionist 'ingathering' of Jews from Europe and the Orient has the same character. Roughly similar groups were to be welded together, on the model of the prenationalist unifications of France and Britain.

This early nation-building was hardly a failure, but the clear tendency of nationalism more recently has been to challenge not only the old empires, especially the colonial empires, but also the composite nation-states. Neither the oldest states (France, Britain) nor the newest (Pakistan, Nigeria) have been safe from such challenges. Secession rather than unification is the current theme. International society today is marked by the proliferation of states, so that 'the majority of the members of the U.N.,' as Eric Hobsbawm has written, 'is soon likely to consist of the late-twentieth-century (republican) equivalents of Saxe-Coburg-Gotha and Schwarzburg-Sonderhausen.' Important transformations of the world economy have opened the way for this process: the rules of viability have radically changed since the 19th century. But the process also represents an extraordinary triumph for the principle of self-determination—with the collective self increasingly defined in ways that reflect the actual diversity of mankind.

Confronted with this diversity, every putative nation-state is revealed as an ancient or modern composition. Self-determination looks to be a principle of endless applicability, and the appearance of new states a process of indefinite duration. If the process is to be cut short, it is unlikely to be by denying the principle—for it appears today politically undeniable—but rather by administering it in moderate doses. Thus autonomy may be an alternative to independence, loosening the bonds of the composite state, a way to avoid their fracture. Instead of sovereignty, national and ethnic groups may opt for decentralization, devolution, and federalism; these are not incompatible with self-determination, and they may be especially appropriate for groups of people who share some but not all of the characteristics of a distinct historical community and who retain a strong territorial base. Whether composite states can survive as federations is by no means certain, but it is unlikely that they can survive in any other way—not, at least, if they remain committed (even if only formally) to democratic government or to some sort of social egalitarianism.

Democracy and equality have proven to be the great solvents. In the old empires, the elites of conquered nations tended to assimilate to the dominant culture. They sent their children to be educated by their conquerors; they learned an alien language; they came to see their own culture as parochial and inferior. But ordinary men and women did not assimilate, and when they were mobilized, first for economic and then for political activity, they turned out to have deep national and ethnic loyalties. Mobilization made for conflict, not only with the dominant groups, but also with other submerged peoples. For centuries, perhaps, different nations had lived in peace, side by side, under imperial rule. Now that they had to rule themselves, they found that they could do so (peacefully) only among themselves, adjusting political lines to cultural boundaries.

So the assumptions of the theoretical tradition have proven true. Self-government has tended to produce relatively homogeneous communities and has been fully successful only within such communities. The great exception to this rule is the United States. At the same time, the Marxist argument, the most significant challenge to traditional wisdom, has proven wrong. Nowhere have class loyalties overridden the commitment to national and ethnic groups. Today, the Soviet Union resembles nothing so much as the empire of the Romanovs: a multinational state held together chiefly by force. Conceivably, if the 'national question' were ever solved, if the existence and continued development of historical communities were guaranteed (as Lenin argued they should be), new patterns of alliance and cooperation might emerge. But for the moment, it must be said that politics follows nationality, wherever politics is free. Pluralism in the strong sense—*One state, many peoples*—is possible only under tyrannical regimes.

American Exceptionalism

Except in the United States. Here too, of course, there are conquered and incorporated peoples—Indian tribes, Mexicans—who stood in the path of American expansion, and there are forcibly transported peoples—the blacks—brought to this country as slaves and subjected to a harsh and continuous repression. But the pluralist system within which these groups have only recently begun to organize and act is not primarily the product of their experience. Today, the United States can only be understood as a multiracial society. But the minority races were politically impotent and socially invisible during much of the time when American pluralism was taking shape—and the shape it took was not determined by their presence or by their repression.

In contrast to the Old World, where pluralism had its origins in conquest and dynastic alliance, pluralism in the New World originated in individual and familial migration. The largest part of the U.S. population was formed by the addition of individuals, one by one, filtered through the great port cities. Though the boundaries of the new country, like those of every other country, were determined by war and diplomacy, it was immigration that determined the character of its inhabitants—and falsified John Jay's account of their unity. The United States was not an empire; its pluralism was that of an immigrant society, and that means that nationality and ethnicity never acquired a stable territorial base. Different peoples gathered in different parts of the country, but they did so by individual choice, clustering for company, with no special tie to the land on which they lived. The Old World call for self-determination had no resonance here: the immigrants (except for the black slaves) had come voluntarily and did not have to be forced to stay (indeed, many of them returned home each year), nor did groups of immigrants have any basis for or any reason for secession. The only significant secessionist movement in U.S. history, though it involved a region with a distinctive culture, did not draw upon nationalist passions of the sort that have figured in European wars.

But if the immigrants became Americans one by one as they arrived and settled, they did so only in a political sense: they became U.S. citizens. In other respects, culturally, religiously, even for a time linguistically, they remained Germans and Swedes, Poles, Jews, and Italians. With regard to the first immigrants, the Anglo-Americans, politics still followed nationality: because they were one people, they made one state. But with the newer immigrants, the process was reversed. Because they were citizens of one state—so it was commonly thought—they would become one people. Nationality would follow politics, as it presumably had in earlier times, when the peoples of the modern world were first formed. For a while, however, perhaps for a long while, the United States would be a country composed of many peoples, sharing residence and citizenship only, without a common history or culture.

In such circumstances, the only emotion that made for unity was patriotism. Hence the efforts of the late 19th and early 20th centuries to intensify patriotic feeling, to make a religion out of citizenship. 'The voting booth is the temple of American institutions,' Supreme Court Justice David Brewer wrote in 1900. 'No single tribe or family is chosen to watch the sacred fires burning on its altars . . . Each of us is a priest.' The rise of ethnic political machines and bloc voting, however, must have made the temple seem disturbingly like a sectarian conventicle. Few people believed politics to be a sufficient ground for national unity. Patriotism was essentially a holding action, while the country waited for the stronger solidarity of nationalism. Whether the process of Americanization was described as a gradual assimilation to Anglo-American culture or as the creation of an essentially new culture in the crucible of citizenship, its outcome was thought to be both necessary and inevitable: the immigrants would one day constitute a single people. This was the deeper meaning that the slogan *From many, one* (*E pluribus unum*) took on in the context of mass immigration. The only alternatives, as the history of the Old World taught, were divisiveness, turmoil, and repression.

The fear of divisiveness, or simply of difference, periodically generated outbursts of anti-immigrant feeling among the first immigrants and their descendants. Restraint of all further immigration was one goal of these 'nativist' campaigns; the second goal was a more rapid Americanization of the 'foreigners' already here. But what did Americanization entail? Many of the foreigners were already naturalized citizens. Now they were to be naturalized again, not politically but culturally. It is worth distinguishing this second naturalization from superficially similar campaigns in the old European empires. Russification, for example, was also a cultural program, but it was aimed at intact and rooted communities, at nations that, with the exception of the Jews, were established on lands they had occupied for many centuries. None of the peoples who were to be Russified could have been trusted with citizenship in a free Russia. Given the chance, they would have opted for secession and independence. That was why Russification was so critical: political means were required to overcome national differences. And the use of those means produced the predictable democratic response that politics should follow nationality, not oppose it. In the United States, by contrast, Americanization was aimed at peoples far more susceptible to cultural change, for they were not only uprooted; they had uprooted themselves. Whatever the pressures that had driven them to the

New World, they had chosen to come, while others like themselves, in their own families, had chosen to remain. And as a reward for their choice, the immigrants had been offered citizenship, a gift that many eagerly accepted. Though nativists feared or pretended to fear the politics of the newcomers, the fact is that the men and women who were to be Americanized were already, many of them, patriotic Americans.

Because of these differences, the response of the immigrants to cultural naturalization was very different from that of their counterparts in the Old World. They were in many cases acquiescent, ready to make themselves over, even as the nativists asked. This was especially true in the area of language: there has been no longterm or successful effort to maintain the original language of the newcomers as anything more than a second language in the United States. The vitality of Spanish in the Southwest today, though it probably results from the continued large-scale influx of Mexican immigrants, suggests a possible exception to this rule. If these immigrants do not distribute themselves around the country, as other groups have done, a state like New Mexico might provide the first arena for sustained linguistic conflict in the United States. Until now, however, in a country where many languages are spoken, there has been remarkably little conflict. English is and has always been acknowledged as the public language of the American republic, and no one has tried to make any other language the basis for regional autonomy or secession. When the immigrants did resist Americanization, struggling to hold on to old identities and old customs, their resistance took a new form. It was not a demand that politics follow nationality, but rather that politics be separated from nationality—as it was already separated from religion. It was not a demand for national liberation, but for ethnic pluralism.

The Practice of Pluralism

As a general intellectual tendency, pluralism in the early 20th century was above all a reaction against the doctrine of sovereignty. In its different forms—syndicalist, guild socialist, regionalist, autonomist—it was directed against the growing power and the farreaching claims of the modern state. But ethnic pluralism as it developed in the United States cannot plausibly be characterized as an antistate ideology. Its advocates did not challenge the authority of the federal government; they did not defend states' rights; they were not drawn to any of the forms of European corporatism. Their central assertion was that U.S. politics, as it was, did not require cultural homogeneity; it rested securely enough on democratic citizenship. What had previously been understood as a temporary condition was now described as if it might be permanent. The United States was, and could safely remain, a country composed of many peoples, a 'nation of nationalities,' as Horace Kallen called it. Indeed, this was the destiny of America: to maintain the diversity of the Old World in a single state, without persecution or repression. Not only *From many, one,* but also *Within one, many.*

Marxism was the first major challenge to the traditional argument for national homogeneity; ethnic pluralism is the second. Although the early pluralists were by no means radicals, and never advocated social transformation, there is a certain sense in which their denial of conventional wisdom goes deeper than that of the Marxists. For the Marxist argument suggests that the future socialist state (before it withers away) will rest upon the firm base of proletarian unity. And like each previous ruling class, the proletariat is expected to produce a hegemonic culture, of which political life would be merely one expression. Pluralists, on the other hand, imagined a state unsupported by either unity or hegemony. No doubt, they were naïve not to recognize the existence of a single economic system and then of a culture reflecting dominant economic values. But their argument is far-reaching and important even if it is taken to hold only that in addition to this common culture, overlaying it, radically diversifying its impact, there is a world of ethnic multiplicity. The effect on the theory of the state is roughly the same with or without the economic understanding: politics must still create the (national) unity it was once thought merely to mirror. And it must create unity without denying or repressing multiplicity.

The early pluralist writers—theorists like Horace Kallen and Randolph Bourne, popularizers like Louis Adamic—did not produce a fully satisfying account of this creative process or of the ultimately desirable relation between the political one and the cultural many. Their arguments rarely advanced much beyond glowing description and polemical assertion. Drawing heavily upon 19th-century romanticism, they insisted upon the intrinsic value of human difference and, more plausibly and importantly, upon the deep need of human beings for historically and communally structured forms of life. Every kind of regimentation, every kind of uniformity was alien to them. They were the self-appointed guardians of a society of groups, a society resting upon stable families (despite the disruptions of the immigrant experience), tied into, bearing, and transmitting powerful cultural traditions. At the same time, their politics was little more than an unexamined liberalism. Freedom for individuals, they were certain, was all that was necessary to uphold group identification and ethnic flourishing. They had surprisingly little to say about how the different groups were to be held together in a single political order, what citizenship might mean in a pluralist society, whether state power should ever be used on behalf of groups, or what social activities should be assigned to or left to groups. The practical meaning of ethnic pluralism has been hammered out, is still being hammered out, in the various arenas of political and social life. Little theoretical justification exists for any particular outcome.

The best way to understand pluralism, then, is to look at what its protagonists have done or tried to do. Ethnic self-assertion in the United States has been the functional equivalent of national liberation in other parts of the world. What are the actual functions that it serves? There are three that seem critically important. First of all, the defense of ethnicity against cultural naturalization: Kallen's pluralism, worked out in a period of heightened nativist agitation and political persecution (see his *Culture and Democracy in the United States*, 1924), is primarily concerned with upholding the right of the new immigrants, as individuals, to form themselves into cultural communities and maintain their foreign ways. Kallen joins the early-20th-century American *kulturkampf* as the advocate of cultural permissiveness. Train citizens, but leave nationality alone! The argument, so far as it is developed, is largely negative in character, and so it fits easily into the liberal paradigm. But Kallen is convinced that the chief product of a liberal society will not be individual selfhood but collective identity. Here surely he was right, or at least partly right. How many private wars, parallel to his intellectual campaign, have been fought on behalf of such identities—in schools, bureaucracies, corporations—against the pressures of Americanization! Most often, when individual men and women insist on 'being themselves,' they are in fact defending a self they share with others. Sometimes, of course, they succumb and learn to conform to standardized versions of New World behavior. Or they wait, frightened and passive, for organizational support: a league against defamation, a committee for advancement, and so on. When such organizations go to work, the pluralist form of the struggle is plain to see, even if legal and moral arguments continue to focus on individual rights.

The second function of ethnic assertiveness is more positive in character: the celebration of this or that identity. Celebration is critical to every national and ethnic movement because both foreign conquest and immigration to foreign lands work, though in different ways, to undermine communal confidence. Immigration involves a conscious rejection of the old country and then, often, of oneself as a product of the old country. A new land requires a new life, new ways of life. But in learning the new ways, the immigrant is slow, awkward, a greenhorn, quickly outpaced by his own children. He is likely to feel inferior, and his children are likely to confirm the feeling. But this sense of inferiority, so painful to him, is also a disaster for them. It cuts them adrift in a world where they are never likely to feel entirely at home. At some point, among themselves, or among their children (the second American generation), a process of recovery begins.

Ethnic celebration is a feature of that process. It has a general and a particular form: the celebration of diversity itself and then of the history and culture of a particular group. The first of these, it should be stressed, would be meaningless without the second, for the first is abstract and the second concrete. Pluralism has in itself no powers of survival; it depends upon energy, enthusiasm, commitment within the component groups; it cannot outlast the particularity of cultures and creeds. From the standpoint of the liberal state, particularity is a matter of individual choice, and pluralism nothing more than toleration. From the standpoint of the individual, it is probably something else, for men and women mostly 'choose' the culture and creed to which they were born—even if, after conquest and immigration, they have to be born again.

The third function of ethnic assertiveness is to build and sustain the reborn community—to create institutions, gain control of resources, and provide educational and welfare services. As with nation-building, this is hard work, but there is a difficulty peculiar to ethnic groups in a pluralist society: such groups do not have coercive authority over their members. Indeed, they do not have members in the same way that the state has citizens; they have no guaranteed population. Though they are historical communities, they must function as if they were voluntary associations. They must make ethnicity a cause, like prohibition or universal suffrage; they must persuade people to 'ethnicize' rather than Americanize themselves. The advocates of religious ethnicity—German Lutherans, Irish Catholics, Jews, and so on—have probably been most successful in doing this. But any group that hopes to survive must commit itself to the same pattern of activity—winning support, raising money, building schools, community centers, and old-age homes.

On the basis of some decades of experience, one can reasonably argue that ethnic pluralism is entirely compatible with the existence of a unified republic. Kallen would have said that it is simply the expression of democracy in the sphere of culture. It is, however, an unexpected expression: the American republic is very different from that described, for example, by Montesquieu and Rousseau. It lacks the intense political fellowship, the commitment to public affairs, that they thought necessary. 'The better the constitution of a state is,' wrote Rousseau, 'the more do public affairs encroach on private in the minds of the citizens. Private affairs are even of much less importance, because the aggregate of the common happiness furnishes a greater proportion of that of each individual, so that there is less for him to seek in particular cares.' This is an unlikely description unless ethnic culture and religious belief are closely interwoven with political activity (as Rousseau insisted they should be). It certainly misses the reality of the American republic, where both have been firmly relegated to the private sphere. The emotional life of U.S. citizens is lived mostly in private—which is not to say in solitude, but in groups considerably smaller than the community of all citizens. Americans are communal in their private affairs, individualist in their politics. Society is a collection of groups; the state is an organization of individual citizens. And society and state, though they constantly interact, are formally distinct. For support and comfort and a sense of belonging, men and women look to their groups; for freedom and mobility, they look to the state.

Still, democratic participation does bring group members into the political arena where they are likely to discover common interests. Why has this not caused radical divisiveness, as in the European empires? It certainly has made for conflict, sometimes of a frightening sort, but always within limits set by the nonterritorial and socially indeterminate character of the immigrant communities and by the sharp divorce of state and ethnicity. No single group can hope to capture the state and turn it into a nation-state. Members of the group are citizens only as Americans, not as Germans, Italians, Irishmen, or Jews. Politics forces them into alliances and coalitions; and democratic politics, because it recognizes each citizen as the equal of every other, without regard to ethnicity, fosters a unity of individuals alongside the diversity of groups. American Indians and blacks have mostly been excluded from this unity, and it is not yet clear on what terms they will be brought in. But political life is in principle open, and this openness has served to diffuse the most radical forms of ethnic competition. The result has not been a weak political order: quite the contrary. Though it has not inspired heated commitment, though politics has not become a mass religion, the republic has been remarkably stable, and state power has grown steadily over time.

Toward Corporatism?

The growth of state power sets the stage for a new kind of pluralist politics. With increasing effect, the state does for all its citizens what the various groups do or try to do for their own adherents. It defends their rights, not only against foreign invasion and domestic violence, but also against persecution, harassment, libel, and discrimination. It celebrates their collective (American) history, establishing national holidays; building monuments, memorials, and museums; supplying educational materials. It acts to sustain their communal life, collecting taxes and providing a host of welfare services. The modern state nationalizes communal activity, and the more energetically it does this, the more taxes it collects, the more services it provides, the harder it becomes for groups to act on their own. State welfare undercuts private philanthropy, much of which was organized within ethnic communities; it makes it harder to sustain private and parochial schools; it erodes the strength of cultural institutions.

All this is justified, and more than justified, by the fact that the various groups were radically unequal in strength and in their ability to provide services for their adherents. Moreover, the social coverage of the ethnic communities was uneven and incomplete. Many Americans never looked for services from any particular group, but turned instead to the state. It is not the case that state officials invaded the spheres of welfare and culture; they were invited in by disadvantaged or hardpressed or assimilated citizens. But now, it is said, pluralism cannot survive unless ethnic groups, as well as individuals, share directly in the benefits of state power. Once again, politics must follow ethnicity, recognizing and supporting communal structures.

What does this mean? First, that the state should defend collective as well as individual rights; second, that the state should expand its official celebrations, to include not only its own history but the history of all the peoples that make up the American people, third, that tax money should be fed into the ethnic communities to help in the financing of bilingual and bicultural education, and of group-oriented welfare services. And if all this is to be done, and fairly done, then it is necessary also that ethnic groups be given, as a matter of right, some sort of representation within the state agencies that do it.

These are far-reaching claims. They have not received, any more than the earlier pluralism did, a clear theoretical statement. They are the stuff of public pronouncements and political agitation. Their full significance is unclear, but the world they point to is a corporatist world, where ethnic groups no longer organize themselves like voluntary associations but have instead some political standing and some legal rights. There is, however, a major difficulty here: groups cannot be assigned rights unless they are first assigned members. There has to be a fixed population with procedures for choosing representatives before there can be representatives acting officially on behalf of that population. But ethnic groups in the United States do not have, and never have had, fixed populations (American Indian tribes are a partial exception). Historically, corporatist arrangements have only been worked out for groups that do. In fact, they have only been worked out when the fixity was guaranteed by a rigid dualism, that is, when two communities were locked into a single state: Flemings and Walloons in Belgium, Greeks and Turks in Cyprus, Christians and Muslims in Lebanon. In such cases, people not identified with one community are virtually certain to be identified with the other. The residual category of intermarried couples and aliens will be small, especially if the two communities are anciently established and territorially based. Problems of identification are likely to arise only in the capital city. (Other sorts of problems arise more generally; these examples hardly invite emulation.)

America's immigrant communities have a radically different character. Each of them has a center of active participants, some of them men and women who have been 'born-again,' and a much larger periphery of individuals and families who are little more than occasional recipients of services generated at the center. They are communities without boundaries, shading off into a residual mass of people who think of themselves simply as Americans. Borders and border guards are among the first products of a successful national liberation movement, but ethnic assertiveness has no similar outcome. There is no way for the various groups to prevent or regulate individual crossings. Nor can the state do this without the most radical coercion of individuals. It cannot fix the population of the groups unless it forces each citizen to choose an ethnic identity and establishes rigid distinctions among the different identities, of a sort that pluralism by itself has not produced.

It is possible, however, to guarantee representation to ethnic groups without requiring the groups to organize and choose their own spokesmen. The alternative to internal choice is a quota system. Thus, Supreme Court appointments might be constrained by a set of quotas: a certain number of blacks, Jews, Irish and Italian Catholics, and so on, must be serving at any given time. But these men and women would stand in no political relationship to their groups; they would not be responsible agents; nor would they be bound to speak for the interests of their ethnic or religious fellows. They would represent simply by being black (Jewish, Irish) and being *there*, and the Court would be a representative body in the sense that it reflected the pluralism of the larger society in its own membership. It would not matter whether these members came from the center or the periphery of the groups, or whether the groups had clearly defined boundaries, a rich inner life, and so on.

This kind of representation depends only upon external (bureaucratic rather than political) processes, and so it can readily be extended to society at large. Quotas are easy to use in admitting candidates to colleges and professional schools and in hiring them for any sort of employment. Such candidates are not elected but selected, though here, too, there must be a fixed population from which selections can be made. In practice, efforts to identify populations and make quotas possible have been undertaken, with state support, only for oppressed groups. Men and women, marked out as victims or as the children and heirs of victims, have been assigned a right to certain advantages in the selection process; otherwise, it is said, they would not be present at all in schools, professions, and businesses. This is not the place to consider the merits of such a procedure. But it is important to point out that selection by quota functions largely to provide a kind of escape from group life for people whose identity has become a trap. Its chief purpose is to give opportunities to individuals, not a voice to groups. It serves to enhance the wealth of individuals, not necessarily the resources of the ethnic community. The community is strengthened, to be sure, if newly trained men and women return to work among its members, but only a small minority do that. Mostly, they serve, if they serve at all, as role models for other upwardly mobile men and women. When weak and hitherto passive groups mobilize themselves in order to win a place in the quota system, they do so for the sake of that mobility, and are likely to have no further raison d'être once it is achieved.

Considered more generally, there is a certain tension between quota systems and ethnic pluralism, for the administrators of any such system are bound to refuse to recognize differences among the groups. They come by their numbers through simple mathematical calculations. It would be intolerable for them to make judgements as to the character of quality of the different cultures. The tendency of their work, then, is to reproduce within every group to which quotas are applied the same educational and employment patterns. Justice is a function of the identity of the patterns among groups rather than of life chances among individuals. But it is clear that ethnic pluralism by itself would not generate any such identity. Historically specific cultures necessarily produce historically specific patterns of interest and work. This is not to say that pluralism necessarily militates against egalitarian principles, since equality might well take the form (socialists have always expected it to take the form) of roughly equal recompense for different kinds of work. It is not implausible to imagine a heterogeneous but egalitarian society: the heterogeneity, cultural and private; the equality, economic and political. Quotas point, by contrast, toward group uniformity, not individual equality. Though it would be necessary for individuals to identify themselves (or to be identified) as group members in order to receive the benefits of a quota system, these identifications would progressively lose their communal significance. The homogenization of the groups would open the way for the assimilation of their members into a prevailing or evolving national culture.

State and Ethnicity

The state can intervene in two basic ways to structure group life. It can encourage or require the groups to organize themselves in corporatist fashion, assigning a political role to the corporations in the state apparatus. This is the autonomist strategy, the nearest thing to national liberation that is possible under conditions of multiethnicity. The effect of autonomy would be to intensify and institutionalize cultural difference. Alternatively, the state can act to reduce differences among groups by establishing uniform or symmetrical achievement standards for their members. Each group would be represented, though not through any form of collective action, in roughly equal proportions in every area of political, social, and economic life. This is the integrationist strategy: it can be applied in a limited and compensatory way to particular (oppressed) groups or more generally to all groups. Applied generally, its effect would be to repress every sort of cultural specificity, turning ethnic identity into an administrative classification.

What the state cannot do is to reproduce politically the pluralist pattern that the immigrants and their children have spontaneously generated, for that pattern is inherently fluid and indeterminate. Its existence depends upon keeping apart what nation-state and corporatist theory bring together: a state organized coercively to protect rights, a society organized on voluntarist principles to advance interests (including cultural and religious interests). State officials provide a framework within which groups can flourish but cannot guarantee their flourishing, or even their survival. The only way to provide such guarantees would be to introduce coercion into the social world, transforming the groups into something like their Old World originals and denying the whole experience of immigration, individualism, and communal rebirth. Nothing like this would appear to be on the American agenda.

The survival and flourishing of the groups depends largely upon the vitality of their centers. If that vitality cannot be sustained, pluralism will prove to be a temporary phenomenon, a way station on the road to American nationalism. The early pluralists may have been naïve in their calm assurance that ethnic vitality would have an enduring life. But they were surely right to insist that it should not artifically be kept alive, any more than it should be repressed, by state power. On the other hand, there is an argument to be made, against the early pluralists, in favor of providing some sorts of public support for ethnic activity. It is an argument familiar from economic analysis, having to do with the character of ethnicity as a collective good.

Individual mobility is the special value but also the characteristic weakness of American pluralism. It makes for loose relations between center and periphery; it generates a world without boundaries. In that world, the vitality of the center is tested by its ability to hold on to peripheral men and women and to shape their self-images and their convictions. These men and women, in turn, live off the strength of the center, which they do not have to pay for either in time or money. They are religious and cultural freeloaders, their lives enhanced by a community they do not actively support and by an identity they need not themselves cultivate. There is no way to change them for what they receive from the center, except when thy receive specific sorts of material help. But their most important gain may be nothing more than a certain sense of pride, an aura of ethnicity, otherwise unavailable. Nor is there anything unjust in their freeloading. The people at the center are not being exploited; they want to hold the periphery. Freeloading of this sort is probably inevitable in a free society.

But so long as it exists—that is, so long as ethnicity is experienced as a collective good by large numbers of people—it probably makes sense to permit collective money, taxpayers' money, to seep though the state/ethnic group (state/church) barrier. This is especially important when taxes constitute a significant portion of the national wealth and when the state has undertaken, on behalf of all its citizens, to organize education and welfare. It can be done in a variety of ways, through tax exemptions and rebates, subsidies, matching grants, certificate plans, and so on. The precise mechanisms do not matter, once it is understood that they must stop short of a corporatist system, requiring no particular form of ethnic organization and no administrative classification of members. A rough fairness in the distribution of funds is probably ensured by the normal workings of democratic politics in a heterogeneous society. Ticket-balancing and coalition-building will provide ethnic groups with a kind of informal representation in the allocative process. Democratic politics can be remarkably accommodating to groups, so long as it has to deal only with individuals: voters, candidates, welfare recipients, taxpayers, criminals, all without official ethnic tags. And the accommodation need not be bitterly divisive, though it is sure to generate conflict. Ethnic citizens can be remarkably loyal to a state that protects and fosters private communal life, if that is seen to be equitably done.

The question still remains whether this kind of equity, adapted to the needs of immigrant communities, can successfully be extended to the racial minorities now asserting their own group claims. Racism is the great barrier to a fully developed pluralism and as long as it exists American Indians and blacks, and perhaps Mexican Americans as well, will be tempted by (and torn between) the anti-pluralist alternatives of corporate division and state-sponsored unification. It would be presumptuous to insist that these options are foolish or unwarranted so long as opportunities for group organization and cultural expression are not equally available to all Americans. A state committed to pluralism, however, cannot do anything more than see to it that those opportunities are *available*, not that they are used, and it can only do that by ensuring that all citizens, without reference to their groups, share equally, or roughly equally, in the resources of American life.

Beyond that, distributive justice among groups is bound to be relative to the vitality of their centers and of their committed members. Short of corporatism, the state cannot help groups unable or unwilling to help themselves. It cannot save them from ultimate Americanization. Indeed, it works so as to permit individual escape (assimilation and intermarriage) as well as collective commitment. The primary function of the state, and of politics generally, is to do justice to individuals, and in a pluralist society ethnicity is simply one of the background conditions of this effort. Ethnic identification gives meaning to the lives of many men and women, but it has nothing to do with their standing as citizens. This distinction seems worth defending, even if it makes for a world in which there are no guarantees of meaning. In a culturally homogeneous society the government can foster a particular identity, deliberately merging culture and politics. This the U.S. government cannot do. Pluralism is thus still an experiment, still to be tested against the long-term historical and theoretical power of the nation-state.

7 Together in Difference: Transforming the Logic of Group Political Conflict

IRIS MARION YOUNG

William J. Wilson, among others, has forcefully argued that race-focused political movements and policies to improve the lives of poor people of colour are misplaced. Race-focused explanations of black and Hispanic poverty divert attention from the structural changes in the US economy that account primarily for the unemployment and social isolation experienced by rapidly growing numbers of inner city Americans. Race-focused policies such as affirmative action, moreover, have benefited only already better off blacks, and fueled resentment among middle class and working class whites. The problems of poor people, whether white or black, male or female, are best addressed, he argues, through a strong class based analysis of their causes and the promotion of universal public programmes of economic restructuring and redistribution.[1]

Group focused movements and policy proposals, these arguments suggest, only continue resentment and have little chance of success. The more privileged white, male, able-bodied, suburban sectors of this society will not identify with economic and social programmes that they associate with blacks, or women, or Spanish speakers or blind people. Only a broad coalition of Americans uniting behind a programme of universal material benefits to which all citizens have potential access can receive the widespread political support necessary to reverse the 1980s retreat of the state from directing resources to meet needs—programmes such as national health service, family allowance, job training and public works, housing construction and infrastructure revitalisation.

This paper was first presented to the Center for Social Theory and Comparative History at the University of California at Los Angeles in June 1991. Thanks to the participants for a lively discussion. Thanks also to David Alexander and Robert Beauregard for comments on an earlier version. Thanks to Carrie Smarto for research assistance.

Iris Young, 'Together in Difference: Transforming the Logic of Group Political Conflict', in *Principled Positions: Postmodernism and the Rediscovery of Value*, ed. Judith Squires (Lawrence and Wishart, London, 1993), pp. 121–50. Reprinted by permission of the author.

Wilson is at least partly right, both about the causes of poverty and deprivation and the necessity of a broad based coalition of diverse sectors of society coming together to cure them. There are nevertheless basic problems with this approach to political organising and policy. Since the working class, broadly understood, is fractured by relations of privilege and oppression along lines of race, gender, ethnicity, age, ablement, and sexuality, experiential differences and group-based distrust will make it difficult to bring this coalition together unless the distrust is openly addressed and the experiential differences acknowledged. If a unified movement were to develop for a universal working class programme, moreover, it is liable to be led by the reflect the interests of the more privileged segments of each fracture. Wilson's own analysis, for example, is seriously male biased; he tends to perceive female-headed households as pathological, and recommends economic and social programmes that assume women's economic connections to men as the most desirable arrangement. Finally, without countervailing restrictions built in, any universal benefits policies are likely to benefit most those already more privileged. Any new job training programme must learn from the CETA (Central Education and Training Agency) experience, for example, how to combat the tendency to train the already most trainable young white men through programmes that better target young single mothers, older people, and poor people of colour. If a political movement wishes to address the problems of the truly disadvantaged, it must differentiate the needs and experiences of relatively disadvantaged social groups and persuade the relatively privileged—heterosexual men, white people, younger people, the able bodied—to recognise the justice of the group based claims of these oppressed people to specific needs and compensatory benefits. Such recognition should not rule out that a programme for social change benefits these relatively more privileged groups, but justice will be served only if the programmes are designed to benefit the less privileged groups more, and in group specific ways. I believe that some theory and practice of socialist, feminist, black liberation and other group based social movements in the last decade has aimed to develop analysis, rhetoric and political practice along these lines.

I conclude from all this that both a unified working-class based politics and a group differentiated politics are necessary in mobilisations and programmes to undermine oppression and promote social justice in group differentiated societies. Given the above dialectic, however, it is not obvious how both kinds of politics can occur. This problem appears in many forms all over the world; societies, classes, social movements, are riddled with inequality, hatred, competition, and distrust among groups whom necessity brings together politically. This paper examines one aspect of this problem, specifically how political actors conceive group difference and how they might best conceive it. Historically, in group based oppression and conflict difference is conceived as otherness and exclusion, especially, but not only, by hegemonic groups. This conception of otherness relies on a logic of identity that essentialises and substantialises group natures.

Attempts to overcome the oppressions of exclusion which such a conception generates usually move in one of two directions: assimilation or separation. Each of these political strategies itself exhibits a logic of identity; but this makes each strategy contradict the social realities of group interfusion. A third ideal of a single polity with differentiated groups recognising one another's specificity and experience requires a conception of difference expressing a relational rather than substantial logic. Groups should be understood not as entirely other, but as overlapping, as constituted in relation to one another and thus as shifting their attributes and needs in accordance with what relations are salient. In my view, this relational conception of difference as contextual helps make more apparent both the necessity and possibility of political togetherness in difference.

In the second and third sections of this paper I bring this theoretical discussion of difference to bear on interpretations of group based political debate in two contexts outside the United States, which until now has been the focus of my thinking on these issues: group conflict in Eastern Europe and the situation of indigenous people in New Zealand.

Group conflict in Eastern Europe appears fairly intractable, with group differentiated unities disintegrating rather than forming. Separatisms have emerged there that exhibit essentialist constructions of group identity and define difference as otherness. Yet social realities dictate the necessary interdependence and interspersion of these groups. In many places in Eastern Europe the tragedy appears to be that group differentiated single polities are necessary, but group exclusions render them impossible.

Recent public debate about the political status of the indigenous Maori people projects more hope for the emergence of a heterogeneous public. Some of the Maori advocates have expressed an ideal of political biculturalism against the more assimilationist rhetoric of the dominant white officials and popular politicians. The Maori movement has succeeded to a certain extent in shifting political rhetoric and policy from this assimilationist position to one that recognises biculturalism in some respects.

Group Difference as Otherness

Social groups who identify one another as different typically have conceived that difference as Otherness. Where the social relation of the groups is one of privilege and oppression, this attribution of Otherness is asymmetrical.

While the privileged group is defined as active human subject, inferiorised social groups are objectified, substantialised, reduced to a nature or essence.[2] Whereas the privileged groups are neutral, exhibit free, spontaneous and weighty subjectivity, the dominated groups are marked with an essence, imprisoned in a given set of possibilities. By virtue of the characteristics the dominated group is alleged to have by nature, the dominant ideologies allege that those group members have specific dispositions that suit them for some activities and not others. Using its own values, experience, and culture as standards, the dominant group measures the Others and finds them essentially lacking, as excluded from and/or complementary to themselves. Group difference as otherness thus usually generates dichotomies of mind and body, reason-emotion, civilized and primitive, developed and underdeveloped.

Gender is a paradigm of this presumption that difference is otherness. Gender categorisation of biological and social group differences between men and women typically makes them mutually exclusive complementary opposites. Western culture, and other cultures as well, systematically classify many behaviours and attributes according to mutually exclusive gender categories that lie on a superior-inferior hierarchy modeled on a mind-body dichotomy. Men are rational, women emotional, men are rule-bound contractors, women are caretakers, men are right-brainers, women are left-brainers. Dichotomous essentialising gender ideologies have traditionally helped legitimate women's exclusion from privileged male places.

The oppressions of racism and colonialism operate according to similar oppositions and exclusions. The privileged and dominating group defines its own positive worth by negatively valuing the Others and projecting onto them as an essence or nature the attributes of evil, filth, bodily matter; these oppositions legitimate the dehumanised use of the despised group as sweated labour and domestic servants, while the dominant group reserves for itself the leisure, refined surroundings, and high culture that mark civilisation.[3]

Not all social situations of group difference have such extremely hierarchical relations of privilege and oppression. Sometimes groups are more equal than this model portrays, even though they may not be equal in every respect. Nevertheless, many such situations of group difference and conflict rely on a conception of difference as Otherness. Some of the conflicting groups in Eastern Europe seem roughly equal in this way and nevertheless see their relation as one of mutual exclusion. I will return to this later.

Whether unequal or relatively equal, difference as otherness conceives social groups as mutually exclusive, categorically opposed. This conception means that each group has its own nature and shares no attributes with those defined as other. The ideology of group difference in this logic attempts to make clear borders between groups, and to identify the characteristics that mark the purity of one group off from the characteristics of the Others.

This conception of group difference as Otherness exhibits a logic of identity. Postmodern critiques of the logic of identity argue that much Western thought denies or represses difference, which is to say, represses the particularity and heterogeneity of sensual experience and the everyday language immersed in it. Rational totalising thought reduces heterogeneity to unity by bringing the particulars under comprehensive categories. Beneath these linguistic categories, totalising thought posits more real substances, self-same entities underlying the apparent flux of experience. These substances firmly fix what does and does not belong within the category, what the thing is and is not. This logic of identity thereby generates dichotomy rather than unity, dichotomies of what is included and what is excluded from the categories. Through this dialectic initial everyday experience of particular differences and variations among things and events become polarised into mutually exclusive oppositions: light-dark, air-earth, mind-body, public-private, and so on. Usually the unifying discourse imposes a hierarchical valuation on these dichotomies, lining them up with a good-bad dichotomy.

The method of deconstruction shows how categories which the logic of identity projects as mutually exclusive in fact depend on one another. The essence of the more highly valued or 'pure' side of a dichotomy usually must be defined by reference to the very category to which it is opposed. Deconstructive criticism demonstrates how essentialised categories are constructed by their relations with one another, and bursts the claim that they correspond to a purely present reality. Deconstruction not only exposes the meaning of categories as contextual, but also reveals their differentiation from others as undecidable: the attempt to demarcate clear and permanent boundaries between things or concepts will always founder on the shifts in context, purpose and experience that change the relationships or the perspectives describing them. Allegedly fixed identities thus melt down into differentiated relations.

Defining groups as Other actually denies or represses the heterogeneity of social difference, understood as variation and contextually experienced relations. It denies the difference among those who understand themselves as belonging to the same group; it reduces the members of the group to a set of common attributes. Insofar as the group categorisation takes one set of attributes as a standard in reference to which it measures the nature of other groups as complementary, lacking, excluded, moreover, it robs the definition of a group's attributes of its own specificity.

The method of deconstruction shows how a self-present identity—whether posited as a thing, a substantial totality, a theoretical system, or a self—drags shadows and traces that spill over that unity, which the discourse representing the identity represses at the same time that it relies on them for its meaning. This process of criticism that reveals the traces, exhibits the failure of discourse to maintain a pure identity, because it appears as internally related to what it claims to exclude. Attempts to posit solid and pure group identities in social life fail in just this way. The practical realities of social life, especially but not only in modern, mass, economically interdependent societies, defy the attempt to conceive and enforce group difference as exclusive opposition. Whatever the group opposition, there are always ambiguous persons who do not fit the categories. Modern processes of urbanisation and market economy produce economic interdependencies, the physical intermingling of members of differently identifying groups in public places and workplaces, and partial identities cutting across more encompassing group identities.

Think, for example, of the social disruptions of an oppositional gender dichotomy. Homosexuality is the most obvious problem here. Enforced heterosexuality is a cornerstone of the gender edifice that posits exclusive opposition between masculine and feminine. The essence of man is to 'have' woman and the essence of women is to depend on and reflect man. Men who love men and women who love women disrupt this system along many axes, proving by their deeds that even this most 'natural' of differences blurs and breaks down.[4] Thus the need to make homosexuality invisible is at least as much existential and ontological as it is moral.

The inability to maintain categorical opposition between social groups appears in examining any social group difference, however. Where there are racial, ethnic, or national group differences there is always the 'problem' of those who do not fit because they are of 'mixed' parentage. The effort to divide such racial or ethnic groups by territory is always thwarted by what to do with those frontier areas where opposing groups mingle residentially, or how to account for and reverse the fact that members of one group reside as a minority population in a neighbourhood, city or territory conceptually or legally dominated by another. The needs of capital for cheap labour increasingly exacerbate this problem of the 'out groups' dwelling in the territory from which they are conceptually excluded. Capital encourages despised or devalued groups defined as Other to accept low paying menial jobs which keep them excluded from the privileges of the dominant group, but cannot keep them physically excluded from land and buildings the privileged claim as theirs. In many parts of the world those defined as 'guest workers' have become a permanent presence, and survive as blatantly ambiguous groups, excluded by definition from the places where they live, but excluded as well from their supposed homelands.[5]

The method of deconstruction consists in showing how one term in a binary opposition internally relates to the other. Group difference conceived as Otherness exhibits a similar dialectic. Frequently the most vociferous xenophobia, homophobia, misogyny arises as a result of a logic that defines a self-identity primarily by its negative relation to the Other. Some gender theorists suggest, for example, that for many men masculinity is primarily defined as what women are not.[6] Racist discourses similarly articulate the purity and virtue of white civilization by detailed fascinated attention to the attributes of the coloured Others, and the white subjects thereby derive their sense of identity from this negative relation to the Other. A group identity formed as a negation of the Other in these ways is fragile and relatively empty, and perhaps for that reason often violently insists on maintaining the purity of its border by excluding that Other.[7] This negative dialectic of group identity denies the subjects so identified a positive specificity. If men were less worried about avoiding invasion by feminine attributes, they might better be able to consider whether there is anything positively specific about masculine experience that does not depend on excluding, devaluing and dominating women.

To challenge this conceptualisation of difference as otherness and exclusive opposition, I propose a conception of difference that better recognises heterogeneity and interspersion of groups. It makes explicit the relational logic I just articulated according to which even the most fixed group identities define themselves in relation to others. A more fluid, explicitly relational conception of difference need not repress the interdependence of groups in order to construct a substantial conception of group identity.[8]

This relational conception of difference does not posit a social group as having an essential nature composed of a set of attributes defining only that group. Rather, a social group exists and is defined as a specific group only in social and interactive relation to others. Social group identities emerge from the encounter and interaction among people who experience some differences in their way of life and forms of association, even if they regard themselves as belonging to the same society. So a group exists and is defined as a specific group only in social and interactive relation to others. Group identity is not a set of objective facts, but the product of experienced meanings.

In this conception difference does not mean otherness, or exclusive opposition, but rather specificity, variation, heterogeneity. Difference names relations of both similarity and dissimilarity that can be reduced neither to coextensive identity nor overlapping otherness. Different groups always potentially share some attributes, experiences, or goals. Their differences will be more or less salient depending on the groups compared and the purposes of the comparison. The characteristics that make one group specific and the borders that distinguish it from other groups are always *undecidable*.

A primary virtue of this altered conception of group difference is that from it we can derive a social and political ideal of togetherness in difference which I think best corresponds to the political needs of most contemporary situations of group based injustice and conflict. Continuing my previous work on this theme, I will call this the ideal of a heterogeneous public.[9] Perhaps the best way to explore the uniqueness of this ideal is to contrast it with the two ideals that tend to surface in contemporary political debate and strategies involving group oppression or group conflict: assimilation and separation.

The tradition of liberal individualism promotes an assimilationist ideal. It condemns group based exclusions and discriminations, along with the essentialist ideologies of group superiority and objectification that legitimate these oppressions. Liberal individualism not only rightly calls these conceptions of group identity and difference into question, it also claims that social group categorisations are invidious fictions whose sole function is to justify privilege. In fact there are no significant categorical group based differences among persons, this position suggests. People should be considered as individuals only, and not as members of groups. They should be evaluated on their individual merits and treated in accordance with their actions and achievements, not according to ascribed characteristics or group affinities which they have not chosen.

Liberal individualism thus proposes an assimilationist ideal as a political goal. The assimilationist ideal envisions a society where a person's social group membership, physical attributes, genealogy, and so on, make no difference for their social position, the advantages or disadvantages that accrue to them, or how other people relate to them. Law and other rules of formal institutions will make no distinction among persons and will assume their moral and political equality. In a society which has realized this assimilationist ideal, people might retain certain elements of group identity, such as religious affiliation or ethnic association. But such group affiliation would be completely voluntary, and a purely private matter. It would have no visible expression in the institutional structure of the society. Workplaces, political institutions, and other public arenas would presume every person as the same, which is to say a free self-making individual.[10]

The assimilationist ideal properly rejects any conception of group difference as otherness, exclusive opposition, and rightly seeks individual freedom, equality and self-development. It wrongly believes, however, that the essentialist substantialising conception of group identity and difference is the only conception. The liberal individualist position associates group based oppression with assertions of group differences as such; eliminating group oppression such as racism, then, implies eliminating group differences.

There are several problems with this assimilationist ideal. First, it does not correspond to experience. Many people who are oppressed or disadvantaged because of their group identity nevertheless find significant sources of personal friendship, social solidarity, and aesthetic satisfaction in their group based affinities and cultural life. While the objectifying, fixed conception of group identity is false, it does not follow that group identity is false altogether. Some group affinities that mean a great deal to people are not tied to privilege and oppression; even among presently privileged groups one can find positive group affinity networks and culturally specific styles that help define people's sense of themselves without being tied to the oppression or exclusion of others. The assimilationist ideal exhibits a logic of identity by denying group difference and positing all persons as interchangeable from a moral and political point of view.

Second, the assimilationist ideal also presumes a conception of the individual self as transcending or prior to social context. As Sandel and others have argued, however, a conception of the self as socially constituted and embedded in particular communities is much more reasonable.[11] The assimilationist ideal carries an implicit normative requirement that the authentic self is one that has voluntarily assumed all aspects of her or his life and identity. Such a voluntarist conception of self is unrealistic, undesirable, and unnecessary. We cannot say that someone experiences injustice or coercion simply by finding themselves in social relationships they have not chosen. If unchosen relationships do not produce systematic group inequality and oppression, and also allow individuals considerable personal liberty of action, then they are not unjust.

The strategy for undermining group based oppression implied by the assimilationist ideal, finally, is not likely to succeed under circumstances where there are cultural differences among groups and some groups are privileged. If particular gender, racial or ethnic groups have greater economic, political or social power, their group related experiences, points of view, or cultural assumptions will tend to become the norm, biasing the standards or procedures of achievement and inclusion that govern social, political and economic institutions. To the degree that the dominant culture harbours prejudices or stereotypes about the disadvantaged groups, moreover, these are likely to surface in awarding positions or benefits, even when the procedures claim to be colour-blind, gender-blind, or ethnically neutral. Behaviourally or linguistically based tests and evaluations cannot be culturally neutral, moreover, because behaviours and language cannot be. When oppressed or disadvantaged social groups are different from dominant groups, then, an allegedly group-neutral assimilationist strategy of inclusion only tends to perpetuate inequality.[12]

Contemporary oppressed or disadvantaged social groups with these criticisms of an assimilationist strategy have often envisioned only one alternative to it, the separatist strategy. Understood in its purist form, separatism says that freedom and self-development for an oppressed or disadvantaged group will best be enacted if that group separates from the dominant society, and establishes political, economic and social autonomy. For many separatist movements this vision implies the establishment of a separate sovereign state with a distinct and contiguous territory. Some movements of cultural minorities and oppressed groups, especially those with residentially dispersed populations, do not find such a state feasible. Radical separatist policies nevertheless call for maintaining and establishing group based political, cultural, and especially economic institutions through which members of the group can pursue a good life as much as possible independently of other groups.

I think that the separatist impulse is an important aspect of any movement of oppressed or disadvantaged groups in a society. It helps establish cultural autonomy and political solidarity among members of the group. By forcing dominant groups who have assumed themselves as neutral and beneficent to experience rejection, moreover, separatism also often threatens and disturbs dominant powers more than other political stances. Sometimes the separatist impulse results in the construction of institutions and practices that do make life better for the oppressed or disadvantaged group, and/or give it more political leverage with which to confront dominant groups. A separatist inspired philosophy of 'women helping women' has established rape crisis centres and battered women's shelters in North America, for example, or women-based economic co-operatives in places such as Chile or India (though in the latter cases the organisers may not call themselves feminist separatists).

Separatism asserted by oppressed groups is very different from the processes of enforced separation, segregation and exclusion perpetrated by dominating groups that assert their superiority. Dominant groups depend for their sense of identity on defining the excluded group as Other and keeping the border between themselves and the Other clear. Separatism is inward looking where chauvinism looks outward; separatism is a positive self-assertion where racism and anti-Semitism are negative; separation of the oppressed is voluntary where their exclusion is coerced. Nevertheless, separatism also submits to a logic of identity structurally akin to that underlying a conception of difference as Otherness. It aims to purify and enclose a group identity and thereby avoid political conflict with other groups.

The aim of self-determination and autonomy propelling separatist movements might be sensible if it were not the case that almost everywhere the groups in conflict are already together, their histories intertwined with mutual influences as well as antagonisms. As I discussed earlier, most social groups today currently reside in patterns interspersed with other groups; where the groups are relatively segregated geographically, there are usually mixed border areas, or some members of a relatively separated group are dispersed elsewhere. Groups that perceive themselves as very different in one context, moreover, often find themselves similar when they together encounter another group. But most important, processes of economic centralisation and diversification, along with urbanisation, have created a necessary economic interdependence among many groups and regions that would much prefer to be separate.

The logic of identity expressed by separatist assertions and movements, finally, often tends to simplify and freeze the identity of its group in a way that fails to acknowledge the group differences within a social group. A strong nationalist separatist movement, for example, may reinforce or increase its domination of women or a religious minority, because it wrongly essentialises and homogenises the attributes of members of the group.

I conclude from these arguments that social movements of oppressed or disadvantaged groups need a political vision different from both the assimilationist and separatist ideals. I derive such a vision from the relational conception of group difference. A politics that treats difference as variation and specificity, rather than as exclusive opposition, aims for a society and polity where there is social equality among explicitly differentiated groups who conceive themselves as dwelling together without exclusions.

What are the elements of such an ideal? First, the groups in question understand themselves as participating in the same society. Whether they like it or not, they move within social processes that involve considerable exchange, interaction, and interdependency among the groups. Their being together may produce conflicts, division, relations of privilege and oppression that motivate their *political* interaction.

Thus, second, to resolve these conflicts the group must be part of a single polity. The polity should foster institutions and procedures for discussing and deciding policies that all can accept as legitimately binding, thereby creating a public in which the groups communicate.

But, third, this public is *heterogeneous*, which means that the social groups of the society have a differentiated place in that public, with mutual recognition of the specificity of the groups in the public. Political processes of discussion and decision-making provide for the specific representation of those groups in the society who are oppressed or disadvantaged, because a more universal system of representation is unlikely to include them in manner or numbers sufficient to grant their perspective political influence. The primary moral ground for this heterogeneous public is to promote social justice in its policies. Besides guaranteeing individual civil and political rights, and guaranteeing that the basic needs of individuals will be met so that they can freely pursue their own goals, a vision of social justice provides for some group related rights and policies. These group institutions will adhere to a principle that social policy should attend to rather than be blind to group difference in awarding benefits or burdens, in order to remedy group based inequality or meet group specific needs.

Group Conflict in Eastern Europe[13]

Scores of group identities pepper what were recently the eight nation-states of Eastern Europe: the Soviet Union, Poland, Czechoslovakia, Hungary, Yugoslavia, Romania, Bulgaria, and Albania. A history of movement, migration, empires, and wars in this region of the world has resulted in a dispersion of many self-identifying groups in several places, not always contiguous. Few places on this earth have escaped such a general process, although the specific histories, of course, vary widely. One group is often dispersed among several of the existing states. Many self-identified nationalities have never had a state in the modern institutional sense. Despite mythologies of pure ethnicities with unitary homelands, virtually every territory has its ethnic and often religious minorities.

With the receding of Communism in this region ethnopolitics has burst on the scene with such passion and violence that it is difficult not to interpret it as a 'return of the repressed'. The policies and practices of the Communist states claimed to have made relations among these groups orderly and co-operative, but this is primarily because limited political freedom repressed some group conflict and claims to autonomy.

The philosophy and policies of these Communist states have certainly had assimilationist tendencies, deriving at least in part from Marxism itself. The Marxist tradition shares with liberalism a modernist Enlightenment orientation which regards ascribed statuses and traditional group based affiliations as conservatising, divisive, and irrational. Historical materialism's theory of social evolution theorises that capitalist development breaks down such status-based social power and distinction, and brings diverse groupings together as workers. The more universal relationships of bourgeois and proletariat emerge, which transcend national, regional and ethnic boundaries. The socialist movement of the nineteenth century was vigorously internationalist, based on this philosophy. Its vision of the future socialist society implied the creation for the first time of a truly universal humanity, not divided by arbitrary boundaries of state, nation or ethne.

In applying the international socialist vision to the concrete context of Eastern Europe, the Bolshevik revolution had to modify this universalist vision. In so doing, the early Russian revolution developed some theory and practice for a state's relation with national minorities that exhibited more sensitivity and progressive tendency than many other places in the world. After World War Two several instances of really existing socialism claimed to have constitutional federations that guaranteed cultural pluralism. There is some reason to think, however, that Communist philosophy regarded such cultural pluralism as a necessary accommodation to existing conditions, and that ethnic affiliation would wither away within the worker's state. Thus Philip Roeder argues, for example, that Soviet Federalism aimed toward assimilation in the long run, even though it accorded special rights to national groups.[14] Yugoslav federalism before the 1970s, to take another example, concretely exemplified the impulse to create a socialist identity that would merge and transcend traditional ethnic identities.

Assimilationist tendencies in Eastern Europe in the last forty years may also be partly attributed to the policies of the major allied powers at the end of World War Two. According to Jonathan Eyal, after 1945 Britain, France and the United States looked at cultural minorities in Eastern Europe and

> concluded that if all citizens were allowed to enjoy their civil rights irrespective of race, language or creed, all would be well. But these were essentially excuses, for both Britain and France entertained few illusions about the future of 'democracy' in Eastern Europe. Rather, they feared that an international system of minorities protection would apply to the West as well as to the East, and they were determined to prevent this from happening.[15]

Against this history of what they perceive either as minority repression or co-optive granting of superficial group rights, many national and ethnic groups have won, and more are demanding, separation from the state jurisdictions in which they have been lodged for more than forty years, and the establishment of their own sovereign polities. Often this separatism has produced its own unifying and repressive consequences, as other ethnic minorities within the territories for which a nationality claims separate sovereignty find themselves excluded from full citizenship recognition and economic opportunity. Ethnic Russians in Lithuania, for example, experience disadvantage and discrimination in the context of Lithunian separatism. In Latvia, ethnic Russians make up a large part of the population, while Latvians account for just over fifty per cent of the inhabitants.[16]

The causes of the terrible wars in Croatia and Bosnia-Herzegovina are clearly multiple and overdetermined, not least of them involving power jockeying and the loss of central government civilian control over the Yugoslav army. But a vociferous notion of difference as Otherness appears to be among these causes. Nationalist movements aim to define a Croat or Serb or Montenegran identity in whole and essential terms, as pure and coherent, and entirely other than that of its neighbours. The groups often tell stories of origins, of the group in its primeval purity, and attach those origins to an original place, from which they now conceive themselves as displaced, or into which others have invaded and do not primordially belong.

Language, national symbols, cultural artifacts such as dress and texts, and above all this constructed primordial history give to the group its essence, which is unique, timeless and unshared by any other group. Where some people outside their region might find the groups nearly indistinguishable, they tend to deny any similarities. The groups from which the group distinguishes itself in order to form its identity come to be constructed as evil Others, all members of the Other group also essentially the same. Because some Croats were fascists and committed genocide during World War Two, in the minds of nationalist Serbs all Croats become natural fascists.

The history of the movement of peoples and the cultural influence and economic interdependence of the peoples of this region seem to me to exemplify the importance of a fluid and relational conception of group difference, which understands groups as overlapping, criss-crossing, and with undecidable borders. Every former Yugoslav Republic has several differently identifying groups within its territory, among which there has been considerable intermarriage, friendship, mutual interaction and influence. The interfusion among groups is profound, which sets the conditions for violent genocide once they, or some of them, decide that they are separate and unique, requiring a separate and homogeneous state and territory.

Thus several of the new constitutions of the former Yugoslav republics, including Croatia and Macedonia, attempt to define the essence of the national identity into their constitutions. According to Robert M. Hayden:

> Constitutional Nationalism both establishes and attempts to protect the constitution of that national as a bounded entity: a sovereign being with its own defining language, culture and perhaps 'biological being', the uniqueness of which must be defended at any cost . . . The cultural concomitants of national identity are also being increasingly viewed as bounded, determinate structures of language, belief, religion, practice. In a return to an old European concatenation, a given nation is seen as having a single, language, a single culture, a single heritage, a single interest.[17]

In these societies where so recently many people had a weak sense of group identity, today in such republics people are forced to locate themselves in one and only one group, having to face serious exclusions if they are not in the nationally dominant group. Such unique and pure identification is tragically impossible for the many people who have married across these boundaries, and for their children. According to Hayden, even in the most homogeneous of the republics, Slovenia, only 73 per cent of the children listed on the 1981 census issues from 'ethnically pure' Slovenian marriages, while in the most bitterly contested areas of Croatia as many as 35 per cent of the children were from mixed Serb-Croat marriages.

In reaction to the assimilationist tendencies they associate with the former Yugoslav Communist state, many of these nationalist groups are asserting a militant separatism, which claims the need for a separate national territory and also claims to include ethnic minorities located in other territories. This separatism raises well grounded fears on the part of national minorities within a national state, who in turn call for their own separate territory. But nowhere is there any territory that contains only one national group. Thus the spiral of separation that breeds more efforts at separation generates only increased hostility. In this region, where the interfusion of groups is so complete and borders of their difference so undecidable, it appears that only forced removal and genocide can homogenise a territory.

The situation of ethnic Albanians in the Serbian province of Kosovo, and the dispute about their status, appears to be typical of many ethnic disputes in the region along the dimensions I have been discussing. Many fear that this conflict will prompt the next war, probably involving several countries in the region. Since the early 1980s, the ethnic Albanians who compose an increasing majority of the province of Kosovo have asserted a separatist claim. They wish to have a separate republic in Yugoslavia, with the same political status as the other six republics. Ethnic Albanians claim that their current status as a province within Serbia has put them at the mercy of Serbian hegemony and hatred. They claim that the Yugoslav and Serbian governments have failed to invest in productive industry in Kosovo, and have instead pursued a development strategy based on extracting raw materials from the province to be used for industrial development elsewhere. Serbs and Montenegrins are favoured by the government in the distribution of public housing in the province, and they hold government office in numbers out of proportion to their numbers in the general population of Kosovo, which together is less than 10 per cent. The Serbian government has systematically repressed expression of Albanian national and cultural experience and symbols, they claim, for most of the last five decades. While these assimilationist policies were relaxed somewhat in the 1970s, the establishment by the Serbian government of a state of emergency in the 1980s has redoubled the oppression of ethnic Albanians.[18]

The Serbs tell a rather different story. Kosovo, they assert, is their original homeland, which those now called Albanians invaded in the seventeenth century. Collaborators with the Italian fascists during the 1930s and 40s, the ethnic Albanians in Kosovo persecuted and killed the Serbs and Montenegrins. Since World War Two, and especially since the early 1980s,

Albanians have suppressed non-Albanian cultural expression, destroyed churches, and created such hardship for Serbs and Montenegrins that tens of thousands have left their homes in Kosovo for neighbouring provinces and republics. The government of Serbia, they claim, has been most generous in its support for Albanian cultural and economic maintenance.[19] As far as I can gather from this distance, the Albanians legitimately claim to be oppressed in Serbia, though there is no excuse for retaliatory violence against Serbs in Kosovo.

I believe that most of the group social movements in Eastern Europe currently protesting their state's policies, engaging in conflicts with other groups, and/or establishing separate states, have claims of justice that deserve a hearing among those with whom they are thrown together or with whom they find themselves in conflict. Separation, involving the establishment of new sovereign jurisdictions, does not offer much of a solution to these problems of privilege, oppression and conflict.

Because of the interfusion of groups in the same territories and multiple group claims over many territories, some groups are harmed no matter how the borders are drawn. As separatist national movements aim to break off their autonomous territory from the larger states of the Soviet Union or Yugoslavia, new minorities within those smaller jurisdictions are inevitably created. The idea of any ethnic or nationally 'pure' polity is a chimera, moreover, and those who see in it ghosts of Nazism have grounds for their fears. The economies of Eastern Europe, finally, are so interdependent that self-sufficiency for any region is a near impossibility. This social and economic interfusion of groups in Eastern Europe implies that they must dwell together in tight political relations, whether they want to or not. Establishing new legal borders and sovereign territories perhaps shifts bargaining power within those relations, but it cannot politically separate the parties. The immediate creation of a new federation of nations of the now independent states that were formerly the Soviet Union attests to the necessity of their remaining together in their difference.

Some commentators appear to draw the conclusion from these horrible conflicts that only a liberal individualist conception of the polity is legitimate. The mistake is to give groups any political recognition at all. People should look on themselves as individuals, simply human beings, and should look on others this way as well. The degree of attachment that people have to group identities makes such a response utopian. As I discussed earlier, it presumes an abstract and voluntarist conception of the self. The only hope for political co-operation, peace and justice in this region, it seems to me, lies in establishing or re-establishing layers of heterogeneous publics that guarantee respect for the cultural specificity and needs of different groups, and which compensate disadvantaged groups, institutionalising means of ensuring that their voice and perspective will be heard. At the time of writing, the principals in the awful war in Bosnia-Herzegovina are conducting talks on a constitutional proposal which perhaps goes a little way toward calling for such a heterogeneously federated polity. Since it is still premised on the separate identities of groups in separate territories, however, it is unlikely to bring a stable peace.

The Maori Movement in New Zealand

During the 1970s and 1980s New Zealand society debated the status of Maori people as a result of a concerted Maori social movement. As described by Andrew Sharp in *Justice and the Maori*, this political debate, by no means over, succeeded at some level in creating a heterogeneous public. Initially, liberal individualist assimilationalist arguments dominated the debate. The Maori movement rejected these arguments, and some of them organised a separatist party. What resulted from the debate, according to Sharp, was the recognition of Maori distinctness within the New Zealand polity and society.

> Although the tension between unity and difference was always likely to be resolved in a way which denied justice to the Maori people (by insisting on seeing them as so many separate individuals who were part of the New Zealand nation), yet they persisted in, and won, a propaganda battle with politicians over their separateness. Perhaps this is the best that can be said of the history of the conflicts of the 1970s and 1980s, with respect to justice.[20]

People of Maori descent (as well as Pacific Islands) suffer disadvantage in New Zealand society along a great many measurable dimensions. Only about ten per cent of the total population, Maori have next to no political influence, even though Parliament seats have been reserved for them for decades. They are outvoted and outnumbered in most areas of common social life, where the dominant European interests and perspectives hold sway *de facto*. In areas of income, longevity, access to health care, housing, education, employment, Maoris fall short compared with whites. Proportionately more Maori than whites are in prison, suffer police abuse, and in general come into contact with law enforcement authorities. Like most indigenous peoples in most other parts of the world the Maori suffer employment discrimination, and they occupy proportionately fewer professional positions in the society than whites.

Before colonial contact there had been no 'Maori' group; there were only individual tribes and village groups. A self-identified Maori people has formed only in the context of confrontation with and differentiation from the European settlers. In 1840 several tribal chiefs signed a Treaty at Waitangi which represented the indigenous people in an agreement with the British crown. Like other European colonial treaties with indigenous peoples, the Treaty of Waitangi recognised the Maori as a distinct people, and promised to reserve land and fishing and hunting rights for them. In return the Maori promised to recognise Crown claims to sovereignty over most of the Aoetorian lands. Like most other such treaties in the rest of the world, the Europeans did not keep their end of the bargain and the Maori had no choice but to keep theirs.

A Maori identity emerged from this encounter with Europeans (called Pakeha by Maori) with very different language, culture, customs and values. This illustrates the idea that social group difference is best described as relational, rather than defined by essences and common attributes. Sharp notes,

> The truth is that the Maori-Pakeha distinction of people and culture is, like any other distinction between groups of people, made, constructed, fashioned from a world of perceptions of similarity and difference which is far more complex than the distinction can express. (p 51)

Sharp also points out that at least at the beginning of the current debate in New Zealand, there was no distinct 'European' identity, no self-conscious pride in European based (primarily British) tradition, no conception of the encounter with the Maori revealing the specificity and relativity of their colonial culture. More often the Europeans viewed the Maori as deviant—backward, uncivilized—from an allegedly culturally neutral set of standards of progress, efficiency, rationality, etc. Many white New Zealanders denied that a group difference between Maori and whites existed any longer. They claimed that generations of living together had made them one nation of New Zealanders, and that in New Zealand people are and should be thought of as individuals, not as members of groups.

In their politicised assertion of positive group difference beginning in the 70s, the Maori vociferously denied this assimilationist picture, but it did have an element of truth that illustrates my point about undecidability in group difference. For while it was and remains possible to say that Maori and Pakeha are different social groups, 'the realities of biological, social and cultural mixing between Maori and Pakeha and their ways of life made a clear distinction between them impossible (p 46).

The Maori asserted that New Zealand politics and society should acknowledge them as a distinct people with a distinct language, culture and way of life. They claimed that because of generations of domination by the Pakeha people they deserved reparations, and they asserted the need for redistribution of New Zealand's resources to provide the Maori with a greater share. They asserted the right to speak their own language in official settings, to administer their own lands and fisheries and to a distinct legal system. They included other planks in the platform for Maori improvement and self-determination, including affirmative action in education and employment, state subsidisation of Maori business and economic development.

Many whites reacted to these assertions of Maori specificity with a liberal individualist response. The political institutions of modern representative democracy do not or should not differentiate citizens. All persons, whatever their social or cultural background, should be considered equal before the law. Law and state policy should be blind to differences of ethnicity or origin, and promote the ability of each individual to achieve whatever they be in competition with others. If those of Maori origin have been disadvantaged and discriminated against, then steps should be taken to remove the barriers to their full inclusion in New Zealand society. But such steps cannot include special recognition for Maori culture and group economy, because that will only continue to keep them marked and disadvantaged. The Maori responded to this reasonable liberalism by claiming that its assimilationist point of view perpetuated cultural imperialism.

> Inequalities were the outcome of monocultural institutions which simply ignore or freeze out the cultures of those who do not belong to the majority. National cultures are evolved which are rooted in the values, systems and viewpoints of one culture only. Participation by minorities is conditional on their subjugating their own values and systems to those of 'the system' of the power culture. The aim should be to attain socio-economic parity between Maori and non-Maori by the provision of resources to meet Maori needs on Maori terms. (p 212)

Separatism was one challenge to the dominant assimilationist position. In 1979 a former minister of Maori Affairs led the founding of a separatist Maori party, which was an important player in the debate. Separatists called for political separation of Maori and Pakeha, with complete Maori sovereignty over Maori lives, land, and fisheries. Perhaps because no single territory could be conceived as the Maori 'homeland', however, and because most Maori are thoroughly interspersed in New Zealand society, with the majority living in cities, complete separation could not be understood as a serious option.

A more realistic Maori political ideal emerged in the doctrine of biculturalism. As defined by Sharp, bilculturalism 'was the doctrine that distributions of things in Aoteraroa/New Zealand should be made primarily between the two main cultures, Maori and Pakeha, and that since Maori and Pakeha were *ethne* worthy of equal respect, the distributions should be equal between them (p 227). Given the power of the Pakeha and the relatively small numbers of Maori, the idea of an equal distribution of political and economic power between the two groups met with insurmountable resistance. Nevertheless, by the late 1980s a general principle of biculturalism was recognised by many people, and institutionalised to some extent in law. The Royal Commission on the electoral system, for example, recommended a multiple member proportional representational system. It also urged that procedures for elections to Hospital Boards, University Councils, City Councils, and Parliament be so modified that Maori representatives might be chosen according to the custom of the Maori themselves (pp 237, 243). Legislation has been enacted which prohibits passage of any bill which is regarded as inconsistent with Maori land holdings. Government reform to recognise biculturalism and give Maori special rights of control over Maori affairs extended beyond legislation, moreover, to the organisation of government bureaucracy.[21]

The debate in New Zealand about what a bicultural society and polity with special rights for the Maori means has not ended, and perhaps cannot end. Specific conflicts of interest between the groups will continue to surface. Disagreements and resentments continue among both groups. Sharp indicates that he believes that the Maori have not yet received justice, especially economic justice. Nevertheless, as I read Sharp's story, the political debate and institutional changes of the 1980s established a heterogeneous public which provides some institutionalised group specific voice for the disadvantaged group and asserts a principle of special rights for the sake of preserving the group's culture and way of life.

Conclusion

I began this paper by referring to a dilemma faced by those seeking change in social policy in the United States toward economic restructing that will be oriented to meeting needs. The dilemma appears to be that a unified class-based social movement is necessary to achieve this change, on the one hand, but justice within and as a result of such a movement requires differentiating group needs and perspectives and fostering respect for those differences, on the other. My analyses of Eastern Europe and New Zealand are partly designed to demonstrate that this sort of dilemma is hardly unique to the context of the United States. All over the world group based claims to special rights, to cultural justice and the importance of recognising publicly different group experiences and perspectives have exploded, often with violence.

In many places the claims, debates and conflicts of this ethnopolitics seem to dwarf other political issues. When they do it is generally no less true there than in the United States that economic structures are a primary case of group disadvantage, where it exists. Some socialists, and some liberals as well, might rightly claim that focus on political group difference and conflict diverts attention from these issues of economic structure.

In this paper I have suggested that the context of economic interdependence provides an important basis for the necessity of groups who define each other as different to maintain a single polity, both in oppositional social movements of civil society or in legislative and other governmental institutions. I have also suggested, however, that the subject of discussion in such a polity should not be restricted to distribution and redistribution of economic resources, or even to issues of control over the means of production and distribution. The way differently identifying groups understand themselves and each other, as well as how their group specific needs and interests intersect with policies and institutions of political decision-making must also be an explicit part of political discourse.

Notes

1. W.J. Wilson, *The Truly Disadvantaged*, University of Chicago Press, Chicago 1987.
2. See Homi K. Bhabha, 'Interrogating Identity: The Postcolonial Prerogative', in David Goldberg (ed), *Anatomy of Racism*, University of Minnesota Press, Minneapolis 1990.
3. For more development of how the conception of difference as otherness connects with disgust, see Chapter 5 of my book, *Justice and the Politics of Difference*, Princeton University Press, Princeton 1990.
4. For an interesting analysis of the structures of enforced heterosexuality and its relation to gender structuring, see Judith Butler, *Gender Troubles*, Routledge, London and New York 1989.
5. Aysegul Bayakan develops a fascinating account of the identity crisis this process has produced among Turks and those of Turkish descent in Germany. 'The Narrative Construction of the Turkish Immigrant in Germany', unpublished manuscript, Women's Studies, University of Pittsburgh.
6. Nancy Chodorow developed this idea in her famous paper, 'Family Structure and Feminine Personality', in Rosaldo and Lamphere (eds), *Women, Culture and Society*, Stanford University Press, 1974; see also Nancy Hartsock, *Money, Sex and Power*, Longman, New York 1983.
7. I have elaborated a description of this process using Julia Kristeva's theory of the abject in Chapter 5 of my book already cited, *Justice and the Politics of Difference*.
8. For a development of this relational conception of difference, see Martha Minow, *Making All the Difference*, Cornell University Press, Ithaca 1990.
9. See my 'Impartiality and the Civic Public: Some Implications of Feminist

Critiques of Moral and Political Theory', in Cornell and Benhabib (eds), *Feminism as Critique*, U. Minnesota, 1987; and *Justice and the Politics of Difference*, Chapters 4 and 6.

10. For a well articulated expression of this assimilationist ideal, see Richard Wasserstrom, 'On Racism and Sexism', in *Philosophy and Social Issues*, Notre Dame University Press, Notre Dame 1980.
11. Michael Sandel, *Liberalism and the Limits of Justice*, Cambridge University Press, Cambridge 1982.
12. For an extended argument that principles and procedures of 'merit' evaluation cannot be group neutral, see *Justice and the Politics of Difference*, Chapter 7.
13. This section has benefited from conversations with Jeff Chekel, Slobodan Pesic, Julie Mostov, and Robert Hayden.
14. Philip G. Roeder, 'Soviet Federalism and Ethnic Mobilization', *World Politics*, Vol. 43, Jan 1991, pp. 196–232.
15. Jonathan Eyal, 'Eastern Europe: What about the minorities?' *World Today*, Vol. 45, December 1989, p. 206.
16. William E. Schmidt, 'Post-Soviet Baltic Republics: Still Stunted and Struggling', *New York Times*, 10 June, 1992.
17. Robert M. Hayden, 'Constitutional Nationalism in the Formerly Yugoslav Republics', *Slavic Review*, Vol. 51, no. 4, Fall 1992; see also Julie Mostov, 'Democracy and the Politics of National Identity', paper presented at meetings of the American Political Science Association, Chicaco, August 1992.
18. See Elez Biber, *Albania: A Socialist Maverick*, Westview Press, Colorado 1990, Chapter 7.
19. See Veselin Kjuretic, 'The Exodus of the Serbs from Kosovo in the Twentieth Century and Its Political Background', Serbian Academy of Sciences and Arts Institute for Balkan Studies, Belgrade; see also Slobodan M. Pesic, 'Paper on Eastern Europe', Matthew B. Ridgway Center for International Studies, University of Pittsburgh, February 1991.
20. Andrew Sharp, *Justice and the Maori*, Oxford University Press, Oxford 1990, p. 43.
21. See Augie Fleras, 'Inverting the Bureaucratic Pyramid: Reconciling Aboriginality and Bureaucracy in New Zealand', *Journal of the Society for Applied Anthropology*, Vol. 48, no. 3, Fall 1989, pp. 214–225.

IV Individual Rights and Group Rights

8 Native Rights as Collective Rights: A Question of Group Self-Preservation

DARLENE M. JOHNSTON

1. Introduction

. . . Reaction to the idea of collective rights is strongly negative in some quarters. Collective rights are seen as inherently dangerous and oppressive. This reaction stems from a perceived clash between individual rights and group rights. Collective and individual interests, however, are not inevitably antagonistic. The supposed antithesis seems to be based on a particular and intolerant conception of the nature of group rights.

Although group rights remain largely misunderstood, recent efforts have been made to ground collective claims in a rights-based theory and to develop a strategy for their adjudication. This paper will rely upon emerging collective rights precepts to establish that native communities are entitled to recognition as rights-bearing entities. The logic of the theoretical foundation will be shown to generate a group right to the territorial integrity of the existing native land base in Canada. The limits of this right and its remedial implications will be explored

2. The Communitarian Contribution

Liberal individualism has been increasingly criticized for its atomization of society and for the isolation and alienation which it produces. Although several traditions flow into this critique, they have in common a yearning for community.[1] No effort is made here to describe in a thorough way the communitarian critique of liberalism. Rather, for the purposes of articulating a theory of group rights, it will be sufficient to focus on the central communitarian insight regarding the nature of the social person.

Darlene Johnston, 'Native Rights as Collective Rights: A Question of Group Self-Preservation', *Canadian Journal of Law and Jurisprudence*, Vol. 2/1 (1989), pp. 19–34. Reprinted by permission of the author.

The communitarians offer a vision of personhood which stands in sharp contrast to the liberal conception of the deontological self. Michael Sandel, in his essay *Liberalism and the Limits of Justice*,[2] explores the deontological ethic from its Kantian foundations to its Rawlsian incarnation. The following passage captures the essence of the deontological project:

The deontological universe and the independent self that moves within it, taken together, hold out a liberating vision. Freed from the dictates of nature and the sanction of social roles, the deontological subject is installed as sovereign, cast as the author of the only moral meanings there are. As inhabitants of a world without telos, we are free to construct principles of justice unconstrained by an order of value antecedently given. . . . And as independent selves, we are free to choose our purposes and ends unconstrained by such an order, or by custom or tradition or inherited status. So long as they are not unjust our conceptions of the good carry weight, whatever they are, simply in virtue of our having chosen them.[3]

By enshrining the parallel priorities of right over good and self over ends, this ethic constructs the 'antecedently individuated self'[4]: a subject which exists prior to and independently of any experience of community.

The communitarians reject this conception of the independent self as failing to capture the reality of human experience. Sandel writes:

To imagine a person incapable of constitutive attachments . . . is not to conceive an ideally free and rational agent, but to imagine a person wholly without character, without moral depth.[5]

In more scathing terms, Christian Bay denounces liberalism for having 'drastically impoverished our appreciation of man's nature and potentialities.'[6] He writes:

Liberals have persistently tended to cut the citizen off from the person; and they have placed on their humanistic pedestal a cripple of a man, a man without a moral or political nature; a man with plenty of contractual rights and obligations, perhaps, but a man without moorings in any real community; a drifter rather than a being with roots in species solidarity.[7]

In contrast to this unattached, isolated and self-interested individual the communitarians offer a more generous and optimistic vision of the person. The dispossessed individual is rescued from the barren deontological universe by a constitutive conception of community.[8] To participate in such a community is to recognize that one's identity is to some extent defined by one's attachments and commitments. According to Sandel:

Where this sense of participation in the achievements and endeavors of (certain) others engages the reflective self-understandings of the participants, we may come to regard ourselves, over the range of our various activities, less as individuated subjects with certain things in common, and more as members of a wider (but still determinate) subjectivity, less as 'others' and more as participants in a common identity, be it a family or community or class or people or nation.[9]

This potential for constitutive attachments is the communitarian remedy for the anomie which pervades liberal society.

The constitutive community holds out the promise that the well-being of the individual and the group may be harmonized. If community is seen as a constituent of individual identity, then enhancing the former need not diminish the latter. Sandel explains:

when 'my' assets or life prospects are enlisted in the service of a common endeavor, I am likely to experience this less as a case of being used for others' ends and more as a way of contributing to the purposes of a community I regard as my own. The justification of my sacrifice, if it can be called a sacrifice, is not the abstract assurance that unknown others will gain more than I lose, but the rather more compelling notion that by my efforts I contribute to the realization of a way of life in which I take pride and with which my identity is bound.[10]

Rather than assuming, as liberalism does, conditions of mutual disinterest, communitarianism posits circumstances of mutual reinforcement.

This strong theory of community has not been without its critics. The limits of communitarianism have been located in its failure to address concrete issues and its propensity for intolerance. The romantic bent of the communitarians is captured by Amy Gutmann's observation that they 'tend to look toward the future with nostalgia.'[11] H.N. Hirsch has no patience with naive and abstract theorizing. In his essay, 'The Threnody of Liberalism', he sets out to expose the dangerous implications built into the renewal of community.[12] Hirsch identifies moral education and homogeneity as factors which are vital to the maintenance of a community. He faults the communitarian scholars for failing to address the negative aspects of such conditions. He maintains that:

both homogeneity and moral education can be politically dangerous in several ways: by encouraging the exclusion of outsiders; by encouraging indoctrination or irrationalism; by compromising privacy and autonomy.[13]

For Hirsch, these are precisely the conditions 'that liberalism is designed to avoid.'[14]

While Hirsch dismisses any strong theory of community as anachronistic and chimerical, Gutmann adopts an integrative approach. She recognizes the 'constructive potential of communitarian values' and suggests that it may be possible 'to discover ways in which local communities and democracy can be vitalized without violating individual rights.'[15] This gesture towards accommodation is important from the perspective of articulating a theory of group rights. Unmitigated communitarianism cannot be expected to generate rights-claims. The communitarian values of benevolence, understanding, and friendship are affirmed as an alternative to the liberal rights-based ethic.[16] To speak of rights is to step outside the community and to revert to the ethics of strangers.

The communitarian impulse to jettison justice must be tempered in order to retain some notion of rights, collective or otherwise. The potential for conflict both within and among communities cannot be ignored. Recognizing, as the communitarians do, that 'to some [we] owe more than justice requires or even permits'[17] is not to say that a rights-based ethic is utterly obsolete in the context of a modern pluralistic society. Although the communitarian agenda does not include the construction of a theory of group rights, Sandel's insight that 'we can know a good in common that we cannot know alone'[18] is an eloquent testimony to the intrinsic value of community which is essential to ground such a theory.

3. A Conception of Groupness

The first conceptual issue to be addressed in the articulation of a theory of group rights is the definition of the right-holder. Much of the animosity against group rights stems from a scepticism that satisfactory criteria can be developed for locating entities entitled to such rights. The sceptics want some assurance of quality control. Otherwise, they fear that collective rights will become a Pandora's box, 'from which all sorts of groupings might spring, demanding rights.'[19] Julius Grey denies that a principled framework for recognition can be established. He maintains that '[t]he beneficiaries and the subjects [of collective rights] cannot be identified, save through unilateral assertion or some other arbitrary process.'[20] The argument from anarchy must be taken seriously by the advocates of collective rights.

Important groundwork for theorizing about group rights was laid by Owen Fiss in his essay, 'Groups and the Equal Protection Clause'.[21] Fiss makes a crucial distinction between haphazard aggregations and social groups. He explains:

> I use the term 'group' to refer to a social group, and for me, a social group is more than a collection of individuals, all of whom, to use a polar example, happen to arrive at the same street corner at the same moment.[22]

Fiss identifies two characteristics which distinguish social groups from mere aggregates. He regards a social group as an 'entity', by which he means that 'the group has a distinct existence apart from its members, and also that it has an identity.'[23] In asserting that groups exist as discrete entities, Fiss rejects the premise of methodological individualism which holds that groups are perfectly reducible into their individual members. He perceives the whole to be qualitatively more than the sum of its parts.

The second characteristic is the condition of 'interdependence'. According to Fiss:

> The identity and well-being of the members of the group and the identity and well-being of the group are linked. Members of the group identify themselves—explain who they are—by reference to their membership in the group; and their well-being or status is in part determined by the well-being or status of the group.[24]

This notion of interdependence prefigures the communitarian conception of the constitutive community. It denies the inevitability of antagonism between the well-being of the group and the well-being of members.

The conception of groupness articulated by Fiss has undergone considerable refinement. The subsequent literature recognizes various species within the genus. Michael McDonald has supplemented the Fissian differentiation of groups and aggregates with the notion of 'self-collection'. He writes:

> In contrast to aggregates, collectivities are 'self-collecting' in the sense that the members engage in rule-following activity of a sort that constitutes the collectivity. The notion of 'self-collection' is intended as an analogue to 'self-reflection'. If self-reflection is basic to individual identity, self-collection is also basic to collective identity. Sometimes the manner of self-collection is formal, as in the rules of incorporation or a nation's constitution. In other cases, it is fairly informal, as in the kind of self-constitutional understanding that unites a discussion group or a tribe.[25]

McDonald suggests a set of left-handed goalies within a hockey league as an example of an aggregate. Such numerical or analytical constructs are 'other-collected' inasmuch as they do not exist independently of our thinking about them.

McDonald argues that there are two fundamentally different forms of self-collection: '(W) self-collection based on will or choice, and (R) self-collection based on *internal* recognition of some significant commonality.'[26] McDonald refers to R-based collectivities as 'natural' and provides examples which include families, communities, and societies. W-based collectivities are described as 'artificial' and examples include clubs, teams, and governments. McDonald considers the Fissian notion of interdependence to be 'much more a matter of recognition than of choice.'[27] The suggestion is that the identity and well-being of R-based collectivities is more intimately connected to that of its members than is the case with W-based collectivities.

This heightened level of interdependence is precisely the distinction that Frances Svensson has in mind when she writes:

Surely there is a politically and morally significant difference between the American Medical Association or the National Rifle Association on the one hand, and the French-speakers of Quebec or the Amish in Pennsylvania on the other. . . .[28]

Svensson describes a group such as the Amish as 'multidimensional', referring to the common bonds of language, religion, ethnicity, race and historical experience. By contrast, the A.M.A. exemplifies a 'undimensional' group, that is, one based on a single bond.[29] Although Svensson links interdependence to dimensional complexity, her examples fall neatly into McDonald's self-collection schema.

The congruence between McDonald's and Svensson's accounts of groupness extends to the implications which flow from their respective indicators of interdependence. McDonald makes a primacy claim for R-based collectivities over W-based collectivities:

My contention is that R-factors are more important because they are more basic or deeper than W-factors in the determination of identity and welfare of the collectivity and, through it, its individual members.[30]

The importance which McDonald attributes to R-based collectivities translates into a stronger claim for recognition. Svensson reaches the same result via dimensional complexity:

Generally speaking, however, the more dimensions a group has, the stronger its claim to special status. It is dimensional complexity which produces such characteristics as endurance over time, stability of identity, systemic interdependence, and relative autonomy, and these in turn play a crucial role in qualifying groups for special status while avoiding the problem of open-endedness.[31]

McDonald also attributes a stabilizing function to his notion of recognition, maintaining that 'R-based collectivities have a certain rigidity or inflexibility with regard to membership that W-based collectivities do not have.'[32]

The counterpositioning of recognition and choice as modes of group identification is also present in Ronald Garet's analysis of groupness. In contrasting voluntary associations (W-based) with ascriptive groups (R-based), Garet isolates another differential in the matrix. He posits an inverse relationship between the voluntariness and the moral importance of a given group:

Many people would consider state, religion or family of birth to be the prominent group-sources of moral obligation in their experience. Yet these are typically among the most ascriptive and least voluntary of groups.[33]

Garet perceives obligation as the correlative of interdependence. He acknowledges that such obligation exists in tension with associational freedom.

Taken together, the variables of interdependence, recognition, dimensional complexity and obligation provide an intricate framework for determining whether a given group is entitled to recognition as a rights-bearing entity. It remains to explore the grounding and nature of the rights which such entities might possess.

4. The Value of Community

Liberal rights theory is predisposed to recognizing two categories of rights holders: individuals and society. There is, however, little conceptual space for the rights of groups. Typically, it is assumed that group interests can be accommodated within the framework of either individual or social rights. Such accommodation requires an element of 'translatability'[34]; group rights are viewed as being perfectly translatable into either individual or social rights. The effect of such translation is to deny the existence of any genuine group rights. Julius Grey, a proponent of the 'no group rights' school, insists that '[a] distinction must be made between 'collective rights' which are meaningless and individual rights, collectively asserted which are a common phenomena.'[35]

Ronald Garet has revealed the limitations of this type of reductionism by providing examples of nontranslatability drawn from American constitutional adjudication. He selects two decisions of the United States Supreme Court: *Wisconsin v. Yoder*[36] (involving a traditional Amish community) and *Santa Clara Pueblo v. Martinez*[37] (involving an American Indian tribe). Both decisions can be described as group-protective. In *Yoder*, the Court created a partial exemption from compulsory schooling legislation in order to avoid the weakening of the traditional way of life of the Amish. In *Santa Clara*, the Court decided, out of deference to tribal sovereignty, that the *Indian Civil Rights Act of 1968* did not create a federal forum for the review of a tribal kinship structure. Relying on these cases, Garet argues that:

> because there are certain things that only groups, and not individuals, can have—such as socialization processes (*Yoder*) and kinship structures (*Santa Clara*)—there are *a fortiori* certain things that only a group can hold a right to have.[38]

Having demonstrated the weakness of the conventional derivative approaches to group rights, Garet sets himself the task of expounding an intrinsic value theory of groups. The result is one of the most sustained and insightful analyses of groupness to be found in the literature.

Analytically, Garet begins with the existential perception that existence is the peculiarly human mode of being; 'the self-formative struggle that distinguishes the human world both ontologically and ethically.'[39] Following

Sartre, Garet views freedom as a structural feature of existence. He writes:

It is in the nature of existence both to make things—products, worlds, identities—and to negate the things made by struggling against them or moving beyond them. It is this struggle or discomfort with the available world that Sartre identified as the freedom which is structurally necessary to existence.[40]

Garet defines existence as a ground of value and of right: 'existence both carries its own moral value (i.e., the intrinsic good) and insists upon that value in the form of the right.'[41] He isolates three necessary components of human being, each of which constitutes an intrinsic moral good: personhood (the individual good), communality (the group good), and sociality (the social good).[42]

The concept of personhood as an intrinsic value capable of bearing rights is a familiar one. Rendered in existential terms:

persons have rights because personhood is a structure of existence; personhood is the face that existence sets against its own past. Infringement of the rights of persons is evil because it constrains the foundational moral possibility of transcending or negating life history by taking responsibility for that history and by choosing anew.[43]

Sociality is similarly a face of existence, albeit a less familiar one. Garet poetically describes sociality as 'a dream that society dreams of itself.'[44] As a structure of existence, sociality is also the ground of a right:

Existence . . . gives rise not only to a personal right—the right not to be made into a determined thing—but also to a social right—the right to move out of the history in which we find ourselves and toward the realization of our common humanity.[45]

Garet has an equally poetic description of communality as 'a kind of provisional, temporary accommodation between a traveller and a destination.'[46] To establish communality as a structure of existence Garet relies upon common intuition:

Not only is groupness an unfathomable *fact* of all our lives, but it is also an unfathomable *value*. We are born into some groups, others we choose, and still others choose us. Life not subject to the call of groupness is as difficult for us to imagine as life not subject to the individuating call of personhood or the sociating call of sociality.[47]

The right which communality asserts is a right of self-preservation; 'the right of groups to maintain themselves and to pursue their distinctive courses.'[48]

The claim that groups are entitled as of right to self-preservation is gaining recognition both domestically and in international law. Yoram Dinstein maintains that 'two collective rights are accorded by general international law to every minority anywhere: the right to physical existence and the right to preserve a separate identity.'[49] In the Canadian context, commentators such as Magnet, McDonald and Monahan argue that collective rights have played an important constitutional role.[50] They agree that the Canadian system of collective rights is designed to guarantee group survival.[51]

What is unique about Garet's treatment of communality is his strict adherence to the principle of non-derivation. He refuses to engage in any form of reductionism.[52] He insists that no hierarchy can be constructed out of the various structures of existence. He maintains that personhood, communality and sociality are symmetrical to one another—'neither derivative from one another nor conceptually ordered, but of equal status and dependent upon a common source.'[53]

To preserve the independence of the three claiming values Garet must acknowledge the potential for conflict. He writes:

> Therein lies the possibilities both of congruence and of tragedy. If it happens that the granting of the group claim also satisfies the claims of individuality or personhood, this is not due to the production of individuality by groups, but to the ultimate common grounding of both individuality and groupness (and sociality) in the structure of the human. If it happens instead that the granting of the group claim obstructs the claims of individuality, then the tragedy is not a choice between immediate and deferred (or specific and general) individuality, but rather a choice between distinct elements of the human good.[54]

The prospect for conflict between the three faces of existence is strikingly demonstrated in both the *Yoder* and *Santa Clara* decisions. Individuality (the claim of the Amish children and the Pueblo women) exists in moral tension with communality (the claim of the Amish community and the Indian tribe) which in turn resists sociality (the claim of the state and the federal government).[55] These examples appear to give substance to the fears voiced by opponents of group rights. The right of groups to self-preservation may, at times, threaten both individual autonomy and general welfare.

While Garet is prepared to acknowledge the 'possibility of tragedy', few critics of group rights will admit to the 'possibility of congruence'. Grey, for example, insists that collective rights 'clash irreconcilably' with individual rights.[56] The desire to avoid conflict, however, will not reduce the moral complexity of existence. The fact of groupness cannot be denied. And the refusal to recognize the value of groupness will leave it hopelessly exposed to the group-destructive potential of sociality. The inclination of the anxious individualist to dismiss the claims of communality should be tempered by the record of atrocities committed against groups in the modern era. The prevalence of collective wrongs such as apartheid and genocide demonstrate the need for collective rights. Garet's intent is not to subjugate personhood but simply to emancipate groupness.

5. A Framework for Adjudication

Garet's ambition in constructing an intrinsic value theory of groups does not extend to providing a mechanism for the adjudication of group claims.[57] His reluctance to offer any scheme for the accommodation of competing claims is consistent with his assertion of equal status for personhood, communality and sociality. To construct a hierarchy of rights would violate the principle of non-derivation; to subordinate one structure of existence to another would deny its intrinsic value. Garet's only prescription for the mediation of conflicting claims is that 'the irreducible groupness of the group rights'[58] be recognized.

With the advent of the *Charter*, a document which enhances the constitutional dimension of Canada's historical commitment to collective rights,[59] the search for an adjudicative framework has assumed a sense of urgency. Some commentators have warned against the wholesale importation of American constitutional theory.[60] Others have embraced the conventional balancing approach designed to reconcile conflicts between individual and social rights.[61] Still others have despaired of finding a principled approach to the judicial resolution of competing claims.[62] Not unexpectedly, committed individualists have insisted on the subordination of collective rights. Grey writes:

> The suggested way of dealing with the danger (of collective rights violating individual rights) is to give a narrow interpretation to the collective rights, to view them as much as possible as individual rights, collectively pursued and, whenever that is not possible, to rank them far behind the basic individual rights.[63]

For their part, ardent collectivitists engage in a reverse form of reductionism. McDonald maintains that collective rights are 'the home in which individual rights must find their place.'[64]

William Pentney has articulated two interpretive principles to facilitate the coexistence of the various categories of rights recognized by the *Charter*. The first principle requires that 'the particular collectivity must not be impaired in its capacity to continue either by the State or by claims on behalf of individuals.'[65] The second principle demands that 'a particular collectivity must respect the maximum individual rights consonant with the preservation of the group.'[66] Although Pentney expressly disavows any intention of constructing a hierarchy of rights,[67] these principles do generate at least a partial ranking. A subset of group rights, that is those which are essential to group survival, are accorded primacy. Pentney writes:

If the collective right being asserted is vital to the continuance of the group, and it cannot be protected by less destructive means, then it is submitted that the collective right must prevail.[68]

Inasmuch as Pentney's approach is purposive and incorporates an element of proportionality, it is an improvement upon cruder forms of subordination. In hard cases, however, it ordains that individual autonomy give way to group survival. To this extent, it remains hierarchical.

Despite Pentney's lapse into superordination, his analysis contains two important insights into the nature of group rights. To begin with, he recognizes that 'collective rights are meaningless without the continued existence and vitality of the group.'[69] This recognition should inform adjudicative strategy, inviting judges to focus on the issue of group impairment. Secondly, Pentney perceives that the content of group rights will be highly particularized, deriving from 'the nature, history and social context of the collectivity.'[70] This attribute of group-specificity has been noted by Kallen and McDonald.[71] Its adjudicative implications are clear: collective rights cannot be asserted in a vacuum. Advocates and adjudicators must demonstrate sensitivity to factual questions. Particular sensitivity is required for dealing with the inevitably subjective element of any group claim. Judges must be cognizant of their group-specific values when they undertake to balance competing claims. Being situated outside the right-claiming entity, there is a risk of devaluing what is experienced as essential to those within.

McDonald has employed Robert Cover's conception of *nomos* to clarify the group-specific nature of group rights. Cover writes:

We inhabit a *nomos*—a normative universe. We constantly create and maintain a world of right and wrong, of lawful and unlawful, of valid and void. . . . In this normative world, law and narrative are inseparably related. Every prescription is insistent in its demand to be located in discourse—to be supplied with history and destiny, beginning and end, explanation and purpose. And every narrative is insistent in its demand for its prescriptive point, its moral.[72]

According to McDonald, each self-collecting group has its own *nomos* which is located within a particular narrative.[73] Within such a narrative an action or event may possess significance which is not translatable.[74] The good adjudicator must struggle against the ethnocentric assumption that the values and interests of his narrative correspond to those of the claiming group.

The typology of group rights remains largely unexplored. The value of communality, as articulated by Garet, grounds the right of groups to self-preservation. But the prescriptions for group survival will be necessarily group-specific. In light of the potential diversity of group claims, it may be premature to attempt to construct a generalized framework for their adjudication. The hazards of reductionism, subordination and ethnocentricity are all too apparent. At this early stage in the development of a collective rights jurisprudence it would be prudent to postpone the construction of an overarching adjudicative apparatus until firm foundational principles are in place. The task of making collective rights meaningful, however, can usefully proceed by way of illustration. An examination of the concrete issues which arise in the context of resolving a specific group claim is a crucial step towards the general recognition and realization of group rights. The remainder of this paper is devoted to such an illustration. The proposed group claim is that of a native community against the group-destructive practice of expropriating their lands.

6. Native Community

According to the 1981 Census, the native population in Canada consists of approximately 552,000 persons. This figure can be divided into the following sub-categories: Status Indians, 350,000; Inuit, 27,000; Non-status Indians, 75,000; and Metis, 100,000.[75] The existence of these legal and quasi-legal categories of native peoples results from a number of factors. One such factor was the *Constitution Act, 1867*. It assigned legislative jurisdiction over 'Indians and Lands reserved for the Indians' to the federal government.[76] In pursuance of its constitutional mandate, Parliament enacted the *Indian Act, 1876*.[77] Throughout its various incarnations, this legislation has erected a complex system of registration which in turn has produced the strictly legal category of Status Indian.

The imposition of legislative distinctions upon Canada's native population has been harshly criticized both for its arbitrariness and for its disintegrative effects.[78] Easily the most controversial element of the registration system was its discriminatory treatment of Indian women who married non-Indians. Such women lost their status and their descendants were not entitled to be registered. However, Indian men who married out retained their status, and their non-Indian wives acquired status, as did their descendants.[79] A most recent revision of the *Indian Act* removes this gender discrimination and restores the status which Indian women lost through marriage.[80] But in dealing with the children of reinstated Indian women, the revised *Indian Act* draws a distinction between band membership and Indian status[81] and creates the anomalous category of an Indian without a band.[82] This latter complication can only have the effect of further fragmenting the native population.[83]

For the purpose of identifying a native community capable of bearing collective rights, the following discussion is restricted in scope to the legal category of Status Indian. This limitation is adopted in order to make the topic manageable. It is not intended to endorse the present stratification of native peoples nor to detract from the moral or legal entitlement of those who fall outside the category of Status Indian. Having simplified the frame of reference it remains to be established that the classification scheme of the *Indian Act* coincides with a conception of groupness that includes a capacity for rights-bearing.

Some commentators, particularly those writing from a sociological perspective, would question whether the legal category of Status Indian corresponds to a natural collectivity. James Frideres writes:

> Culture and race no longer affect the definition of an Indian: today's definition is a legal one. If someone who exhibits all the racial and cultural attributes traditionally associated with 'Indianness' does not come under the terms of the *Indian Act*, that person is not an Indian in the eyes of the federal and provincial governments.[84]

This argument focuses on the under-inclusiveness of the legal distinction, a feature which cannot be denied. But that is not to say that those Indians covered by the legal definition do not share racial and cultural attributes. The legal parameters do not operate to exclude significant commonality.

Evelyn Kallen draws a distinction between ethnic groups and ethnic categories, placing Indians in the latter. She maintains that:

> the relevant distinction is between arbitrary, artifical categories of classification, designed for analytic purposes (conceptual constructs) or designed for statistical ends (numerical constructs), on the one hand, and actual *sui generis* social collectivities organized on the ethnic basis (ethnic groups) on the other. Ethnic categories may be represented empirically by loosely connected, dispersed aggregates, as in the historical case of the Canadian Indian . . . The Canadian Indian did not exist prior to contact with Europeans.[85]

It is possible to treat the concept of Indian status as a numerical construct: for example, the number of Status Indians enumerated in the 1981 Census was 350,000. At this level of abstraction Indians do appear to resemble an aggregate more than a group. This is because the category is, by definition, individuated. According to s. 2(1) of the *Indian Act*, '"Indian" means a *person* who pursuant to this Act is registered as an Indian or is entitled to be registered as an Indian.'[86] The *Act*, however, does contemplate the existence of collective entities in the form of Indian bands. It provides that:

> 'band' means a body of Indians
> (a) for whose use and benefit in common, lands, the legal title to which is vested in Her Majesty, have been set apart before, on or after the 4th day of September, 1951,
> (b) for whose use and benefit in common, moneys are held by Her Majesty, or
> (c) declared by the Governor in Council to be a band for the purposes of this Act;[87]

Admittedly, the fact of a legislative definition does not settle the question of whether an Indian band constitutes a social group. If such a body were purely a creature of statute, then it would not represent what Kallen describes as '*sui generis* ethnocultural collectivities' and could not ground cultural group rights.[88]

At this point it is helpful to recall McDonald's distinction between 'self-collecting' collectivities and 'other-collected' aggregates. He states that '[i]n contrast to aggregates, collectivities are 'self-collecting' in the sense that the members engage in rule-following activity of a sort that constitutes the collectivity.'[89] Under this view, in order to find collectivity status it is necessary to establish that Indian bands are 'self-collecting'. This task is facilitated by historical considerations.

Prior to the recent *Indian Act* amendment which created the hybrid category of 'Indian without a band', virtually every Status Indian was affiliated with a band.[90] As of 1984, there were 573 bands in Canada, varying in size from fewer than one hundred to more than eight thousand members.[91] Historically, band designations could occur in one of two ways: by entering into a land cession treaty with the Crown or by voluntary registration. While the latter can be viewed as an individuated form of affiliation, the former is a peculiarly collective act. Arguably those bands whose designations stem from their collective surrender of their traditional lands may be characterized as self-constitutional. Treaty activity, however, was far from uniform. For a variety of historical reasons, Indians in the Atlantic provinces, Quebec, British Columbia, and the Yukon did not enter into land cession treaties.[92] As a result, only fifty per cent of Status Indians belong to bands which engaged in the 'self-collecting' act of taking treaty.[93] This is not to say, however, that non-treaty bands do not constitute collectivities. Often the original designation goes back several generations and the descendants participate in a collective identity. Admittedly the power of the Governor in Council simply to declare that a body of Indians constitutes a band for administrative purposes runs contrary to the notion of 'self-collection'. And on occasion, this power was exercised arbitrarily, without regard for cultural differences.

In spite of these disparities, it is predominantly the case that band designations correspond to existing socio-cultural realities. These groups of Indians share, at a minimum, a common interest in land. The reserve is a closed spatial area which, in setting the band apart from outsiders, reinforces the collective identity.[94] This spatial dimension of the band often coincides with common cultural and linguistic characteristics and a shared historical experience. Renan's observation that 'peoplehood is cemented by shared memories of common suffering'[95] is particularly apt in the context of native communities. These communities exist independently of their designations by outsiders. If the Governor in Council decided to revoke all band designations, the communities to which they correspond would not cease to exist.

The correspondence, albeit imperfect, between band designations and ethnocultural collectivities suggests that Indian bands are entities capable of bearing collective rights. McDonald would place Indian bands within the category of R-based collectivities. He writes:

> In traditional societies, we would expect values to be based more on recognition than on choice, with the result that collective and individual identity and well-being would be less open to volition than in, say, liberal individualistic societies. This, I claim, marks a major difference between native communities and our own.[96]

Svensson also regards native communities as the paradigm for multidimensional groups. She points to the level of interdependence and obligation as indicators of communality within Indian societies:

> Members of the community are expected to participate in communally-oriented functions, and to respect the authority of the community and its traditions and values; withdrawal from participation is equated with withdrawal from the community, since membership can mean nothing other than participation.[97]

Both McDonald and Svensson regard native communities as possessing a strong claim to recognition as rights-bearing entities.

As noted earlier, the content of group rights may vary with the nature, history, and social context of a given collectivity.[98] Nevertheless it is possible to make some observations which apply to native communities generally. Among the characteristics basic to Indian societies, for example, are the ethic of sharing and the consensual approach to decision-making.[99] Thomas Berger, in the course of conducting the MacKenzie Valley Pipeline Inquiry, came to appreciate that '[t]he value of egalitarianism has important implications for the way decisions are made within native society.'[100] Berger discovered that '[i]n the native villages there was an implicit assumption that everyone shared in forming the community's judgment on the pipeline.'[101]

What is perhaps most characteristic of Indian societies is the primary significance of the land to their existence. An understanding of the native concept of land is therefore essential in order to give content to the rights of native collectivities.

7. The Native Concept of Land

Native people view their relationship with the land as central to their collective identity and well-being. Within the native world view, people and land and culture are indissolubly linked. The following testimony of a Fort McPherson Indian given at the hearings of the MacKenzie Valley Pipeline Inquiry captures the essence of the native people's relationship to the land:

> It is very clear to me that it is an important and special thing to be an Indian. Being an Indian means being able to understand and live with this world in a very special way. It means living with the land, with the animals, with the birds and fish, as though they were your sisters and brothers. It means saying the land is an old friend and an old friend that your father knew, your grandfather knew, indeed your people always have known . . . we see our land as much, much more than the white man sees it. To the Indian people our land is really our life. Without our land we cannot—we could no longer exist as people. If our land is destroyed, we too are destroyed. If your people ever take our land, you will be taking our life.[102]

This special relationship with the land appears to be universal among indigenous peoples. The *Cobo Report*, a comprehensive United Nations study into the problems facing indigenous peoples, acknowledges the importance of land:

> It is essential to know and understand the deeply spiritual and special relationship between indigenous peoples and their land as basic to their existence as such and to all their beliefs, customs, traditions and culture. For such peoples, the land is not merely a means of production. The entire relationship between the spiritual life of indigenous peoples and Mother Earth, and their land, has a great many deep-seated implications. Their land is not a commodity to be acquired, but a material element to be enjoyed freely.[103]

Distinctive practices flow from the native conception of land. Native people regard themselves as trustees of the land for future generations and, as a result, cannot contemplate its permanent alienation.[104]

History demonstrates that there is a strong correlation between the loss of their traditional lands and the marginalization of native people. Displaced from the land which provides both physical and spiritual sustenance, native communities are hopelessly vulnerable to the disintegrative pressures from the dominant culture. Without land, native existence is deprived of its coherence and distinctiveness.

The right of native communities to self-preservation, the foundational right accorded to collective entities capable of bearing rights, would be meaningless without a right to the continued possession and enjoyment of their land. Native communality therefore requires the assertion of a right against the group-destructive practice of alienating native land. And if the right to self-preservation does generate a restriction on the alienation of native land, the *Indian Act* regime governing the use and disposition of reserve lands should incorporate such a restriction.

To some extent, the *Indian Act* reinforces the communal land use practices of native people in its definition of the Indian interest in reserve lands. In *Joe v. Findlay* the British Columbia Court of Appeal confirmed the communal nature of this interest:

The legal title to the reserve lands vests in Her Majesty the Queen in right of Canada. By virtue of the interpretation of s. 2 and s. 18 of the Indian Act . . . the use and benefit of reserve lands accrues to and comes into existence as an enforceable right . . . vested in the entire band for which such reserve lands have been set apart. . . . This statutory right of use and benefit, often referred to in the cases as a usufruct (not a true equivalent borrowed from Roman law) is a *collective right* in common conferred upon and accruing to the band members as a body and not to band members individually.[105]

This recognition of a collective right inhering in the band as a group should have important implications for the alienation of reserve lands.

The *Indian Act* supports the cultural survival of native communities by placing important restrictions on the disposition of reserve lands. Section 37 declares that:

Except where this Act otherwise provides, lands in a reserve shall not be sold, alienated, leased or otherwise disposed of until they have been surrendered to Her Majesty by the band for whose use and benefit in common the reserve was set apart.[106]

There is an element of consent built into the surrender requirement: a surrender is void unless it is assented to by the majority of the electors of the band.[107] In prohibiting the alienation of reserve lands without the consent of the band, the surrender provisions ensure the preservation of the land base which is so essential to the continued existence of a native community.

The *Indian Act*, however, provides for an exception to the general inalienability of reserve lands. Subsection 35(1) permits the expropriation of reserve lands. It reads:

35(1) Where by an Act of the Parliament of Canada or a provincial legislature, Her Majesty in right of a province, a municipal or local authority or a corporation is empowered to take or to use lands or any interest therein without the consent of the owner, the power may, with the consent of the Governor in Council and subject to any terms that may be prescribed by the Governor in Council, be exercised in relation to lands in a reserve or any interest therein.[108]

What is most striking and disturbing about this provision is the complete and absolute discretion vested in the Governor in Council. There is no indication of any factors which should inform the decision to consent to the expropriation of reserve lands. Subsection 35(2) directs that the procedure for the compulsory taking will be governed by the statute which confers the expropriation power upon the authority in question.[109] Typically, such legislation will have been drafted to accommodate a balancing of the rights of individual property owners against the public interest. It is doubtful that such legislation will contemplate the communal nature of the band's interest in reserve lands. The tribunal involved will have to be careful not to translate the collective rights involved into individual rights.

There is no guarantee, however, that the matter will ever come before a tribunal. Subsection 35(3) provides that:

> Whenever the Governor in Council has consented to the exercise by a province, authority or corporation of the powers referred to in subsection (1), the Governor in Council may, in lieu of the province, authority or corporation taking or using the lands without the consent of the owner, authorize a transfer or grant of such lands to the province, authority or corporation, subject to any terms that may be prescribed by the Governor in Council.[110]

Should the Governor in Council opt to make a grant of the reserve lands in lieu of a compulsory taking, the band will be denied the procedural protections which are available to all other property owners. And on the face of the section, there is no necessity for the Governor in Council even to seek the band's input into the decision to consent to the taking. As it stands, s. 35 poses a serious threat to the integrity of reserve communities. If the federal government is going to take seriously the right of native peoples to self-preservation, then it must introduce restraints upon the group-destructive practice of expropriating reserve lands.

This is not to say that expropriation must be prohibited in all cases. The right that a band may assert against the compulsory taking of its land is not absolute. To confer paramountcy upon such a claim in the abstract would be to deny the equal status of communality and sociality. There may be exceptional circumstances in which sociality will be able to assert a stronger claim. What is essential, however, is a structured opportunity for native input into the decision which has such group-destructive potential. There must be some guarantee that the collective nature of the right asserted and its centrality to the continued existence of the native community will be given due weight.

In addition to modifying the procedure to accommodate native participation, the federal government should revise the scheme for compensation. Subsection 35(4) presently contemplates the payment of money as compensation for the compulsory taking of reserve land.[111] Once again, the conventional procedures may not be designed to take account of the unique interest which a band possesses in reserve lands. Generally, owners are awarded an amount of money which reflects the fair market value of their property. But to assume that the value which native people place on their land can be translated into money is to misunderstand completely the native conception of land. To native people land is not a commodity which can be bought and sold. Land has an intrinsic value which cannot be reduced into monetary terms. Money cannot replace a way of life which is intimately connected with the land. The only adequate form of compensation would be the provision of replacement lands. These would have to be equal in extent, quality and legal status in order to allow the continuation of the native way of life.[112]

The right of native communities to self-preservation, therefore, has significant implications both for the legitimacy of the expropriation of reserve lands and for the appropriateness of compensation. It is with the native conception of land that the valuation and accommodation must begin.

Notes

1. See H.N. Hirsch, 'The Threnody of Liberalism: Constitutional Liberty and the Renewal of Community' (1986), 14 *Political Theory* 423 for a succinct discussion of the work of five prominent scholars in the communitarian tradition: MacIntyre, Sandel, Walzer, Tribe, and Auerbach.
2. Michael J. Sandel, *Liberalism and the Limits of Justice* (Cambridge: Cambridge University of Press, 1982).
3. Ibid. at 177.
4. Ibid. at 147.
5. Ibid. at 179.
6. Christian Bay, 'From Contract to Community: Thoughts on Liberalism and Postindustrial Society' in F.R. Dallmayr, ed., *From Contract to Community* (New York: Marcel Dekker Inc., 1978) at 30.
7. Ibid.
8. Sandel, *supra*, note 2 at 150.
9. Ibid. at 143.
10. Ibid.
11. Amy Gutmann, 'Communitarian Critics of Liberalism' (1985), 14 *Philosophy and Public Affairs* 308 at 322.
12. Hirsch, *supra*, note 1.
13. Ibid. at 435.
14. Ibid.
15. Gutmann, *supra*, note 11 at 321.
16. Michael J. Sandel, 'Morality and the Liberal Ideal' *The New Republic*, May 7, 1984, at 15–17.
17. Sandel, *supra*, note 2 at 179.
18. Ibid. at 183.
19. Vernon Van Dyke, 'Collective Entities and Moral Rights: Problems in Liberal-Democratic Thought' (1982), 44 *Journal of Politics* 21 at 32.

20. Julius H. Grey, 'Equality Rights: An Analysis' *Canadian Bar Review*, forthcoming.
21. Owen M. Fiss, 'Groups and the Equal Protection Clause' (1976), 5 *Philosophy and Public Affairs* 107.
22. Ibid. at 148.
23. Ibid.
24. Ibid.
25. Michael McDonald, 'Collective Rights and Tyranny' (1986), 56 *University of Ottawa Quarterly* 115 at 120.
26. Michael McDonald, 'Indian Status: Colonialism or Sexism?' (1986), 9 *Canadian Community Law Journal* 23 at 37.
27. Ibid. at 41.
28. Frances Svensson, 'Liberal Democracy and Group Rights: The Legacy of Individualism and Its Impact on American Indian Tribes' (1979), 27 *Political Studies* 421 at 434.
29. Ibid.
30. McDonald, *supra*, note 26 at 41.
31. Svensson, *supra*, note 28 at 435.
32. McDonald, *supra*, note 26 at 43–44.
33. Ronald R. Garet, 'Communality and Existence: The Rights of Groups' (1983), 56 *Southern California Law Review* 1001 at 1045.
34. Ibid. at 1007.
35. Grey, *supra*, note 20.
36. 406 U.S. 205 (1972).
37. 436 U.S. 49 (1978).
38. Garet, *supra*, note 33 at 1038.
39. Ibid. at 1002.
40. Ibid. at 1066.
41. Ibid. at 1002.
42. Ibid. at 1003.
43. Ibid. at 1068.
44. Ibid. at 1033.
45. Ibid. at 1069.
46. Ibid. at 1072.
47. Ibid. at 1070.
48. Ibid. at 1002.
49. Yoram Dinstein, 'Collective Human Rights of Peoples and Minorities' (1976), 25 *International and Comparative Law Quarterly*, 102 at 118.
50. J.E. Magnet, 'Collective Rights, Cultural Autonomy and the Canadian State' (1986), 32 *McGill Law Journal*, 170 at 173; Michael McDonald, 'The Personless Paradigm' 37 *University of Toronto Law Journal* (1987), 212 at 224–225; Patrick Monahan, *Politics and the Constitution* (Toronto: Carswell, 1987) at 95.
51. See Magnet, Ibid. at 176; Monahan, Ibid. at 111–112; Michael McDonald, 'The Forest in the Trees: Collective Rights as Basic Rights' (*unpublished*) at 6.

52. Query whether McDonald, Ibid. at 18, lapses into reductionism when he says that we must decide 'whether we value groups for the sake of individuals or the reverse.' See also text at note 64 *infra*.
53. Garet, *supra*, note 33 at 1065.
54. Ibid. at 1052–1053.
55. At first glance, sociality does not appear to be relevant to the *Santa Clara* decision. Garet, however, argues that sociality is very much at stake: 'The interpersonal inequality created by the membership rule hardly seems consistent with a norm of equal sharing in society' (at 1036).
56. Grey, *supra*, note 20 at 13.
57. Garet, *supra*, note 33 at 1005.
58. Ibid. at 1050.
59. *Constitutional Act, 1982* [en. by the *Canada Act, 1982* (U.K.), c. 11, s. 1] Part I, Canadian Charter of Rights and Freedoms. See ss. 16–23 (minority language and education rights): s. 25 (aboriginal rights); s. 27 (multicultural heritage); s. 29 (confessional schools).
60. See Monahan, *supra*, note 50 at 95; Michael McDonald, 'Collective Rights "In a Free and Democratic Society"' (1986, *unpublished*) at 3–7.
61. See Van Dyke, *supra*, note 19 at 22.
62. F.L. Morton, 'Group Rights v. Individual Rights in the Charter: The Special Cases of Natives and Quebecois' in N. Nevitte and A. Kornberg, eds., *Minorities and the Canadian State* (Oakville, Ontario: Mosaic Press, 1985) at 73.
63. Grey, *supra*, note 20 at 15.
64. McDonald, *supra*, note 26 at 48.
65. W.F. Pentney, *The Aboriginal Rights Provisions in the Constitution Act, 1982* (Saskatoon: Native Law Centre, 1987) at 52.
66. Ibid. at 53.
67. Ibid. at 51–52.
68. Ibid. at 53.
69. Ibid. at 57.
70. Ibid. at 56.
71. Evelyn Kallen, 'Multiculturalism, Minorities and Motherhood: A Social Scientific Critique of Section 27' in J.H. Grey, ed., *Multiculturalism in Canada: A Legal Perspective* (Toronto: Carswell, 1987) at 124; McDonald, *supra* note 51 at 7–8.
72. Robert M. Cover, 'The Supreme Court 1982 Term: Foreward: Nomos and Narrative' (1983), 97 *Harvard Law Review* 4 at 4–5.
73. McDonald, *supra*, note 51 at 15.
74. Ibid. at 17.
75. *Indian and Native Programs: A Study Team Report to the Task Force on Program Review* (Ottawa: Min. of Supply and Services, 1985) at 1.
76. (U.K.), 30 & 31 Vict., c. 3, s. 91(24) (formerly *British North America Act, 1867*). The Supreme Court of Canada has ruled that Parliament's constitutional mandate in respect of 'Indians' includes 'Eskimos': In *re Eskimos*, [1939] S.C.R. 104.

77. S.C. 1876, c. 18.
78. See, for example, James S. Frideres, *Native People in Canada: Contemporary Conflicts*, Second Edition (Scarborough, Ontario: Prentice-Hall Canada Inc., 1983) at 13; Bradford W. Morse, *Aboriginal Peoples and the Law: Indian, Metis and Inuit Rights in Canada* (Ottawa: Carleton University Press, 1985) at 4–5.
79. For a discussion of this aspect of the former *Indian Act* see: Kathleen Jamieson, *Indian Women and the Law: Citizens Minus* (Ottawa: Min. of Supply and Services, 1978).
80. R.S., c. 1–6 as amended c. 10 (2nd Supp.): 1974–75–76, c. 48; 1978–79, c. 11; 1980–81–82–83, cc. 47, 110; 1985, c. 27. See 'Definition and Registration of Indians', ss. 5–17. The enfranchisement provisions are also revoked with similar provisions for reinstatement.
81. Ibid.
82. See McDonald, *supra*, note 26 at 47 for a discussion of the divisive potential of the 'new Indian-without-band' status.
83. In contrast to the divisive *Indian Act* regime, a gesture towards native reunification may be found in s. 35(2) of the *Constitution Act, 1982* which states that '[i]n this Act, 'aboriginal peoples of Canada' includes the Indian,Inuit and Metis peoples of Canada.' *Supra*, note 59 at Part II, The Rights of the Aboriginal Peoples of Canada.
84. Frideres, *supra*, note 78 at 7.
85. Evelyn Kallen, *Ethnicity and Human Rights in Canada* (Toronto: Gage Publishing Limited, 1982) at 65–66.
86. *Supra*, note 80, emphasis added.
87. Ibid.
88. Kallen, *supra*, note 85 at 66.
89. McDonald, *supra*, note 25 at 120.
90. Frideres, *supra*, note 78 at 138.
91. Ibid. at 140.
92. Ibid. at 9.
93. *Supra*, note 75 at 9.
94. Frideres, *supra*, note 78 at 142.
95. As cited in Dinstein, *supra*, note 49 at 104.
96. McDonald, *supra*, note 26 at 42.
97. Svensson, *supra*, note 28 at 431.
98. *Supra*, note 70 and accompanying text.
99. Thomas R. Berger, 'The Persistence of Native Values' in J.E. Goldstein and R.M. Bienvenue, eds., *Ethnicity and Ethnic Relations in Canada: A Book of Readings* (Toronto: Butterworths, 1980) at 87–89.
100. Ibid. at 87.
101. Ibid. at 88.
102. As cited in Berger, *supra*, note 99 at 84.
103. United Nations. Commission on Human Rights, Sub-Commission on Prevention of Discrimination and Protection of Minorities. *Study of the*

Problem of Discrimination Against Indigenous Populations. Special Rapporteur Jose R. Martinez Cobo. (E/CN.4/sub.2/1986/7/Add.4, para. 196–197).

104. Kallen, *supra*, note 85 at 68.
105. (1981), 3 *W.W.R.* 60 at 62, emphasis added.
106. *Supra*, note 80, s. 37.
107. Ibid. s. 39.
108. Ibid., ss. 35(1).
109. Ibid., ss. 35(2).
110. Ibid., ss. 35(3).
111. Ibid. ss. 35(4).
112. The failure of the *Alaska Native Claims Settlement Act, 1971*, which treats native land as a corporate asset susceptible to taxation and alienation, stands as a stark reminder of the hazards of imposing foreign concepts upon the traditional native lifestyle. For a discussion of the disintegrative effects of *ANCSA* see: Thomas R. Berger, *Village Journey: The Report of the Alaska Native Review Commission* (New York: Hill and Wang, 1985) at 45.

9 Some Confusions Concerning Collective Rights

MICHAEL HARTNEY

1. Introduction

In recent years, there has been an increased interest in considering collectivities to be moral agents and holders of collective rights. Peter French and others have argued that corporations are agents and bear moral responsibility for their actions.[1] Virginia Held makes similar claims about nations.[2] She also believes that we have 'obligations to humanity collectively, to bring about its continued existence, and perhaps also to such lesser groups within it as our fellow nationals or conceivably the ethnic group to which we belong or the family or clan of which we are a member'[3] and that in some of these cases—humanity, nations—the obligation correlates with a collective right. Perhaps, the area where claims of collective rights have aroused the greatest interest is that of the alleged rights of minority groups within some larger political unit. Thus, in recent political debate in Canada, collective rights have been ascribed or invoked in relation to Quebec and to aboriginal peoples. It is with this last group of alleged collective rights that I will be particularly concerned in this paper.

While the term 'collective right' has become familiar through these political debates, one would be hard pressed to find references to collective rights in any dictionary or encyclopaedia of philosophy or in any standard work on political philosophy. Among philosophers, the term is still very much of a novelty, and even very recent books on rights contain no reference at all to the term.[4] Two recent authors who do discuss the question of collective rights, and accept the possibility of their existence, are Joseph

Earlier versions of this paper were read at the annual conference of the Canadian section of the International Association for Philosophy of Law and Social Philosophy, and at the Universities of Waterloo and Western Ontario. I profited from comments made on these occasions, as well as at the Vancouver seminar on collective rights organized by the Network on the Constitution in April 1991.

Michael Hartney, 'Some Confusions Concerning Collective Rights', *Canadian Journal of Law and Jurisprudence*, Vol. 4/2 (1991), pp. 293–314. Reprinted by permission of the author.

Raz[5] and Wayne Sumner.[6] In both cases, the discussion is brief and the concept of a collective right is clearly not central to the theory of rights being expounded.

This new concern for collective rights is the result of a recent interest in the value of communities. Proponents of collective rights for minority groups often seem to move in a rather cursory way from the claim that communities are good things to the claim that communities have rights:

1. Communities are goods (i.e., have value).
2. Therefore, they ought to be protected.
3. Therefore, communities have rights (to existence, etc.).

In such an abbreviated form, the argument could be challenged in a number of ways:

1. Proposition 3 is ambiguous as it does not distinguish between moral and legal rights: moral and legal rights have separate existence-conditions and so the argument is insufficient as it stands.

2. Proposition 3 cannot be true since collectivities cannot have any rights (either moral or legal, or both).

3. Even if the argument is restricted to moral rights, and it is conceded that collectivities can have moral rights, not every good generates a right to it; hence, additional premisses are needed to yield 3.

4. It is not necessary to vest rights (either moral or legal) in collectivities in order to protect them; this goal can be achieved by vesting the appropriate rights in individuals. Hence, 3 does not follow from the premisses.

5. It is not desirable to vest rights (either moral or legal) in collectivities, since (1) this will have undesirable moral consequences, such as the violation of individual rights, or (2) the creation of a category of rights distinct from, and potentially conflicting with, individual rights is misleading since it distracts us from the fact that the ultimate reason for the need to protect collectivities is their contribution to the welfare of individuals. Hence, 3 does not follow from the premisses.

All of these criticisms allege that the argument for collective rights involves certain confusions. I wish to examine some of these alleged confusions in this paper. I suggest that the current debate around collective rights is actually a conflation of three different issues.

1. The first is about the value of the existence of certain groups and the importance of protecting these groups against forces which might weaken or destroy them, perhaps even to the extent of outweighing certain rights of individuals (either within the group or outside of it). This we might call the *value-of-groups* question. It can be raised and answered without making use of the terminology of collective rights. It is encapsulated in premisses 1 and 2 above.

The other issues presuppose the moral importance of groups.

2. The second issue is whether the moral importance of the existence of certain groups results in *moral* rights for these groups. There are in fact two questions here: (1) whether it makes any sense to speak of groups as right-holders (the *conceptual* question), and (2) whether certain communities do have collective moral rights protecting their existence (the *substantive* question). We might believe in the moral importance of communities, and yet deny that these communities have any collective moral rights for a variety of reasons, e.g., because rights are not the appropriate way of protecting groups, or because groups cannot be rights-holders, or because the rights protecting the existence of groups are better vested in the individual members of the group rather than in the group itself.

3. The third issue is whether this protection of groups should take the form of vesting certain *legal* rights directly in the relevant groups and not merely in their members. Again there are two questions here, the conceptual one about the possibility of collective legal rights, and the substantive one about the desirability of protecting groups by vesting legal rights in them rather than in their members. This is a separate issue from either of the first two: one could believe in the moral importance of certain communities, and even accept the existence of collective moral rights, and yet deny (for either conceptual or substantive reasons) that the way to protect them is by creating collective legal rights; conversely, in order to accept the possibility or the desirability of legal rights for communities, one need not believe in the possibility or the desirability of collective moral rights.

The first confusion therefore to be avoided in discussing collective rights is the conflation of these three issues. My main concern in this paper is with the second issue, that of collective moral rights, but I will have a few things to say about the other two (in sections 2 and 4). In my discussion of both legal and moral collective rights, my focus will be mainly on the conceptual questions—are such rights possible?—rather than the substantive ones—do (or should) communities have rights?

2. The Value of Communities

Most proponents of collective rights, at least in recent political debate in Canada, seek to ascribe them to groups such as ethnic, linguistic and religious minorities. There have not been very many attributions of collective rights to groups identified by class or gender. Why should some groups be singled out in this way? Various authors have psychological or ontological explanations for the peculiarity of these groups: these explanations are often intended to explain why these groups can be rights-holders. Michael

McDonald calls them 'self-collecting'[7] or groups with 'shared understandings'.[8] In Canada, the focus on these groups is perhaps due to the fact that the constitution provides for special treatment for some of these groups: native peoples have a special legal status under the *Indian Act*, and s. 25 of the *Canadian Charter of Rights and Freedoms* protects 'any aboriginal, treaty or other rights or freedoms that pertain to the aboriginal peoples of Canada'; both the French and English languages are given recognition and protection by s. 133 of the *Constitution Act 1867* and ss. 16–23 of the *Charter* guarantee education in the minority language in each province; and finally s. 93 of the *Constitution Act 1867* guarantees to the Catholic minority in Ontario and the non-Catholic minority in Quebec the right to a separate publicly funded school system.

In this paper, I will not be concerned with the question whether certain features set these groups apart from all others, but it is worthwhile to point out that there are important differences among them. (1) There are differences in the extent to which we can choose to belong to them: one can choose one's religion, but not one's ethnic origin.[9] (2) There are differences in the extent to which one can belong to more than one group simultaneously: one can belong to more than one language group but not to more than one religion (inasmuch as the differences among religions lies in mutually incompatible beliefs), with ethnicity somewhere in the middle (since one can be of mixed ethnic origin). (3) Finally, ethnic, linguistic and religious groups differ considerably in the extent to which they can be said to act collectively, with linguistic groups standing at one end of the spectrum, and those religions with a decision structure at the other. In spite of these differences, I will call these groups 'communities' for ease of exposition; in so doing, I am not conceding that some important features distinguish them from all other groups.

Much of the energy of defenders of collective rights seems to be spent arguing for the moral importance of communities, and charging opponents of collective rights with denying any value to communities, or subscribing to a incorrect ontology of groups. Some of this energy is probably misplaced, since few people deny the basic premiss that human flourishing is not possible without human relations, and therefore outside of communities. Disagreements about the importance of communities are about the reason for the importance of communities and the degree of this importance. (1) Views about the importance of communities to human well-being range from the mild view that some community life is necessary for human flourishing to the strong view that one's very identity is bound up with the communities to which one belongs. (2) People disagree about whether the source of the value of a community is to be found in its moral features—for example, that it fosters autonomy or that it is tolerant—with the consequence that some communities may be harmful rather than beneficial to individuals, or whether the source of its value is the fact that it is the community into which one was born or to which one has always belonged (with the consequence that there are no external standards by which one can judge communities, and the only thing that matters is that it is *one's own* community). These are important questions, but as my main interest lies elsewhere. I will only give a cursory answer to them.

For some people, the moral requirement that communities are to be protected seems to be based on a form of moral skepticism which eschews any judgments about the relative merits of various communities: since no community can be said to be better than any other, protecting the survival of a community is a way of recognizing that the moral code of this community is just as valid as any other. The difficulties with such a position are well-known: one cannot derive a non-skeptical injunction to be tolerant from moral skepticism. A different argument would be that members of a community are entitled to live according to their own moral code (whether or not it is better than any other). While we readily recognize the right of individuals to live by their own lights, such a right is limited to behaviour which is mainly self-regarding, and society is entitled to step in when an individual's personal code of behaviour has undesirable consequences on others. In the case of a community, the potential for undesirable consequences for the lives of individuals is there from the very beginning, and so there can be no moral grounds for autonomy, if this means that society has no duty to intervene to protect the interests of individuals within the community.

Some of the stronger claims that one's very identity is bound up with the community to which one belongs suggest that ceasing to belong to the community one was born into would have disastrous effects on one's 'identity' and would leave one as impoverished individual. Such a thesis is surely false. Many people who undergo a radical change of community—e.g., by emigrating from their native land and leaving behind the society into which they were born, or by undergoing a religious conversion—experience the change as a liberation and think themselves better off for it. If claims about identity and rootedness imply that such changes are always for the worse, then they are mistaken and dangerous, for they serve to keep people imprisoned in unsatisfying cultures.

The important point to be made is that, whatever their views on these controversial matters, people generally believe that communities are important because of their contribution to the well-being of individuals. Such a view is part of what might be called *value-individualism*: only the lives of individual human beings have ultimate value, and collective entities derive their value from their contribution to the lives of individual human beings.[10] The opposite theory we might call '*value-collectivism*': the view that a collective entity can have value independently of its contribution to the well-being of individual human beings. Such a position is counter-intuitive, and the burden of proof rests on anyone who wishes to defend it. Most communitarians and defenders of collective rights do not appear to subscribe to such a view, since the point they are trying to make against those they perceive to be their opponents is the importance of communities for human lives.[11]

Now it is true that it makes sense to say that something is for the good of a group even if it is not for the good of its individual members. That the group continues to exist, or that it increases in size, appears to be good for the group (whether or not its members benefit). This is true, but morally irrelevant. If we posit some goal to be achieved, then we can make conditional judgments of value with respect to that goal: such judgments are not unconditional, since they are independent of the moral value of the goal: a strategy may be a good strategy for committing a heinous crime. Any teleological system has inherent goals, and so can be said to benefit or to be harmed according to whether its goals are fostered or hindered: thus watering a plant does it good. But such conditional judgments of value carry no weight in our moral deliberations until they are connected up with judgments about intrinsic value, and these always depend ultimately on the well-being of individual human beings. Thus, though fostering the growth of a group may be good for the group, it is morally irrelevant unless it is also good for the members of the group.

Because of value-individualism, we can say that all goods are *individual* as far as their ground or justification is concerned. But this does not mean that goods cannot be called collective from some other point of view.

1. The *availability* of some goods is collective: it is impossible for the distribution of the benefit to be controlled voluntarily by anyone other than each potential beneficiary. (E.g., the general beneficial features of a society: that it is tolerant, cultivated, beautiful, prosperous, respectful of persons, etc.) The central feature of such goods is *non-excludability*. We can call them 'non-excludable goods' or 'public goods'.[12] If we wish to call them (or some subset of them) 'collective goods', it must be understood that this refers to their availability: perhaps 'collectively available goods' would be less confusing.

2. Some goods consist in a *collective activity*: the good is not some end-product of the activity, but the very activity itself. Such is the good of friendship, or of a game or a cultural activity in which one takes part. Though these may have some sort of external pay-off (such as the salary of a professional sportsman) the very participation in the activity is itself a good, and one which can be enjoyed only with others. These are what Réaume calls '*participatory goods*'.[13]

3. Some goods contribute to the well-being of individuals because of the latter's *membership* in a certain community or group. We could call them '*group* goods'. The most important of these will typically be collectively-available goods. E.g., if self-determination for a given ethnic group is a good, then it is collectively available to every member of that group: one could call it a group collective good. To the extent that membership in the group contributes to the individual's well-being, the existence and the activity of the group is itself a public and a participatory good, but only for the members of the group.

Recent discussions of the collective dimensions of certain goods have enriched our understanding of the ways in which things can be good and has countered a mistaken perception that all goods are enjoyed individually in the manner of consumer goods. But this heightened awareness of the collective dimensions of certain goods does not detract from the truth of value-individualism, that all goods are good to the extent that they contribute to the well-being of individual human beings. There may be collective dimensions to the value of communities—some of their benefits may be publicly available to their members and some of these benefits may be participatory—but the community has no value other than its contribution to successful lives of its members (and perhaps also of non-members).

Value-individualism is a not a thesis about the ontology of groups, but about the ground of value. Value-individualism does not imply ontological individualism, i.e., the view that groups are reducible to their members. Even if ontological individualism is false, it does not follow that the value of the group has any foundation other than the well-being of individuals, just as the fact that most entities in the universe are not identical with individual human beings does not entail that their value (if any) has some other ground than their contribution to the lives of individual human beings. The refutation of ontological individualism—on which communitarians and defenders of collective rights expend much energy—is relevant to the question whether groups can have rights of their own, not the question whether groups are morally important.

Value-individualism has consequences for the notion of an *interest*. Can there be collective interests? There is something which could be called the aggregate interest of a group, i.e., the sum of the interests of its members. It may be in the interest of a few members of a group that the value of the Canadian dollar stay high, and in the interest of most members of the group that it should fall; the aggregate interest is that it should fall. The concept of aggregate interest is applicable to any collection of individuals, and not just to communities or groups with a certain psychological or sociological unity. This may be what some people have in mind when they speak of collective interests, but for most users of the term it is surely something which is not reducible to a set of individual interests.

There are two concepts of a collective interest which meet this last condition. The first is that of an interest shared by members of a group in such a way that the interest is non-individualizable. The other is of an interest of a group over and above the interests of its members. The difference between the two concepts is that in the second case members of the group have individual interests which can conflict with the group interest, but not in the first.[14]

Réaume believes the interest in a participatory good is collective in the first sense because such goods can only be enjoyed with others: '. . . the individual has no interest as an individual in . . . these goods';[15] 'The interests of the group, because they are interests in the maintenance and development of a participatory good, cannot be reduced to a set of individualized interests'.[16] But this is unconvincing. Take the example of an orchestra. It is a good for its members, a participatory good. It is also a—non-participatory—good for members of the community who enjoy the music produced by the orchestra. (It also contributes to the existence of certain diffuse public goods, such as a heightened appreciation of music in the community.) Now, it seems uncontroversial that individual members of the community who enjoy good music have an interest (as individuals) in the existence of the orchestra. If so, it is hard to see why the actual (or potential) members of the orchestra do not have an interest *as individuals* in the existence of the orchestra. If the orchestra ceases to exist, their lives are impoverished, as are those of the members of the potential audience. The fact that the good is participatory for one class of persons and not for the other does not affect the nature of their interest in the good if its value consists in its contribution to the well-being of individuals. Whether this contribution is joint or separate is irrelevant to the fact that people's lives are enriched by it. Furthermore, it may cease to be in the interest of one of the members of the orchestra to belong to it, while the interest of the others remains unaffected: in that sense, the interest of one member is severable from that of the others.

The other concept of a collective interest is that of an interest of a group over and above that of the members of the group, such that the group interest might conflict with those of the members. Now it is clear that the aggregate interest of a group can conflict with the individual interest of some of its members. If a collective interest is to be more than a mere aggregate interest, it must be possible, in principle, for it to conflict with the interest of *most* of the members of the group. Does it make any sense to say that the group as such has an interest in subsisting and growing, even though it would be better for most of its members that the group cease to exist? Just as we can meaningfully make use of concepts such as 'good' and 'benefit' with respect to any assumed goal (and hence to any teleological system), it may be that we can do the same with the concept of an interest, and so speak of the interest of a plant in surviving and also of the interest of a group in surviving.[17] But the ascription of such an interest is what I have called 'conditional': it presupposes a postulated goal. It can become unconditional, and hence morally relevant, only if it is connected up with the interests of human beings. Consequently, there seems to be no way in which there could be a collective interest which is morally relevant: whatever interest there is in the survival of a group, it is a derivative interest, derived from the aggregate interest of its members in its survival (and perhaps, in certain cases, from the interest of non-members in its survival) . . .[18]

3. Rights

If we assume that communities are valuable and ought to be protected, the next issue is whether this protection can, or should, take the form of rights. This issue involves two sets of distinctions. The first is the distinction between moral and legal rights; they have separate existence-conditions, and it is an important thesis of this paper that the debate about collective rights is flawed by a failure to discuss each kind of right separately.[19] The second distinction is that between the conceptual question whether rights—moral or legal—can ever inhere in collectivities, and the substantive question whether the protection of communities requires that they be endowed with rights (moral or legal). Before addressing the conceptual question about collective rights, it is necessary to say something about the nature of rights.

Legal Rights. Law differs from ordinary life or moral discourse in that the truth of any legal statement depends ultimately on the acts of certain *authorities*. Whatever is legal or illegal is so because it was *made so* by legal authorities. The ultimate touchstone therefore of all legal statements (and of the meaning of legal terms) is therefore the acts (and especially the utterances) of these legal authorities. It is because courts have defined terms such as '*mens rea*' and 'malice' (as in 'malice aforethought') in a certain way that these terms have the meaning they have; whether this agrees with the moral meaning of 'guilty' or 'malice' is irrelevant to the legal meaning of the terms. No argument, philosophical or otherwise, can ever prevail against the pronouncement of the competent legal authority.

This is especially true of the term 'right'. The utterance of a legal authority (legislature, official, court) that a right is being conferred is conclusive evidence that a legal right has been conferred. Whatever legal authorities say is a legal right, is a legal right, whether this agrees with what philosophers would say about moral rights.[20] If a statute says that trees have rights, then trees have certain legal rights, whether we consider this to be morally defensible or even morally possible. The utterances of legal authorities constitute the raw data upon which our theory of legal rights must build. This theory must make room for all the rights and the kinds of rights which utterances of legal authorities say have been conferred.

Hohfeld,[21] following Salmond,[22] claimed that legal authorities used the term 'right' to refer to four different properties or statuses: the correlate of a legal duty ('claim'),[23] the absence of duty ('privilege' or 'liberty'), the capacity to change legal relations ('power'), and protection against a change in one's legal position ('immunity'). I believe Hohfeld's analysis accurately reflects the usage of legal authorities, and therefore is the correct analysis of legal rights, whether this agrees with what philosophers have to say about moral rights. Consequently, there are four different uses of the term 'right' in the law, and when we come to ask whether groups can have legal rights, we will in fact be asking four different questions.

Moral rights. In ordinary language, we use the term 'right' in at least two ways: we say that someone has (or does not have) the right *to* something (e.g., to life or to the repayment of a loan), and we also say that someone has (or does not have) the right to *do* such and such.[24] In the first instance, the existence of the right concerns the behaviour of someone other than the right-holder, since to say that I have a right to something is to say (at least) that someone has the duty to act in a certain way towards me. In the second instance, it is the right-holder's behaviour which is in question, and to say that he has a right to act in this way is to say (at least) that he is morally free to do so, i.e., that it is not wrong for him to do so. These two uses of the term 'right' correspond in part to Dworkin's 'strong' and 'weak' senses of 'right' respectively.[25] They also correspond to the first two uses of the term 'right' in Hohfeld's analysis of legal rights, and for that reason they are often called 'claim-rights' and 'liberty-rights' respectively.[26]

Most of the recent literature of rights focuses on the 'strong' sense of the term. The standard interpretation of a claim-right is that another person is under a duty to act in a certain way with respect to the 'thing' to which the first person has a right. Other philosophers think that there is more to it than that, e.g., Sumner favours the view that rights are 'packages of Hohfeldian normative advantages',[27] i.e., that they can imply duties, powers, immunities, etc. But whether a right-to-something merely implies a duty in others or is a package of normative advantages, the core idea of right-to language appears to be that of a good or interest protected by a duty: some things are considered to be goods, and to say that one has a right to such a thing is a way of saying that one's interest in such a thing is deserving of protection.[28]

The minimal form of this protection is a duty imposed on others to foster or protect the good in question; it may also involve a 'package of normative advantages' with respect to the good in question.

Not all goods or interests generate rights; it is only when there is a particularly important moral reason for protecting the good or interest in question that we speak of there being a right to it. This idea is expressed in Dworkin's well-known claim: 'Individual rights are political trumps held by individuals. Individuals have rights when, for some reason, a collective goal is not a sufficient justification for denying them what they wish, as individuals, to have or to do, or not a sufficient justification for imposing some loss or injury upon them'.[29] Or in Raz's claim that a right exists if an aspect of a single person's well-being is a sufficient reason for holding some other person(s) to be under a duty.[30] Political theories will differ in their estimate of the importance of certain goods or interests for human well-being, and therefore in their ascription of particular rights, but the central idea remains that of important interests of individuals protected against aggregative moral considerations. That is why Dworkin rejects the idea that society could have the right to do whatever is in the public benefit or the majority within society could have the right to preserve whatever environment it wishes to live in, since such 'rights' would simply annihilate any competing individual rights.[31]

Whatever weight is to be assigned to the public benefit or the protection of a social environment congenial to the majority, it cannot amount to a right.

Thus, not all goods (or interests) generate rights; only those which are central to the well-being of individuals do so. Goods (or interests) may generate duties (e.g., of protection) but these duties do not correlate with rights, unless there is some special moral reason for protecting these goods. There is an important difference here between legal and moral rights. In order to determine whether a certain legal right exists, one determines first whether the law has imposed a legal duty on someone, and then whether that duty can be interpreted as owed *to* somebody; since the law can create duties for all sorts of reasons, including relatively unimportant ones, one can have a legal right to something relatively unimportant, and the importance of this thing or of the reason for the legal duty do not tell us whether there is a right to it. On the other hand, a moral right implies a good (or interest) sufficiently important that it warrants protection by duties on others. Thus, there are no unimportant moral duties, and an estimate of the importance of the good or interest in question is central to the determination of the existence of a moral right. We have all sorts of legal rights which do not correlate with any moral right.

Since moral rights protect important goods and since things have value—

morally relevant value—only to the extent that they contribute to the well-being of beings whose life is of ultimate value (i.e., human beings), then only human beings can be the holders of moral rights. Suppose we agree that *A* has a moral duty not to kill *B*'s dog. If we want to speak of a moral right here, the right belongs not to the dog, but to *B*. Though it is the dog's life which is being protected by the duty and the right, the reason why it warrants protection is its contribution to *B*'s life, and so it is *B* who has a moral right that the dog shall live.

4. Collective Legal Rights

If the Hohfeldian analysis of legal rights is correct, then when we come to ask whether groups can have legal rights, we have to ask a number of different questions: whether they can be the beneficiaries of legal duties, or agents subject to legal duties (since a legal liberty is the absence of a legal duty), or holders of a legal power or of a legal immunity. Now, these questions are open to two interpretations. They may ask whether groups can have rights (in any of these senses) given the present state of the law of a given jurisdiction, or whether they could *ever* have any of these kinds of rights.

The answers to the first set of questions are to be found by what could be called legal analysis. The acts and utterances of legal authorities are examined in order to determine whether they have ever conferred legal rights (in any sense of the term) on groups, and also in order to determine whether the concepts implied in the acts of legal authorities could allow rights to be conferred on groups without modifying the concepts in question. There are at least two *loci classici* which are appealed to in support of the claim that Canadian law has conferred legal rights on groups: the reference in s. 93(1) of the *Constitution Act 1867* to 'any right or privilege with respect to denominational schools which any class of persons have by law in the province at the union', and the reference in s. 25 of the *Constitution Act 1982* to 'any aboriginal, treaty or other rights or freedoms that pertain to the aboriginal peoples of Canada'. Whether these authoritative legal texts (and any other less explicit ones) are most plausibly interpreted as conferring rights (or perhaps as acknowledging the conferral of rights) collectively on groups rather than distributively on the members of the groups is a question I leave to better legal minds. The answer will depend on such matters as the purposes thought to be pursued by the legislative authorities, the provision of legal means by which the rights are to be exercised or enforced collectively, and so on.[32]

Quite apart from the questions raised by these well-known constitutional texts, the law uses a variety of techniques to allow more than one person to share in a given legal status: there are rules about partnerships, about unincorporated societies, about joint tort-feasors; there are various forms of ownership such as joint tenancy and tenancy in common. In virtue of these rules, people can share certain legal powers, or can be jointly liable for misdeeds. But these various forms of joint status work well if the number of individuals involved is small. The law's favourite device for dealing with larger numbers is the corporation. This involves the creation of a fictitious being to which legal personality is granted. It follows from this that a corporation is not a collectivity from the point of view of the law. As many authors point to corporations (and states) as obvious instances of collectivities invested with legal rights[33] it is important to dispel the confusion between the two points of view from which a corporation (or a state) can be considered.

From the point of view of the sociologist, a corporation is a group of people engaged in certain tasks related to each other in certain ways. But from the point of view of the law, a corporation is a fictitious person separate from all the persons making up the sociological group. This fictitious person has legal rights and duties, but they are different from the legal rights and duties of the people who make up the corporation in the sociological sense. The fictitious person has assets and property, but they are not the assets and property of the members, either individually or collectively. The fictitious person can act, can buy and sell, enter into contracts and commit crimes and torts; this is possible only because the acts of certain natural persons within the corporation are considered by the law to be the acts of the corporation, and the legal effects of these acts are imputed to the fictitious person and not to the individuals who actually performed them.

Thus, a University is a corporation in the legal sense. If it refuses to pay me my salary, I cannot sue my faculty colleagues on the grounds that they are part of the University in the sociological sense. This is quite different from a case of joint liability (e.g. a partnership or joint tort-feasors) where I may sue any one of the individuals for the whole amount, and it is then up to that unfortunate individual to try and recover from the others. The fiction of incorporation shields the members of the corporation in the sociological sense from legal liability.[34]

To sum up then: in the sociological sense, a corporation is a group, but it cannot act collectively, own property, make contracts or commit torts. In the legal sense, a corporation can do all these things, but it is not a group: it is a single—fictitious—person, distinct from all the members of the group and from the group itself. Thus, in the following syllogism,

1. Corporations and states have legal rights,
2. Corporations and states are collective entities,
3. Therefore, [some] collective entities have legal rights,

premiss 1 above is false and premiss 2 is true from the sociological point of view, while from the legal point of view premiss 1 is true and 2 is false.

The comments just made about corporations also apply to the State. In one sense, a State can be understood as a community of persons: this we can call the sociological sense. But in the legal sense, the State is something different from the sum of the citizens. In a democratic regime, citizens take part in the functions of the State; it is then easy to equate the State with the totality of the citizens. But legally speaking, the State is a legal person distinct from its citizens. It helps to speak of the 'government' rather than the State (understanding 'government' to include all the functions of the State and not just the executive branch). In a dictatorship, a single person exercises all the legal powers of government: it is no less a government than a democratic regime with elected officials, public debates, the pressure of public opinion, etc. From the point of view of the law, government need not be collective in order to be government.

The same of course is true of lesser public bodies, such as a municipality. And if an Indian band has corporate status, then we must distinguish between the band as a community of persons and the legal corporation which bears the same name. Whatever legal rights the corporation possesses are not collective rights.

In the last few paragraphs, we have been examining the question whether the law as it presently stands allows groups to be holders of legal rights. This has to be distinguished from the question whether the law could *ever* vest legal rights in groups. The answer to the former question might be 'no', but the answer to the latter is surely 'yes' given the legal omnipotence of legal authorities. Whether the concept of a legal claim-right implied by the present state of Canadian law allows trees to have claim-rights, nothing prevents Canadian legal authorities from conferring such rights on trees (and thereby, perhaps, changing the concept of a legal claim-right). Of course, unless the conferral of rights on trees is to be otiose, the relevant authorities must provide for some way in which these rights are to be exercised or legally enforced (since trees cannot do so themselves). But the law has laid down similar provisions in the past for human beings who were unable to act on their own (such as infants and the mentally incompetent), and so there is nothing unusual about this. Thus, the answer to the conceptual question is that groups can have legal rights (in all the various senses of the word) if legal authorities decide to confer such rights on them.

This leaves us with the question whether it is desirable that legal authorities confer rights on communities. If we assume that communities are valuable and deserve protection, then this becomes a question of legal technique: it is a matter of deciding whether vesting legal rights in communities is the best way of achieving the desired goal.[35] To this question I offer no answer, except to point out that to create a legal corporation and to vest legal rights in it is not to create collective legal rights (if we understand by a collective right a right which vests in a collectivity as such).

5. Moral Rights and Communities

Thus far, we can say the following:

1. Religious, ethnic and linguistic communities can be important to the well-being of their members.
2. It is conceptually possible for legal rights to be vested in groups. Whether communities should be protected in this way remains an open question.

One way in which we could try to bridge the gap between 1 and 2 is through the concept of a collective moral right. If communities have moral rights to survival, this would seem to provide some justification for endowing them with legal rights. The question is then the logical possibility of the existence of collective moral rights. Now, we have also established the following points:

3. Moral rights (in the strong sense) protect goods or interests which are of fundamental importance to the well-being of individuals by imposing duties on others.
4. Individuals have moral rights against other members of society and against the government: they impose duties on others not to harm (or to promote) their fundamental interests, and on the government to provide for the protection of these interests by appropriate political and legal measures. While certain collective goals may have moral importance, and citizens may have moral duties to promote these collective goals, we do not say that the government (or the state, or 'society') has moral rights against the citizens (with respect to these collective goals).

Now, a religious or ethnic or linguistic community within a larger political society occupies an intermediate position between the individual and the whole of society (or the government): with respect to the latter, it stands in roughly the same position as the individual citizen, i.e., as part to whole, but in relation to its own members, it stands as whole to part. And so a useful way of determining the moral status of a community *vis-à-vis* the whole of society and *vis-à-vis* its own members is to consider the relative moral positions of individual citizens and society (or the government).

Consider first the community as a part of society. Individuals have moral rights against fellow citizens and against the government, moral rights which protect their fundamental interests. If the existence of that community is a good for its members (and so it is in their interest that it continue to exist), then it is possible that both the government and other members of society have duties to protect it, and the members of the community have a moral right to the continued existence of their community. (Whether such duties and rights exist is determined by the same considerations which determine whether any other duties or rights exist: the importance of the interest in question, etc.) The community itself can be said to have rights against members of society at large and against the government only if it has interests distinct from those of its members. I have argued that there are no such interests. And so, even if the government and individual members of society have certain duties with respect to the preservation of the community in question, these duties are owed to (and the rights are held by) the individual members of the community.

Consider now the community as a whole with respect to its components, the individual members of the community. We do not say that the whole of society has rights against its members, rights which could override the individual rights of the members. While there are important moral considerations such as the 'common good', they do not normally outweigh individual rights. On the other hand, other members of society may have rights which must be respected and which may impose limits on the pursuit of one's own rights, but these are rights of individuals, not of society. The same can be said of a community with respect to its members. If it has any valid moral claims, they cannot be such as to override (except perhaps in exceptional circumstances) the rights of its members. The only moral claims which might normally outweigh the rights of an individual member would be the rights of the other members. If a member wishes to leave the group, it is not a valid reason against his doing so that the group is now smaller than it was before. If there could ever be a valid moral reason against his doing so, it must be because reducing the size of group makes it more difficult for the rest of the members to benefit from the existence of the group.[36] But the reason is therefore one based on the interest of individuals in the continued existence of the group, not on any collective consideration.

Therefore, a community considered as a part of society does not have rights against society as a whole, and considered as a whole in relation to its members, it does not have rights against them. Either there are no rights (as society has no rights against its members), or the rights are those of individuals.

In the preceding paragraphs, I have been asking whether communities have the necessary features in order to be rights-holders. But perhaps I should go about it in another way, and ask whether certain rights have features which makes it impossible for them to be held by individuals, with the consequence that, if these rights are to exist, they must be held by collectivities. Three circumstances have been suggested as implying that a right cannot be individual: (1) when the object of the right is collective; (2) when the interest protected by the right is collective; (3) when the exercise of the right is collective.

The object of the right. The claim here is that if there is a right to an object *X* and this object is a collective good, then the right inheres in the collectivity rather than the individuals. This claim can take a number of forms.

A. 'If there is a right to a good which is a feature which only a group can have, then the right must belong to the group (and not to any individual within it)'. Garet makes such a claim: 'because there are certain things that only groups, and not individuals, can have—such as socialization processes . . . and kinship structures . . ., there are *a fortiori* certain things that only a group can hold a right to have'.[37] This claim has implausible consequences: since a fair system of criminal justice is something only a group, and not an individual, can have, it would follow that individuals cannot have any right to a fair system of criminal justice, and that no individual's right would be violated if the system were not fair.

B. 'If there is a right to a public (i.e., collectively available) good, then it cannot belong to an individual'. This is the view Raz argues for (though he is concerned with a sub-class of public goods, i.e., those which are inherently public).[38] As Réaume has pointed out,[39] the incompatibility Raz establishes between the public nature of the good and the individual nature of the subject of a right is a contingent one, and turns on the seriousness of the burden which others would have to bear to ensure the good. But this test applies to all goods: it could rule out an individual right to an individual good, just as it could allow in an individual right to a collective good. Raz believes that no individual right to a public good appears to pass the test.

C. Réaume's own principle is: 'If there is a right to a good which cannot be enjoyed by a single indiviual (i.e., a participatory good), it cannot belong to a single individual'.[40] Here the argument is not substantive but conceptual: since the interest in a participatory good is not individualizable, no one individual can be said to have an individual right to the good. I have criticized (in section 2 above) the claim there are no individual interests in participatory goods.

The interest served. This principle can take a strict and a loose form. The strict form is: 'Any right which is meant to serve the interests of a group as such (rather than the interest of its members) inheres in the group and not in its members'.[41] As it presupposes that there is a group interest over and above that of the members, this form of the principle is untenable. The looser form reads: 'Any right which is meant to serve the interests of individuals because of their membership in a certain group inheres in the group rather than the individuals'. It is perfectly possible for interests of members of groups (whether they be communities in the sense we have been using, or other identifiable groups, such as women, handicapped people, etc.) to generate rights, but there is no reason to think that the rights cannot inhere in the individuals. The interests are those of individuals, and so the rights are individual. A physically handicapped may have a moral right to special treatment, but it is the individual person who receives the treatment and not the whole group of physically handicapped persons.

The exercise of the right. In virtue of this principle, any right which cannot be exercised individually cannot inhere in individuals.[42] This principle is clearly too broad. The right to assemble and associate freely cannot be exercised by a single person, and yet it is an individual right. In the first place, single individuals can be prevented from assembling or associating with others; in such a case, that individual is the only one whose right is being violated (since no one else is being interfered with). Secondly, the collective right would have to be located in the totality of the citizenry, and there are good reasons not to ascribe rights to the whole of society.

Thus, there does not appear to be any category of right which cannot, in principle, be held by individuals. And so, the conclusion is that, conceptually, there are no moral rights which inhere in collective entities.

6. Alternative Concepts of a Collective Right

Throughout this paper, I have been taking the term 'collective right' in its literal sense, i.e., as a right which inheres in a group or collective entity rather than in an individual. I have concluded that morally speaking there can be no such rights. But there are perhaps other interesting ways of understanding the term. Terms such as 'civil rights' or 'contingent rights' serve to mark off the kind of right in question from other kinds of rights on the basis of some feature of the right other than the nature of the *subject* or *holder* of the right. The same might be possible with the term 'collective right'. Earlier, I discussed the claims that a right inheres in a group if its object or the interest served or its exercise were collective. We could reformulate this claim to say that a right will be called 'collective', not if it inheres in a group, but simply because its object or the interest served or its exercise is collective. In other words, the adjective 'collective' serves to identify a class of rights on the basis of some other feature than the nature of the holder.

But not all these suggested alternative definitions of a collective right are helpful or useful. For instance, there seems little point in calling every right which can only be exercised jointly with other people a collective right. For then even the right to get married would be a collective right, and this diverges too much from established usage. On the other hand, it would not be far-fetched to call a right to a collective good or a right designed to serve the interest of members of a group a collective right. This may be all that defenders of rights-inhering-in-collectivities are looking for.[43]

As a matter of fact, one of these alternative definitions has gained an important foothold in Canadian law. In his commentary on s. 27 of the *Canadian Charter of Rights and Freedoms*,[44] Tarnopolsky drew a distinction between rights which all individuals possess simply in virtue of being human beings ('individual rights' or 'human rights') and rights which individuals possess in virtue of their membership in a certain kind of group ('group' rights).[45] Individual rights are rights to be treated like any other human being; group rights are rights to be treated differently. Thus, both kinds of rights are held by individuals; the difference turns on whether the right is universal or limited to a group. Tarnopolsky added that individual rights require governments to refrain from interfering in people's lives, while group rights require them to provide services. The term 'group rights' also appears in the opinion of the majority judges (one of whom was Tarnopolsky) in *Reference re an Act to Amend the Education Act*;[46] in fact, the educational rights of Ontario Catholics are even called 'group collective rights'. The notion of a right reserved to members of a certain group is clearly a very different concept from that of a right inhering in a collective entity; to avoid confusion, one could recommend using the term 'group right' for the former and 'collective right' for the latter. Unfortunately, the French version of Tarnopolsky's Charter commentary translated 'group right' by 'droit collectif'.[47] Tarnopolsky's concept has been taken up both by legal writers[48] and by other judges.[49]

Thus, there are alternative concepts of a collective right available to those who accept my argument that moral rights cannot inhere in groups, and yet wish to keep the term. Nevertheless, it is doubtful whether a multiplicity of uses of the term 'collective right' is conductive to clear thinking.[50]

7. Conclusion

I have granted (1) that communities are important for the well-being of individuals, (2) that legal rights can vest in collective entities, and that there may be substantive reasons for endowing communities with them, and (3) that it is conceivable that members of communities could have individual moral rights to the preservation and protection of their communities. This may be all that defenders of collective rights are really looking for. My objection is to the claim that moral rights can inhere in collectivities as such, and the objection is grounded in the belief that the use of this terminology leads to confusion and to moral mistakes. As evidence of this last claim I offer the following brief survey of the current uses of the term 'collective rights' in the language debates in Quebec.

The term is used in three different, quite incompatible, ways, but all three arguments are meant to justify legislation restricting the use of English in Quebec.

1. The first argument is that, while members of the English-speaking minority in Quebec possess certain individual rights, the French-speaking majority also have rights, that these rights are collective, and that they override the individual rights of the English-speaking minority. This argument often takes the form of an appeal to 'democracy' and majority rule, to the 'collective right' of the majority to see its preferences prevail. In summary then, (1) it is the majority which is supposed to have these collective rights, (2) they are rights against the minority; and (3) they override the individual rights of this minority. This is nothing more than the claim that 'society' or 'the majority' has rights against minorities and individuals, and as such, is untenable.

2. Another argument conceives of French-speaking Quebeckers as a minority within Canada, and it is as a threatened minority that they possess collective rights to survival: these rights then justify a special status for Quebec within Canada, and ultimately legislation restricting the use of English within Quebec. Thus, (1) the collective rights belong to a minority; (2) they are rights against the majority within Canada (and secondarily against the anglophone minority within Quebec); and (3) they override the individual rights of Anglo-Quebeckers. That the preservation of the French language in Canada is an important thing (both for francophones and others) can readily be conceded; that this fact may create moral duties in governments and individuals to take appropriate measures is also a possibility; but that these duties correlate with rights of the francophone community is a mistake. Rights protect interests, and the relevant interests in this case are those of individual francophones whose life will be impoverished if French disappears or is weakened. If there are any rights to the preservation of a cultural environment in which French can flourish, the rights belong to those individuals who have an interest in the survival of French. (Some francophones may have no such interest.) The interests at stake here will inevitably conflict with other interests in society. The only way to

determine which interests are to prevail is to determine the importance of the interests for the lives of the individuals affected and the number of individuals affected. This means weighing individual interests (or rights) against individual interests (or rights). The weight of the interest in the preservation of the French language is no greater than that of the individuals concerned. The use of the term 'collective right' here is a rhetorical device intended to give greater weight to the francophone interests than would otherwise be the case.

3. The third argument is unusual, and was invoked by counsel for the Government of Quebec before the Quebec Superior Court in *Attorney-General of Quebec* v. *Quebec Association of Protestant School Boards.*[51] According to section 23 of the *Canadian Charter of Rights and Freedoms*, a parent has the right to have his or her children educated in the minority language of the province in which they reside, provided that parent was educated in that language in Canada. On the other hand, the Quebec Language Charter (usually referred to as Bill 101) allows this right only to those who were educated in English *in Quebec.* When Bill 101 was challenged on the grounds that it violated the constitutional rights of English-Canadians who now live in Quebec but were educated in English elsewhere in Canada, counsel for the Government of Quebec used the following argument to show that no constitutional rights were being violated.

Section 23 of the Canadian Charter guaranteeing the right to education in the minority language is intended to ensure the survival of the minority group in each province. Hence, it must not be understood as conferring on every person falling within its terms an individual right to education in the minority language, but rather on the whole minority group a collective right to sufficient educational establishments to ensure its survival. Certain members of the minority group can be deprived of the benefit in question (i.e., education in their language) without endangering the existence of the whole group. When this happens (and that is what Bill 101 does), the group's survival is not threatened, and so its right has not been violated, and consequently no violation of the Charter has occurred.

Thus, in this argument, (1) the collective right belongs to the anglophone minority in Quebec and not to Franco-Quebeckers, and (2) it affords less protection than would an individual right, thus allowing the francophone majority to deny access to English-language schooling to some anglophones. But this argument—taken as a moral argument rather than an attempt at interpreting a legal text to achieve a certain legal result—presupposes that there exists a collective interest which is something over and above the interests of the members of the group, and that the right in question is meant to serve that collective interest rather than the interests of the individuals. That is like arguing that there is some value in having clean air over and above the fact that human beings need clean air, and that this value is being preserved as long as there is some corner of the globe where clean air still exists, even if people are dying everywhere else from a lack of it. Here the term 'collective right' is being used, not to give greater weight to the interests it is meant to protect, but to give them *less* weight than would otherwise be the case.[52]

A concept which can be applied both to a majority group and to a minority group, and both to enhance and to diminish the weight of the interest of the group to which it is applied, and in each case with the end of defending the very same political goal, is hardly conducive to clear thinking.

Notes

1. P.A. French, 'The Corporation as a Moral Person' (1979) 16 *American Philosophical Quarterly* 297; 'Crowds and Corporations' (1982) 19 *American Philosophical Quarterly* 271; *Collective and Corporate Responsibility* (New York: Columbia Univ. Press, 1984); 'Corporate Moral Agency', in W.M. Hoffman & J.M. Moore, eds., *Business Ethics: Readings and Cases in Corporate Morality* (New York: McGraw-Hill, 1984) 163.
2. V. Held, *Rights and Goods* (Chicago and London: University of Chicago Press, 1984) at 255.
3. Ibid. at 244.
4. For instance, A. White, *Rights* (Oxford: Clarendon Press, 1984); J. Waldron, introduction to J. Waldron, ed., *Theories of Rights* (Oxford: Oxford University Press, 1984) 1; J. Nickel, *Making Sense of Human Rights* (Berkeley and Los Angeles: University of California Press, 1987); J.J. Thomson, *The Realm of Rights* (Cambridge, Mass. and London: Harvard University Press, 1990).
5. J. Raz, *The Morality of Freedom* (Oxford: Clarendon Press, 1986) at 207–09.
6. L.W. Sumner, *The Moral Foundation of Rights* (Oxford: Clarendon Press, 1987) at 209–11.
7. M. McDonald, 'Collective Rights and Tyranny' (1986) 56 *University of Ottawa Quarterly* 115 at 120.
8. M. McDonald, 'Should Communities Have Rights? Reflections on Liberal Individualism' *Canadian Journal of Law and Jurisprudence*, Vol 4/2 (1991) at 219. Others use a different terminology: see examples in D.M. Johnston, 'Native Rights as Collective Rights: A Question of Group Self-Preservation' (1989) 2/1 *Canadian Journal of Law and Jurisprudence* 19 at 22–24.
9. In certain countries, ethnicity can be not only an ethnological but also a legal concept. In Canada, there is at least one situation in which one can choose to change one's legal ethnicity: one can become legally an aboriginal by marrying an aboriginal.
10. The term 'value-individualism' here is to be distinguished from what Raz calls 'moral individualism' (Raz, *supra*, note 5 at 198), which is the view that

collective goods can have only instrumental value. See pp. 200–01 of *The Morality of Freedom* for the distinctions Raz draws between three different categories of intrinsically valuable things.

11. Cf. McDonald, *supra*, note 8 at 236: 'This, however should not lead us to think that collective autonomy is valuable only as a means of enhancing individual autonomy. On my view collective autonomy, like individual autonomy, is valuable in its own right; hence, one should not be valued simply as a means to the other.' Is this a criticism of what Raz calls moral individualism, or is McDonald attributing ultimate value to groups?
12. See Raz, *supra*, note 5 at 198–99; D. Réaume, 'Individuals, Groups, and Rights to Public Goods' (1988) 38 *University of Toronto Law Journal* 1.
13. Réaume, ibid. at 10.
14. Some authors use the term 'collective interest' to refer, not to an interest of a collective entity, but to an interest [of individuals] in a collective good. E.g., 'The interests that are protected are inherently collective or social interests, in particular the interest that human beings have in belonging to nurturing, identifying collective groups', McDonald, *supra*, note 8 at 229. This can be a source of confusion.
15. Réaume, *supra*, note 12 at 11.
16. Ibid. at 24.
17. Note that there are two ways in which a group can cease to exist: if its members cease to exist, and if its members cease to belong to it. The moral implications of each of these two ways are different, and so we should be wary of comparing the demise of a group to the demise of an individual.
18. M. McDonald (*supra*. note 7 at 120–21) makes the following point about the claim that the beneficiaries of the right to minority language education are the individuals who 'sit in the classroom':

    > That the children of a linguistic minority sit in the classroom is certainly true, but it does not of necessity follow that the benefits derived from their education accrue to them rather than to their linguistic collectivity. Imagine, for example, that these particular children would do better individually through linguistic assimilation than by stubbornly maintaining their mother tongue. Yet their assimilation might well involve the demise of that linguistic collectivity in that area or even the world.

    Is the suggestion here that the 'linguistic collectivity' can have an interest over and above the aggregate interest of all of its members? Or is it simply (and uncontroversially) that the interests of some of the members of the group can be at odds with the aggregate interest of the group?
19. Contributors to the debate often argue for 'collective rights' without qualification, or shift from moral rights to legal rights in the course of the discussion. For instance: M. McDonald, *supra*, note 8; D.M. Johnston, *supra*, note 8.
20. This does not mean that every utterance by a legal authority is authoritative; it is so only if it is not rejected by some higher authority.
21. W.N. Hohfeld, *Fundamental Legal Conceptions* (New Haven: Yale University Press, 1919).

22. In the 1902 edition of his *Jurisprudence*, Salmond had already drawn most of the Hohfeldian distinctions. Perhaps it is time he be given some credit for this important conceptual work.
23. It is one of the weaknesses of the Hohfeldian analysis of legal rights that all duties must correlate with rights and therefore must be owed *to* someone. The same failing characterizes Carignan's paper on collective rights, where the need to find correlates for all sorts of legal duties causes the author to ascribe all sorts of collective rights to society or to the state: P. Carignan, 'De la notion de droit collectif et de son application en matière scolaire au Québec' (1984) 18 *Revue juridique Thémis* 1.
24. The difference between the two expressions is even more striking in French, where there is a difference not only in the preposition but also in the use of the article: 'avoir droit *à* quelque chose', 'avoir *le* droit *de* faire ceci'.
25. R. Dworkin, *Taking Rights Seriously* (London: Duckworth, 1977) at 188ff.
26. Many philosophers reject the idea that 'the right to do something' is a bare liberty, and insist that for there to be a right, there must be something more, such as the protection of this liberty (i.e. a duty on others not to interfere). E.g., H.L.A. Hart 'Are There Any Natural Rights?' in J. Waldron, ed., *Theories of Rights* (Oxford: Oxford University Press, 1984) 77 at 87, n. 14; J. Feinberg, *Social Philosophy* (Englewood Cliffs: Prentice-Hall, 1973) at 58; Sumner, *supra*, note 6 at 35. If these claims are meant to reflect ordinary usage, then they are clearly wrong. It is certainly true that one can always *interpret* (often with considerable plausibility) a person's statement that 'A has the right to do x' to mean more than 'It is not wrong for A to do x', but it does not follow that this is what most people actually mean by it. And the best evidence that this is *not* what most people mean by it is that the *negative* use of the right-to-do terminology—i.e., the denial that *A* has the right to do *x*—cannot plausibly be interpreted as a statement about other people's duties: 'you have no right to do *x*' simply means 'it is wrong for you to do *x*'. If this is true of negative right-to-do statements, then it is highly likely that people sometimes use positive right-to-do statements in the same way. But of course philosophers who resist the idea that 'the right to do something' can be nothing more than a bare liberty, may not be appealing to ordinary usage, but proposing to reform it. They may believe that the only proper or useful or fruitful use of the term is to refer to a claim-right. Hohfeld of course was of the same opinion.
27. Sumner, *supra*, note 6 at 45.
28. It has been traditional to say that there are two interpretations of a right: for one school (the Will or Choice view), the core-idea of a right is that of a protected choice, while for the other (the Interests or Benefit view), the core-idea is that of a protected interest or benefit. These two views can be reconciled if one recognizes that autonomy or possibility of choice is a good, and that it is in one's interest (in the broad sense that it contributes to one's well-being) to have such a possibility.
29. Dworkin, *supra*, note 25 at xi.
30. Raz, *supra*, note 5 at 166.

31. Dworkin, *supra*, note 25 at 194.
32. The concept of a collective right can be used in two ways. One is to argue for certain political or legal initiatives: we could call this the justificatory use of the term, and it is characteristic of the moral context. The other use is to explain the present state of the law: legal authorities confer rights without bothering about the theoretical questions implied by their activity, and the theorist then arrives on the scene and explains what has gone on as the conferral of a right on a group collectively rather than on discrete individuals.
33. For instance, Carignan, *supra*, note 23; V. Van Dyke, 'Collective Entities and Moral Rights: Problems in Liberal Democratic Thought' (1982) 44 *Journal of Politics* 21.
34. It should also be pointed out that a legal corporation need not involve more than one person (at any one time): such is the corporation sole of English Law, which is usually an office held successively by a number of persons. Perhaps the corporation sole could be interpreted as a diachronous rather than a synchronous collectivity, i.e., a collectivity over time, but this does not appear to be very promising since the various members of this 'collectivity' never act collectively, and the interaction among the members goes in only one direction. Nevertheless, this example does raise interesting questions about the diachronous character of other collectivities.
35. Some of the debates about collective rights *sans plus* are no doubt about questions of legal technique, e.g., A. Buchanan, 'Assessing the Communitarian Critique of Liberalism' (1989) 99 *Ethics* 856 at 862ff, and McDonald, *supra*, note 8 at 229ff.
36. Whether such a consideration has sufficient moral force to outweigh an individual's autonomy rights is a substantive question I do not address.
37. R. Garet, 'Communality and Existence: The Rights of Groups' (1983) 56 *Southern California Law Review* 1001 at 1038.
38. Raz, *supra*, note 5 at 198–203.
39. Réaume, *supra*, note 12 at 6.
40. Ibid. at 7–13.
41. This is the principle explicitly argued for by counsel for the Quebec government in *Attorney-General of Quebec* v. *Quebec Association of Protestant School Boards*, discussed below at note 51. A number of legal writers define collective (or group) rights in terms of the protection of 'group interests' without indicating clearly whether they are using the latter term strictly or loosely: e.g., J.E. Magnet, 'Collective Rights, Cultural Autonomy and the Canadian State' (1986) 32 *McGill Law Journal* 170; F.L. Morton, 'Group Rights versus Individual Rights in the Charter: the Special Cases of Natives and the Quebecois' in N. Nevitte & A. Kornberg, eds., *Minorities and the Canadian State* (Oakville, Ont.: Mosaic Press, 1985) 71.
42. This principle has been invoked (or sometimes tacitly assumed) by a number of writers on collective legal rights: e.g., Y. Dinstein, 'Collective Human Rights of Peoples and Minorities' (1976) 25 *International and Comparative Law Quarterly* 102 at 115. On the other hand, it was rejected by Justice McIntyre

of the Supreme Court of Canada in *Reference re* Public Service Employee Relations Act, [1987] 1 S.C.R. 313 at 397.

43. Some of the legal writers cited earlier (note 41) as defending the view that a right inheres in a group if its purpose is to serve the interest of that group, may in fact have been defending the weaker thesis that a right will be called 'collective' if its purpose is to serve the interest of a group.
44. 'This Charter shall be interpreted in a manner consistent with the preservation and enhancement of the multicultural heritage of Canadians'.
45. W.S. Tarnopolsky, 'The Equality Rights', in W.S. Tarnopolsky & G.-A. Beaudoin, eds., *The Canadian Charter of Rights and Freedoms: Commentary* (Toronto: Carswell, 1982) 395 at 437–39.
46. (1986) 53 O.R. (2nd) 513.
47. G.-A. Beaudoin & W.S. Tarnopolsky, eds., *La charte canadienne des droits et libertés* (Montréal: Wilson et Lafleur/Sorej, 1982) at 553.
48. E.g., M. Lebel, 'Les droits linguistiques et la Charte canadienne des droits et libertés' (1983) 18 *Les cahiers de l' ACFAS* 31 at 48.
49. In *Edwards Books and Art Ltd.* v. *the Queen*, [1986] 2 S.C.R. 713 at 808–9, Justice Wilson of the Supreme Court of Canada invokes Tarnopolsky's concept when she states that, in allowing merchants who close on Saturday for religious reasons to open on Sunday, the Ontario statute prohibiting Sunday shopping grants a group right to the merchants who keep the Sabbath on Saturday.
50. Carignan, *supra*, note 23, has a particularly luxuriant classification of collective [legal] rights, which commits most of the sins denounced in the present paper:
    1. Rights vested in collective entities:
        A. In the whole of society
        B. In groups within society:
            1. Incorporated groups
            2. Unincorporated groups
        C. In groups through their members.
    2. Rights which can be implemented only collectively:
        A. Which can be exercised only collectively
        B. Which can be enforced only collectively.
51. [1982] C.S. 673; 140 D.L.R. (3rd) 33.
52. This 'weak' concept of a collective right is completely at odds with the more usual concept invoked in debates about language. McDonald appears not to have noticed the fact since he cites Mr. Justice Deschênes' criticism of this concept as an instance of 'outright hostility to all group rights': McDonald, *supra*, note 8 at 226.

10 Are There Any Cultural Rights?

CHANDRAN KUKATHAS

I

I shall advance the thesis that if there are any moral rights at all, it follows that there is at least one natural right, the equal right of all men to be free.

—H.L.A. Hart, 'Are There Any Natural Rights?'

At least since the American civil rights movement, many people have become more aware of the harm suffered by ethnic or cultural minorities laboring under discriminatory practices or inequities which have developed over decades, if not centuries. The conditions of the American black and the American Indian, the Canadian Inuit, the New Zealand Maori, and the Australian Aborigine have been the subject of various administrative and legislative initiatives. And the political claims of the Basques in Spain, the French Canadians in Canada, and the Tamils in Sri Lanka have been gaining wider prominence. In more recent times, however, one particular concern has begun to receive greater attention: the cultural health of some of these ethnic minorities. Increasingly, the impact of the larger society on the cultural integrity and durability of ethnic minorities has come to be a matter of debate, if not concern. And to a significant extent, it is cultural integrity which now forms the basis of the moral claims, and political demands, advanced by these minorities. In particular, some of those who describe themselves as 'indigenous peoples' swamped by settler cultures—Polynesian Fijians, Maori New Zealanders, and American Indians, for

I wish to thank audiences at Bowling Green State University and the Federalist Society of the University of Toledo Law School where versions of this essay were first read. For helpful comments and suggestions I am grateful to Richard Mulgan, Philip Pettit, Brian Beddie, John Gray, Stephen Macedo, Emilio Pacheco, and Robert Goodin. I am especially indebted to William Maley for his criticism and advice. I would like to acknowledge the generous support of the Institute for Humane Studies through its F. Leroy Hill Fellowship. Thanks are also due to the Social Philosophy and Policy Center at Bowling Green State University for providing the collegial but interruption-free environment in which work on this essay was completed.

Chandran Kukathas, 'Are There Any Cultural Rights?', *Political Theory*, Vol. 20 (1992), pp. 105–39 (minus 109, 129–32). Reprinted by permission of Sage Publications, Inc.

example—call not simply for improvements in their economic conditions but for protection of their cultural practices.

These developments have not been without significance for political theory, and liberal theory in particular. In the light of this modern 'ethnic revival,' many have come to question the relevance of liberal political thinking. Liberalism, with its stubborn insistence on viewing society in individualist terms, is said to be incapable of coping with the phenomena of group loyalty and cultural reassertion. The disdain for liberal thinking is forcefully expressed by Anthony Smith in the introduction to his study of *The Ethnic Revival*:

> The dissolution of ethnicity. The transcendence of nationalism. The internationalisation of culture. These have been the dreams, and expectation, of liberals and rationalists in practically every country, and in practically every country they have been confounded and disappointed. . . . Today the cosmopolitan ideals are in decline and rationalist expectations have withered. Today, liberals and socialists alike must work for, and with, the nation state and its increasingly ethnic culture, or remain voices in the wilderness.[1]

Much of this criticism has emerged in the wake of a growing conviction that there is no prospect of individuals abandoning their particular loyalties for a universalist humanism. Thus one has to accept the conclusion 'well known to great masses of people for a long time but not to generations of elite humanist scholars and strivers for human perfectibility: namely, that our tribal separatenesses are here to stay. . . . They are not about to dissolve into any new, larger human order.'[2] The problem with liberalism, it is held, is that its individualist outlook leads it to neglect those communal interests which are so much more important than liberals recognize. Vernon Van Dyke, for example, has argued in a series of papers that 'the liberal emphasis on the individual precludes a proper theory of the state, which suggests in principle that liberalism cannot be trusted to deal adequately with the question of status and rights for ethnic communities.'[3] Frances Svensson, drawing on Van Dyke's work, similarly complains that 'liberal democratic theory, in its almost exclusive emphasis on individual rights and its neglect of communal interests, has created a context in which no balance has been possible between the claims of individuals and multidimensional communities.'[4]

Reservations about liberalism have been expressed by its friends as much as by its detractors. John Gray, for example, suggests that liberal thinking makes a fatal error in regarding people not as 'Sikhs or Poles, Palestinians or Israelis, Blacks or Wasps, but merely persons, rights-bearing (and, doubtless also, gender-neutral) ciphers.'[5] Indeed, he maintains that 'the sustaining myths of liberal modernity—myths of global progress, of fundamental rights and of a secular movement to a universal civilization—cannot be maintained even as useful fictions in the intellectual and political context of the last decade of our century.'[6] For Gray, this means that we should abandon liberalism and look to other, more coherent ways of theorizing.

A somewhat different response comes from Will Kymlicka in his important study, *Liberalism, Community, and Culture*. Kymlicka too concedes that liberalism, 'as commonly interpreted . . . gives no independent weight to our cultural membership, and hence demands equal rights of citizenship, regardless of the consequences for the existence of minority cultures.'[7] Yet he proposes to reinterpret the liberal tradition, to show that a respect for minority rights is indeed compatible with liberal equality: 'Post-war liberal clichés need to be rethought, for they misrepresent the issue, and the liberal tradition itself.'[8]

In this essay, I propose to take issue with these writers. I shall argue that while we are right to be concerned about the cultural health of minority communities, this gives us insufficient reason to abandon, modify, or reinterpret liberalism. Far from being indifferent to the claims of minorities, liberalism puts concern for minorities at the forefront. Its very emphasis on *individual* rights or *individual* liberty bespeaks not hostility to the interests of communities but wariness of the power of the majority over minorities. There is thus no need to look for alternatives to liberalism or to jettison the individualism that lies at its heart. We need, rather, to reassert the fundamental importance of individual liberty or individual rights and question the idea that cultural minorities have collective rights.

It ought, however, to be emphasized that to take this view is not to imply that groups or cultural communities do not have interests or, indeed, that particular peoples cannot have legitimate grievances which need to be addressed as a matter of justice. The primary thesis advanced here is not that groups do not matter but rather that there is no need to depart from the liberal language of *individual* rights to do justice to them.

To defend this thesis, I begin, in the next section, to put the case for the liberal standpoint, taking issue with those who challenge its individualist premises. The third section then turns to develop my case in response to those who wish to see liberal theory modified to take cultural claims into consideration, after which the fourth section takes on the question of what such a view amounts to and attempts to account for the place of cultural minorities in liberal society. The fifth section reviews various important objections before the conclusions of this essay are given a final formulation.

II

Liberal political theories, it is widely held, assume or argue that the good society is one which is not governed by particular common ends or goals but provides the framework of rights or liberties or duties within which people may pursue their various ends, individually or cooperatively. It is a society governed by law and, as such, is regulated by right principles. These are principles of justice, which do not themselves presuppose the rightness or betterness of any particular way of life. Although liberals are not commonly skeptics about questions about the good life, they emphasize that no one should be forced to accept any particular ideal of the good life. The liberal response to the multiplicity of religious and moral traditions in modern society has thus been to advocate toleration, as far as possible, of different ways of living.

This response has received a variety of justifications from liberal thinkers, who have founded their conclusions on claims of natural right or arguments about original contracts or calculations of utility. Despite this variety, there is a core of common assumptions to be found in liberal arguments.[9] First, liberal theory is *individualist* in asserting or assuming the moral primacy of the person against the claims of any social collectivity; second, it is *egalitarian* because it confers on all such individuals 'the same moral status and denies the relevance to legal or political order of differences in moral worth among human beings'; and third, it is *universalist* because it affirms the moral unity of the human species and accords 'a secondary importance to specific historic associations and cultural forms.'

These characteristically liberal assumptions—particularly the first and third—have long been the targets of criticism from communitarian quarters. Typically, these criticisms have made the point that liberalism's individualist premises are unacceptable because any conception of an individual presupposes some view of society and community since individuals are social beings. This objection has acquired a more distinctive flavor, however, in an argument that groups occupy an intermediate position between the individual and the state and deserve special moral recognition. Vernon Van Dyke in particular has objected that 'modern liberal political theorists focus on relations between the individual and the state as if no groups count that are intermediate.'[10] He takes to task for this neglect a variety of contemporary theorists from John Plamenatz and John Rawls to Carole Pateman and Hanna Pitkin.[11] Making the point that, as a matter of political fact, ethnic groups of all sorts are indeed accorded 'rights' in many countries, Van Dyke offers a number of reasons why it is important that, 'alongside the principle that individuals are right-and-duty-bearing units, a comparable principle should be accepted for the benefit of ethnic communities.' . . .[12]

Van Dyke, like many others, is right to say that liberal theory subordinates the claims of the community to those of the individual. But subordination is not neglect. What needs to be established now is that liberal theory does have good reason for elevating the individual, yet does not go so far as to disparage the interests of communities—interests which cannot be reduced to the interests of individuals. That is the task of the rest of this section. It ought now to be made clear, however, that in advancing the arguments that follow I am in fact not only defending liberal theory *simpliciter* but developing *a particular* liberal theory.

Contrary to a commonly held and often expressed view, liberal theory does not begin with the assumption that the world is made up of isolated, atomistic individuals. (Even the most individualistic of thinkers, Hobbes, was moved to put forward his political theories by the actions of particular groups or interests in society—the warring factions during the upheavals of the 1640s.) Individuals invariably find themselves members of groups or associations which not only influence their conduct but also shape their loyalties and their sense of identity. There is no reason for any liberal theorist to deny this. What has to be denied, however, is the proposition that fundamental moral claims are to be attached to such groups and that the terms of political association must be established with these particular claims in mind.

The primary reason for rejecting the idea of group claims as the basis of moral and political settlements is that groups are not fixed and unchanging entities in the moral and political universe. Groups are constantly forming and dissolving in response to political and institutional circumstances. Groups or cultural communities do not exist prior to or independently of legal and political institutions but are themselves given shape by those institutions.[13] As Donald Horowitz has put it, 'Ethnic identity is not static; it changes with the environment.'[14]

The importance of this point cannot be too strongly emphasized. Scholars, like Anthony Smith, who are critical of liberalism have insisted on 'the "naturalness" of ethnicity' and criticize recent scholarship for starting 'from the premiss that nations and nationalism are peculiarly modern phenomena, and that there is nothing "natural" or inborn about national loyalties and characteristics.'[15] Yet the work of Horowitz shows quite clearly that this criticism is mistaken. There is an 'interactive quality' to the variables related to group identity: culture, boundaries, conflict, and the policy outcomes of conflict.[16] Ethnic identity has a contextual character: Group boundaries 'tend to shift with the political context.'[17]

For example, in the former Indian state of Madras, cleavages within the Telugu population were not very important. Yet as soon as a separate Telugu-speaking state was carved out of Madras, Telugu subgroups quickly emerged as political entities. Similarly, many ethnic groups were the product of subgroup amalgamation in the colonial period in Asia and Africa. The Malays in Malaysia, for example, emerged as a 'distinct' group only after colonialists created specific territories out of loose clusters of villages and regions; much the same can be said for the Ibo in Nigeria and the Moro in the Philippines. Indeed, Horowitz suggests that some 'such groups were "artificial" creations of colonial authorities and missionaries, who catalyzed the slow merger of related peoples into coherent ethnic entities. They did this by the way they categorized those they encountered and by the incentives they established to consummate the amalgamation.'[18] Of course, it was not only colonialism that shaped these identities. The Malays, for instance, despite the fact that their numbers were drawn from island peoples as far away as Sumatra, Sulawesi, Borneo, and Java, as well as Malaya, developed their highly cohesive identity partly because of the appearance of *Chinese* immigrants.[19] But the important point remains: Group formation is the product of environmental influences, and among these environmental factors are political institutions.

This is not to say that culture is unimportant, but it is not fundamental, even for the constitution of group identity. Legal rights can themselves be important determinants. In the late 1960s in Assam, Bengali Muslims found it advantageous to declare Assamese their language in part to become eligible for land reserved for indigenes.[20] As Horowitz observes, 'Culture is important in the making of ethnic groups, but it is more important for providing *post facto* content to group identity than it is for providing some ineluctable prerequisite for an identity to come into being.'[21]

Now, the causes of group formation do not render group interests illegitimate. But they do point to why it may not be appropriate to try to answer questions about what political institutions are defensible by appealing to the interests of existing groups. Often, those interests exist, or take their particular shape, only because of certain historical circumstances or because particular political institutions prevail and not because they are a part of some natural order. There is no more reason to see particular interests as fixed than there is to see particular political arrangements as immutable. Liberal political theories thus typically take as their starting points the existence of a plurality of interests—often competing, if not in actual conflict—and ask how or by what principles of political order might adjudicate between or accommodate competing claims. But recognizing that many interests, cultural or otherwise, might have well-founded claims, liberal theory tries to look at the problem of divining political rules from a standpoint which owes its allegiance to no particular interest—past, current, or prospective.

For this reason, liberal theory looks at fundamental political questions from the perspective of the individual rather than that of the group or culture or community. Such collectives matter only because they are essential for the well-being of the individual. If the condition of the community or the culture made no difference to the life of any individual, then the condition of the collective would not matter.[22] None of this implies that there is such a thing as 'individual' in the abstract. Individuals do not exist in the abstract any more than interests do. But interests *matter* only because individuals do. Thus, while groups or cultures or communities may have a character or nature which is not reducible to the nature of the individuals who inhabit them, their moral claims have weight only to the extent that this bears on the lives of actual individuals, now or in the future.[23] Liberal political theories rest on the assumption that while the interests given expression in groups, cultural communities, or other such collectives do matter, they matter ultimately only to the extent that they affect actual individuals.

So groups or communities have no special moral primacy in virtue of some natural priority. They are mutable historical formations—associations of individuals—whose claims are open to ethical evaluation. And any ethical evaluation must, ultimately, consider how actual individuals have been or might be affected, rather than the interests of the group in the abstract. It is not acceptable to evaluate or choose political institutions or to establish legal rights on the basis of the claims or interests of cultural communities because those very institutions or rights will profoundly affect the kinds of cultural communities individuals decide to perpetuate or to form. Groups may generate entitlements, but entitlements can also create groups. Historical priority does not confer on a community the right to continued existence (even though it may be the source of other valid claims—to which I return later).

This last (unqualified) sentence would be challenged immediately by a defender of cultural rights, raising the following objection. If institutions or legal rights are to be established, why not choose conservatively and protect existing cultural communities? Granted that the choice of laws and institutions can indeed alter the composition of groups, is there not a case for establishing rights that protect actual cultural communities on which individuals depend? After all, the breakdown or disintegration of such communities, bringing social dislocation and anomie, is scarcely a good—for group or individual. So, there appears to be good reason to recognize the right of groups to guard themselves against the intrusions of the outside world and to determine their own destiny.

Yet this case is not as straightforward as it appears, for reasons that have much to do with the mutable nature of cultural communities. In recognizing this, it is important to note not only that group composition changes over time but that most groups are not homogeneous at any given moment. Within cultural communities there may be important differences and conflicts of interest. Internal divisions can take two forms: divisions between subgroups within the larger community and divisions between elites and masses, which may have quite different interests. Differences of interest between subgroups might be observed, for example, in the experiences of groups such as the Yoruba of Nigeria, the Lozi of Zambia, and the Bakongo of Zaire, Angola, and Congo (Brazzaville). In each of these cases, the group was formed in response to internal differentiation among subgroups, many of whom fought each other. It was only in opposition to colonialism that their leaders sought to minimize subgroup cultural differences, standardize language, and take other measures to assimilate the many interests into a united association with political strength. Although many of these movements of assimilation met with great success, subgroup identities have remained, and in some cases, subgroup conflict persists.[24]

The more important conflict of interest within groups, however, is that between the masses and elites. This conflict is starkly revealed within ethnic cultural communities confronted by modernization. Under these circumstances, elites have 'distinctive interests that relate to modernity: good jobs, urban amenities, access to schools, travel, prestige.'[25] In some cases, there is no doubt that elites use their advantages to further their personal ends, in some cases manipulating ethnic sentiment in pursuit of their career aspirations.[26] In others, however, matters are more complex. Aboriginal representatives of the National Aboriginal Consultative Committee established by the Australian Commonwealth government were often suspected by their people of succumbing to 'white' patronage, even when they were innocent.[27] To some extent this was the product of ignorance: In many cases, Aborigines did not understand agreements entered into on their behalf by their 'representatives.' And it is not always easy for those uninitiated into the ways of bureaucracies to understand how difficult it is to avoid being 'swallowed up.'[28] Yet these cases also reveal the real gap that sometimes exists between the interests of the elite and the interests of the mass of group members.

This poses a particular dilemma for cultural minorities seeking self-determination within the larger society and wishing to preserve their cultural integrity. To be self-determining in the larger society requires a measure of political power, and this means becoming involved in the political processes of the nation. Elites from minority cultures must invariably mix with the educated elites from other minorities and from the dominant society. But in this process, the interests of the minority elite become further removed from those of their cultural community. If their cultural community itself undergoes changes, however, the prospect of preserving cultural integrity diminishes.

The cultural community and its elite may, of course, share a common interest in the symbolic standing of the group as a whole. If both gain from the growth of collective self-esteem, then the masses might welcome the prestige derived from the success of wealthier or higher-status group members. One Malay leader has, in fact, defended policies of preferential treatment in these terms, arguing that although the benefits fall disproportionately to the Malay elite, the masses, knowing of Malay group success, enjoy a vicarious satisfaction more highly prized than personal material gain.[29] Yet while it may indeed be the case that 'the distribution of prestige is a real and rational object of conflict'[30] among ethnic groups, securing this goal can serve to heighten the divisions within the community. Indeed, it could be argued that the masses may be more interested in jobs and economic progress whereas the elites, who already enjoy these material benefits, have a greater interest in symbolic traditionalism.[31]

From a liberal point of view, the divided nature of cultural communities strengthens the case for not thinking in terms of cultural rights. Cultural groups are not undifferentiated wholes but associations of individuals with interests that differ to varying extents. So within such minorities are to be found other, smaller minorities. To regard the wider group as the bearer of cultural rights is to affirm the existing structures and therefore to favor existing majorities. Minorities within a cultural community which might over time have formed quite different coalitions with other interests may find that their interests are to a significant degree subject to control by the larger rights-bearing community. More important, it restricts the opportunity of minorities within the group to reshape the cultural community, whether directly or through its interaction with those outside the group. Liberal theory is generally concerned to avoid entrenching majorities or creating permanent minorities.

To say this is to recognize that it is not always the case that the entire cultural community is eager, or even willing, to preserve cultural integrity at any price. Often, individuals or groups within the community wish to take advantage of opportunities which have produced the unintended consequence of changing the character of the community. Thus, for example, while Aboriginal elites have argued that land rights granted to Aborigines as a people ought to reserve those lands for Aboriginal communities in perpetuity, some individual Aborigines argue that those communities should be free to use the land as an economic asset to be bought and sold.[32] Here, there is undeniably a conflict between the interests of the cultural community as a whole—at least as conceived by elites within it—and those of (groups of) individual members. Liberal theory does not look to give precedence to the views of those who claim to speak in the interests of the cultural community as a whole, even if they are in the majority, because the interests of the minority cannot be discounted.

In the end, liberalism views cultural communities more like private associations or, to use a slightly different metaphor, electoral majorities. Both are the product of a multitude of factors, and neither need be especially enduring, although they can be. The possibility that they might be, however, does not justify entrenching the interests they manifest.

One significant objection raised here is that this individualist view is fundamentally an assimilationist one which is destructive of minority cultures because it ignores their need for special protection. The most forceful assertion of this criticism of liberalism has been Van Dyke's, and it is worth expounding more fully. Liberal doctrine, he argues, is at least integrationist if not assimilationist and finds permanent communalism unacceptable. The trouble is, permanent communalism may be exactly what some groups, notably 'indigenous peoples,' actually want.[33] Liberal 'ideology,' however, is inclined to 'break up reservations, destroy tribal relations, settle Indians on their own homesteads, incorporate them into the national life, and deal with them not as nations or tribes or bands but as individual citizens,' despite the fact that 'many Indians do not want to be integrated into mainstream society.'[34] Van Dyke quotes from the manifesto of the Indians who made the Longest Walk (1978): '"How do we convince the U.S. government to simply leave us alone to live according to our ways of life? . . . We have the right to educate our children to our ways of life. . . . We have the right to be a people. These are inherent rights. . . . Our fight today is to survive as a people."'[35]

All this leaves Van Dyke in no doubt that the individualist perspective, as he characterizes it, 'gives an advantage to members of the dominant group' who find it easier to establish rapport with those with influence and power and 'tend to obtain disproportionate representation in the various elites.'[36] (Elite members co-opted from minorities, he adds, tend not to be 'representative,' often because they have abandoned the culture from which they sprang.[37]) Moreover, individualism, 'combined with the usual stress on person merit,' tends to be destructive of minority cultures because the schools are likely to promote the dominant culture and undermine all others. The minority person is likely to find his culture disparaged: 'The whole attitude is an attack on the existence of the group and the self-respect of its members. It means oppression, and perhaps exploitation as well.'[38]

But this outlook is mistaken both in its characterization of the liberal view, and in its assertions about liberalism's implications. There is no reason why liberals should press for assimilation or integration of cultures or find communalism unacceptable. Nor is there a good case, from a liberal point of view, for destroying tribal communities to force Indians to enter the mainstream of national life. This is not to say that no liberal thinker has defended views which might be used to justify such intentions, but there is no good reason to suppose that any liberal must go along with them. On the contrary, there is every reason, from a liberal point of view, to accede to the Indians request to 'leave us alone to live according to our ways of life.' What follows is the outline of a liberal point of view which does precisely this, without invoking claims about group rights.

From a liberal point of view the Indians' wish to live according to the practices of their own cultural communities has to be respected not because the culture has the right to be preserved but because individuals should be free to associate: to form communities and to live by the terms of those associations. A corollary of this is that the individual should be free to dissociate from such communities. If there are any fundamental rights, then there is at least one right which is of crucial importance: the right of the individual to leave a community or association by the terms of which he or she no longer wishes to live. Cultural communities should, then, be looked on in this way: as associations of individuals whose freedom to live according to communal practices each finds acceptable is of fundamental importance.

This view appears to place great weight on the nature of cultural communities as *voluntary* associations. To some extent, this is so—but to a very small extent. Most cultural communities are not voluntary associations in any strong sense. Membership is usually determined by birth rather than by deliberate choice, and in many cases, there is no option of entry for those born outside—even though, as we have seen, groups will seek to redefine the boundaries of membership (and of group identity) when circumstances are propitious. Cultural communities may be regarded as voluntary associations to the extent that members recognize as legitimate the terms of association and the authority that upholds them. All that is necessary as evidence of such recognition is the fact that members choose not to leave. Recognition in these austere terms would, of course, be meaningless without the individual having one important right against the community: the right to be free to leave. That has to be the individual's fundamental right; it is also his only fundamental right, all other rights being either derivative of this right, or rights granted by the community.[39]

This view of the rights of the individual gives a great deal of authority to cultural communities. It imposes no requirement on those communities to be communities of any particular kind. It does not require that they become in any strong sense 'assimilated,' or even 'integrated' into the mainstream of modern society. It in no sense requires that they be liberal societies; they may indeed be quite illiberal. There is thus no justification for breaking up such cultural communities by, for example, driving tribes off their lands or forcibly resettling them. The wider society has no right to require particular standards or systems of education within such cultural groups or to force their schools to promote the dominant culture. If members of a cultural community wish to continue to live by their beliefs, the outside community has no right to intervene to prevent those members acting within their rights.

Yet at the same time, this view does not give the cultural community any fundamental right. The basis of the community's authority is not any right of the culture to perpetuation, or even existence, but the acquiescence of its members. Those members have the inalienable right to leave—to renounce membership of—the community. This right is more potent than it might at first appear because it implies that in many circumstances, individuals within the cultural community are free to leave *together or in association with others* and to reconstitute the community under modified terms of association. Cultural communities without the broad support or commitment of their members will thus wither; yet communities within which there are only isolated pockets of discontent with its cultural norms might well prevail.

This version of the liberal individualist standpoint seeks, then, to strike a balance between the claims of the individual and the interests of the community. It recognizes the existence of cultural groups but denies that they are in any sense 'natural,' regarding them rather as associations of individuals drawn together by history and circumstance. As such, they have certain acquired interests, but these are in no way equivalent to the interests of all their members. The mutability of such communities reflects their nature as associations of individuals with different interests. The interests of the community as a whole and the interests of particular (groups of) individuals within may well conflict. The liberal individualist view outlined here, by regarding the group as having its moral basis in the acquiescence of individuals with its cultural norms, rejects the idea that the group as such has any right to self-preservation or perpetuation. Nonetheless, by seeing the right of association as fundamental, it gives considerable power to the group, denying others the right to intervene in its practices—whether in the name of liberalism or any other moral ideal.

But the thesis, as it stands, will be subjected to numerous objections from defenders of cultural rights and liberals alike and needs to be refined and given more careful expression. Some especially prominent criticisms are addressed in the following sections.

III

Criticisms of the standpoint expounded here come from two general directions: from those who think culture has been given too little recognition and from those who think it has been given too much. These objections have to be met. Somewhat fortuitously, they both appear in Will Kymlicka's recent study, *Liberalism, Community, and Culture,* that argues for a liberalism which gives special weight to claims of cultural membership. So I shall try to meet the criticisms in question by addressing some of the arguments advanced in Kymlicka's work.

Kymlicka maintains that liberals have been wrong to regard the idea of collective rights for minority cultures as theoretically incoherent and practically dangerous.[40] In his view, liberals can and should embrace the idea of cultural rights without denying liberalism's individualist premises—individualist premises of the kind I discussed earlier.[41] The right way to look at the issue, he suggests, is not to see a conflict between individual rights and group rights, or 'respect for the individual' and 'respect for the group.' The real conflict, which does indeed pose a dilemma, is between two kinds of respect for the individual. Individuals might be due respect as members of a distinct cultural community—in which case 'we must recognize the legitimacy of claims made by them for the protection of that culture'—or they might be due respect as citizens of the common political community—in which case 'we must recognize the importance of being able to claim the rights of equal citizenship.'[42] The demands of citizenship and the demands of cultural membership can pull in different directions because 'differential citizenship rights may be needed to protect a cultural community from unwanted disintegration.'[43] For Kymlicka, the solution to this dilemma lies not in rejecting liberalism but in reconciling minority rights with 'liberal equality,' thereby providing an individualist justification of differential (cultural) rights.[44] And this means showing 'that membership in a cultural community may be a relevant criterion for distributing the benefits and burdens which are the concern of a liberal theory of justice.'[45]

In trying to show this, Kymlicka in effect mounts a case for thinking that culture has been given too little recognition in liberal theorizing. Certainly, the protection he wishes to give cultural communities exceeds that given them by the liberal theory advanced earlier in this essay. So the two considerations on which he defends cultural rights call for careful examination. The first consideration is the value of culture and cultural membership. Culture matters, Kymlicka argues, because the range of options open to us to choose is determined by our cultural heritage. It is within cultures, through examples and stories, that we learn about the kinds of life it is possible to lead, and we 'decide how to lead our lives by situating ourselves in these cultural narratives, by adopting roles that have struck us as worthwhile ones, as ones worth living (which may, of course, include the roles we were brought up to occupy).'[46] Cultural structures are thus important because they provide 'the context of choice.'[47] The fundamental reason for supporting cultural membership is 'that it allows for meaningful individual choice.'[48] Liberals should be concerned with the fate of cultural structures because it is 'only through having a rich and secure cultural structure that people can become aware, in a vivid way, of the options available to them, and intelligently examine their value.'[49] Concern for the cultural structure thus 'accords with, rather than conflicts with, the liberal concern for our ability and freedom to judge the value of our life-plans.'[50]

The second consideration on which Kymlicka bases his defense of cultural rights is liberal equality. Cultural minorities, such as the Inuit, he argues, suffer a particular disadvantage inasmuch as they 'can face inequalities which are the product of their circumstances or endowment, not their choices or ambitions.'[51] Their cultural communities are often undermined by decisions of people outside the community. Cultural minorities, compared with the majority culture, operate in unequal circumstances, and this, Kymlicka insists, is the case for all members of such minorities; thus 'all Inuit people face the same inequality in circumstances.'[52] His conclusion is that 'only if we ground collective rights in unequal circumstances can we distinguish the legitimacy of Aboriginal rights from the illegitimacy of attempts of assorted racial, religious, class, or gender groups to gain special status for their preferred goals and practices.'[53]

Although Kymlicka's outlook is also a liberal individualist one, his position is clearly quite different from that advanced in this essay. While I have tried to play down concern for group rights by describing cultural communities as having their legitimate basis in individual freedom of association, Kymlicka wishes to emphasize group interests and sees them as having their basis in liberal concerns about choice and equality. Like Van Dyke, he is motivated by a concern for the plight of ethnic minorities, and 'indigenous' peoples in particular. His theory is, however, untenable both from a liberal point of view and from the perspective of someone concerned with the interests of cultural minorities.

The problem stems from the attempt to justify cultural rights, which need to be given some foundation consistent with liberal theory. Kymlicka's foundation is essentially an argument about the primary importance of individual *autonomy*. Cultural rights protect autonomy. They do this inasmuch as they look to guarantee the stability of the cultural environment within which the individual is able to exercise the capacity to make meaningful choices. Unfortunately, many cultures do not place such importance on choice. This is an ideal which finds especial favor among the adherents of the liberalism of J.S. Mill. As Kymlicka himself notes, 'For Mill the conditions under which people acquired their ends were important: it mattered whether their education and cultural socialization opened up or closed off the possibility of revising their ends.'[54] Yet many cultures, including those of a number of the 'indigenous peoples' referred to, do not place such value on the *individual's* freedom to choose his ends. Often, the individual and his interests are subordinated to the community. Moreover, the individual might be expected to accept uncritically the long-standing practices of the cultural group. Critical reflection need play no part in their conceptions of the good life.

Consider, for example, the following account by Kenneth Maddock of the nature of Australian Aboriginal society:

> On Anderson's view of freedom we would have to say either that Aboriginal society traditionally was servile in spirit or that it was not the kind of society in which attitudes of servility and independence could arise. Now the absence of opposition and criticism cannot be explained by an absence of inequality or disenfranchisement. It seems rather that explanation must be sought in the Aboriginal acceptance of a utopian conception of society according to which an order having been laid down all that remains to do is to conform to it. This anti-historical view of how things have come to be as they are is bound up with the disjoining of creativity, which is imputed to the powers, and tradition, fidelity to which is urged upon humans. When ideas like this take root—and the initiatory process is calculated to ensure they do—all prospect of opposition and criticism vanishes.[55]

Here we have a society in which the values of order and conformity are inculcated through ritual, with creativity and critical reflection of the fundamental nature of individual commitment to these values thereby extinguished. If these practices are to be allowed to continue in the wider society, the justification cannot be one which emphasizes the importance of preserving the context of choice. If choice and critical reflection are most highly valued, then it is cultural interference rather than cultural protection that is required. If we disdain interference, then choice ceases to be a consideration.

Having embraced choice as critically important, Kymlicka is drawn down the path of interference. This is revealed in his response to the problem of the Pueblo Indians raised by Svensson.[56] The problem arose when some members of this culture, following conversion to Christianity, chose to withdraw from certain communal functions while continuing to demand their 'share' of community resources. The result was the ostracizing of, and denial of resources to, those apostates who had thus violated Pueblo religious norms. Objecting to this treatment, the Christian converts appealed to the 'Indian Bill of Rights' (Title II, added to the 1968 Civil Rights Act) for religious protection. Other Indians objected to the extension of the Indian Bill of Rights to the Pueblos as destructive of their traditions, in which religion was an integral part of community life. Kymlicka's response is that 'the restriction on religious liberty *couldn't* be defended on [his] account of minority rights' because, first, 'there is no inequality in cultural membership to which it could be viewed as a response' and, second, the 'ability of each member of the Pueblo reservation . . . to live in that community is not threatened by allowing Protestant members to express their religious beliefs.'[57] To complaints by scholars like Svensson that for many in the Pueblo, 'violation of religious norms is viewed as literally threatening the survival of the entire community,'[58] Kymlicka responds that the only real evidence for such a claim is the dislike that the majority feels for the dissident practice. In this regard, he likens the complaint to Lord Devlin's claim that the acceptance of homosexuality undermines the English community. The mistake made here by people like Devlin, he suggests, is that of seeing anything that changes the *character* of the community as *undermining* the community.

Kymlicka makes the basis for his own view very clear: 'If the goal is to ensure that each person is equally able to lead their chosen life within their own cultural community, then restricting religion in no way promotes that.'[59] He is in no doubt that were the theocracy ended, each majority member of the Pueblo would still have 'as much ability to use and interpret their own cultural experiences,' and that 'supporting the intolerant character of a cultural community undermines the very reason we had to support cultural membership—that it allows for meaningful individual choice.'[60]

Yet the important question is, why make 'meaningful individual choice' the basis for supporting cultural membership—particularly when this value is not recognized as such by the culture in question? Many cultural minorities besides the Pueblo Indians do not place individual autonomy or choice high in the hierarchy of values. To the extent that they have had to go so far as to defend their cultural integrity against invasion or exploitation, they have invoked the independence of their community's way of life and the importance of retaining their *identity*.[61] By insisting that the cultural community place a high value on individual choice, the larger society would in effect be saying that the minority culture must become much more liberal.

Kymlicka does not reject this conclusion, arguing that 'finding a way to liberalize a cultural community without destroying it is a task that liberals face in every country, once we recognize the importance of a secure cultural context of choice.'[62] Yet from the perspective of persons seeking to preserve the group identity or the cultural integrity of the minority community, this is surely unacceptable. First, they might raise an objection that Hume noted: that it is all too easy to judge societies by standards they do not recognize.[63] More important, however, they would surely object that to elevate individual choice and suggest the course of 'liberalizing' their cultures 'without destroying them' is to fail to take their culture seriously. If their culture is not already liberal, if it does not prize individuality or individual choice, then to talk of liberalization is inescapably to talk of undermining their culture. Culture is not simply a matter of colorful dances and rituals, nor is it even a framework or context for individual choice. Rather, it is the product of the association of individuals over time, which in turn shapes individual commitments and gives meaning to individual lives—lives for which individual choice or autonomy may be quite valueless. To try to reshape it in accordance with ideals of individual choice is to strike at its very core.

Furthermore, it is not clear why it should be permissible to intervene in existing cultural practice even if the result is not the destruction of the culture but 'merely' the reshaping of its 'character.' What many cultural communities are asking for, as the American Indian manifesto quoted earlier suggests, is to be left alone.[64] Moreover, they wish the reshaping of their community to take place, as far as possible, by the terms set by their own practices. If the change in character takes place as a result of dissident members of the minority community invoking 'rights' granted them by the dominant culture, then the change constitutes not a response of the community to the new circumstances confronting it but a change enforced by the wider society interfering in its internal practices.

Although these arguments may justifiably be put against Kymlicka, it must also be borne in mind that none of this is to suggest that cultural communities can be insulated from the wider society. As T.S. Eliot suggested, this is an illusion which can only be maintained 'by a careful fostering of local "culture," culture in the reduced sense of the word, as everything that is picturesque, harmless and separable from politics, such as language and literature, local arts and customs.'[65] There must, of necessity, be some political contact between the dominant and the minority culture, and change is inescapable for both. The problem here is to establish the principles that account for the place of minority cultures within the larger society. The problem is not that of finding ways to insulate minority cultures against change.

The argument against Kymlicka is that his account of the place of cultural minorities seeks to entrench cultural rights on a basis which itself undermines many forms of cultural community, specifically those that fail in their practices to conform to liberal norms of tolerance and to honor the liberal ideal of autonomy. Cultural minorities are given protection—provided they mend their ways. In the end, it is only culture in Eliot's 'reduced sense of the word' that is protected. Thus from the perspective of a defender of the interests of cultural minorities, Kymlicka's view has to be found wanting.

But his position is also inadequate from a liberal point of view. Here the problem stems from his desire to give cultural minorities differential rights on the basis of liberal equality. His contention is that cultural minorities are specially disadvantaged because they can face inequalities which are the result of circumstance rather than choice and that, in cases such as that of the Inuit, all members of the minority face the same inequality of circumstances as compared with the majority culture. Yet both parts of this contention look dubious in the extreme. First, there is no good reason to think that only minorities can face inequalities which are not the product of their choices. Anyone born physically or mentally disabled, for example, could make this claim no matter what his culture, as indeed might anyone born into poverty. If there is a reason to give cultural minorities special rights, lack of control over circumstances surely is not one of them.

Second, the idea that *all* minority members face the *same* inequality of circumstances seems absurd. Even if the Australian Aborigines are collectively and, on average, the worst off in the society (and they are if we look to the standard range of social indicators—from infant mortality to rates of imprisonment), there are many (even if, arguably, not enough) Aborigines who are better off—richer, better educated, more powerful—than the majority of Australians. So, why not give other disadvantaged Australians the same rights? Again, there seems to be no case here for special cultural rights.

If these two empirical propositions are the basis of Kymlicka's call for cultural rights, then that call looks extremely dubious from the point of view of the liberal idea of equal treatment.

In sum, Kymlicka's theory seems both to grant cultural minorities too much recognition and to give them too little. It gives them too much insofar as liberal equality does not appear to sanction special rights, and it gives them too little insofar as regarding choice or autonomy as the fundamental liberal commitment disregards the interests of cultural communities which do not value the individual's freedom to choose. If so, then it cannot mount a serious liberal challenge to the individualist view elaborated in this essay.

IV

Now it might, at this point, be objected that it is odd to criticize Kymlicka—or any other liberal view which seeks to incorporate cultural rights—for failing to respect some minority cultures, because the theory advanced in this essay maintains that cultures should not be given special protection, that there are no cultural rights. It is therefore worth reiterating that the point of this essay is not to disparage the interests of minorities but to argue that it is not necessary to abandon or modify liberal theory to do justice to their concerns. It is on the basis of this objective that Kymlicka's theory was questioned and found wanting from the perspectives of both cultural minorities and liberalism. The problem now is to explain more carefully what this liberalism amounts to and how it accounts for the place of cultural minorities in the wider society.

What should have become clear from the criticisms raised against Kymlicka is that the liberal view advanced here is individualist in quite a different way from some others. It begins with the relatively innocuous, shared assumption that moral evaluation is individualistic in the sense that what counts, ultimately, is how the lives of actual individuals are affected. 'It is individual, sentient beings whose lives go better or worse, who suffer or flourish, and so it is their welfare that is the subject-matter of morality.'[66] But unlike some other liberal views, including Kymlicka's, it does *not* go on to impose severe restrictions on what is to count as (a legitimate form of) human flourishing. It does not go on to suggest that human flourishing requires that the individual be capable of autonomy or have the capacity to choose his or her way of life on the basis of critical reflection on a range of options. Rather, it is content to accept that what matters most when assessing whether a way of life is legitimate is whether the individuals taking part in it are prepared to acquiesce in it.

These premises are somewhat austere. They may be more austere even than those on which Loren Lomasky chooses to defend his own conception of liberal basic rights: the idea of individuals as project pursuers.[67] Lomasky is critical of the idea of grounding liberal rights in the ideal of individual autonomy—and for good reason: With the defence of autonomy often comes a disregard for actual practices and ways of life.[68] For this reason, he argues that what is most important and requires recognition is that individuals are project pursuers. Projects may not be chosen: 'A person's commitments may be unarticulated and not at all the product of conscious deliberation culminating in a moment of supreme decision. They may rather be something that he has gradually and imperceptibly come to assume over time in much the same way that one takes on distinctive vocal inflections or the cast of one's face.'[69] Nonetheless, project pursuit is 'partial.' 'To be committed to a long-term design, to order one's activities in light of it, to judge one's success or failure as a person by reference to its fate: these are inconceivable apart from a frankly partial attachment to one's most cherished ends.' Thus, Lomasky maintains, an 'individual's projects provide him with a *personal*—an intimately personal—standard of value to choose his actions by. His central and enduring ends provide him reasons for action that are recognized as his own.'[70]

But even to take personal project pursuit as fundamental to our nature excludes a part of human practice because some cultures are not able to accept the idea that *individual* projects can provide any sort of standard of value. Consider, once again, Maddock's portrait of Australian Aboriginal society:

If we take human culture to be humanly created, then we are forced to the conclusion that there is among Aborigines a profound resistance to crediting themselves with their own cultural achievements. Their plan of life is held to have been laid down during The Dreaming by the powers and occasionally to have been modified since by the intervention of these powers, as when one appears to a man in a dream and communicates a new song or rite. Aborigines claim credit only for fidelity to tradition or, as they put it, for 'following up The Dreaming'. It is powers alone who are conceived as creative, men being passive recipients of unmotivated gifts. As men deny the creativity which is truly theirs, they can account for their culture only by positing that to create is to be other than human. To be human is to reproduce forms.[71]

In such a society, it would seem, individuals are not project pursuers; although they might be said to display commitments, they do not regard themselves as possessing *personal* goals.[72] Nonetheless, there may be enough reason to respect that way of life into which they have been inducted and which is the only life they know.

The theory advanced here looks to recognize as legitimate cultural communities which do not in their own practices conform to individualist norms or recognize the validity of personal projects. Yet at the same time, it is a liberal theory inasmuch as it does not sanction the forcible induction into or imprisoning of any individual in a cultural community. No one can be *required* to accept a particular way of life. Thus if, as has often happened, some members of a particular culture on making contact with the wider society wished to forsake their old ways, they would be free to do so, and the objections of their native community would not be recognized. In this respect, minorities within cultural minorities receive some protection. On the other hand, if those members wished not to leave their community but to assert rights recognized by the wider society but not by their culture, they receive no recognition. What is given recognition first and foremost is individual freedom of association (and dissociation). The practices of communities of individuals, the majority of whom accept the legitimacy of the association, must also be accepted, the views of dissidents notwithstanding.

The implications of this view deserve to be spelled out in concrete terms. In the case of the Old Order Amish of Wisconsin, raised by Van Dyke, for example, it means that they would have the right to live by their traditional ways. Their right not to send their children to public schools beyond the eighth grade would be grounded not in the First Amendment guarantee of freedom of religion but in the principle of freedom of association. (Indeed, the obligation of Amish parents to send their children to public schools at all becomes questionable.)

A similar conclusion would be defended in the case of gypsy children. Section 39 of the British Education Act of 1944 makes it an offense for a parent not to send a child to school regularly but includes a special provision for gypsy children of no fixed abode. Because their parents move constantly in search of seasonal work, they are required to attend only half the number of school sessions. But because gypsy custom does not value schooling, the parents believing they can educate a child satisfactorily through informal instruction in the ways of their culture, only a minority of children receive any formal primary education. Their freedom to associate and live by their own ways, however, would, by my argument, make this permissible. The argument put by Sebastian Poulter that because 'at present many gypsy children are being denied the sort of education which would fit them to make a rational choice of lifestyle as adults,' there may be reason to convict the parents under the Education Act and override 'this particularly harmful aspect of gypsy tradition and culture'[73] would be rejected. There is no more reason to insist that gypsy parents offer their children a 'rational choice' of life-style through public education than there is to require that other parents offer their children the opportunity to become gypsies.

In the case of the Pueblo Indians, it means that if the community refuses to accept the conversion of some of its individual members to Protestant Christianity, those individuals have to choose between abiding by the wishes of the community or ceasing to be a part of it. They may, of course, seek to change the Pueblo stance from within, but they may not appeal to any outside authority. As members of American society, they have freedom of religion; as Pueblo, they do not. The case of the individual Muslim wishing to deny that there is no other god but Allah and that Muhammad is his messenger is precisely analogous. As a citizen of a liberal society, he has the right of free speech; as a Muslim, however, he has no right to challenge Islam's fundamental tenet or to deny that the Quran was a part of God's essence by, say, embracing the metaphysical doctrines of the Mu'tazila.[74] The individual would therefore have to choose between being a part of the Muslim community and retaining his right of free speech. The community would be entitled to ostracize the individual who refuses to conform to its norms; it would not, however, be entitled to inflict any greater penalty.[75]

As these examples illustrate, the liberal view advanced here gives communities a considerable amount of power over the individuals who constitute their membership. Despite the individualist premises, some very strong 'communitarian' conclusions have been reached. Communities undoubtedly are important, but it is not necessary to reject individualist premises so as to give them some recognition. To do this, however, the primacy of freedom of association is all-important; it has to take priority over other liberties—such as those of speech or worship—which lie at the core of the liberal tradition. Otherwise, 'illiberal' communities cannot perpetuate themselves or even form.

This last point perhaps indicates more sharply what kind of liberal theory is being defended here. It is a theory which sees a liberal society as one that need not be made up of liberal communities. If society is, in Rawls's phrase, a 'social union of social unions,'[76] there is no necessity that these all be liberal social unions. What is of crucial importance, however, is that each community enjoy a certain amount of independence and integrity: that they are in fact the social unions *of those individuals* and not simply the categories within which society places particular groups. For each social union to have any significant measure of integrity, it must *to some extent* be impervious to the values of the wider liberal society.

Yet the qualification 'to some extent' is an important one. no community within a wider society can remain entirely untouched by the political institutions and the legal and moral norms of the whole. (One of the weaknesses of Robert Nozick's conception of utopia is that it suggests the possibility of a society of wholly independent communities unaffected by the workings of the other social unions or the society as a whole.[77]) For a number of reasons, most cultural communities will be profoundly affected by the wider community. The most important reason is the very fact of the society recognizing the freedom of the individual to leave his community. Once the individual has the option to leave, the nature of his community is transformed, particularly if the formal right comes with substantive opportunities.

The case of the New Zealand Maori provides an illustration of this point. Maori society before contact with Europeans was, as Richard Mulgan explains, a very strongly nonindividualist culture. Groups and their welfare were the prime values, and individuals found their identity as part of the group, existing to serve collective ends. Individuals could justifiably be subordinated or sacrificed for the good of the community. Yet today, Maori social life is much less collectively oriented, with many Maori living in urban areas away from their tribal settings. Indeed, Maori identity has become much more a matter of individual personal choice. The cause of this change was the possibility of leaving the community. A precontact Maori would never have contemplated leaving the clan or village, but this is no longer the case. As Mulgan remarks 'Once the possibility of leaving with impunity becomes a practicable and the fact of staying becomes a deliberate decision the ethical balance between individual and group has shifted irrevocably in the individual's direction. Today loyalty to the group and submersion in its activities and purposes can never be recovered.'[78]

In the theory defended here, although cultural communities may seek to protect themselves against the intrusions of the wider society, they may not take any action they like to enforce group loyalty. Thus, in recognizing the right of exit, they would also have to abide by liberal norms forbidding slavery[79] and physical coercion. More generally, they would be bound by liberal prohibitions on 'cruel, inhuman or degrading treatment.'[80] Cultural groups that persisted in violating such norms would therefore disappear as their dissident members exercised their enforceable claims against the community.

Cultural communities, however much they tried to distance themselves from the larger society, would be affected by it to the extent that their ways of life might have external effects. Even communities that are geographically separate and remote might generate environmental externalities. In such cases, they would not be able to invoke the right of free association as a defense against prosecution for damages, for example. This, again, might well have the effect of fundamentally altering the practices within the community.

Indeed, cultural communities would be more profoundly affected by the wider society to the extent that they opt to coexist more closely with it. For example, an Indian immigrant community which had chosen (whether separately or collectively) to settle in the midst of English society might be determined to retain certain customs or practices but would be subject to established legal provisions for, say, testator's family maintenance. In this respect, such communities would be open to legal challenge by their own members who dissent from the rulings of the community. It would also affect the community's understanding of the marriage contract and possibly its understanding of the obligations of children to their parents.

The idea of accounting for the claims of minority cultural communities by taking freedom of association, and the corollary right of exit for a community, as fundamental may perhaps now be seen in fuller light. Although formulated earlier as a freedom which seems to offer purely formal guarantees, it is clearly one that has some substantive bite. Thus without establishing cultural rights, it may be possible to account for the legitimate claims of cultural minorities in a liberal social order. Before pressing this conclusion any more strongly, however, it is necessary to look at some lingering worries and to say a little more about the nature of the society which provides the context for this theory.

V

. . . Thus far, the objections of those who wish to see greater recognition of group rights have been addressed. From another quarter, however, would come objections that even the individualist view defended here gives too much weight to the interests of cultural minorities. The fundamental concern of those who hold this view is well expressed by Poulter in his discussion of toleration of immigrant cultures. 'Cultural tolerance,' he writes, 'obviously cannot become "a cloak for oppression and injustice within the immigrant communities themselves," neither must it unduly strain and endanger the integrity of the 'social and cultural core' of English values as a whole.'[81] Here is a clear statement of the view that minority cultural communities must conform to the standards of morality and justice of the wider society—first, for the sake of justice within the minority community, and second, for the sake of the stability and social unity of the society as a whole. Does the view defended in this essay run the risk of upholding injustice within minority communities—perhaps to the extent that this will undermine the stability of society as a whole?

If to do justice is to give each person his or her due, the answer to the first part of this question depends on what we think a person is due. The problem is that different cultural communities have different conceptions of what individuals are due or entitled to, and in many cases, these conceptions will not value those freedoms and equalities which figure prominently in liberal conceptions of justice. Here, then, it has to be admitted that by liberal standards there may be injustice within some cultural communities: Freedom of worship may not be respected; women may have opportunities closed off to them; and the rights of individuals to express themselves may be severely restricted.

Yet it must also be borne in mind that the probability and the extent of 'injustice' is tempered by two factors. The first is that the acceptability of cultural norms and practices depends in part on the degree to which the cultural community is independent of the wider society. Tribal communities of Indians or Aborigines which are geographically remote and have little contact with the dominant society might well live according to ways which betray little respect for the individual. Yet cultural communities that are more fully integrated into the mainstream of society would not find it so easy because their members will also be a part of the larger legal and political order. They might, for example, be tied to that order not only by the fact of citizenship but by the fact that they own property, trade, and use public services. This makes it more difficult to maintain different standards of justice partly because community members (especially of the younger generation) may reject them in favor of the societywide norms but also because individuals are not free to change their cultural allegiances as convenient. We cannot choose to be Quakers only in wartime.

To take a practical example, people from the Indian subcontinent settling in Britain, may not be entitled to enforce the arranged marriages of unwilling brides. Under section 12 of the Matrimonial Causes Act of 1973, a marriage can be annulled if it took place under 'duress,' and the case of *Hirani v. Hirani* in 1982 established that the threat of social ostracism could place the individual under duress to a sufficient degree to determine that the marriage was not entered into voluntarily.[82] The immigrant community, while entitled to try to live by their ways, have no right here to expect the wider society to enforce those norms against the individual.[83]

The second factor tempering the probability and the extent of 'injustice' is the principle upholding individual freedom of association and dissociation. If an individual continues to live in a community and according to ways that (in the judgment of the wider society) treat her unjustly, even though she is free to leave, then our concern about the injustice diminishes. What is crucially important here, however, is the extent to which the individual does enjoy a *substantial* freedom to leave. As was indicated at the end of the preceding section, the freedom of the individual to dissociate from a community is a freedom with considerable substantive bite. Yet there are certain conditions which make this possible, and these ought, in conclusion, to be brought out more explicitly, for they go a little way further to indicating what kind of social and political order is upheld by the theory advanced here.

The most important condition which makes possible a substantive freedom to exit from a community is the existence of a wider society that is open to individuals wishing to leave their local groups. A society composed of tribal communities organized on the basis of kinship, for example, would not make the freedom of exit credible: The individual would have to choose between the conformity of the village and the lawlessness (and loneliness) of the heath. Exit would be credible only if the wider society were much more like a market society within which there was a considerable degree of individual independence and the possibility of what Weber called social closure was greatly diminished.

More important still, the wider society would have to be one in which the principle of freedom of association was upheld, and this seems unlikely in a social order in which the other liberal freedoms were not valued. This suggests that it may be necessary that the wider society itself be one that could be described as embodying a liberal political culture.

Notes

1. Anthony D. Smith, *The Ethnic Revival* (Cambridge: Cambridge University Press, 1980), 1. Liberal hopes are described as 'delusions,' resting 'on a systematic underestimation of one of the fundamental trends of the last two centuries.'
2. Harold R. Isaacs, *Idols of the Tribe: Group Identity and Political Change* (New York: Harper & Row, 1975), 216.
3. Vernon Van Dyke, 'The Individual, the State, and Ethnic Communities in Political Theory,' *World Politics* 29 (April 1977): 343–69, at 344. See also 'Justice as Fairness: For Groups?,' *American Political Science Review* 69 (June 1975): 607–14; 'Collective Entities and Moral Rights: Problems in Liberal Thought,' *Journal of Politics* 44 (1982): 21–40; *Human Rights, Ethnicity, and Discrimination* (Westport and London: Greenwood, 1985).

4. Frances Svensson, 'Liberal Democracy and Group Rights: The Legacy of Individualism and Its Impact on American Indian Tribes,' *Political Studies* 27 (1979): 421–39, at 438.
5. John Gray, 'Mill's and Other Liberalisms,' in his *Liberalisms: Essays in Political Philosophy* (London and New York: Routledge, 1989), 217–38, at 234.
6. Ibid., 235.
7. Will Kymlicka, *Liberalism, Community, and Culture* (Oxford: Oxford University Press, 1989), 152.
8. Ibid., 211: 'A government that gives special rights to members of a distinct cultural community may still be treating them *as individuals*; the provision of such rights just reflects a different view about how to treat them as individuals.'
9. In the account that follows, I borrow freely from John Gray's discussion in *Liberalism* (Milton Keynes: Open University Press, 1985), x.
10. Van Dyke, 'The Individual, the State,' 361.
11. Ibid., 363–4. See also his paper on Rawls, 'Justice as Fairness.'
12. Van Dyke, 'The Individual, the State,' 363.
13. A finer distinction needs to be made with regard to certain cultural groups such as the American Indians or the New Zealand Maori that did, in some sense, exist as cultural groups before European political institutions were established in their territories. This distinction is discussed further on in the essay.
14. Donald L. Horowitz, *Ethnic Groups in Conflict* (Berkeley: University of California Press, 1985), 589.
15. Smith, *The Ethnic Revival*, 85.
16. Horowitz, *Ethnic Groups in Conflict*, 73; see also chap. 2 passim.
17. Ibid., 66.
18. Ibid., 66–67.
19. Ibid., 68. See also Alfred P. Rubin, *The International Personality of the Malay Peninsula: A Study of the International Law of Imperialism* (Kuala Lumpur: Penerbit Universiti Malaya, 1974).
20. Horowitz, *Ethnic Groups in Conflict*, 195.
21. Ibid., 69.
22. A more detailed defense of this individualist standpoint may be found in Chandran Kukathas and Philip Pettit, *Rawls:* A Theory of Justice *and its Critics* (Oxford: Polity Press, 1990), 12–16. For a contrary view, see Charles Taylor, 'Irreducibly Social Goods,' in *Rationality, Individualism and Public Policy*, edited by Geoffrey Brennan and Cliff Walsh (Canberra: Australian National University, 1990), 45–63; but see the reply by Robert E. Goodin, 'Irreducibly Social Goods: Comment 1,' 64–79.
23. Note that I have not made the stronger assertion that it is only the lives of individuals *within* the group that can relevantly be taken into account.
24. On this, see Horowitz, *Ethnic Groups in Conflict*, 71.
25. Ibid., 101. Bitter jokes about the two most dangerous tribes in Africa, the Wabenzi (those who drive Mercedes cars) and the Bintu (those who have 'been to' Europe and America) suggest that there is an awareness of the differences of interest.
26. Ibid., 225, and more generally chap. 5.

27. See Judith Wright, *We Call for a Treaty* (Sydney: Collins/Fontana, 1985), 292–99.
28. A complaint made by a senior Aboriginal public servant, Charles Perkins, responding to Aboriginal complaints about his ineffectiveness. See Scott Bennett, *Aborigines and Political Power* (Sydney: Allen & Unwin, 1989), 103.
29. 'With the existence of the few rich Malays at least the poor can say their fate is not entirely to serve rich non-Malays. From the point of view of racial ego, and this ego is still strong, the unseemly existence of Malay tycoons is essential.' Mahathir bin Mohamad, *The Malay Dilemma* (Kuala Lumpur: Federal Publications, 1981), 44. See also Thomas Sowell, *Preferential Policies: An International Perspective* (New York: Morrow, 1990), 48–51.
30. Horowitz, *Ethnic Groups in Conflict*, 226.
31. I owe this point to Richard Mulgan, who suggests that the urbanized Maori in New Zealand might provide an example of elite interests.
32. One Aboriginal businessman thus complained: 'Land is granted to appease the non-Aboriginal conscience in the large cities, but Aborigines are not allowed to use it freely because paternalists do not think the black man is sufficiently mature to behave responsibility. For example, Aborigines are prohibited from selling, leasing or trading their land—thus shut out of the activities that would make their land an economic asset.' Bob Liddle, 'Aborigines Are Australian too,' in *A Treaty with the Aborigines?*, edited by Ken Baker (Melbourne: Institute for Public Affairs, 1988), 14.
33. Van Dyke, 'Collective Entities,' 29.
34. Ibid., 29. The internal quotation is from a Commissioner of Indian Affairs, as quoted by Frances Svensson, *The Ethnics in American Politics: American Indians* (Minneapolis: Burgess, 1973), 73.
35. Ibid., 29. The internal quotation is from *Congressional Record*, July 27, 1978, H7458.
36. Van Dyke, 'The Individual, the State,' 365.
37. Ibid., 365.
38. Ibid.
39. There are also rights which the individual might have as a member of the wider society. Some of these might be exercised by an individual while living in a cultural community within that society; other rights might not be open for the individual to take up without leaving his cultural community. For example, an individual might not be free to exercise the right to marry whomsoever she wishes if such a right is recognized by the wider society but not by her religious community—unless she chooses to leave her religion. This issue is discussed more fully later.
40. Kymlicka, *Liberalism*, 144.
41. Thus the question that Kymlicka poses himself (on p. 162) is 'How can we defend minority rights within liberalism, given that its moral ontology recognizes only individuals, each of whom is to be treated with equal consideration?'
42. Ibid., 151.

43. Ibid., 151–52.
44. Ibid., 164; 'Aboriginal rights, at least in their robust form will only be secure when they are viewed, not as competing with liberalism, but as an essential component of liberal political practice.'
45. Ibid., 162.
46. Ibid., 165.
47. Ibid., 178.
48. Ibid., 197.
49. Ibid., 165.
50. Ibid., 167.
51. Ibid., 190.
52. Ibid., 240.
53. Ibid., 241.
54. Ibid., 19. See J.S. Mill, *On Liberty in Utilitarianism; On Liberty; Essay on Bentham*, edited with an introduction by Mary Warnock (London: Fontana, 1985), chap. 3.
55. Kenneth Maddock, *The Australian Aborigines: A Portrait of Their Society* (Ringwood: Penguin, 1972), 193–94. John Anderson's account of freedom, referred to at the beginning, suggested that freedom in a community is measured by the degree to which its ruling order meets with opposition and its ruling ideas with criticism, and that the servility of a community is measured by the extent to which political opposition is suppressed. This is discussed by Maddock on 192–93.
56. Svensson, 'Liberal Democracy,' 430–34.
57. Kymlicka, *Liberalism*, 196.
58. Svensson, 'Liberal Democracy,' 434.
59. Kymlicka, *Liberalism*, 196.
60. Ibid., 196–97.
61. I have discussed the importance of identity with regard to the Australian Aborigines in *Without Oppression or Disputation: Aboriginal Identity and the Origins and Growth of the Protest Movement of the 1960s* (Canberra: B.A. Honors thesis, Department of History, Australian National University, 1978).
62. Kymlicka, *Liberalism*, 170. Elsewhere, Kymlicka writes of 'helping the culture to move carefully towards a fully liberal society' (p. 170) and promoting 'the longer-term idea of full liberal freedoms' (p. 171).
63. 'There are no manners so innocent or reasonable, but may be rendered odious or ridiculous, if measured by a standard unknown to the persons; especially if you employ a little art or eloquence, in aggravating some circumstances, and extenuating others, as best suits the purpose of your discourse.' David Hume, 'A Dialogue,' in Hume, *Enquiries Concerning Human Understanding and Concerning The Principles of Morals*, edited by L.A. Selby-Bigge, revised by P.H. Nidditch (Oxford: Clarendon, 1975), 330.
64. It must, in fairness, be noted that Kymlicka is not suggesting that there is any reason to think that there is always a case for practical intervention by, say, the courts in cultural community affairs. He notes in the case of the Pueblo

Indians, for example, that the dispute may be best resolved by tribal courts 'if that is the consensus amongst the Pueblo.' See *Liberalism*, 197. What precisely is meant here by consensus, however, is perhaps in need of fuller explanation.

65. T.S. Eliot, *Notes Towards the Definition of Culture* (London: Faber, 1962), 93.
66. Kymlicka, *Liberalism*, 242.
67. Loren Lomasky, *Persons, Rights, and the Moral Community* (Oxford University Press, 1987).
68. Ibid., 248–50.
69. Ibid., 42.
70. Ibid., 27–8.
71. Maddock, *The Australian Aborigines*, 129.
72. Here I am not sure how strongly Lomasky wants to insist that projects are what provide personal standards by which individuals make choices. Elswhere in his book he seems to suggest that any display of commitment may be taken as evidence of the existence of a project. See, for example, p. 45 where he says that all 'patterns of motivated activity that form the structure of a scrutable life . . . merit recognition as projects.' If so, there may be less reason for disagreement between us.
73. Sebastian Poulter, 'Ethnic Minority Customs, English Law and Human Rights,' *International and Comparative Law Quarterly*, 36 (1987): 589–615, at 600–1.
74. The Mu'tazila were an eighth-century Arab-Muslim school whose 'larger philosophy, developed under the influence of Greek thought, betrayed the majority sentiment of the Arab-Muslim milieu about the nature of God and his creation. For other Muslims, Muhammad and the Quran, not reason, were the central experiences of Islam.' See Ira M. Lapidus, *A History of Islamic Societies* (Cambridge: Cambridge University Press, 1988), 107 and 105–108 more generally.
75. Certainly not the death penalty, as *some* Muslims have advocated in the case of Salman Rushdie.
76. John Rawls, *A Theory of Justice* (Oxford: Oxford University Press, 1971), 527–30.
77. See Robert Nozick, *Anarchy, State and Utopia* (Oxford: Blackwell, 1974), part 3.
78. Richard Mulgan, *Maori, Pakeha and Democracy* (Auckland: Oxford University Press, 1989), 64.
79. This would include 'voluntary slavery.' For an argument showing why the individual has no right to sell himself into slavery, see Thomas W. Pogge, *Realizing Rawls* (Ithaca and London: Cornell University Press, 1989), 48–50.
80. See Poulter, 'Ethnic Minority Customs,' 602, for a discussion of this notion as it has affected British legislation through European Convention, Art. 3 and the International Covenant on Civil and Political Rights, Art. 7.
81. Poulter, 'Ethnic Minority Customs,' 593.
82. Ibid., 599–600.
83. The community could, of course, continue to ostracize the dissenting member. It is perhaps impossible to prevent the oppression and injustice resulting from the withdrawal of love or affection or social acceptance.

11 Internal Minorities and their Rights

LESLIE GREEN

'*Because* the persecuting majority is vile, says the liberal, *therefore* the persecuted minority must be stainlessly pure. Can't you see what nonsense that is? What's to prevent the bad from being persecuted by the worse?'[1]

The Problem: Minorities within Minorities

We acknowledge the rights of minorities in order to protect some of their urgent interests, even against the otherwise legitimate claims of the majority. Thus ethnic, cultural, religious, or sexual minorities end up with rights that are, in a certain way, rights against the majority. But these minority groups are rarely homogeneous; they often contain other minorities. The Scots are a minority nation within the United Kingdom, and the Gaelic-speaking are a minority among Scots. Mennonites are a religious minority, and gays are a minority among Mennonites. In this paper, I want to explore the moral standing of such internal minorities, as I shall call them.

The issue is urgent in both theory and practice. Some of the ways in which we try to ensure that minorities are not oppressed by majorities make it more likely that those minorities are able to oppress their own internal minorities. For example, we sometimes accord religious or cultural minorities special rights to self-determination. But as students of international relations know, the right to non-interference in internal matters is the first refuge of a government intent on violating rights. In a parallel way, the special rights of minority groups can empower them to make decisions that persecute their own internal minorities. What then should be done?

This problem is relevant to any political theory that attaches significant weight to the value of personal autonomy, but it is especially important to modern liberalism. It is often said that liberals are atomistic individualists, concerned to protect people against the predations of the state and thus

---

blind to important values of solidarity and community. The picture is familiar enough to need no elaboration. Nonetheless it is wrong. For the individuals in the historically dominant forms of liberalism are not isolated monads; they are members of families, churches, ethnic groups, nations, and so on. Indeed, it was group-based strife—particularly seventeenth-century wars of religion—that gave birth to central elements of the liberal tradition. The struggles to secure civil liberties, limit the powers of government, and the like were motivated less by social atomism than by what we might call molecularism—acknowledgement that among the most significant constituents of civil society are overlapping social groups. And for liberals this is not merely a brute fact to be noticed and accommodated; it is something to be fostered and celebrated, for it is partly through such associations that people find value and meaning in their lives. Liberals (and even some libertarians[2]) defend political freedom in order to promote experiments in living, but those experiments are normally joint ventures.

Misguided emphasis on the supposed atomism of the liberal tradition has thus occluded a more important risk: liberalism may become an uncritical booster of civil society. So far from being unrelentingly individualistic, it is prone to a naive collectivism of the middle range. For the social groups that it protects and promotes can themselves be enemies of liberal values, as my epigraph from Christopher Isherwood suggests. Liberal theory and practice secure the family from the interference of the state but rarely protect women or children from the predations of the family.[3] They secure religious liberty but permit religions to oppress their minority members. These issues are not well framed in the language of atomism.

Some liberals have noticed the problem. J.S. Mill, for example, was alive to the risks of social, and not just political, tyranny (although, as we shall see, his response to it was not always adequate). But others have ignored it. They suppose that if the point of a liberal society is to provide for conditions of freedom in which diverse social groups may flourish then it should not interfere with their internal constitutions. Fundamental principles of political morality are thus applied only at the molecular level. Here, I examine and criticize some sources of that view.

Rights and Minority Groups

To grasp the problem better, it helps to consider the nature of rights. X has a right, as I understand it,[4] only if X has an interest sufficiently important to warrant holding others to be under some duties to respect or promote that interest. Rights are thus not merely correlates of duties on the part of others; they are the ground of such duties.

When we speak of minority rights, whether in morality or in law, we may have in mind one of two things. The first is the rights that people have *even when* they are in the minority. The rights of communists to organize politically, or of gay men to sexual liberty, are of this sort. The fact that a communist or a gay man is properly held to enjoy these rights is not something that flows in any essential way from membership in a social group; it derives from an urgent, but individuated, interest. To be sure, freedom of political association and sexual liberty are valuable in part because of the forms of social interaction that they make possible. But they are individuated interests inasmuch as the individual's stake in these goods is itself sufficiently important to warrant holding others duty-bound. The interests command respect without waiting on the reinforcement of numbers.

In contrast, the second sort of rights is one that people have only *because* they are members of a certain minority group. The right of the Aboriginal inhabitants of North America to self-government is of this sort; the value of group membership is part of the ground of the right. Such rights exist because some of our most urgent interests lie not merely in individuated goods such as personal liberty and exclusive property but also in collective goods. These include things, such as clean air and national defence, that are public goods in the economists' sense: they are inexcludable and non-rival in consumption. If they are available for some, then there is no convenient way to prevent others from receiving them, and the quantity consumed by one person does not perceptibly limit the amount available to others. Other collective goods, though excludable, are non-rival in a deeper sense; their collective production or enjoyment is part of what constitutes their value. Self-government is like that, and so is life in a cultured society. These are supplied jointly, but only to those who participate; yet the fact of being in it together is part of their value.

While some theorists deny that collective interests of either sort can ground rights, I do not think that that position can be sustained, and I have argued against it elsewhere.[5] Certainly, there is no ground for the view that collective interests are, as a class, less urgent than individual interests. An individual's interest in some of the most central liberal rights, such as freedom of expression, is often quite weak; most people have greater interests in a healthy physical environment or in a climate of mutual tolerance. It is true that, in the case of collective interests, the benefits of rights are assignable only to a class (so that we cannot give a fully individuated answer to the question, 'For whose sake is this duty imposed?'). But that does not make them weak or diffuse, and the relevant class may be reasonably determinate. In such instances, it is hard to resist the conclusion that collective interests warrant holding others duty-bound and thus that they ground rights.

It is, of course, open to dispute just which collective interests are this important—that is a major question of substantive moral philosophy. For example, I think that there is a moral right to clean air, and to a tolerant society, and sometimes to national self-determination, but not to a tradition of epic poetry or to general cultural survival. It is also a matter for argument whether these are appropriately thought of as 'collective rights.' But we do not need to resolve these issues here. It is enough that individuals have interests as members of a certain social group, in collective goods that serve their interests as members, but the duty to provide which would not be justified by the interests of any one individual taken alone.[6]

It seems to me that membership in some minority groups—for instance, certain ethnic, national, cultural, or religious communities—is bound up with significant collective interests of this kind. In such cases, in addition to the usual individual rights to personal liberty and associative freedom, there are further special rights to powers and resources needed for the existence of the group. Will Kymlicka has given one argument for such rights in the case of cultural minorities.[7] Our most important interest is in leading a good life, and as a necessary component of that we need the capacity to frame, pursue, and revise our conceptions of the good life. Testing and choosing for ourselves among the options are a major part of life's value. But no one chooses the options themselves; no one chooses the context of choice. And that being so, the cultural resources with which we find ourselves are among our unchosen circumstances of life. Through no fault of our own, and sometimes through no fault of anyone, the culture in which we begin provides an insecure foundation on which to build. If, for example, one is born to the cultural resources of most people of Canada's First Nations, one will find much of one's energy just going to secure those forms of community, language, and culture that others are able to take for granted. Even if one will ultimately kick away the ladder on which one has ascended, it must be strong enough to bear the initial weight. The special rights of minority cultures—the powers, liberties, and rights that go to strengthen them—can thus be understood and justified as a kind of ex ante compensation. They are not a compromise with the requirements of justice, but a consequence of them.

Notice that on this argument there is nothing about minority status as such that generates rights. It is just that the most vulnerable are those with the least powers and resources, and they are often, though not invariably, in the minority. Minority status is one imperfect correlate of social marginality. Some minorities, such as the rich, are extremely powerful; some majorities, such as women, are not. (That is why there is an affinity between the rights of women and the rights of minorities.) The main context in which minorities are disadvantaged as such is in majoritarian decision procedures such as voting, and those procedures are usually not the only way of settling things. (So while the rich might be outvoted, they are rarely outbid.)

The argument from the value of cultural membership is one source of the special rights of minority groups; another familiar one is based on the interest in national self-determination. It might be objected,[8] however, that there are lots of cultural, ethnic, and religious minorities, yet we do not want to endorse endless special rights of the sort that we ascribe to Aboriginal peoples. That would be rights inflation, and it would introduce so many constraints on decision making that nothing could get done.

The objection contains both truth and falsehood. Of course, the self-government model is unlikely to be appropriate for all minorities. But that is only one extreme example of the kind of rights at issue. Other options include granting groups limited autonomy in certain areas (for instance, over education), exempting them from certain general obligations (such as military service), giving recognition to their divergent practices (as in marriage), supporting their distinctive institutions, and so on. These lesser forms of protection may not give the minorities everything that they want, or even need. But to have a right, it is not necessary that one have an interest so dominating that it warrants imposing a whole set of duties adequate for sufficient promotion of the interest. (Few rights of any sort are powerful enough to guarantee the interests that they protect.) The definition requires only that it be important enough to warrant imposing *some* duties on others (or depriving them of some powers, etc.). It is reasonable to suppose that different minorities are in different positions, some entitled to substantial support, others to a minimum. And the minimum might be small enough or of such a character that it would be wrong to institutionalize it in the legal system, for that is always a further question. I am going to say little about these issues here, for we have enough problems just at the level of theory. But it is worth bearing in mind that questions of institutional design always need to be argued separately.

The Rights of Internal Minorities

If minority groups do have such rights, then it might seem that so must internal minorities. It is just a matter of logic: they too are minority groups, and they have two different majorities to contend with. So members of internal minority or marginal groups have, first, individual rights. Aboriginal women, for example, have a right to fair participation in the political institutions that govern them. And second, they may have collective rights as members of an internal minority group: if cultural membership can ground special rights, then so can membership in a sub-culture. Thus English-speaking Quebecers have, in addition to their individual rights of freedom of association and of expression, a collective right to the resources needed for their cultural and linguistic security.

The highly controversial character of the two examples just mentioned should already be enough to suggest that the argument cannot move so swiftly. It is often denied that Aboriginal women or anglophone Quebecers have the moral rights in question: their interests are thought to be embraced or excluded by the rights of the respective minorities of which they form parts. It is said that the patriarchal structure of some bands need not yield to the claims of women or that the *visage linguistique* of Quebec need not accommodate English. Now, it would be unsurprising if those views came from conservative or traditionalist quarters; what is interesting is that they are also endorsed by some liberals. The latter say that the autonomy of the bands frees them from having to conform to colonial European views about democracy, or that respect for the distinctive character of Quebec's society includes respect for its decisions about how to control its cultural environment. Familiar liberal values thus apply among, but not necessarily within, minority groups. How might liberals defend that double standard?

Two Claims

In both theory and popular ideology, two claims seem to be most persuasive. They centre on purported disanalogies between the situation of minority groups and that of their internal minorities. The first is that if members of internal minorities do not like the way that a minority group is treating them, they can exercise their powers of exit and simply leave the group. Consider the case of Rev. Jim Ferry, the Canadian Anglican priest dismissed for disobeying his bishop's order to abandon his gay lover. It may be heart-rending that Anglicans are entitled so to discriminate against sexual minorities; but some argue, if gays do not like it, they are free to leave the church. (And often do.) In contrast, a minority group is not free to leave the state or the broader society. Ferry is free to join another church or none; but where are Anglicans as a whole supposed to go?[9] States exercise compulsory jurisdiction, and even when they allow exit, they do so on their own—not necessarily favourable—terms. And one generally leaves a state only to go to another,[10] admission to which is even more closely regulated. In contrast, the minority groups that compose civil society are not like states or inclusive societies; they generally do allow exit, so those who regard themselves as harshly treated by their group are free to disaffiliate or assimilate to the majority. While Anglicans therefore have rights to religious freedom, gay Anglicans have no comparable rights to sexual freedom, at least not if they wish to hold holy office. Because religious liberty properly includes a measure of self-determination for sects, we should tolerate such local illiberalisms, goes the argument.

The second claim is that the internal minority—minority relationship differs from that between minority and majority with respect to relative power. One reason why we want to protect minorities is that they are relatively powerless to protect themselves. The majority is strong; the minority is not. So, while giving the First Nations special rights against the Canadian majority strengthens the weak as against the strong, to give other special rights to, say, Metis or urban Indians is to strengthen them as against an *already weak* group. Or again, to give the province of Quebec special powers to promote use of French strengthens that minority as against the continental majority; but to give special powers or immunities to Quebec's English would strengthen their hand as against the French, who are a weak group in the continental context.

This objection is frequently voiced by activists who, having suffered the real consequences of their political vulnerability and internalized an identity of weakness, are now told that they are oppressors of their own minorities. A lesbian feminist complains of bisexual activists: 'Who or what has the power in the bisexual vision? Can activists really think that lesbian feminists *oppress* them? . . . Given our vulnerability, the priorities of bisexual declarations are baffling: do oppression and phobia from the gay world warrant more attention than, say, Jesse Helms or global capitalist patriarchy?'[11] The question of 'priorities' and of what kind of oppression warrants more attention might suggest that it is just a matter of rank: first we deal with the oppression of minorities, then we get to the internal minorities. It is understandable why Aboriginal women, Quebec's anglophones, and bisexual women might not want to wait for self-government, Quebec independence, or gay liberation to have their say. But in fact the second objection is not intended in this way. The asymmetries in power are thought to undercut, and not merely delay, the rights of internal minorities. The belief is that internal minorities should not have, because they do not need, rights against the minorities themselves.

If these objections hold good, then internal minorities do not have the same sort of rights as the minority groups themselves. And if that is so, then a liberal regime is compatible with the existence and protection of minority groups that treat some of their members badly and that, to be more exact, act towards internal minorities in ways that would be condemned if practised by the larger community against the minorities. There is no doubt that if Anglicans were subjected to the distress and humiliation to which they subjected Rev. Ferry, they would regard it as a clear violation of religious freedom. If the French language were proscribed in the circumstances in which English is in Quebec, it would be thought outrageous. If all Aboriginal bands were excluded from national political power in the way in which the patriarchal bands exclude women, it would be a corruption of democracy. So we need to ask: are these objections—the arguments from exit and from relative power—really compelling enough to deny rights to internal minorities in question?

Exit and Justice

Let us consider first the argument from exit. Its root appeal rests in the liberty principle itself: people ought not to be prevented from doing those things that they freely and competently choose, provided that they do not harm others. The apparent setback to the interests of internal minorities is thus tolerable, for they freely and completely choose to adhere to the minority groups of which they are members. The harms suffered, if any, are not done to 'others.'

The argument is sound only if members of minority groups do in fact have a fair chance to leave if mistreated. To see how rarely that is the case, one must assess the real prospects for exit.

Consider a clear violation of individual rights by a minority group.[12] David Thomas, a member of the Lyackson Indian Band in British Columbia, was forcibly and without consent captured and initiated into the ceremony of 'spirit dancing,' in the course of which he was assaulted, battered, and wrongfully confined. His captors (all members of other bands) defended their actions on the ground that they had a collective Aboriginal right to continue their traditions of spirit dancing, notwithstanding that this practice violated Thomas's individual rights to personal security. The court did not agree with them, and Thomas won his lawsuit. The judge held: 'He is free to believe in, and to practice, any religion or tradition, if he chooses to do so. He cannot be coerced or forced to participate in one by any group purporting to exercise their collective rights in doing so. His freedoms and rights are not subject to the collective rights of the aboriginal nation to which he belongs'.[13] Setting aside the legal issues, what exactly is the relationship between Thomas and the nation 'to which he belongs'?

Membership in this minority group, like that in many others, is partly ascriptive. Thomas was an Indian within the meaning of the Indian Act, but that was not his doing. He was also recognized by the nation as one of its own, but he testified that he had lived off the reserve most of his life, was not raised in the traditional religion or culture, knew little about it, and did not want to learn any more. And, of course, he did not consent to the initiation ceremony. Nonetheless, his abductors did not think that he had exercised any relevant power of exit: they still saw him as subject to their traditions. But what else could Thomas have done? Left the area? Repudiated his family? When membership is partly ascriptive in this way, exit is difficult and hardly a good substitute for rights.

J.S. Mill encountered this problem in his argument for tolerating the Mormon practice of polygamy, which he thought violated the rights of Mormon women: 'No one has a deeper disapprobation than I have of this Mormon institution; both for other reasons, and because, far from being in any way countenanced by the principle of liberty, it is a direct infraction of that principle, being a mere riveting of the chains of one half of the community, and an emancipation of the other from reciprocity of obligation towards them.'[14] It is important to notice how substantial these vices are. Polygamy violates both liberty and justice because it upsets a fair reciprocity of obligation. That is, it violates women's rights in the only sense of the term that Mill recognizes. But Mill says that the practice should none the less be tolerated, because exit from it is possible: 'Still it must be remembered that this relation is as much voluntary on the part of the women concerned in it, and who may be deemed the sufferers by it, as is the case with any other form of the marriage institution.'[15]

Now Mill was, as we know, not exactly thrilled by the ordinary monogamous marriage, so to say that polygamy is no less voluntary than that is not saying much. (Indeed, he calls women's acquiescence in it 'surprising' and thinks it explained by their belief that any form of marriage to a man is better than being single.) But, provided that Mormons 'allow perfect freedom of departure to those who are dissatisfied with their ways,'[16] they should be tolerated.

To test the force of this argument, we need to notice what Mill means by 'tolerating polygamy.' This does not bring any obligation to recognize Mormon marriages, nor to release others from their own obligations on the strength of Mormon views. Mill merely says, 'I cannot admit that persons entirely unconnected with them ought to step in and require that a condition of things with which all who are directly interested appear to be satisfied, should be put to an end. . . .'[17] That is, he takes the argument from exit to justify tolerating polygamy in the sense of not extirpating it.

That is indeed one kind of toleration; but it is an uninterestingly special case. There are perfectly good reasons for doubting that outsiders should undertake a crusade against polygamy—reasons that have nothing to do with the argument from exit. For example, the crusade may well fail or backfire. In any case, there may be no question of putting polygamy to an end; we might simply be wondering about whether it is permissible to impose restraints and safeguards on the practice—for instance, to ensure that women who refuse it are not shunned or impoverished, to guarantee that men in such unions do fulfil their obligations, and to provide for easy divorce. Any of these limitations would be at odds with Mormon practices of the time; yet all of them would go some way to respecting the rights of Mormon women.

A more interesting question, then, is whether the freedom to exit obviates the rights that these measures would protect. Let us suppose, with Mill, that Mormon women are free to remain unwed and (unlike David Thomas) may leave the jurisdiction of the group. In this sense, then, the church is a voluntary association: one is free to exit. But entry is a different matter. Adult converts are a minority in most religions. So the position of these women is more complex than the notion of 'voluntary association' might suggest. They are not like members of a tennis club who assessed the options and then freely joined and who remain free to resign. On the contrary, they typically found themselves members of an institution whose character is largely beyond their control but that structures their lives.

That being so, the meaning and costs of departure are different from what Mill's argument might suggest. For reasons that Hume gave[18] and with which Mill was certainly familiar, the mere existence of an exit does not suffice to make it a reasonable option. It is risky, wrenching, and disorienting to have to tear oneself from one's religion or culture; the fact that it is possible to do so does not suffice to show that those who do not manage to achieve the task have stayed voluntarily, at least not in any sense strong enough to undercut any rights they might otherwise have.

So the exit argument is a poor one. Mill began by conceding that what is at issue here is justice: polygamy upsets a fair reciprocity of obligation between men and women. But it is no part of a liberal theory that justice can be secured merely by providing for exit. If a certain social structure is unjust, it cannot become just merely by becoming avoidable. True, when exit is unavailable things are even worse, but that does not prove that when exit is available things are all right. What we would have expected here from Mill is not a weak and formalistic appeal to the principle *volenti non fit injuria*, but rather a rejection of the practice's claim to impose obligations at all, along the lines of his rejection of slavery contracts.[19] That he does not do so results from his identifying toleration of a practice with not eliminating it. Had he considered that the minority might protect the interests of women in other ways, he would have had to confront the conflict more directly.

These examples suggests ways in which the real prospects of leaving a minority group differ from the model of voluntary association. And the examples are not idiosyncratic: the minority groups that are most prized as experiments in living are precisely those in which membership is an 'organic' relation, where entry is not voluntary, membership is partly ascriptive, and exit, when possible, is costly. Under these conditions, internal minorities still need their rights.

Relative Power

Now I turn to the second objection to recognizing the rights of internal minorities—namely, that the groups against which they seek rights are, by definition, weak ones.

The reply here turns on getting absolute and comparative judgments of power into the right perspective. It is true that minority groups often have inadequate resources and that that is a reason for recognizing their special rights to begin with. But although that is so, many internal minorities are even worse off, and in ways that make them vulnerable to the minority.

First, there is a delicate question of political culture. It has often been noted that the disadvantage in which minority groups live is not always a fertile field for tolerance. In Christopher Isherwood's novel *A Single Man*, the gay protagonist puts it this way: 'While you're being persecuted, you hate what's happening to you, you hate the people who are making it happen; you're in a world of hate. Why, you wouldn't recognize love if you met it!'[20] And even in a world of love, Freud thought, hate must find some expression: 'It is always possible to bind together a considerable number of people in love, so long as there are other people left over to receive manifestations of their aggressiveness. . . .'[21]

To be sure, these pessimistic thoughts are speculative, and one cannot discount bias on the part of those who routinely suspect all minorities of intolerance. The capacity for intolerance is quite widely spread; Mill called the tendency to compel social conformity 'one of the most universal of all human propensities.'[22] And not everyone thinks that this tendency is most likely to become malignant in tight-knit social groups. On the contrary, some have argued that such groups actually promote tolerance. Espousing the view that it is in fact an anomic, mass society that nurtures hatreds, Michael Sandel writes, 'Intolerance flourishes most where forms of life are dislocated, roots unsettled, traditions undone.'[23] That might suggest that it is liberal society itself, not the minority groups, that is the problem.

These claims are hard to adjudicate and can rapidly descend into what Robert Nozick calls 'normative sociology'—the study of what the causes of social problems *ought* to be. Still, I think that there is ground for worry here. If one has learned to expect that one will be attacked from above, it is natural to fear that one may also be assaulted from below and to strike preemptively. These fears undermine trust in others, and trust is important in sustaining tolerance. Moreover, it is hard to build defences that shelter from one direction only—institutions and practices that promote solidarity, unanimity, and so on keep both majorities and internal minorities in check, whether that is their intention or not.

So we need not postulate special psychological mechanisms to predict a deficit of internal tolerance among some minorities: the circumstances of their lives simply make it extremely prudent to strive for unity. Inasmuch as there is strength in numbers, the minority will seek to avoid costly internal dissent. And the majority will also find it convenient if there is one authoritative voice that speaks for the minority. As a result, there is strong pressure for minorities to discipline themselves in these ways. And that is in fact what happens. The political development of Aboriginal associations in Canada follows the normal career of modern pressure-group politics, just as the US gay liberation movement formed itself fairly explicitly on the civil rights movement that preceded it. When minorities are thus organized and disciplined, they are given a clear voice and become stronger; but they often silence and disempower internal minorities in doing so.

A probable consequence of this process is that internal minorities will be among the most vulnerable groups in a society. Minorities are badly off, but internal ones are often even worse off. They suffer from being members of minority groups who need to defend themselves not only from the majority but also from other members of their own minority.

The reply to the second objection thus rests on complex factual questions about power and strategy, the answers to which are not always clear. Aboriginal women are doubly marginalized. But what should we say, for example, of anglophone Quebecers? That they were a historically powerful group does not seem in doubt. But are they still? It is sometimes thought that their power is somehow transmitted to them from other English-speaking groups. It is often said, for example, that Quebec is the last hope for the French language in North America, whereas if English were to perish in the province it would still flourish elsewhere. Is that relevant? After all, it is no solace to francophones that their language will always survive in Paris; why should English Montrealers feel reassured that their language will still be spoken in Boston?

These issues are obviously complex. My point is this. Neither the absolute weakness of a minority group, nor its relative weakness *vis-à-vis* the majority, proves that it is also weak *vis-à-vis* its own internal minorities. Moreover, there is good reason to suppose that it will often be stronger. I conclude, therefore, that the argument from relative power is no better than the argument from exit and that at least some internal minorities are entitled to rights in just the way that the minority groups themselves are, and for the same reasons.

Conflicts of Rights

If this thesis is correct, then minority rights are more dense than they appear. People have rights as members of a minority group, but members of the minority have rights as individuals *and* sometimes also as members of an internal minority.

The density of these rights makes conflicts among them nearly inevitable. Giving special rights to Indian bands does not have much chance of weakening or diminishing the cultural context of the Canadian majority. But securing the individual rights of native women within an Aboriginal community may well weaken it, as may securing the collective rights of groups within some bands. So here we have a genuine case of conflicing rights, in which to satisfy one is to set back another.

How are these conflicts to be resolved? I can say nothing about it here, and it is silly to look for a general theory. Everything depends on the character and weight of the particular rights involved and on the social context. But I want to stress that the existence of conflicts is what is at issue, for it has significant consequences for the relationship between liberalism and minorities.

Both protection of special minority interests and the limits on that protection flow from a single source. So while liberals can defend, for example, the value of cultural membership—including collective rights in one sense of that term—they cannot defend every culture. It is the liberal hope that people will, through experiments in living, articulate lives that are rich with value and meaning. At the same time, it is a requirement of liberal theory that they do so within the limits imposed by justice. As Kymlicka rightly says: 'Each person should be able to use and interpret her cultural experiences in her own chosen way. That ability requires that the cultural structure be secured from the disintegrating effects of the choices of people outside the culture, but also requires that each person within the community be free to choose what they see to be most valuable from the options provided (unless temporary restrictions are needed in exceptional circumstances of cultural vulnerability).'[24]

I think that is roughly correct but want to raise a question about its implications for the character of minority groups in a liberal society. If internal minorities are to have their rights, will not the whole point of different experiments in living be defeated? Are we to be able to experiment provided that we stay away from the dangerous elements of patriarchy, or nationalism, or homophobia—that is, provided that minority groups remain, so to speak, nice?

Clearly, much variation will be possible; there are many different ways of being nice. But could the Pueblo, for instance, remain theocratic? Kymlicka says that his argument for protecting culture provides no ground for restricting the religious freedom of the Peublo because they could survive with a Protestant minority. There could be no legitimate reason for restricting religious freedom, since there is no inequality in cultural membership to which it might be a response.[25]

Perhaps the Pueblo could remain Pueblo even with a Protestant minority; but that is only because it is in this case possible to prise apart culture and religion. It is a lucky thing if that is so, but it is easy to think of contrary examples, especially when one looks to cultural or religious minorities that cannot be defined by a certain linguistic or ethnic character. Many religions, for example, simply incorporate as central elements doctrines that are inconsistent with respect for the rights of women, children, sexual minorities, and so on. Here, to liberalize is to change.

Now, it is true that any theory of cultural integrity must allow for a distinction between changes in and changes of a culture. Conservatives often complain that the former amounts to the latter, that any change is a fundamental threat to 'our ways.' That is not a credible position. Many cultures incorporate as part of their fabric disputes about what their ways really are. But still, I think of no way of showing ex ante that the distinction will always fall neatly along the line demarcated by respect for rights. It may just be true of some groups that respect for the rights of their internal minorities would undermine them. And if so, there will be genuine and tragic conflict to face.

There is therefore no doubt that some ways of understanding group life—for example, most types of religious and cultural fundamentalism—will fare poorly under any regime that strives to respect personal autonomy. It is not that such ways of life will entirely vanish, but they will be deeply transformed if they survive, perhaps in the sort of way that Scots Calvinists became moderate presbyterians in North America. That may worry some who believe that a liberal regime must be 'neutral' among competing conceptions of the good. Certainly the consequences of a liberal political order will not be neutral among experiments in living. It is true that the reason that liberty-limiting fundamentalisms (for example) fare poorly is not that the liberal order disapproves of their way of life nor that they refuse to conform to community standards. They fare poorly because they are ill-adapted to the environment of liberal justice. But that distinction, native to modern liberalism, is foreign to them.

Yet without respect for internal minorities, a liberal society risks becoming a mosaic of tyrannies; colourful, perhaps, but hardly free. The task of making respect for minority rights real is thus one that falls not just to the majority but also to the minority groups themselves.

Notes

1. Christopher Isherwood *A Single Man* (New York: Farrar, Straus, Giroux 1964) 72.
2. Robert Nozick *Anarchy, State and Utopia* (Oxford: Blackwell 1974) chap. 10.
3. See Susan Moller Okin *Justice, Gender, and the Family* (New York: Basic Books 1989).
4. I follow Joseph Raz *The Morality of Freedom* (Oxford: Clarendon Press 1986) 166 ff.
5. See Leslie Green 'Two Views of Collective Rights' *The Canadian Journal of Law and Jurisprudence* 4 (1991) 316–27. See also Denise Réaume 'Individuals, Groups, and Rights to Public Goods' *University of Toronto Law Journal* 38 (1988) 1–27.
6. The conditions follow Raz *Morality of Freedom* 208.
7. Will Kymlicka *Liberalism, Community, and Culture* (Oxford: Clarendon Press 1989). Kymlicka does not consider the collective character of the interest in cultural survival. He treats it instead as a fully individuated interest in a certain comparative good—not having a worse cultural endowment than others—thus connecting it with a certain doctrine about equality. That thesis is not essential to the present argument.
8. By for example, John R. Danley 'Liberalism, Aboriginal Rights, and Cultural Minorities' *Philosophy and Public Affairs* 20 (1991) 169, 176, 177.
9. For Ferry's account, see James Ferry *In the Courts of the Lord* (Toronto: Key Porter Books, 1993). Anglicans are not, I think, an oppressed minority among Canadian religions and have little incentive to depart. But some religious minorities, such as Puritans, Mennonites, Hutterites, and Doukhobors, did leave oppressive states. Their success in attaining religious freedom elsewhere was mixed.
10. Setting aside the interesting case of carving a new state out of the territory of the old. For a helpful discussion of the issues, see Allen Buchanan *Secession: The Morality of Political Divorce from Fort Sumter to Lithuania and Quebec* (Boulder, Col.: Westview Press 1991).
11. Ara Wilson 'Just Add Water: Searching for the Bisexual Politic' *Out/Look* 16 (1992) 30.
12. *Thomas v. Norris*, [1992] 2 C.N.L.R. 139.
13. Ibid. at 162.
14. J.S. Mill *On Liberty* in his *Utilitarianism* ed. M. Warnock (London: Fontana 1962) 224.
15. Ibid.
16. Ibid.
17. Ibid.
18. David Hume 'Of the Original Contract' in his *Essays: Moral, Political, and Literary* (London: Oxford University Press 1963) 452–73.
19. Mill *On Liberty* 235–6.

20. Isherwood *A Single Man* 72.
21. S. Freud *Civilization and Its Discontents* (Harmondsworth: Penguin 1971) chap. 5.
22. Mill *On Liberty* 216.
23. M.J. Sandel 'Morality and the Liberal Ideal' in J.P. Sterba ed. *Justice: Alternative Political Perspectives* 2nd edn. (Belmont, Calif.: Wadsworth 1992) 224.
24. Kymlicka *Liberalism, Community, and Culture* 198.
25. Ibid. 196.

V Minority Cultures and Democratic Theory

12 Self-Determination versus Pre-Determination of Ethnic Minorities in Power-Sharing Systems

AREND LIJPHART

Introduction

In this paper, I want to make three main points. The first of these is that the basic principles of consociational democracy—or power-sharing democracy—are so obviously the appropriate answer to the problems of deeply divided (plural) societies that both politicians and social scientists have repeatedly and independently re-invented and re-discovered them. Secondly, these principles must be thought of as broad guidelines that can be implemented in a variety of ways—not all of which, however, are of equal merit and can be equally recommended to divided societies. My third and most important point will be that an especially important set of alternatives in applying the consociational principles is the choice between self-determination and pre-determination of the constituent groups in the power-sharing system, that is, the groups that will be the collective actors among whom power will be shared.

To give a brief preview of the last proposition, the terms 'self-determination' and 'pre-determination' describe the alternatives very well and in an almost self-explanatory way, but my use of the former differs from the most common usage. Self-determination deviates from the concept of '*national* self-determination'—the idea that nations should have the right to form separate sovereign states—in two fundamental respects. It refers to a method or process that gives various rights to groups *within* the existing state—for instance, autonomy rather than sovereignty—and it allows these groups to manifest themselves instead of deciding in advance on the identity of the groups. Needless to say, my concept of pre-determination is

Arend Lijphart, 'Self-Determination versus Pre-Determination of Ethnic Minorities in Power-Sharing Systems' in *Language and the State: The Law and Politics of Identity*, ed. David Schneiderman (Les Éditions Yvon Blais, Inc., Montreal, 1991), pp. 153–65. Reprinted by permission of the publishers.

completely unrelated to the superficially similar theological concept of pre-destination. Like self-determination, it refers to an internal process, but in contrast with self-determination, it means that the groups that are to share power are identified in advance. Both in contemporary and historical cases of consociationalism, pre-determination is more common, but I shall argue that self-determination has a number of great advantages and ought to be given much more attention by constitutional engineers who are trying to devise solutions for divided societies.

As a final introductory remark, let me define a few other basic concepts. I shall use the terms *deeply divided society* and *plural society* as synonyms. A plural society is a society that is sharply divided along religious, ideological, linguistic, cultural, ethnic, or racial lines into virtually separate subsocieties with their own political parties, interest groups, and media of communication. These subsocieties will be referred to as *segments*. As the definition of plural society indicates, the segments can differ from each other in several ways: in terms of religion, language, ethnicity, race, and so on. The most common of these is *ethnicity*, but the different categories overlap considerably. Ethnic differences imply cultural differences and often linguistic differences as well. Furthermore, cultural differences frequently include religious differences. Even when, as in the plural societies of Lebanon and Northern Ireland, the segments are mainly described in religious terms, the differences between them encompass a great deal more and can also be legitimately described as ethnic differences. I shall therefore make the general assumption that segments are ethnic segments and, in particular, ethnic minorities. Finally, let me emphasize that I shall use the terms *consociational* democracy and *power-sharing* democracy synonymously and interchangeably.

Re-discovering and Re-inventing Consociationalism

Three answers have been given to the question of how to provide peace and democracy in plural societies. The first is that this is an impossible task: successful democracy is assumed to require a minimum of homogeneity and consensus and hence cannot be established in plural societies. This answer has been given by social scientists from John Stuart Mill to Alvin Rabushka and Kenneth A. Shepsle. Mill states:

> Free institutions are next to impossible in a country made up of different nationalities . . . Among people without fellow-feeling, especially if they read and speak different languages, the united public opinion, necessary to the working of representative government, cannot exist.[1]

On the basis of similar arguments (although couched in modern game-theoretic terminology), Rabushka and Shepsle contend that 'stable democracy [cannot] be maintained in the face of cultural diversity' and that to argue otherwise reveals wishful thinking.[2]

The main problem with the Mill and Rabushka-Shepsle argument is not that it is not logical but that there are numerous cases of plural societies where democracy has worked reasonably well. The argument requires two amendments. First, it must be stated in terms of probability: democracy is less likely to be successful in plural than in homogeneous societies instead of in absolute and apodictic possible/impossible terms. Second, as I shall show in greater detail below, social scientists are not the only people who can understand the logic of this proposition. Politicians in plural societies can also grasp it and may want to try to take special measures to strengthen the probability of successful democracy. This means that the proposition can be turned into a self-denying prediction.

The second answer is that democracy in divided societies is possible provided that there is a majority that is firmly in control. A good example is Northern Ireland in the period from 1921 to 1972 when political power was firmly in the hands of the Protestant majority segment.[3] My objection to this second answer is not that it is empirically incorrect but that it seems highly questionable that we can speak of democracy in such cases. In Northern Ireland, Protestant majority rule spelled majority dictatorship rather than democracy in anything but the most superficial sense of the term.

The third answer is that peace and democracy are indeed possible in even the most deeply divided societies, provided that, instead of majority rule, consociational democracy is used. I discovered this answer in the late 1960s on the basis of my case study of the Netherlands and a subsequent extension of this study to Belgium, Switzerland, and Austria.[4] I have defined consociational democracy in terms of four basic principles: two primary principles (grand coalition and segmental autonomy) and two supplementary or secondary principles (proportionality and minority veto).

A grand coalition is an executive in which the political leaders of all significant segments participate. It may take various institutional forms. The most straightforward form is that of a grand coalition cabinet in a parliamentary system. In presidential systems, it may be achieved by distributing the presidency and other high offices among the different segments. These arrangements may be strengthened by broadly constituted councils or committees with important coordinating and advisory functions.

Segmental autonomy means the delegation of as much decision-making as possible to the separate segments. It complements the grand coalition principle: on all issues of common interest, the decisions should be made jointly by the segments; on all other issues, decision-making should be left to each segment. A special form of segmental autonomy that is particularly suitable for divided societies with geographically concentrated segments is federalism. If the segments are geographically intermixed, segmental autonomy will have to take a mainly non-territorial form.

Proportionality is the basic standard of political representation, civil service appointments, and allocation of public funds. As a principle of political representation, it is especially important as a guarantee for the fair representation of minority segments. There are two extensions of the proportionality representation of small segments and parity of representation (when the minority of minorities are over-represented to such an extent that they reach a level of equality with the majority or largest group).

The minority veto is the ultimate weapon that minorities need to protect their vital interests. Even when a minority segment participates in a grand coalition executive, it may be overruled or out-voted by the majority. This may not present a problem when only minor issues are being decided, but when a minority's vital interests are at stake, the veto provides essential protection.

While I was discovering consociationalism in the Netherlands, two other scholars were independently discovering the same phenomenon in Australia and Switzerland: Jürg Steiner in the latter country and Gerhard Lehmbruch in a comparative study of the two countries.[5] But I should really use the word 're-discover,' because another social scientist had preceded us by a few years: Sir Arthur Lewis in his pathbreaking short book on West Africa.[6] Lewis defined the kind of democratic system he deemed desirable for the West African plural societies—which he did not give a distinct label—more narrowly than I have above, but it is clearly consociational: elections by proportional representation (leading to a multiparty system of ethnically based parties), broad and inclusive coalition cabinets, and autonomy for the different ethnic groups by means of a decentralized federal system. The term 'consociation' goes back much farther; it was coined in the early seventeenth century by political theorist Johannes Althusius.[7] But Althusius was mainly an early federalist thinker and he cannot be regarded as a consociationalist. Lewis is clearly the intellectual originator of the theory.

What I have just stated requires one slight modification. Lewis formulated his concept of democracy on the basis of what he thought was needed, but not practised, in West Africa apparently in complete ignorance of the empirical examples of power-sharing elsewhere in the world. This means that he did not discover it; he invented it. Or, more precisely, he *re*-invented it. Politicians in different countries and at different times had already invented or re-invented it before him. The prize for the original invention should probably be given to the 'peaceful settlement' of 1917 in the Netherlands, which was a comprehensive, thoroughly consociational arrangement, adopted at the same time that full democracy was being adopted.[8] Subsequently, it was re-invented in Lebanon in 1943 (National Pact), Austria in 1945 (grand coalition in what Lehmbruch has called 'proportional democracy'), Malaysia in 1955 (government by the Alliance), Colombia in 1958 (the system of co-participation and pre-set alternation in the presidency), Cyprus in 1960 (the independence constitution), and Belgium in 1970 (drastic constitutional changes setting up a kind of 'linguistic federalism').[9] What is striking about these repeated re-inventions of consociationalism is that, although they are substantively so similar, they appear to have occurred completely independently of each other. There is no evidence that the later instances of the establishment of power-sharing were based on the lessons of earlier cases. The fact that, without the benefit of social learning, plural societies have repeatedly opted for consociational democracy as a solution to the problem of deep divisions, adds considerably to the strength of consociationalism as a general model.

Varieties of Power-Sharing

In my previous writings, I have emphasized that consociational democracy does not mean one specific set of rules and institutions.[10] Instead, it means a general type of democracy defined in terms of four broad principles, all of which can be applied in a variety of ways. For instance, as indicated earlier, the grand coalition can be a cabinet in a parliamentary system or a coalitional arrangement of a president and other top office-holders in a presidential system of government. The Swiss seven-member federal executive, which is based on a hybrid of parliamentary and presidential principles, is an additional example. Segmental autonomy may take the role of territorial federalism or of autonomy for segments that are not defined in geographical terms. Proportional results in elections may be achieved by the various systems of formal proportional representation (PR) or by several non-PR methods, such as Lebanon's method of requiring ethnically balanced slates in multi-member district plurality elections.[11] The minority veto can be either an absolute or a suspensive veto, and it may be applied either to all decisions or to only certain specified kinds of decisions, such as matters of culture and education. There is also the general difference, applicable to all four consociational principles, between laying down the basic rules of power-sharing in formal documents—such as constitutions, laws, or semi-public agreements—and relying on merely informal and unwritten agreements and understandings among the leaders of the segments.

I have come to believe that one of the most important differences between consociational arrangements—and also one of the most important choices that consociational engineers have to make—is the difference between pre-determination and self-determination of the segments of a plural society. Should these segments be identified in advance, and should power-sharing be implemented as a system in which these pre-determined segments share power? This appears to be the simplest way of instituting consociationalism, although, as I shall show below, it entails several problems and drawbacks. The alternative, which is necessarily somewhat more complicated, is to set up a system in which the segments are allowed, and even encouraged, to emerge spontaneously—and hence to define themselves instead of being pre-defined.

The crucial importance of this set of alternatives has become especially clear to me as a result of my thinking about the best way of setting up a democratic power-sharing system in South Africa. The first problem, of course, is to induce the different groups in South Africa to start negotiations on a peaceful and democratic solution for their country, and the second problem will be to secure agreement on the principle of power-sharing. Assuming that these problems can be solved, I have tried to address the next question: what kind of power-sharing system should be adopted? Here the main problem is that, while there is broad agreement that South Africa is a plural society, the identification of the segments is both objectively difficult and politically controversial. The root of this problem is that the South African system of minority rule has long relied on an official and strict classification of its citizens in four racial groups (African, White, Coloured, and Asian) and the further classification of the Africans into about a dozen ethnic groups. The racial classification has served the allocation of basic rights: for instance, the current 'tricameral' system allows Whites, Coloureds, and Asians to elect separate chambers of parliament, and excludes Africans from the national franchise. The ethnic classification has been the basis of the 'grand apartheid' system of setting up, and encouraging the eventual independence, of a series of ethnic homelands (formerly called Bantustans).

As a result of this policy of artificially forcing people into racial and ethnic categories, it has become quite unclear what the true dividing lines in the society are. The South African government appears to continue to think mainly in terms of race when it speaks of group rights and a sharing of power among groups. My own feeling is that the ethnic groups, including the two White ethnic groups of Afrikaners and English-speakers, are the strongest candidates to be considered the segments of the South African plural society, but I admit right away that the situation is more complicated. For instance, the English-speaking Whites appear to be a residual group rather than a cohesive and self-conscious ethnic segment. Another example concerns the Coloureds: should they be considered a separate segment or, since most of them speak Afrikaans and have an Afrikaans cultural background, do they form a single ethnic segment together with the White Afrikaners? Others have argued that modernization, industrialization, and urbanization have had a 'melting pot' effect, and that South Africa today is no longer a plural society and has become a 'common society'.[12]

Furthermore, the White government's insistence on African ethnic differences in connection with its widely despised homelands policy has had the ironic effect of making ethnicity highly suspect among most Africans. This sentiment is expressed clearly in Archbishop Desmond Tutu's statement: 'We Blacks (most of us) execrate ethnicity with all our being.'[13] Similarly, the African National Congress, the most powerful Black party in South Africa (although officially banned), both rejects ethnicity, since it regards ethnicity as a White divide-and-rule policy, and denies even its existence and hence its political relevance.

How can we resolve these disagreements about the identity of the segments and about whether South Africa is a plural society or not? My answer is that these disagreements do not need to be resolved, since we can design a consociational system on the basis of self-determined segments. First of all, I recommend elections by a relatively pure form of PR which will allow representation for even very small parties. Its rationale is based on the definition of a plural society that I gave earlier. This definition implies that one of the tests of whether a society is genuinely plural is whether or not its political parties are organized along segmental lines. We can turn this logic around: if we know that a society is plural but cannot identify the segments with complete confidence, we can take our cue from the political parties that form under conditions of free association and competition. PR is the optimal electoral system for allowing the segments to manifest themselves in the form of political parties. The beauty of PR is not just that it yields proportional results and permits minority representation—two important advantages from a consociational perspective—but also that it permits the segments to define themselves. Hence the adoption of PR obviates the need for any prior sorting of divergent claims about the segmental composition of South Africa or any other plural society. The proof of segmental identity is electoral success. We can go one step further: PR elections can also provide an answer to the question of whether South Africa is a plural society or not. If it is a plural society, the successful parties will be mainly segmental (and presumably ethnic) parties; if it is not a plural society, the parties that will emerge will be non-segmental policy-oriented parties. PR treats all groups, segmental or non-segmental, in a completely equal and even-handed way.

All of the consociational principles can now be instituted on the basis of self-determination. A grand coalition can be prescribed by requiring that the cabinet be composed of all parties of a specified minimum size in parliament; since these will be segmental parties, the cabinet will automatically be an inter-segmental grand coalition. The proportional allocation of public service jobs and public funds can also be based on the relative strengths that the several segments have demonstrated in the PR elections. And instead of granting a minority veto to all pre-determined segments, such a veto can be given to any group of legislators above a certain specified percentage.

Segmental autonomy can be organized along similar lines. Any cultural group that wishes to have internal autonomy can be given the right to establish a 'cultural council,' a publicly recognized body equivalent to a state in a federation. One of its main responsibilities will be the administration of schools for those who wish to receive an education according to the group's linguistic and cultural traditions. The voluntary self-segregation that such schools entail is acceptable as long as the option of multicultural and multiethnic education is also made available and provided that all schools are treated equally. It should be emphasized that this kind of non-territorial self-determined segmental autonomy can either be an alternative or an addition to geographically-based federalism. The two are eminently compatible. In the South African case, territorial federalism makes a great deal of sense because many of the ethnic segments have clear geographical strongholds and also because of the great diversity of the country in other respects. At the same time, however, there is so much group inter-mixture that territorial federalism by itself is insufficient to satisfy the demands of segmental autonomy.

In their book *South Africa Without Apartheid* Heribert Adam and Kogila Moodley make similar recommendations.[14] And such proposals have also been formally placed on the political agenda of South Africa by the Progressive Federal Party (PFP). In its constitutional plan adopted in 1978, the PFP proposes the following procedure to effect a grand coalition cabinet: The lower house of a bicameral legislature will be elected by PR, and the lower house will in turn elect the prime minister by majority vote. Then a power-sharing cabinet will be formed by requiring that the prime minister appoint cabinet members 'proportional to the strength of the various political parties' in the lower house and that 'in doing so the Prime Minister will have to negotiate with the leaders of the relevant parties'. Segmental autonomy is proposed by the PFP in the following self-determined form: 'A cultural group may establish a Cultural Council to assist in maintaining and promoting its cultural interests and apply to have that council registered with the Federal Constitutional Court'. These cultural councils will be publicly recognized bodies almost on a par with the states in the federal system that the PFP recommends; in the federal senate, where the states will be represented by equal numbers of senators, each cultural council will be able to name one senator, too.[15]

The PFP proposal of cultural councils was inspired by the Belgian example of non-territorial federalism (or, more accurately, partly non-territorial federalism), but it differs significantly from the Belgian model in that Belgian cultural councils are based on pre-determination: three, and only three, councils—Dutch, French and German—were established. Similarly, the Belgian constitution prescribes that the cabinet be composed of equal numbers of Dutch-speakers and French-speakers—again an example of pre-determination of segments. There are a number of other well-known examples of pre-determined segments, particularly the Greek and Turkish segments which are explicitly specified in the 1960 Cypriot constitution and Maronites, Sunnis, Shiites, and other religious sects recognized in the 1943 National Pact in Lebanon. However, the pre-1970 Belgian system of inter-religious and inter-ideological consociationalism was largely of the self-determined kind. The same generalization applies to the Dutch, Swiss and Austrian cases of consociational democracy.

A final, particularly interesting, but much less well-known example of self-determination is the 1925 Law of Cultural Autonomy in Estonia. Under its terms, each ethnic minority with more than 3,000 formally registered members had the right to establish autonomous institutions under the authority of a cultural council elected by the minority. This council could organize, administer, and supervise minority schools and other cultural institutions such as libraries and theatres, and it could issue decrees and raise taxes for these purposes. The councils also received state and local subsidies, and public funding was provided for the minority schools at the same level as for Estonian schools. The German and Jewish minorities quickly took advantage of the law and set up their own autonomous cultural authorities. As Georg von Rauch writes, 'these cultural authorities soon proved their worth, and the Estonian government was able to claim, with every justification, that it had found an exemplary solution to the problem of its minorities'.[16]

Advantages of Self-Determination

In the case of South Africa, because of special South African conditions and circumstances, self-determination of the segments is almost certainly the only way in which a consociation can be successfully established and operated. In most other cases, self-determination and pre-determination may both be reasonable options for consociational engineers. I would argue, however, that self-determination has a number of great advantages over pre-determination and hence that, unless there are compelling reasons to opt for pre-determination, the presumption should be in favor of self-determination. In this final section of my paper, let me list the advantages of self-determination:

1. The very first point in favor of self-determination is that it avoids the problem of invidious comparisons and discriminatory choices. Deciding which groups are to be the recognized segments in a power-sharing system necessarily entails the decision of which groups are not going to be recognized. In Lebanon, for instance, should the Moslem and Christian communes or the Maronites, Sunni, Shiite, Greek Orthodox, etc., sub-communes be made into the basic building blocks of the power-sharing system? In Belgium, since the small German-speaking minority was given its own cultural council, should not the Spanish, Turkish, and Moroccan minorities be given the same privilege? Even in cases that appear to be completely clear and uncontroversial, I would still argue that self-determination has no disadvantages compared with pre-determination in this respect.

2. The problem of potential discrimination is especially serious in countries where there are two or more large segments, which will obviously be recognized as participants in the power-sharing system, but also one or more very small minorities. These minorities run the risk of being overlooked, disregarded, or worse. Cyprus provides a good illustration. During the negotiations about the constitution and the electoral law, the question of how to define membership in the Greek majority community and in the Turkish minority community and the question of how to deal with the other, much smaller, minorities such as the Armenians and Maronites were discussed with 'extraordinary intensity,' as S.G. Xydis reports. Xydis speculates that the Turkish Cypriots may have been 'anxious to prevent any other minority in Cyprus from acquiring the status similar to that of the Turkish community with all its political implications'.[17]

3. Pre-determination entails not only potential discrimination against groups but, as a rule, also the assignment of individuals to specific groups. Individuals may well object to such labelling. If fact, the very principle of officially registering individuals according to ethnic or other group membership may be controversial, offensive, or even completely unacceptable to many citizens. Self-determination avoids the entire problem of placing people in groups and of establishing procedures for making decisions in individual cases. The New Zealand system of guaranteed Maori representation in parliament can serve as an example here. For many years, Maoris were

placed on separate voter registers and voted for Maori candidates in four exclusively Maori districts. This entailed the problem of deciding whether particular individuals should be placed on Maori or the general voter registers and the additional problem that many Maoris preferred not to be singled out for this special treatment. In order to alleviate these problems, it was decided that the special Maori seats would be retained but that, for Maoris, registration on the Maori register would be optional. Clearly the entire problem could be solved by the introduction of PR; reserved Maori seats would no longer be necessary. This is what New Zealand's Royal Commission on the Electoral System proposed in 1986.[18]

4. Self-determination gives equal chances not only to all ethnic or other segments, large or small, in a plural society but also to groups and individuals who explicitly reject the idea that society should be organized on a segmental basis. In the Lebanese case, Theodor Hanf has suggested that the consociational arrangement could be strengthened considerably if secularly-oriented groups and individuals could be recognized on a par with the traditional religious communities:

> A formula which makes group membership optional instead of obligatory could perhaps reduce the fear of those who wish to preserve their group identity, and perhaps prevent pressure being exerted upon those who do not wish to define themselves as members of a specific community but as Lebanese.[19]

A system of self-determination would obviously make this possible. In the Netherlands, the self-determined system of segmental schools, primarily designed to accommodate the main religious groups, has also been taken advantage of by small secular groups interested in particular educational philosophies to establish, for instance, Montessori schools.

5. In systems of pre-determination, there is a strong temptation to fix the relative shares of representation and other privileges for the segments on a permanent or semi-permanent basis. Examples are the 1:1 (Dutch-French) ratio of representation in the Belgian cabinet, the 7:3 (Greek-Turkish) ratio in the Cypriot cabinet and legislature, and the 6:5 (Christian-Moslem) ratio in the Lebanese parliament. Especially in Lebanon, this fixed ratio has become extremely controversial and it is one of the underlying causes of the breakdown of consociationalism in that country. Self-determination has the advantage of being completely flexible, since it is based on the numbers of people supporting the different parties and registering as members of cultural groups. It is naturally and continually self-adjusting.

6. Even when ethnic groups are geographically concentrated, the boundaries between different ethnic groups never perfectly divide these groups from each other. This means that territorial federalism can never be a perfect answer to the requirements of ethnic and cultural autonomy. And,

if we opt for autonomy on a non-territorial—that is, individual—basis, the most satisfactory method is to let the individuals determine their group membership for themselves. This consideration is becoming more and more important as individual mobility in modern societies increases and dilutes the geographical concentration of ethnic groups.

7. Finally, let me make an argument which is partly at variance with the main thrust of my reasoning so far. In many cases, the main segments of a plural society may be absolutely clear and uncontroversial, and these segments may want to be recognized as formally and specifically as possible. In these circumstances, it may make sense to use a combination of pre-determination and self-determination: for instance, a two-tier system of pre-determination of the large segments and self-determination of any other group that may aspire to similar, though not necessarily identical, rights of representation and autonomy. While my main argument remains that self-determination is to be preferred to pre-determination, many of the advantages of self-determination can be attained by using self-determination as a complementary method to pre-determination.

Are there any disadvantages to self-determination? The only genuine drawback is that it precludes the application of the principle of minority overrepresentation. As indicated earlier, the principle of proportionality is already favorable to minorities, especially small minorities, but it may be extended even further by giving minorities more than proportional representation. The 7:3 ratio in Cyprus is an example of such overrepresentation since the actual population ration of the Greek and Turkish segments is closer to 8:2. The advantage that minorities derive from overrepresentation should not be exaggerated, however. The stronger protection for minorities in power-sharing systems is provided by guaranteed representation, guaranteed autonomy, and, if necessary, the use of the minority veto. Compared with these strong weapons, overrepresentation is no more than a marginal benefit.

Notes

1. John Stuart Mill, *Considerations on Representative Government* (New York: Liberal Arts Press, 1958) at 230.
2. Alvin Rabushka and Kenneth A. Shepsle, 'Political Entrepreneurship and Patterns of Democratic Instablity in Plural Societies' (April 1971) 12:4 *Race* at 462.
3. See Ian Lustick, 'Stability in Deeply Divided Societes: Consociationalism versus Control' (April 1979) 31:3 *World Politics* at 325–44.
4. Arend Lijphart, *The Politics of Accommodation: Pluralism and Democracy in the*

Netherlands (Berkeley: University of California Press, 1968); Arend Lijphart, 'Typologies of Democratic Systems' (1968) 1:1 *Comparative Political Studies* at 3–44.

5. Jürg Steiner, *Amicable Agreement versus Majority Rule: Conflict Resolution in Switzerland* (Chapel Hill: University of North Carolina Press, 1974); Gerhard Lehmbruch, *Proporzdemokratie: Politisches System und politische Kultur in der Schweiz und in Österreich* (Tübingen: Mohr, 1967).
6. W. Arthur Lewis, *Politics in West Africa* (London: Allen and Unwin, 1965).
7. Johannes Althusius, *Politica Methodice Digesta* (1603).
8. See also Hans Daalder, 'The Consociational Democracy Theme' (July 1974) 26:4 *World Politics* at 604–21.
9. See Arend Lijphart, *Democracy in Plural Societies: A Comparative Exploration* (New Haven: Yale University Press, 1977) passim.
10. See Arend Lijphart, 'Consociation: The Model and Its Applications in Divided Societies,' in Desmond Rea, ed., *Political Co-Operation in Divided Societies: A Series of Papers Relevant to the Conflict in Northern Ireland* (Dublin: Gill and Macmillan, 1982) at 166–186. See also Heinz Kloss, 'Territorial prinzip, Bekenntnixprinzip, Verfügungsprinzip: Über die Möglichkeiten der Abgrenzung der Volklichen Zugehrigkeit' (1965) 22 *Europa Ethnica* at 52–73.
11. Arend Lijphart, 'Proportionality by Non-PR Methods: Ethnic Representation in Belgium, Cyprus, Lebanon, New Zealand, West Germany, and Zimbabwe' in Bernard Grofman and Arend Lijphart, eds., *Electoral Laws and Their Political Consequences* (New York: Agathon Press, 1986) at 113–123.
12. Heribert Adam and Kogila Moodley, *South Africa Without Apartheid: Dismantling Racial Domination* (Berkeley: University of California Press, 1986) esp. at 196–214.
13. Desmond Mpilo Tutu, *Hope and Suffering: Sermons and Speeches* (Grand Rapids, Michigan: Eerdmans, 1984) at 121.
14. *Supra*, note 12 at 215–263.
15. Arend Lijphart, *Power-Sharing in South Africa* (Berkeley: Institute of International Studies, University of California, 1985) at 66–73.
16. Georg von Rauch, *The Baltic States: Estonia, Latvia, Lithuania—The Years of Independence 1971–1940* (Berkeley: University of California Press, 1974) at 141–142.
17. Stephen G. Xydis, *Cyprus: Reluctant Republic* (The Hague: Mouton, 1973) at 490–492.
18. Arend Lijphart, 'The Demise of the Last Westminster System? Comments on the Report of New Zealand's Royal Commission on the Electoral System' (August 1987) 6:2 *Electoral Studies* at 97–103.
19. Theodor Hanf, 'The "Political Secularization" Issue in Lebanon' in *The Annual Review of the Social Science of Religion*, Vol. 5 (Amsterdam: Mouton, 1981) at 249.

13 Democracy and Difference: Some Problems for Feminist Theory

ANNE PHILLIPS

When feminists have challenged the proclaimed gender neutrality of 'malestream' political thought, they have frequently lighted on the abstract individualism of supposedly ungendered citizens as a target for their critique. In Zillah Eisenstein's *The Female Body and The Law*, this provides the starting point for a new theory of equality that no longer relies on us being treated the same; in Carole Pateman's *The Sexual Contract* it underpins a critique of contractual models as necessarily premised on a masculine notion of the body as separable from the self; in Susan Moller Okin's *Justice, Gender, and the Family* it is developed into a vision of a genderless society as the precondition for fully just relations.[1]

My concern here is with the further implications for democracy, and more specifically, with the arguments that subsequently open up over group identities and group representation. The feminist challenge to the abstract, degendered individual has combined with the earlier critique of those who took class as the only or only interesting social divide, to usher in a new politics based around heterogeneity and difference. Not just 'the' sexual difference: the most innovative of contemporary feminist writing moves beyond a binary opposition between male and female towards a theory of multiple differences. The myth of homogeneity is then seen as sustaining a complex of unequal and oppressive relations; and group identities and group specificities are increasingly regarded as part of what must be represented or expressed.

The argument shares some common ground with issues long familiar to theorists of democracy, where group affiliation and group organisation is frequently presented as a counterweight to the hierarchy of advantages that otherwise attach to citizens as individuals. In their *Participation and Political Equality*, for example, Sidney Verba, Norman Nie and Jae-on Kim suggest that systematic inequalities in individual political influence can be at least

Anne Phillips, 'Democracy and Difference: Some Problems for Feminist Theory', *Political Quarterly*, Vol. 63/1 (1992), pp. 79–90. Reprinted by permission of Blackwell Publishers.

partially off-set by the power of organisation. In particular, they argue, political equality is fostered by explicit confrontation around class, religion, race or other social cleavages, for where conflicts of interests become part of the organisational basis of political mobilisation, this helps boost the participation of otherwise disadvantaged groups.[2] If we take this line of argument seriously, however, then it makes a case for much stronger conclusions about institutionalising group representation. Democracy implies equality, but when it is superimposed on an unequal society, it allows some people to count for more than others. Group organisation by those less advantaged can in principle equalise the weighting, but given the tendency for those with greater individual resources also to monopolise the group-based resources, things rarely work out this way. If equal weighting is to be desired, and group representation is potentially a means of achieving it, then why not develop formal representation for disadvantaged groups in order to guarantee them a more equal weight?

When the discussion deals solely with class, people have been reluctant to follow it through to any such conclusion, for while the systematic inequities that class introduces into democratic politics are frequently deplored, they are somehow in the end accepted. The issues become more pointed when they concern groups defined by their ethnicity or gender, these being aspects of ourselves for which we can hardly be held responsible, characteristics we can do nothing about. And yet our democracies are significantly skewed towards the representation of white men, who make up the overwhelming majority of our politicians and who determine what gets on the political agenda. Collective action has only mildly modified this pattern. Should we not call for more formal representation of group identities or group interests in order to counteract the current balance of power?

This is one of the questions that feminism raises for democracy, though I would not want to suggest that it is the only—or even the major—concern. Feminism is associated with a richly textured and layered vision of democracy, in which the precise institutions for political representation have tended to play a subordinate role; feminist theorists have scored many telling points against the abstract individualism of ungendered citizens, but few have derived from this specific recommendations on the difference sexual difference should make.[3] The most fully developed policy recommendation is the call for quota systems to achieve parity between the sexes—in parliaments, political parties, trade unions, corporate structures, and so on—which need not (and I will argue should not) rely on any substantial notion of 'representing women'. The case for group representation is as yet implicit in feminist theorising on democracy, while the notion of group interests has already provoked substantial feminist critique.[4] That said, the feminist emphasis on heterogeneity and differences is beginning to introduce new issues into democratic theory and practice, and I will use this essay to explore some of the problems thus raised.

The starting point is that institutionalising group representation seems to conflict with what has been the movement of democracy, which is typically away from group privilege and group representation, and towards an ideal of citizenship in which each individual counts equally as one. The French Revolution shattered the principle of representation according to estates; in all countries that lay claim to the title of democracy, the transition to universal suffrage contested and eliminated the various group definitions—by property, by education, by sex or by race—that had previously organised the distribution of power. Democracy, in this sense, has been viewed as a challenge to special interest groups, and not only because these tend to confirm dominant interests. Many contemporary radicals see the ideals of democracy as pointing towards a politics in which people will transcend their localised and partial concerns, getting beyond the narrow materialism of special interest to address the needs of the community instead. This is the foundation stone, for example, of Benjamin Barber's *Strong Democracy*, where the case for a more active and participatory democracy rests on the transformative powers of democratic discussion and talk. Liberal democracy, he argues, accepts all too readily the notion of pre-given, frozen, interests that can only be counted, protected or suppressed. Strong democracy, by contrast, would bring people into direct engagement with other arguments, needs and concerns, and this more active involvement would help thaw out the rigidity of their initial positions. People might still arrive at the meeting with their minds fixed only on themselves or their group, but after fuller exposure to other people's worries, would develop a more collective approach.[5]

This version of democracy has obvious attractions when set alongside the damning complacencies of twentieth century pluralism, which argued that politics was and always would be a matter of competition between interest groups, and that democracy was sufficiently guaranteed by the chance for any group to compete. But it remains open to precisely the charge that is levelled against pluralism: insufficient attention to political equality. When society is ordered in a hierarchical fashion (as is any society we have yet been privileged to meet) then those groups that have been silenced or marginalised or oppressed will look to ways of enhancing their own representation. They will have little time for appeals to them to set aside their own parochial concerns and consider the issues more broadly. Feminists, for example, have had weary dealings with those who claim that the emphasis on sex is divisive, or that it helps rigidify barriers we might all prefer to see removed. Their response has been typical of previously silenced constituencies: the groups that are dominant need their powers stripped away; but others need to amplify their collective voice.

Group Representation

This is the central message in Iris Marion Young's recent critique of Benjamin Barber, and indeed her work serves as the clearest example of a feminist case for group representation. Extending considerably beyond issues of gender, Young calls on democracies to set up procedures that would ensure additional representation for all oppressed groups. The mechanisms she proposes include public funding to enable such groups to meet together and formulate their ideas; the right to generate their own policy proposals that would then have to be considered by decision-makers; and veto powers over matters that are most directly that group's concern. (Two examples she suggests of this last are a veto power for women over legislation affecting reproductive rights, and a veto power for Native Americans over the use of reservation lands.) She has many potential groupings in mind, and her suggested list for the United States is somewhat daunting in its implications. It includes 'women, blacks, Native Americans, Chicanos, Puerto Ricans and other Spanish-speaking Americans, Asian Americans, gay men, lesbians, working class people, poor people, old people, and mentally and physically disabled people'.[6]

The argument deals explicitly with equalising political influence, for it is only oppressed groups that would qualify for this addition to their political weight. The theoretical underpinning, however, is Iris Young's critique of impartiality, which extends beyond the more quantitative aspects of equality to address the conservatism of an undifferentiated norm. We have inherited from the Enlightenment an ideal of universal citizenship which, however badly practised, claims to deal with us in our essentially 'human' concerns. The vision of democracy that is associated with this claims to treat us as abstract individuals or citizens, regardless of our sex, race or class. More even than this, it calls on us to treat ourselves and others in the same selfless way. We are allowed to voice, but are not encouraged to press, our own specific concerns. Fairness is then conceived as a matter of putting oneself in the other person's shoes—but, as a number of recent feminist theorists have noted, there is an unfortunate asymmetry in this. The injunction may sound positive enough when addressed to those in comfortable positions of power, who do indeed need shaking out of their specific and narrow concerns. The same injunction can be totally disabling for those less fortunately placed. When an oppressed group is called upon to put its own partial needs aside, it is being asked to legitimate its own oppression.

Though he approaches the issues from an opposite theoretical direction, Will Kymlicka deals with related question when he discusses the relevance of liberalism to culturally plural societies, his main concern being to justify group rights for any aboriginal community. What he means by this is 'a stable and geographically distinct historical community with separate language and culture rendered a minority by conquest or immigration or the redrawing of political boundaries'.[7] As he describes it, current legislation in Canada and the USA gives such communities a distinct—and in some ways preferential—legal status. Non-Native Americans, for example, have only restricted mobility, property or voting rights in the reservation lands of the United States; non-Indian Canadians are similarly restricted in their access to reservation land. In the Canadian North, where the inhospitable environment is enough to discourage permanent settlement by non-Inuit Canadians, the problem is not so much pressure on the land, as the fact that extensive development projects for exploiting natural resources have brought with them large numbers of transient workers, who at any point in time are likely to outnumber the original—and permanent—community. Since these 'migrant' workers may stay for as long as seven years, they are able to vote and thereby influence the allocation of local resources, but they may as a consequence tailor local provision to their own requirements. (One of the issues here is whether schoolchildren should be taught in one of Canada's two official languages: however transient the development workers, they surely have a right to ensure their children are educated in either French or English, but this may speed the disintegration of Inuit culture and language.) The problem Kymlicka poses is whether minority groups can therefore insist on special status and group rights in order to protect their cultural heritage.

He argues that they can, and in one of the many irritants to those who seek a close connection between philosophy and politics, he rests his argument on a very different foundation from that suggested in recent feminist debate. While Iris Young employs a critique of impartiality to underpin her case for group representation, Kymlicka appeals to the principle of neutral concern as his basis for what are on the face of it rather similar conclusions. Liberalism, he argues, is best understood in its classically individualist terms of enhancing our choices over the kind of life we should lead, and it is a tradition that encourages self-examination. Liberals believe that people can (and should) detach themselves from whatever traditions or values they have inherited, for 'no particular task is set for us by society, and no particular cultural practice has authority that is beyond individual judgment and possible rejection'.[8] 'Cultural structures', however, provide the essential context within which people become aware of the options open to them and can then intelligently judge their worth. Where a cultural community is threatened with disintegration, this then puts its members at a severe disadvantage—and it is in order to rectify this inequality that these communities require special status or special protection. One possible political implication is given in recent proposals by aboriginal leaders in the Canadian North: for a three-to-ten-year residency qualification before citizens acquire rights to vote or hold public office; for a guaranteed 30% aboriginal representation in regional government; and for veto power over legislation affecting crucial aboriginal interests.[9] This last overlaps directly with one of Iris Young's proposals.

In both cases, the crucial arguments relate to political equality, and the distorting consequences of trying to pretend away group difference or affiliation. Political equality is not guaranteed by the equal right to vote, nor gender neutrality by the abstractions of the liberal individual. Abstract individualism imposes a unitary conception of human needs and concerns, and this serves to marginalise those groups who may differ from the dominant norm. The needs of women then appear as a 'special case' (though women make up half the population); ethnic differences are subsumed under 'the problem of ethnic minorities' (as if ethnicity is only a characteristic of minority—deviant—groups); the pauperisation of pensioners is treated as just one of many pressure group preoccupations (though most of us will eventually be old). The dominance of a norm is so powerful that it obscures the startling fact that most people lie outside its boundaries. As Iris Young indicates, we would like a politics that is more honest than this: 'we must develop participatory democratic theory not on the assumption of an undifferentiated humanity, but rather on the assumption that there are group differences and that some groups are actually or potentially oppressed or disadvantaged.'[10]

Problems of Group Narrowness and Closure

The case seems overwhelming, and it calls out for some hard thinking about the institutional changes that would meet such complaints. Precisely what these should be is more difficult to decide, for it comes up against the worrying problems of group narrowness and group closure. No-one (I imagine) would want to flee the abstractions of an undifferentiated humanity only to end up in its opposite; no-one would favour the kind of politics in which people were elected only to speak for their own group identity or interests, and never asked to address any wider concerns. Even setting aside what we would lose in terms of competing notions of the common good, such a development could mean shoring up communal boundaries and tensions, which could be as oppressive as any universal norm. If cultural diversity is positive, there is no advantage in restricting its range.

It is worth noting that even in drawing attention to the plurality of groups and cultures, both Young and Kymlicka express reservations over what defines a community or group. Young, in particular, is scathing on the authoritarianism implicit in notions of the 'community', which all too often serve to iron out multiple identities, and impose another kind of oppressive norm.[11] Kymlicka hovers around similar reservations when he notes that some aboriginal women's groups have called for an external review of aboriginal self-government, thereby indicating their sense of isolation or suppression within the aboriginal community. Neither theorist warms to the notion of a group identity that is pre-given or fixed. Young explicitly rejects the idea that group identities are defined by some essential set of common attributes; observes that most people have multiple group identifications; and that groups come into being and then fade away. Kymlicka deals only with the historically specific case of aboriginal communities, and he remains agnostic over how far his arguments could be extended beyond such groups. A close reading of his argument suggests, however, that he looks forward to a time when members of the aboriginal community might choose alternatives to their aboriginal identity, and abandon their original group.

Both then recognise the problem of closure, the risk that institutionalising forms of group representation could block further development and change. But if this *is* a problem—and I think it is—it surely should be given more weight. What distinguishes these arguments from the everyday talk of pressure groups is the case they make for institutional recognition: not just the softer versions of letting groups carry on with their organisation and campaigns, but a harder insistence on getting funding and recognition and powers. The more substantial the powers, however, the more it matters that we might get the groups wrong. Do we say, for example, that wherever a group feels itself oppressed or discriminated against, then there is a *prima facie* case for guaranteeing that group some form of representation? Such feelings could after all be misplaced (one example suggested to me being the men who have been deprived of their hot suppers by the fact that their wives go out to work). And what if the procedures become counter-productive, strengthening rather than weakening a divide? Nigeria, for example, has experimented extensively with quota systems and federal structures in order to balance demands between different ethnic groups, but there is a strong body of opinion that regards this as perpetuating a damaging three-way competition, recurrently reproduced between three major parties. The smaller ethnic groups were seriously disadvantaged in the first constitution; the subsequent proliferation of states only intensified what Richard Joseph describes as 'prebendal politics', an unhealthy jostling for resources, and offices, and power.[12] Where societies are divided between advantaged and disadvantaged groups, it does seem crucial to establish mechanisms that will equalise the balance of power. But such mechanisms can perpetuate the problem, and may not respond readily enough to change.

No-one to my knowledge argues for the extreme reversal of current liberal democratic practice that would substitute group representation for the more general representation by political parties. The issue is more one of complementarity, as in Iris Young's suggestions for strengthening the input of groups into the formulations of public policy. But any call for funding or special status draws attention to the difficulties in establishing which groupings are relevant, and this lends weight to a more cautious approach. There is a powerful argument for enhancing procedures for group consultation, and for concentrating these on groups who have been disadvantaged in the current distribution of political influence. There is a much more shaky case for giving such groups definitive power.

The difficulties in defining what are the appropriate groups are compounded by the additional problems of group representation. It is hard to see what counts as 'representing' a group, for there are few mechanisms for establishing what each group wants. We cannot say, for example, that getting more women elected to local or national assemblies therefore secures the representation of women. Politicians are not elected by women's constituencies, and apart from canvassing opinion within their own parties, and perhaps consulting their own coterie of friends, they do not have a basis for claiming to speak 'for women'. One response would be to create more substantial mechanisms for consultation and group organisation—perhaps along the lines that Iris Young suggests. But then anything that relies on people going to meetings (a women's forum, for example) potentially founders on the limited numbers who are likely to attend. The people who go to meetings are often a pretty 'unrepresentative' bunch!

Gender Quotas

The problems of accountability combine with the risks of freezing what are multiple and shifting identities to set severe limits to the notion of group representation, favouring a weaker version of group consultation over the stronger versions that might include veto power. The same problems do not, however, apply to the case for political quotas, which can be and should be distinguished. The extraordinary mismatch between the kind of people who get elected and the gender and ethnic composition of the population they claim to represent remains as a serious blot on the practices of democracy. These problems can be tackled without a notion of group representation.

The case for gender quotas has been pursued with particular success by women active in political parties in the Nordic countries, largely, but not exclusively, those on the left of the political spectrum. In the course of the 1970s a number of parties adopted the principle of at least 40% female representation at all levels of elected delegation within the party itself: the Swedish Liberal and Communist Parties in 1972; the Norwegian Liberal Party in 1974, and Socialist Left Party in 1975; the Danish Socialist People's Party in 1977.[13] In the following decade there was a push to extend this to the level of female representation in national parliaments, the mechanisms being relatively straightforward in electoral systems that operate a party list system and elect according to proportional representation. In 1980, parties in both Norway and Sweden proposed legislation that would commit *all* political parties to a minimum of 40% women on their electoral lists; failing the success of this bid, various parties introduced the practice unilaterally.[14] In 1983, for example, the Norwegian Labour Party introduced a 40% quota for candidates in local and national elections, while among the parties that remained ideologically opposed to the principle of a quota system, there was also substantial movement. The Norwegian Conservative Party espouses 'competence' rather than formal quotas, but women nonetheless made up 30% of its national representation by the mid-1980s.

The results have proved rather spectacular. While Britain has only just managed to lift itself above the 5% barrier in its proportion of women MPs, the Nordic countries stand out as a relative haven for women politicians. By 1984 women had taken 15% of the parliamentary seats in Iceland; 26% in Norway and Denmark; 28% in Sweden and 31% in Finland.[15] In 1985, Norway took the world record, very largely as a result of the quota introduced by the Norwegian Labour Party and the fact that Labour then won the general election. Women made up 34.4% of the Storting (the national assembly); held eight out of 18 cabinet posts; contributed 40.5% of the membership of County Councils; and 31.1% of the membership of municipal councils.

Though feminists have employed a variety of arguments in pressing the case for political quotas, the crucial one does not—and I believe should not—rest on a notion of group representation. More than anything, it is an argument in terms of political equality. When the composition of decision-making assemblies is so markedly at odds with the gender and ethnic make-up of the society they represent, this is clear evidence that certain voices are being silenced or suppressed. If there were no substantial obstacles in the way of equal participation, then those active in politics would be randomly distributed according to their ethnicity or gender; the fact that the distribution is so far from random therefore alerts us to these obstacles and the necessity for some countervailing force. The argument can be enhanced by all manner of predictions about how the composition of our decision-making assemblies will be enriched by a wider range of opinions and knowledges and concerns. But the argument is not strengthened—if anything it is weakened—by the more substantial notion of 'representing' a new constituency or group. Accountability is always the other side of representation, and, in the absence of procedures for establishing what any group wants or thinks, we cannot usefully talk of their political representation.

The difficulties that bedevil group representation do not therefore affect the case for political quotas—or indeed for whatever alternative mechanisms could help establish political parity. The one point of overlap—and it is a difficult one—is in thinking about how far one should extend the principle of what I shall call 'mirror' rather than political representation: what exactly are the groups that should count? The standard case against quota systems is a *reductio ad absurdum* that pretends the list will go on and on, and, while I would want to resist the dishonesty of those who prefer no change, the objection contains the kernel of a serious concern. If the arguments in favour of ethnicity and gender are so decisive, what justifies us in stopping at these two: surely the same kind of points could be made in terms of religion, of sexuality, of class? In each case the failure to 'reflect' the distribution of characteristics through the population as a whole should alert us to obstacles that are preventing equal participation. In each case there is then an argument for guaranteeing proportional representation. Where exactly are we supposed to draw the line, and what is the basis for any distinction?

The answer at one level is simple: it is politics that defines the pertinent categories, which therefore the quite legitimately change. This is true even in terms of what I am presenting as the more 'permanently' relevant categories, and perhaps helps explain why the case for parity between women and men has so far met with greater success than the parallel case for parity between different ethnic groups.[16] In the case of Britain, for example, the all-embracing concept of 'black' people rapidly dissolved into a distinction between the Asian and Afro-Caribbean communities, and then subsequently into finer distinctions between a wide variety of ethnic groups. What is this context then counts as 'adequate' ethnic representation? Such questions can hardly be answered in isolation from politics and political mobilisations, and any attempt to settle the matter in advance would freeze the relevant categories at a premature moment of discussion and debate. The same argument would apply to any further extensions of mirror representation. Religious affiliation, for example, becomes more or less pertinent depending on the politics of the society in question, and it would be inappropriate to rule it in or out as a matter of abstract principle. I am not entirely happy with this resolution, for when politics becomes sole arbiter, this edges too close to an abdication of judgement. These are matters that require much closer discussion.

The general conclusions I draw involve a modification—but also a modified defence—of liberal democracy as we know and loathe it. It is indeed dangerous to pretend that who or what we are is irrelevant, to ask people to submerge their group differences in an abstract citizenship, to say that politics should be only a matter of ideas. Such complacency leaves democracy too much at the mercy of existing power relations, which will just reproduce existing patterns of power. More specifically, the composition of political representation does matter, and we need the kind of institutional changes that will guarantee proportionality—at least by ethnicity and gender. But we should detach the arguments, for example, for more women in politics—for parity between women and men—from the arguments for representing women as a group. The case still stands whether these women 'represent' women or not.

The issues raised in recent feminist discussions of group difference and group representation relate to and extend what has been a long history of debate on democracy, and cannot but concern those who query the inadequacies of what currently passes for political equality. Our societies are not homogeneous: they are structured around systemic inequalities and recurrent exclusions. We exist not just as abstract citizens, but also as members of variously privileged or disadvantaged groups. Political organisation based around the dominant cleavages—whether these are by gender or class or ethnicity or religion—is rightly viewed as one possible means of redressing the balance, and my argument in this paper is not against such collective action *per se*. Nor is it an argument against careful consideration of the ways of enhancing group involvement in the process of policy formation, and ways of weighting this towards those groups who have been most excluded. And on what seems to me the more straight-forward issue of equalising individuals' access to political élites, I believe the time for reform is long overdue. My reservations refer exclusively to that more ambitious step of institutionalising group representation, for in exploring the possible extension of feminist arguments into a case for formal and substantial group representation, I have come to the conclusion that the potential risks outweigh the gains.

Notes

1. Zillah Eisenstein, *The Female Body and the Law*, University of California Press, 1989; Carole Pateman, *The Sexual Contract*, Polity Press, 1989; Susan Moller Okin, *Justice, Gender, and the Family*, Basic Books, New York, 1989.

2. Sidney Verba, Norman H. Nie and Jae-on Kim, *Participation and Political Equality*, Cambridge University Press, 1978.
3. For a fuller discussion of the relationship between feminist and democratic theory, see my *Engendering Democracy*, Polity Press, Oxford, 1991.
4. See, for example, Irene Diamond and Nancy Hartsock, 'Beyond Interests in Politics: a comment on Virginia Sapiro's "When are Interests Interesting?"', *American Political Science Review*, 1981, 75(3); Anna G. Jonasdottir, 'On the Concept of Interests, Women's Interests, and the Limitations of Interest Theory', in K.B. Jones and A.G. Jonasdottir (eds.), *The Political Interests of Gender*, Sage, Beverley Hills, 1988; Rosemary Pringle and Sophie Watson, '"Women's Interests" and the Post-Structuralist State', in Michèle Barrett and Anne Phillips (eds), *Destabilizing Theory: Contemporary Feminist Debates*, Polity Press, Oxford, forthcoming 1992.
5. Benjamin Barber, *Strong Democracy: Participatory Politics For A New Age*, University of California Press, 1984. For an earlier argument that follows similar lines see Sheldon Wolin, *Politics and Vision*, Little Brown and Company, 1960.
6. Iris Marion Young, 'Polity and Group Difference: A Critique of the Ideal of Universal Citizenship', *Ethics*, 1989, Vol. 99, p. 261.
7. Will Kymlicka, *Liberalism, Community, and Culture*, Clarendon Press, Oxford, 1989, p. 258.
8. Ibid., p. 50.
9. Ibid., p. 147.
10. Young, *op. cit.*, p. 261.
11. Iris Marion Young, 'The Ideal of Community and the Politics of Difference', in Linda Nicholson (ed.), *Feminism/Postmodernism*, Routledge, London, 1990.
12. Richard A. Joseph, *Democracy and Prebendal Politics in Nigeria*, Cambridge University Press, 1987.
13. Torild Skard and Elina Haavio-Mannila, 'Mobilization of Women at Elections', in Elina Haavio-Mannila *et al.*, *Unfinished Democracy: Women in Nordic Politics*, Pergamon Press, Oxford, 1985.
14. Torild Skard and Elina Haavio-Mannila, 'Women in Parliament', in *Unfinished Democracy*, 1985.
15. Joni Lovenduski, *Women and European Politics: Contemporary Feminism and Public Policy*, Wheatsheaf, 1986, p. 152.

16. At its 1990 conference, for example, the Labour Party finally committed itself to the principle of quotas to achieve at least 40% female representation at all levels within the Party, and to the aim of parity between the sexes in the Parliamentary Labour Party over the next ten years or the next three general elections. But there are as yet no agreed mechanisms for achieving the latter: no simple matter within the framework of single member constituencies, and local constituency choice.

VI Controversies

14 The Rushdie Affair: Research Agenda for Political Philosophy

BHIKHU PAREKH

Among the different mechanisms upon which a civilization relies to preserve and perpetuate itself, telling its complex history in the form of a story is one of the most common. Since civilizations vary greatly in their systems of values, conceptions of man and society and social structures, they are amenable and grant cultural legitimacy to different patterns of story-telling. In some, the community constitutes the hero of the story, and its collective deeds form its content; in others, the pride of place is assigned to privileged groups or individuals.

Although the history of European civilization has been told in several different stories, the most popular and influential stresses the heroic deeds of remarkable individuals and centres around the themes of blasphemy, martyrdom, resurrection and the triumph of good over evil after an initial setback. The story begins with Socrates, widely accepted as the first uncompromising champion of critical reason and independent thought. When accused, among other things, of impiety and undermining the Athenian gods, he preferred death to the loss of intellectual independence. He triumphed in his death and became the founder of the tradition of free inquiry in general and philosophy in particular. Jesus of Nazareth, accused of blasphemy by his own people and killed by the Romans at their instigation, became the founder of a great religion. His small band of largely illiterate followers, persecuted for refusing to honour Roman gods, eventually converted the mighty Roman empire. The story goes on in this vein weaving its narrative around such defiant dissenters as Copernicus, Galileo, Martin Luther and Spinoza, all in one form or another accused of and in varying degrees persecuted for alleged acts of blasphemy. In each of these increasingly successful revolts against God or His earthly representatives, the central figure incarnates and realizes one or other of the cherished

Bhikhu Parekh, 'The Rushdie Affair: Research Agenda for Political Philosophy', *Political Studies*, Vol. 38 (1990), pp. 695–709 (minus 708–9). Reprinted by permission of Blackwell Publishers.

values of European civilization and supposedly takes mankind a step further towards its ultimate goal. The community suppressing him is rarely if ever judged right. Indeed it is almost always presented as reactionary, backward looking, an enemy of truth. All progress in history is seen as a result of battles between individual sources of light and communal sources of darkness.

Salman Rushdie's case beautifully fits into this story and apparently confirms its central message. He too has been condemned to death for revolting against the God of his people and had to go into presumably permanent hiding. His case also has several other features that add to its fascination. Rushdie's revolt was inspired by the European tradition of independent thought and scepticism, a tradition with a long record of hostility to his ancestral way of life. The people placed in charge of executing the death sentence on him are those for whose dignity and material interests he has a long record of fighting and whose current anger deeply puzzles and pains him. If his ungrateful coreligionists were ever to succeed in assuaging their murderous wrath, he would be the first western martyr in the cause of literature, especially the novel. Rushdie thus stands at the centre of such large battles as those between Christianity and Islam, secularism and fundamentalism, Europe and its ex-colonies, the host society and its immigrants, the post and pre-modernists, art and religion, and between scepticism and faith.

Not surprisingly, what I shall call the Rushdie affair has given rise to several important questions of considerable interest to political philosophers. I propose to tease out and comment on some of them.

Text

Rushdie's *The Satanic Verses* is a story of migration and metamorphosis and, at a different level, of death and resurrection. It uses the brilliantly articulated experience of migration to explore the nature and constitution of the self, including the way it is related to and constantly re-forms itself in response to changes in its natural and social environment, language, memories, hopes and fears. As Rushdie put it:

> I wanted to write a novel which at its most fundamental level is about metamorphosis—the nature of it, the process by which it happens, its effect on the metamorphosed self and on the world around it, and its link with the act of travelling. Not least because the pressures exerted by migration are one of the classic contemporary locations of metamorphosis—what I call 'translation': a carrying across of the self into another place and another language. I am fascinated by how the classic roots of the self in language, society and place are disrupted by the act of migration:

you suddenly find yourself in a new culture with different rules, and a new language, and for a while you flounder. The self is forced to find different principles on which to invent itself. That's what I was really trying to write about.[1]

Imaginative exploration of reality can take many forms, depending on the level of abstraction adopted by the author. Rushdie adopts a relatively low level of abstraction. He fantasizes and redefines real, recognizable men and women and does not create wholly new characters and images. His characters are not products of what Kant called 'pure' or 'transcendental' imagination, but real people subjected to the free play of fantasy. *The Satanic Verses* is thus a work of fantasy, not of pure fiction, of an imaginatively reinterpreted but not a radically reconstituted reality.[2]

Rushdie's fascinating blend of magic realism and fantasized history has great literary merits. It is ideally equipped to explore areas of life dominated by neither fact nor fantasy alone but by a blend of the two, or where reality itself has become fantastic. It is also suited to exploring the birth and spread of momentous historical movements in which great individuals and masses activate their own and each other's myths and fantasies, generate powerful emotions, and shape their fantasized present in the light of a fantasized past and future. Not surprisingly, *The Satanic Verses* delineates with unparalleled intensity and precision the structure and dynamics of the immigrant's everyday life, including the experiences of self-alienation, the joys and torments of harbouring multiple selves, and the 'fantastic reality' in which he is forced to live.

Rushdie's method also has its dangers. If a writer is not careful, he or she might end up treating recognizable men and women as *mere* objects of fantasies, as people whom he knows better than they do themselves, as *manipulable* material for the free play of his imagination. He might then become not just disrespectful and irreverent, but supercilious and dismissive, a shade crude, even perhaps exhibitionist, scoring cheap points off half-real characters. If he seeks to explore such forms of experience as religion and sexuality, which for different reasons arouse powerful emotions and require great sensitivity, he runs the risk of violating their integrity, even vulgarizing them, and outraging conventional norms of good taste. The danger is particularly great in the case of religion. It is the realm of the sacred and the holy *par excellence* and involves strong feelings of piety and reverence, which can be easily offended if subjected to the indelicate play of an undisciplined fantasy.

In two complex chapters which form part of a dream of one of the central characters of *The Satanic Verses*, Rushdie explores the birth and triumph of Islam. He delineates Mahound's (that is, Muhammed's) dilemmas, states of mind, dreams, inevitable compromises with the old pre-Islamic world, reactions to the reactions of that world to his new discipline, and so on in a most perceptive and vivid manner. But he does not always find it easy to remain restrained and sensitive. Anger, irreverence and even thinly veiled contempt inform his exploration and suffuse his choice of images, metaphors, language and sequence of events.

Muhammad is present as a 'Businessman' constantly doing deals with the archangel and God. His God 'is really a Businessman' who offers him convenient bargains and helps him out of embarrassing situations. The archangel is no less 'obliging' and even reduces the initial quota of 40 prayers a day to five in recognition of Muhammad's and his followers' difficulties. Islam is a 'revelation of convenience' and could easily have had a different code of moral and spiritual discipline if that had suited Muhammad better.

Muhammad is called a 'smart bastard', a debauchee who, after his wife's death, slept with so many women that his beard turned 'half-white' in a year. Muslims deeply respect Bilal, the emancipated black slave who was the first convert to Islam. Here, he is an 'enormous black monster, with a voice to match his size'. Muhammad's three revered colleagues, including Bilal, are 'those goons, those f—ing clowns', the 'trinity of scum'. Like any great religious text, the Koran is full of rules and injunctions about forms of worship, helping the poor, concern for those in need, moral purity, self-discipline and surrender to the will of God. *The Satanic Verses* mockingly reduces it to a book 'spouting' rules about how to 'fart', 'f—' and 'clean one's behind', and why only two sexual positions are legitimate, one of them being sodomy (that tired anti-Muslim canard yet again).

Another passage relates to Mahound's twelve wives. When Ayesha, his young and favourite wife, protested against his taking on so many wives, the novel goes on:

> Who can blame her? Finally he went into—what else? One of his trances and out he came with a message from the archangel. Gibreel had recited verses giving him full divine support. God's own permission to f— as many women as he liked. So there: What could poor Ayesha say against the verses of God? You know what she did say? This: Your God certainly jumps to it when you need him to fix things up for you.

There is also a brothel scene in which twelve whores take the names of Muhammad's wives.[3] Rushdie has argued that it was intended to provide a profane antithesis to (and thus to highlight and accentuate) the holy. But since the holy has been treated in a mocking manner throughout the novel, the brothel scene cannot be its antithesis; rather, it is a further expression of the same approach.

Debate

Soon after the publication of *The Satanic Verses* Muslims all over the world began to campaign against it. Although the anger was universal, the campaign (for reasons we cannot discuss here) was largely confined to South Asia, especially India and Pakistan, and to the South Asian, mainly Pakistani, Muslims settled in Britain, particularly in the Midlands and parts of Yorkshire. Muslim spokesmen in Britain were initially confused and stated their case badly.[4] Some complained that the book had 'hurt' them, 'offended' their 'feelings' and was guilty of gross 'blasphemy'. Although the concept of blasphemy is uniquely Christian and has no analogue in Islam, Muslim spokesmen continued to use the term, both because it made most sense to their intended audience and because it enabled them to take advantage of the existing law against it. Some of them also said that Rushdie was guilty of apostasy, a uniquely Islamic concept with no analogue in other religions. The Arabic words *riddah* and especially *irtidad*, usually translated as apostasy, mean 'turning back' on Islam, forsaking it for unbelief or another religion, and convey the ideas of cultural treason or treachery and violation of a solemn commitment. The white critics rejoined that the charge of apostasy implied that a Muslim was *never* at liberty to give up his faith, and that this contradicted the Koranic stress on the voluntary nature of religious belief and its condemnation of hypocrisy, denied a man's right to change his mind, and went against the all too human experience of occasional loss of faith. Undeterred, some Muslim spokesmen continued to accuse Rushdie of apostasy. Some others argued that a quiet or private rejection of Islam was permissible but not its aggressive and public condemnation. The latter amounted to declaring a 'war' on the 'House of Islam' and could not be forgiven. Yet others conceded the point of the criticism and preferred to stress Rushdie's blasphemy and the offence he had caused to their feelings.

Over time Muslim spokesmen developed a better-argued and more coherent critique of *The Satanic Verses*. First, *The Satanic Verses* was a wholly 'untruthful' account of Islam and spread 'utter lies' about it. Had the book not stayed so recognizably close to history the 'gross inaccuracies' would not have mattered. Under the circumstances they did, so Muslims had a right to stand up for the integrity and honour of their faith. This explains why Muslim leaders agreed to withdraw their campaign if the book added a note disclaiming its historical character.

Secondly, *The Satanic Verses* was 'abusive', 'insulting', 'scurrilous', 'vilifactory' in its treatment of men and women whom Muslims considered holy and of whose sacred memories they considered themselves custodians.

It discussed their religion in a most 'obscene', 'indecent', 'filthy' and 'abominably foul' language and violated all norms of civilized discussion. Muslim spokesmen contended that they were complaining not about their subjective feelings of hurt, but against Rushdie's violation of the norms governing a critical discussion of religion and his transgression of *Hodud* (limits which no decent man should cross). They said they did not mind a serious critique of their religious beliefs. Libraries were full of them and their authors were rarely harmed, but they did mind Rushdie's tone, attitude and language.

The third Muslim complaint related to the way the book had demeaned and degraded them in their own and especially others' eyes. It reinforced many of the prejudices created against them by the Orientalists and gave grounds for a few more into the bargain. It made them objects of ridicule and presented them as barbarians following a fraudulent religion created by a cunning manipulator and devoid of a sound system of morality. As a Muslim as well as a scholar of Islam, Rushdie owed it to his people to counter the 'myths' and 'lies' Christians had spread about them over the centuries, or at least to refrain from lending them his authority. Instead, he had joined the Orientalist discourse, lowered Muslims in their own and others' esteem, and harmed their moral and material interests.

Muslims began to insist that for these and other reasons *The Satanic Verses* had no place in a 'civilized society' and should be banned. When their noisy but peaceful protests got nowhere, a small group of them burned a copy of it.[5] Rather than stimulate a reasoned discussion of their grievance, the book-burning incident led to a torrent of denunciation. Muslims were called 'barbarians', 'uncivilized', 'fanatics', 'fundamentalists' and compared to the Nazis. Many a writer, some of impeccable liberal credentials, openly wondered how Britain could 'civilize' them and protect their innocent progeny against their parents' 'medieval fundamentalism'. No one cared to point out that only a few months earlier, several Labour Members of Parliament had burnt a copy of the new immigration rules outside the House of Commons without raising so much as a murmur of protest, or that on occasion the Prime Minister's effigy had been hanged with such silly slogans as 'Hang the Bitch'.

Muslim protests in Britain were now beginning to attract international attention. Some Muslim leaders unwisely internationalized the issue by making representations to Muslim heads of state. In response to these and other factors, the late Ayatollah Khomeini made his notorious intervention and pronounced a death sentence on Rushdie. His *fatwa* marked a turning point in the development of Muslim consciousness. Tolerant and even a little timid until then, the British Muslims suddenly experienced a sense of power. They had managed to extract a statement of regret from Rushdie, they now commanded media attention, they were courted by the British government, and they had succeeded in shifting national attention from themselves to *The Satanic Verses*. The sense of power, combined with a mean desire for revenge at having been ignored for so long, generated a new mood of aggressive intolerance. In their new mood, they escalated their demands. They now insisted that the book should not be issued in paperback edition and be withdrawn from public libraries, as well as that the existing law of blasphemy which protected the Anglican church be extended to other religions as well. A few pursued their case for separate Muslim schools with increased vigour and some even pressed for the recognition of the Muslim civil law.

As for the white British, especially liberal public opinion, its response was along predictable lines. *The Satanic Verses* was 'only a novel' and it was wholly wrong to view it as history. Muslims were being unjustifiably 'touchy' and 'prickly' and should learn to accept criticism and even occasional ridicule. Free speech was deeply cherished by British Society and was non-negotiable; Muslims must either respect it or emigrate to where they felt more comfortable. They had freely chosen to migrate to Britain and had a moral duty to accept its way of life. It was wrong of them to insist on retaining their cultural separateness. They were, of course, free to practise their religion provided they ensured that it remained confined to the private realm and did not interfere with their civil and political obligations. If they refused to integrate and become assimilated into British society, they could not legitimately complain of racial discrimination. British society was based on a shared conception of who belonged to it and accepted the obligation to treat all its members equally and fairly. It was 'only natural' for it not to extend the obligation to those refusing to assimilate into and accept without reservation its dominant way of life. John Patten, Minister of State at the Home Office, sent a widely acclaimed letter to Muslim leaders outlining the essentials of the British way of life and urging them to become British.[6]

This is where the matter stands at present. Old arguments, some of which were sketched earlier, continue to be rehearsed on both sides, but for all practical purposes they have ceased to matter. Rushdie, still defiant though a little mellowed, remains in hiding. Muslims continue to sulk and feel alienated but are no longer clear about what they want. After the sale of millions of copies, the ban on *The Satanic Verses* no longer makes sense. They would like its long-delayed paperback edition to be dropped altogether, although that is not in the hands of the government. There is little chance that the latter will relax Rushdie's security and allow any of the diminishing band of Muslim hotheads to get their hands on him and assuage their anger. For its part, the government is convinced that Muslims were and are wrong to feel so strongly about the 'novel' and that time and their eventual exhaustion offer the only way out of the impasse.

Status of the Immigrant

The Rushdie affair has directly or indirectly raised several large issues. I shall highlight some of those that should interest political philosophers.

First, the Rushdie affair has raised in a novel form the old question of the nature and implications of the membership of a political community. When Muslims were campaigning against *The Satanic Verses*, they were constantly reminded of the terms of engagement between immigrants and the host society. They were told that in coming to settle in Britain they had consented to its way of life and incurred an obligation to abide by its laws, norms and values. They were to respect and adjust to the British way of life rather than expect it to adjust to them. If they found it oppressive or inhospitable, they were free and indeed honour bound to leave the country.

Muslim spokesmen interpreted the concept of consent differently. Consent was a bilateral relationship and entailed commitment on both sides. As immigrants they did have an obligation to obey the laws of the land, but British society too had obligations to them. By not only admitting but positively recruiting them to help rebuild its post-war economy in full knowledge of who they were and what they stood for, Britain had consented to and incurred an obligation to respect at least the fundamentals of their way of life. It was true that British society might find some of their practices and values unacceptable, even as they might find some of its practices offensive. The way out lay in negotiating a consensus in a spirit of goodwill and mutual tolerance. To insist that they and the other minorities should accept the British way of life amounted to treating them as second-class citizens bearing the burdens but lacking the rights of equal citizenship. Furthermore, asking the immigrants to acknowledge the authority of the established system of government and to obey its laws was one thing; to ask them to accept the prevailing form of life and become British in their ways of thought and life was altogether different. To equate the two was to confuse the state with the nation, a form of authority with a culture. Immigrants owed loyalty to the British state, but not to British values, customs and way of life. So long as their customs and practices did not prevent them from discharging their basic obligations as citizens, they were at liberty to preserve and even fight for them. By defining their political obligations so widely as to include adherence to British culture, the British state was guilty of violating their cultural and moral integrity. This was not only unacceptable in itself but also incompatible with Britain's claim to be a liberal society.

Whatever view one takes of the Muslim arguments and the political theory underpinning them, the nature of the relationship between immigrants and the host society and of their mutual obligations and claims clearly requires greater attention than it has been traditionally given. Almost every major western state has a large and growing immigrant population. Immigrants come for a variety of reasons, ranging from search for asylum to their active recruitment by the state, and each generates distinct claims and obligations. They also come from different countries, ranging from ex-colonies to fellow-members of such international organizations as the European Community. In each case they stand in different historical and contractual relations to the receiving country. Again, some immigrants are or see themselves as short-term residents anxious after a few years to return to their countries of origin or to move elsewhere; some are or see themselves as long-term residents anxious eventually to return to their countries of origin and in the meantime to remain and work within, but not to become full members of, the host society; some others want to remain members of their countries of origin as well as become full members of the host country; yet others have completely broken with their countries of origin.

There is nothing improper in any of these and other choices immigrants make, and almost all western countries accept and make room for them. Many countries allow dual nationality. Many more permit immigrants to own property and invest capital in their countries of origin, and even to claim tax relief for remittances made to their close relations there. Many countries also recognize that so long as their citizens remain loyal to them, there is nothing wrong if they are also deeply committed to and even champion the interests of some other to which they feel culturally attached, as in the case of the Jews. In short, citizenship today is a much more differentiated and far less homogeneous concept than has been presupposed by political theorists. It therefore requires a more nuanced and diversified theory of political obligation than has been offered so far.

Immigrants' rights vary greatly and bear little relation to their obligations in most western countries. In Britain they long enjoyed full citizenship rights on arrival. During the past few years, they have ceased enjoying full rights of citizenship even after becoming citizens. If, for example, they marry outside Britain, they are allowed to bring in their spouses only under the most stringent and discriminatory conditions. Germany grants different status to different categories of immigrants. While it is clear about their obligations, it is vague and confused about their rights. In the Netherlands and Sweden, until immigrants acquire full citizenship they may participate in local but not national elections, and are required to refrain from political and even trade union activities. They are, as in classical Athens and Rome, only permitted to present their grievances through officially accepted indigenous citizens and organizations. In hardly any European country do the rights of millions of Helots match their obligations or even form a coherent pattern. The simple-minded distinction between citizens and non-citizens is no longer adequate. We need a more differentiated theory of rights and obligations that *both* safeguards the dignity and basic interests of all, be they full citizens or fresh immigrants, yet acknowledges their differential status and claims on society.

Equality Before the Law

Secondly, the Rushdie affair has brought into sharp relief some of the ambiguities of the concept of equality before the law. When Muslim leaders contended that the British anti-blasphemy law, which only protected Anglican Christianity, discriminated against them, they provoked a variety of responses.[7] Some, mainly conservatives, rejected the criticism. Britain was, they insisted, a Christian *society* in the sense that Christianity meant something to most of its people, was a source of many of their moral values, and regulated births, marriages, deaths and other important events of their lives. More to the point, Britain was a Christian *state*, the product of a historical settlement between the state and the Church of England which made Christianity an integral part of the former's corporate identity. Christianity thus enjoyed a special political status and could not be treated on a par with other religions. A man's moral obligation to treat all men and women equally did not undermine or supersede his obligation to treat his wife, parents and children in a special and privileged manner. The state was no different. A measure of discrimination was built into its very structure, which the principle of equality before the law must recognize and respect. Lord Jacobovitz, the Chief Rabbi, endorsed this view when he said that Britain was right to privilege Christianity and that the Jews would be wrong to demand the protection of the anti-blasphemy law.[8]

Muslim spokesmen rejected this argument on three grounds. First, no historical settlement could claim permanence. It was a product of its time and subject to negotiation in the light of new circumstances. Secondly, such an argument would justify all manner of privileges and practices and rule out progress. Thirdly, the principle of equality required that all religions should be treated equally, irrespective of their age, history or popular support.

Others, mainly liberals, conceded the Muslim charge of discrimination but responded in two different ways. Some advocated the extension of the anti-blasphemy law to all major religions, whereas others pleaded for its abolition. In either case they thought that the principle of equality before the law was respected. Muslim leaders endorsed the former but attacked the latter course of action on the ground that the abolition of the anti-blasphemy law was discriminatory and unfair. To retain it all these years and to abolish it just when another religion demanded its protection was mean and hypocritical. It granted formal or negative and not substantive or positive equality. Furthermore, if the Church of England did not now require the protection of the law, it did not have to take advantage of it, but there was no reason to deny it to those in need of it. Muslim spokesmen also argued that their religion was under particular threat in the current climate and that it was perfectly fair to grant special protection to the weak. After all, the anti-discriminatory legislation protecting women and the ethnic minorities was based on that principle, and so at a different level was the welfare state.

We have then four different interpretations of the concept of equal treatment of all religions. First, there is the conservative view, according to which the state is not to persecute or suppress any religion but remains at liberty to privilege one that is an integral part of its history and identity. Secondly, there is the strong liberal view that the state should protect all religions equally. Thirdly, there is the weak liberal view that it should protect no religion. And fourthly, we have the Muslim view that the state should protect all religions; but if for some reason it cannot, it should protect the one under threat in the same way that it grants extra protection to individuals under threat or in special need. I am not concerned here to assess the validity of the four interpretations but only to point out that the concept of equal treatment is far more complex than is generally appreciated. The apparently fair and even-handed liberal conception sometimes has opposite consequences, and being individual-centred many of our theories of equality come to grief when applied to *groups*, which call for a very different conception of equality.

The courts of law in Britain have also had to decide how to interpret the requirement of equal treatment so that one takes full account of relevant differences between individuals while scrupulously avoiding giving privileges to any; that is, how to be *discriminating* without becoming *discriminatory*. A few cases illustrate the point.

In *R.* v. *Bibi* (1980), the Court of Appeal reduced the imprisonment of a Muslim widow, found guilty of importing cannabis, from three years to six months on the grounds that, among other things, she was totally dependent on her brother-in-law and was socialized by her religion into subservience to the male members of her household. In *R.* v. *Bailey* and *R.* v. *Byfield* (1982), the moral codes of men brought up in the West Indies were taken into consideration in sentencing them for having sexual intercourse with girls under 16. In *R.* v. *Abesanya* (1983), the Nigerian mother who had scarred the cheeks of her fourteen- and nine-year-old sons in accordance with tribal custom was convicted but granted an absolute discharge. Her children had been willing parties, the cuts had been made in a ceremonial atmosphere and were unlikely to leave permanent marks, and the mother did not know that her conduct was contrary to English laws. In *Malik* v. *British Home Stores* (1980), it was decided that in appropriate circumstances Asian women but not white women could wear trousers at work. In *Dawkins* v. *Crown Supplies* (1989), it was decided that a Rastafarian cannot be refused employment merely because he is unwilling to cut off his dreadlocks. In all these cases a person's cultural background made a difference to his or her treatment by the courts. The law was *pluralized*, and departures from the norm of formal equality were made in different ways and guises, so as to reconcile the apparently conflicting demands of legal uniformity and cultural diversity, of formal equality and fairness.

The British Parliament too has recognized that the principle of equality before the law should accommodate important cultural and religious differences in furtherance of the principles of individual liberty, religious tolerance and promotion of social harmony. Under the Shops Act 1950, Jews may open their shops on Sundays without being in breach of the Sunday trading laws, provided that they register with the local authority. Under the Slaughter of Poultry Act (1967) and the Slaughterhouses Act (1979), Jews and Muslims may slaughter poultry and animals in abattoirs according to their traditional methods. Under the Motor-cycle Crash-helmets Act (1976), Sikhs are excused from wearing crash helmets provided they are wearing turbans. The law on carrying knives in public places contained in the Criminal Justice Act (1988) exempts those carrying them for religious reasons. In none of these cases was it felt that equality under the law was isolated. Jews are hardly offered real equality under the Sunday trading laws, as otherwise they would be reduced to opening their shops on only five days a week when others have the advantage of an extra day. Under certain circumstances, equality rules out uniformity and requires differential treatment. Such treatment neither confers privileges on those involved, nor amounts to reverse discrimination.

Communal Libel

The third important issue raised by the Rushdie affair relates to the concept of what I shall call communal libel or defamation. In most societies libel is an offence. Broadly speaking it consists in making public, untruthful and damaging remarks about an individual that go beyond fair comment. Libel is an offence not so much because it causes pain to, or offends the feelings of, the individual concerned, for the damaging and untruthful remarks made in private do not constitute libel, as because they lower him in the eyes of *others*, damage his *social* standing, and harm his *reputation*.

An individual is not a free-floating atom but a member of a specific community and his identity is at once both personal and social. His self-respect is therefore necessarily tied up with, and partly grounded in, the general respect for his community. To say that 'all Jews are mean, unreliable, rapacious and selfish' is to implicate and demean every one of them. Or to say that 'all blacks are thick, stupid and sexy', or that 'all Indians are effeminate, devious and liars' is to degrade every black man and every Indian. Such untrue and damaging remarks, which nurture and perpetuate perverse stereotypes, lower the social standing of the communities involved, demean them in their own and others' eyes, and treat them less equally than the rest. In so far as they go beyond fair comment they amount to communal libel or defamation. Communal libel can cause deep moral injury and lead to such things as self-alienation, self-hatred and compensatory aggression, movingly described by black, Jewish and Asian writers. Human beings feel ontologically insecure and fail to develop the vital qualities of self-respect, self-confidence and a sense of their own worth if they are constantly insulted, ridiculed, subjected to snide innuendoes, and made objects of crude jokes on the basis of their race, colour, gender, nationality or social and economic background. To accuse the protesting victims of being prickly, oversensitive or unable to share a good laugh is to betray a lack of elementary moral sensitivity. Ugly actions occur within the framework of, and draw their legitimacy from, an ugly moral climate. The latter is built up and sustained by, among other things, gratuitously offensive remarks, each in itself perhaps good-humoured and tolerable but collectively devastating and corrupting. A humane and sensitive society based on mutual respect ought to find ways of discouraging them.

In several countries the concept of ethnic libel is incorporated in their legal systems. In 1989 the government of New South Wales in Australia passed a law declaring unlawful acts which 'incite hatred towards, serious contempt for, or serious ridicule of' persons and groups on the ground of their race.[9] In so far as it punishes incitement to 'racial hatred' and not just racially discriminatory actions, even the British Race Relations Act of 1976 is informed by a diluted version of ethnic libel.

The law has its obvious limits and becomes counter-productive if enacted or applied with excessive zeal. Its role is largely symbolic and educational. By affirming the community's collective disapproval of certain forms of utterances, it both reassures the minorities and lays down norms of public debate made effective by selective enforcements. Since the law can play only a limited part in creating a humane and gentle society, we need to explore other ways. A powerful press council along the lines recently proposed in Britain, non-punitive and declaratory laws laying down what may or may not be said publicly but attaching no penalties, and vigilant citizens' forums bringing to bear the organized pressure of enlightened public opinion on those responsible for corrupting and lowering the level of public discourse, indicate the direction in which we need to move.

The concept of communal libel does, of course, raise difficult questions, but these are not unanswerable. The British Race Relations Act of 1976 and the subsequent court cases show that ethnic groups can be defined without much difficulty. Libel laws the world over have found reasonably satisfactory ways of distinguishing between libel and legitimate and fair comment, and the distinction can be applied with suitable modification to groups as well. We do, of course, need to decide whether the protection against libel should be confined to racial and ethnic groups or extended to religious and even perhaps to other groups. If the Jews and blacks are to be protected against vilifactory, degrading and provocative remarks, what about the Muslims and even the capitalists? Although we cannot even begin to answer these questions here, they are not as insuperable as they seem. The law is concerned not to eliminate all injustices and inequalities but only those that are currently recognized to be unfair or oppressive, and is rightly selective. Again, it could be argued that groups based on natural, unalterable, visible and easily identifiable characteristics are qualitatively different from, and more vulnerable than, those based on beliefs, interests, preferences, sentiments and social relations, and merit a differential treatment.

Grounds of Free Speech

The fourth important question raised by the Rushdie affair relates to the nature, grounds and limits of free speech. Not only Rushdie and his supporters but almost the entire white community thought that Muslim demands involved unacceptable restraints on free speech and could not be conceded. Rushdie spoke for them all when he said:[10]

How is freedom gained? It is taken: never given. To be free, you must first assume your right to freedom. In writing *The Satanic Verses*, I wrote from the assumption that I was, and am, a free man.

What is freedom of expression? Without the freedom to offend, it ceases to exist. Without the freedom to challenge, even to satirise all orthodoxies, including religious orthodoxies, it ceases to exist. Language and the imagination cannot be imprisoned, or art dies, and with it, a little of what makes us human.[10]

These and other remarks, which are typical of much present and past liberal writing on the subject, make strange reading and highlight some of the limitations of the liberal discourse on free speech. Rushdie reduces speech, a publicly orientated and interpersonal act, to expression, a subjectivist and personal act and shifts the focus from a shared public realm to the individual's right or need to express himself. He says, further, that *he* is free to offend others and satirize their deeply held beliefs but does not explain why *they* should put up with the offence. His right to free expression entails, and is made possible by, a corresponding obligation on them to refrain from interfering with it and to suffer patiently whatever hurt his utterances might cause them. Rushdie does not explain why they should accept such an obligation and how it serves their 'human' interests. Again, he looks at the question of free speech almost entirely from the standpoint of a writer. He assumes that the writer's interests are morally paramount and that what is good for him or her *is* or *must be* good for society as a whole. He is not alone in taking this view. While he universalizes the concerns and interests of a novelist, such earlier advocates of free speech as Milton, Locke, J.S. Mill, Kant and Schelling universalized those of the poet, the philosopher, the scientist or the artist. They are all united in the belief that intellectuals or men of ideas are the moral leaders or vanguard of society, that what is good for them is *eo ipso* good for all, and that only a society conducive to their pursuits is truly human. All this may or may not be true but it needs to be argued rather than uncritically assumed or asserted. In this area as in others, liberalism displays a deep and rarely acknowledged paternalist, even authoritarian impulse. It assumes that all 'civilized' and 'sensible' men want minimum restraints on free speech and that those who do not are ignorant, barbarians, benighted and need to be ignored, suppressed, morally blackmailed or politically manipulated. What is more, hardly any of the illustrious defenders of free speech appreciated the simple fact that since they earned their living by, and had a vested interest in, free speech, they lacked the necessary measure of objectivity and impartiality in this matter and could be guilty of exaggeration and bias.

That Rushdie's assertion of a writer's more or less unrestrained right to express himself as he pleases runs into difficulties can be illustrated by a hypothetical example. Imagine a novelist writing about the tragic victims of Auschwitz. Suppose he mocks and ridicules them, trivializes their suffering, and presents them as a despicable lot thoroughly deserving the mindless brutality inflicted on them. He creates scenes of collective debauchery, wife-swapping, incest and cannibalism, and presents Jewish women as offering themselves and their young children to the Nazi guards in return for a few more days of life. Not only the Jews but all decent men and women would feel deeply outraged by such a 'literary' work, rightly complaining that it takes unacceptable liberties with Jewish collective memories and insults the honour and integrity of the pathetically helpless victims. Since the law is a blunt instrument and since we are rightly uneasy about giving government the power to censor creative writing, we may not ask for such a work to be banned. But we would be right to express our sense of outrage against it and our disapproval of, and even contempt for, the author in the strongest possible terms. We would feel that he had misused his freedom, taken undue advantage of society's tolerance, and violated the unspoken conventions regulating the exercise of his literary freedom. In other words, his freedom of expression *has* to be balanced against the rights of others to their individual and collective self-respect. The law's reluctance to restrain him does not mean that he is at liberty to ignore the moral constraints of good taste and respect for his fellow human beings.

Suppose the deeply hurt Jews mounted a strong protest against the hypothetical book and demanded that it be banned, in the same way that Muslims have done against *The Satanic Verses*. On what grounds would we feel justified in telling them that although understandable, their demand is wrong and that they should patiently suffer the deep hurt and anguish caused by the book? Many of the traditional arguments are of little avail. The author cannot claim that he was pursuing *truth* or furthering the cause of human *progress*. He cannot invoke the writer's right of *self-expression* because the very basis and rationale of the right is in dispute. If he or his defenders were to say that his act was an isolated aberration which should be put up with in the larger interest of human freedom, they would have a case but not a very strong one. Those affected, in this case the Jews, might ask why *they* should be asked to bear the moral and emotional cost of preserving freedom and how they can be sure that the book will not set a precedent and their acquiescence not be used against them in future. They might rejoin too that if society agreed that the book was offensive, it should at least express its collective disapproval of it, even if it is not prepared to ban it.

All this is not to deny that free speech is one of the highest values and that it can be adequately defended, merely that the traditional liberal defence is not wholly satisfactory. It considers the question largely from the standpoint of intellectuals and uncritically assumes that what is good for them is necessarily good for society as a whole. This is not only philosophically suspect but also too elitist and paternalist to carry conviction in a democratic society, especially one in which not just sizeable minorities but evidently the 'moral' majority also feels intensely protective about its deeply held beliefs, values and practices, and demands to know why it should put up with iconoclastic attacks on these by 'irresponsible' intellectuals taking 'perverse pride' in knocking established values, as a Catholic bishop put it at the height of the Rushdie controversy. The rise of the morally authoritarian

New Right, and some of the recent restrictions on free speech imposed by the Thatcher government evidently with popular support, indicate the increasing dissatisfaction with the traditional celebration of free speech. Political philosophers can ill afford to ignore these ominous signs. In justifying free speech, as with such other rights as the right to liberty and property, liberal writers have tended to concentrate on the beneficiaries, ignoring those who stand little chance of enjoying these rights and who for the most part only bear their corresponding burdens. We need to look at the question of free speech from the standpoint of the community rather than the intellectual and show if, how and why it is in *its* interest to allow maximum possible freedom not only to the press but also to its iconoclastic intellectuals. Many a liberal writer, including J.S. Mill, Constant and de Tocqueville, saw the need for this, but despaired of finding an answer. Free speech, they argued, was and will always remain an elite value constantly threatened by and in need of vigorous political defence against the masses. In an age far more democratic than theirs, such an authoritarian despairing answer will not do. Free speech in all its forms needs to be defended in democratic terms; that is, in terms of the vital moral and cultural interests of the community as a whole, or else it will remain dangerously precarious. . . .

Notes

1. Salman Rushdie, 'Between God and Devil', *The Bookseller* (31 March 1989).
2. For a further discussion, see my 'The holy text and the moral void', *New Statesman and Society* (22 March 1989).
3. Of all the controversial material in the book, this episode seems to have aroused the greatest anger and anguish among Muslims.
4. For these and following statements of Muslim views, see Lisa Appignanesi and Sara Maitland (eds.), *The Rushdie File* (London, Fourth Estate, 1989); and Shabbir Akhtar, *Be Careful With Muhammed! The Salman Rushdie Affair* (London, Bellow Publishing, 1989). The London-based Muslim journal *Impact* is a source of useful information on Muslim views. The Commission for Racial Equality organized three seminars on the Rushdie affair attended by major spokesmen of all points of view and had several official consultations with Muslim leaders. As its then Deputy Chairman, I attended all these and draw on my notes of the proceedings.
5. For a detailed discussion see my 'The Rushdie affair and the British press: some salutary lessons', in Bhikhu Parekh (ed.), *Free Speech* (London, Commission for Racial Equality, 1990).
6. The letter is included as Appendix D in Bhikhu Parekh (ed.), *Law, Blasphemy and the Multi-Faith Society* (London, Commission for Racial Equality, 1990).
7. Parekh (ed.), *Law, Blasphemy and the Multi-Faith Society*, especially the contributions by Simon Lee, Keith Ward and Alan King-Hamilton.

8. Appignanesi and Maitland (eds.), *The Rushdie file*, p. 138.
9. See Appendix F in Parekh (ed.), *Law, Blasphemy and the Multi-Faith Society*.
10. 'In Good Faith', *Independent* (11 Feb. 1990). In this long article Rushdie offers a spirited defence of *The Satanic Verses* against its Muslim critics. See also the two replies by Michael Dummett and myself in the *Independent* (18 Feb. 1990).

15 The Capacity of International Law to Advance Ethnic or Nationality Rights Claims

S. JAMES ANAYA

1. Introduction

In all areas of the globe, segments of humanity are clinging to bonds of race, language, religion, kinship, and custom, and are projecting those bonds into the political future. In all too many instances, recent events remind us, the interactive patterns of ethnic and national groupings are oppressed by structures of human organization grounded in the modern system of states. The native tribes of the American continents, the Quebecois, the Baltic peoples, the Eritreans, the Kurds, and the Basques are all examples of groups that have been challenging the state structures that engulf them.

Comprehensively formulated, claims of ethnic or nationality groups can be divided into two categories. One category corresponds to claims of nondiscrimination and equal treatment for the members of the group within the context of a larger social setting. Examples of such claims are in the civil rights movement that coalesced in the 1950s and 1960s in the United States and in the campaign against apartheid in South Africa. International law has provided clear support for these claims. The nondiscrimination ideal has been firmly embedded and elaborated in major international legal instruments, such as the United Nations Charter,[1] the Universal Declaration of Human Rights,[2] the International Human Rights Covenants,[3] and the International Covenant on the Elimination of all Forms of Racial Discrimination.[4]

The second category is comprised of those claims in which ethnic

Delivered at the 1990 Conference of the U.S.S.R.–U.S.A. Scholars Dialogue on Human Rights and the Future, which was jointly sponsored by the U.S.S.R. Academy of Sciences through its Institute of State and the American Council of Learned Societies, in Moscow (June 19–21, 1990).

James Anaya, 'The Capacity of International Law to Advance Ethnic or Nationality Rights Claims', 75 *Iowa Law Review*, 837–44 (1990). Reprinted with permission.

communities seek some degree of separation or autonomy from the rest of the population of the state in which they are located. Examples include the secessionist efforts of the Baltic peoples in the Soviet Union and attempts at greater autonomy on the part of Indian tribes of North America and other indigenous peoples around the world.

Although the words 'all peoples have the right to self-determination' have made their way into the texts of major multilateral treaties,[5] international law has yet to clearly embrace claims for political autonomy beyond the context of classical colonialism. Still, the affirmation of self-determination of peoples has provided a wedge for ethnic autonomy claims to make their way prominently into contemporary international legal and political discourse. My comments focus on this second category of ethnic and nationality claims and on the institutional capacities of international law to embrace a theory of self-determination to uphold them.[6]

2. The Historical Sovereignty Approach to Autonomy Claims

Ethnic group claims of autonomy take on one or a combination of two basic approaches. One I will call the *historical sovereignty* approach. Under this approach, self-determination is invoked to restore the asserted 'sovereignty' of an historical community that roughly corresponds to the contemporary claimant group. This approach generally accepts the premise of Western theoretical origins of a world divided into territorially defined, independent or 'sovereign' states. However, this approach perceives an alternative and competing political geography based on an assessment of historically based communities. Thus, for example, representatives of North American Indian tribes often rely on assertions of pre-Columbian nationhood or sovereignty in making claims for greater political autonomy.

There are at least three aspects of international law limiting this approach. The first limitation is in the so-called doctrine of *intertemporal* law, which judges historical events according to the law in effect at the time of their occurrence.[6] However unfortunately, international law has operated in historical periods to validate the acquisition of territory by states regardless of the wishes of the indigenous population. Dominant earlier formulations of the doctrines of conquest and effective occupation, for example, upheld the empire building that led to the current political configuration of the Americas.[7]

There are, of course, situations in which the doctrine of intertemporal law is not an impediment. In the situation of the Baltic republics, for instance, a quite persuasive case has been made that their forced annexation into the Soviet Union in 1940 was an illegal usurpation of the republics' status as independent sovereign states, both under contemporary norms and the norms of international law applicable at that time.[8] In the same vein, a good case can be made that the international law of the sixteenth through the mid-nineteenth centuries embraced the treaties concluded during that period between the European powers and many American Indian tribes.[9] Most of these treaties upheld the tribes' powers of self-governance, although within diminished spheres. Assessing the vitality of these treaties for the purposes of contemporary international law, however, is complicated by the intervening period in the late nineteenth and early twentieth centuries in which international law appears to have rejected the international status of treaties with non-European aboriginal peoples.[10]

A second aspect of international law that limits its capacity to embrace ethnic autonomy claims along the historical sovereignty approach is the matter of *recognition*. Recognition is a phenomenon of international legal process which 'may validate situations of dubious origin.'[11] That is, when a preponderance of states, international organizations, and other relevant international actors recognize a state's boundaries and corresponding sovereignty over territory, international law upholds the recognized sovereignty as a matter of traditional held foundational principle.[12] International legal process thus hardly questions whether the territory was acquired by lawful means, leaving little room for groups within the cloak of a recognized sovereign to assert competing sovereignty solely on the basis of historical conditions or events.

As with the doctrine of intertemporal law, recognition may not be a major obstacle in limited circumstances. Again, the Baltics provide an example. The United States and the Western European countries declined to recognize the annexation of the Baltic republics by the Soviet Union in 1940 and established an official position of nonrecognition of Soviet sovereignty over them.[13] This position apparently has not changed, even though no major power has come forward and expressly welcomed any of the Baltic nations into the community of independent states, as Lithuania, the most independence minded of them, repeatedly has requested.

A third aspect of international law that limits the historical sovereignty approach to ethnic autonomy claims, and perhaps the most significant institutional limitation, is a normative trend within international legal process toward *stability through pragmatism* over instability, even at the expense of traditional principle.[14] Sociologists estimate that today there are around 5,000 discrete ethnic or national groupings in the world,[15] and each of these groups is defined—and defines itself—in significant part by reference to history. This figure dwarfs the number of the independent states in the world today, approximately 176. Further, of the numerous stateless cultural groupings that have been deprived of something like sovereignty at some point in their history, many have likewise deprived other groups of autonomy at some point in time. If international law were to fully embrace ethnic autonomy claims on the basis of the historical sovereignty approach, the number of potential challenges to existing state boundaries, along with the likely uncertainties of having to assess competing sovereignty claims over time, could bring the international system into a condition of legal flux and make international law an agent of instability rather than stability.

Accordingly, the major contemporary international organizations and tribunals have resisted a model of self-determination that would realign state boundaries and create new ones according to a simple formula of historical community. The United Nations did not promote the decolonization of Africa and Asia through a policy of restoring precolonial political units based primarily on tribal affiliations. Rather, U.N. policy was to pursue the independence of the colonial territories whose boundaries were widely acknowledged to be artificial in relation to the indigenous population.[16] The Organization of African Unity also adopted this policy after some debate.[17]

The International Court of Justice followed in this direction in the *Western Sahara Case*.[18] The case involved the decolonization of the Saharan territory formerly under Spanish rule. The Court, in an Advisory Opinion, acknowledged that colonial political communities linked peoples of the Western Sahara with adjoining Morocco and Mauritania through historical spheres of influence and allegiance.[19] But the Court held that such 'legal ties' should not influence the application of the principle of self-determination in the decolonization of the Western Sahara. Instead, the Court favored a model of self-determination by which the future status of the territory would be determined through the free and genuine expression of the will of its contemporary inhabitants.[20]

Given all these considerations, my view is that international law cannot easily embrace claims of ethnic or nationality group autonomy primarily based on accounts of the pre-existence and wresting of sovereignty.

3. The Human Rights Approach to Autonomy Claims

A second approach, suggested by the International Court of Justice in the *Western Sahara Case*, focuses on contemporary human interaction and values, and, I believe, holds greater possibilities for the advancement of autonomy claims through international law. I will call this second approach the *human rights* approach.

Under this approach, self-determination is not linked fundamentally to historically derived 'sovereign' entities which are described in somewhat static terms and projected into the future. Rather, self-determination arises within international law's expanding lexicon of human rights concerns and accordingly is posited as a fundamental right that attaches collectively to groups of living human beings. In the decolonization context, the international community preferred a human rights approach, which succeeded in breaking down the colonial empires that extended into Africa, Asia and elsewhere. In that context, relevant actors conceived of self-determination as the right of the contemporary inhabitants of colonized territories to be free from outside domination, a right derived from notions of freedom, equality, and peace.[21] Independent statehood for the colonial territories, understandably, was the norm.

In applying the principle of self-determination to the context of contemporary ethnic autonomy claims within the human rights approach, other evolving human rights concepts come into play—especially the concept of cultural integrity. An emergent human right of cultural survival and flourishment within international law is signaled by the United Nations Charter,[22] article 27 of the Civil and Political Rights Covenant,[23] the Convention Against Genocide,[24] and the UNESCO Declaration of Principles of Cultural Co-operation.[25] Joining the human values of freedom, equality, and peace with those represented in the principle of cultural integrity can provide potent justification for ethnic autonomy claims. In the context of indigenous peoples, for example, a U.N. study has concluded that self-governance is

> an inherent part of their cultural and legal heritage which has contributed to their cohesion and to the maintenance of their social and cultural tradition. . . . Self-determination, in its many forms, is thus a basic pre-condition if indigenous peoples are to be able to enjoy their fundamental rights and determine their future, while at the same time preserving, developing and passing on their specific ethnic identity to future generations.[26]

Despite its appeal, the human rights approach raises a specter of destabilization contrary to international law's normative trends, if phrased in absolutist terms insisting on a right to choose independent statehood even in cases when the right-holders may in fact desire some lesser status. It is thus helpful, and perhaps imperative, to move beyond the independent statehood rhetoric if self-determination is to be meaningful in the context of most current ethnic autonomy claims.

In my view, self-determination should not be equated with a right to independent statehood. Under a human rights approach, the concept of self-determination is capable of embracing much more nuanced interpretations and applications, particularly in an increasingly interdependent world in which the formal attributes of statehood mean less and less. Self-determination may be understood as a right of cultural groupings to the political institutions necessary to allow them to exist and develop according to their distinctive characteristics. The institutions and degree of autonomy, necessarily, will vary as the circumstances of each case vary. And in determining the required conditions for a claimant group, decisionmakers must weigh in the human rights of others. While not precluded, independent statehood will be justified only in rare instances. Such a formulation of self-determination, I believe, will advance global peace and stability consistent with international law's normative trends.

Even when understood in such nonabsolutist terms, the human rights approach to ethnic autonomy claims continues to face impediments arising from within the fabric of international law. I see two remaining, but not insurmountable, problems. First, there is the *individualistic bias* toward human rights conceptions within modern international law which impedes the recognition of collective or group rights. This bias results from traditional Western liberal political philosophy that has provided the major impetus for the development of human rights in international law.[27] As I have discussed elsewhere, the Western liberal perspective

> acknowledges the rights of the individual on the one hand and the sovereignty of the total social collective on the other, but it is not alive to the rich variety of intermediate or alternative associational groupings actually found in human cultures, nor is it prepared to ascribe to such groupings any rights not reducible either to the liberties of the citizen or to the prerogatives of the state.[28]

International legal and political discourse, however, has made significant movement toward greater realization of collective or group rights. An important example is in the treatment of indigenous peoples' concerns within the United Nations and its affiliate, the International Labour Organization. The recent draft Universal Declaration on the Rights of Indigenous Peoples,[29] developed by a working group of the U.N. Human Rights Commission, and the ILO Convention on Indigenous and Tribal Peoples,[30] adopted by the 1989 International Labour Conference, both address indigenous peoples' rights as rights of collectivities. Also, the African Charter on Human and Peoples' Rights[31] elaborates upon the group rights of the family and 'peoples' as distinct from individual or states' rights.

A second limitation, related to the matter of recognition discussed above, is in the classical international law *doctrine of state sovereignty*.[32] The doctrine of sovereignty—together with its corollaries of territorial integrity, exclusive jurisdiction, and nonintervention—impedes the capacity of international law to regulate matters within the spheres of authority asserted by states recognized by the international community. Sovereignty is especially jealous of matters of social and political organization. I believe, however, that to the extent a claim for ethnic autonomy can be posited as a human rights concern, state sovereignty impediments can be overcome.

Within modern international law, the doctrine of sovereignty increasingly has become subject to the human rights values embraced by the international community. In a global community that remains organized substantially by state jurisdictional boundaries, sovereignty principles continue, in some measure, to advance human values of stability and ordered liberty. But since the atrocities and suffering of the two world wars, international law has not much upheld sovereignty principles when they serve as an accomplice to the subjugation of human rights or act as a shield against international concern that coalesces to promote human values. The proliferation of a floor of human rights norms that are deemed applicable to all states as to their own citizens and the decolonization process itself both demonstrate the yielding of sovereignty principles to human rights imperatives in modern international law.[33]

4. Conclusion

International law is not easily disposed to aid autonomy claims that challenge state structures simply on the strength of alternative visions of sovereignty founded primarily on evaluations of history. Such an approach imposes great tensions upon the institutional framework of international law. International law, I believe, can best accommodate ethnic autonomy claims if they are justified on human rights grounds and avoid absolutist assertions of independent statehood. To be sure, ethnic communities are the product of both present and past conditions and events. Historical phenomena can have great relevance to the contemporary life of a community and thus be meaningful in terms of human rights. A human rights approach does not necessarily exclude consideration of historical conditions, but it refocuses such consideration into a larger assessment of the requirements for the present day realization of human values. Through its human rights discourse, modern international law is hospitable to such as assessment and its concern for the values implicated in ethnic and nationality rights claims.

Notes

1. *E.g.*, U.N. Charter art. 1, para. 3 (affirming 'respect for human rights and for fundamental freedoms for all without distinction as to race, sex, language or religion').

2. *E.g.*, Universal Declaration of Human Rights art. 2, G.A. Res. 217 A(III), 3(1) U.N. GAOR at 71, U.N. Doc. A/810 (1948) ('Everyone is entitled to all the rights and freedoms set forth in this Declaration, without distinction of any kind, such as race, colour, sex, language, religion, political or other opinion, national or social origin, property, birth or other status.').
3. International Covenant on Civil and Political Rights, Dec. 16, 1966, art. 2(1), G.A. Res. 2200 (XXI), 21 U.N. GAOR Supp. (No. 16) at 52, U.N. Doc. A/6316 (1967) (entered into force Mar. 23, 1976); International Covenant on Economic, Social and Cultural Rights, Dec. 16, 1966, art. 2(2), G.A. Res. 2200 (XXI), 21 U.N. GAOR Supp. (No. 16) at 49, U.N. Doc. A/6316 (1967) (entered into force Jan. 3, 1976).
4. International Convention on the Elimination of All Forms of Racial Discrimination, Mar. 7, 1966, G.A. Res. 2106A (XX), 20 U.N. GAOR Supp. (No. 14) at 47, U.N. Doc. A/6014 (1965) (entered into force, Jan. 4, 1969).
5. *E.g.*, International Covenant on Civil and Political Rights art. I, supra note 3; International Covenant on Economic, Social, and Cultural Rights art. 1, supra note 3; *see also* U.N. Charter art. 1(2).
6. *See* Island of Palmas (Netherlands v. U.S.), 2 R. Int'l Arb. Awards 829, 845 (1928) ('a juridical fact must be appreciated in the light of the law contemporary with it, and not of the law in force at the time when a dispute in regard to it arises. . . .').
7. *See, e.g.*, I.C. Hyde, *International Law Chiefly as Applied and Interpreted by the United States* 163–71, 175 (1922) ('states were agreed that the native inhabitants possessed no rights of territorial control which the European explorer or his monarch was bound to respect'); J. Westlake, *Chapters on the Principles of International Law* 129–66 (1894) (discussing territorial sovereignty in relation to 'uncivilized' regions); *see also* Eastern Greenland (Den. v. Nor.), 1933 P.C.I.J. (ser. A/B) No. 53 (determining territorial sovereignty over Eastern Greenland without regard to the indigenous Inuit population); Cayuga Indians (Gr. Brit. v. U.S.), 6 R. Int'l Arb. Awards 173, 176 (1926) (holding that an Indian 'tribe is not a legal unit of international law').
8. *See* 'Materials of the International Scientific Conference on Legal Assessment of the USSR-Germany Pacts of August 23 and September 28, 1939', 39 *Proceedings of the Estonian Academy of Sciences* 97 (1990).
9. *See* Clinebell & Thompson, 'Sovereignty and Self-Determination: The Rights of Native Americans Under International Law', 27 *Buffalo L. Rev.* 666, 679–93 (1978); Morris, 'In Support of the Right of Self-Determination for Indigenous Peoples Under International Law', 29 *German Y.B. Int'l L.* 277, 291 (1986).
10. *See* Island of Palmas, supra note 6, at 831 ('*contracts between a State* . . . and *native princes or chiefs of peoples* not recognized as members of the community of nations, . . . are not, in the international law sense, treaties or conventions capable of creating rights and obligations . . .'); *see also* supra note 7.
11. M. Shaw, *Title to Territory in Africa* 23 (1986); *see also* I. Brownlie, *Principles of Public International Law* 163–64 (3d edn. 1979) (discussing acquiescence and recognition).

12. *See* I. Brownlie, supra note 11, at 287.
13. B. Kaslas, *The Baltic Nations: The Quest for Regional Integration and Political Liberty* 274–83 (1976) (discussing the history of relations between the Baltic states and the Soviet Union and the reaction of the United States and Western Europe).
14. *See generally* L. Chen, *An Introduction to Contemporary International Law* 3–14 (1989) (discussing the importance of a global context for decisionmaking).
15. R. Stavenhagen, 'Problems and Prospects of Multiethnic States', *The United Nations University Annual Lecture Series* No. 3, at 5 (1986).
16. *See* C. Mojekwu, 'Self-Determination: The African Perspective', in *Self-Determination: National, Regional, and Global Dimensions* 221, 228–29 (Y. Alexander & R. Friedlander eds., 1980).
17. *See* ibid. at 230–31; Ramphul, 'The Role of International and Regional Organizations in the Peaceful Settlement of Internal Disputes (with Special Emphasis on the Organization of African Unity)', 13 *Ga. J. Int'l & Comp. L.* 371, 377–78 (1983).
18. Western Sahara, 1975 I.C.J. 12 (1975).
19. Ibid. at 45–49, 64–65.
20. Ibid. at 68. The Court, however, held that the 'legal ties' it found did not amount to ties of 'territorial sovereignty,' thus leaving open the possibility that a certain showing of historical sovereignty could govern the application of the principle of self-determination, at least in the decolonization context in which the sovereignty of the colonial powers over overseas territories no longer was propped up by the phenomenon of international recognition.
21. *See* Declaration on the Granting of Independence to Colonial Countries and Peoples, Dec. 14, 1960, G.A. Res 1514 (XV), 15 U.N. GAOR Supp. (No. 16) at 66, U.N. Doc. A/4684 (1961).
22. U.N. Charter arts. 13, 55, 57, and 73 (affirming cultural cooperation and development as among the purposes of the U.N.).
23. International Covenant on Civil and Political Rights, art. 27, supra note 3 (recognizing the right of the members of 'ethnic, religious or linguistic minorities . . . to enjoy their own culture, to profess and practise their own religion [and] to use their own language').
24. Convention on the Prevention and Punishment of the Crime of Genocide, Dec. 9, 1948, 78 U.N.T.S. 277 (entered into force Jan. 12, 1961) (defining, at article II, genocide as 'acts committed with intent to destroy, in whole or in part, a national, ethnical, racial or religious group, as such . . .').
25. Declaration of the Principles of International Cultural Cooperation, Proclaimed by the General Conference of the United Nations Educational, Scientific and Cultural Organization at its fourteenth session on Nov. 4, 1966, reprinted in United Nations, Human Rights: A Compilation of International Instruments at 409, U.N. Doc. ST/HR/1/Rev.3 (1988) (affirming a right and duty of all peoples to protect and develop the cultures throughout humankind).
26. U.N. Sub-Commission on Prevention of Discrimination and Protection of Minorities: Study of the Problem of Discrimination Against Indigenous

Populations, U.N. Doc. E/CN.4/Sub.2/1986/7/Add.4 at 20 (1987) (Jose R. Martinez Cobo, Special Rapporteur).

27. *See generally* Weston, 'Human Rights', in *Human Rights in the World Community: Issues and Action* (R. Claude & B. Weston eds., 1989) (discussing the Western liberal origins of modern human rights conceptions).
28. Anaya, 'The Rights of Indigenous Peoples and International Law in Historical and Contemporary Perspective', 1989 *Harv. Indian L. Symp.* 191, 198 (1990).
29. U.N. Doc. E/CN.4/Sub.2/1989/33.
30. International Labor Organization Convention (No. 169) Concerning Indigenous and Tribal Peoples in Independent Countries, International Labour Conference, Draft Report of the Committee on Convention 107 at 25–33, Provisional Record (No. 25) 76th Session (1989), in *Basic Documents In International Law and World Order* 489 (B. Weston, R. Falk, & A. D'Amato, 2d edn., 1990).
31. African Charter on Human and Peoples Rights, June 26, 1981, O.A.U. Doc. CAB/LEG/67/3 Rev. 5, 21 I.L.M. 59 (1982) (entered into force Oct. 21, 1986).
32. *See generally* I. Brownlie, supra note 11, at 287–97 (characterizing sovereignty as the 'basic constitutional doctrine of the law of nations').
33. *See* Anaya, supra note 28, at 211–15.

16 Aliens and Citizens: The Case for Open Borders

JOSEPH H. CARENS

Borders have guards and the guards have guns. This is an obvious fact of political life but one that is easily hidden from view—at least from the view of those of us who are citizens of affluent Western democracies. To Haitians in small, leaky boats confronted by armed Coast Guard cutters, to Salvadorans dying from heat and lack of air after being smuggled into the Arizona desert, to Guatemalans crawling through rat-infested sewer pipes from Mexico to California—to these people the borders, guards and guns are all too apparent. What justifies the use of force against such people? Perhaps borders and guards can be justified as a way of keeping out criminals, subversives, or armed invaders. But most of those trying to get in are not like that. They are ordinary, peaceful people, seeking only the opportunity to build decent, secure lives for themselves and their families. On what moral grounds can these sorts of people be kept out? What gives anyone the right to point guns at *them*?

To most people the answer to this question will seem obvious. The power to admit or exclude aliens is inherent in sovereignty and essential for any political community. Every state has the legal and moral right to exercise that power in pursuit of its own national interest, even if that means denying entry to peaceful, needy foreigners. States may choose to be generous in admitting immigrants, but they are under no obligation to do so.[1]

I want to challenge that view. In this essay I will argue that borders

This paper was first written for an APSA seminar on citizenship directed by Nan Keohane. Subsequent versions were presented to seminars at the University of Chicago, the Institute for Advanced Study, and Columbia University. I would like to thank the members of these groups for their comments. In addition I would like to thank the following individuals for helpful comments on one of the many drafts: Sot Barber, Charles Beitz, Michael Doyle, Amy Gutmann, Christine Korsgaard, Charles Miller, Donald Moon, Jennifer Nedelsky, Thomas Pogge, Peter Schuck, Rogers Smith, Dennis Thompson, and Michael Walzer.

Joseph Carens, 'Aliens and Citizens: The Case for Open Borders', *Review of Politics*, Vol. 49/2 (1987), pp. 251–73 (minus 254, 256–7). Permission granted by the editors of *The Review of Politics* at the University of Notre Dame.

should generally be open and that people should normally be free to leave their country of origin and settle in another, subject only to the sorts of constraints that bind current citizens in their new country. The argument is strongest, I believe, when applied to the migration of people from third world countries to those of the first world. Citizenship in Western liberal democracies is the modern equivalent of feudal privilege—an inherited status that greatly enhances one's life chances. Like feudal birthright privileges, restrictive citizenship is hard to justify when one thinks about it closely.

In developing this argument I will draw upon three contemporary approaches to political theory: first that of Robert Nozick; second that of John Rawls; third that of the utilitarians. Of the three, I find Rawls the most illuminating, and I will spend the most time on the arguments that flow from his theory. But I do not want to tie my case too closely to his particular formulations (which I will modify in any event). My strategy is to take advantage of three well-articulated theoretical approaches that many people find persuasive to construct a variety of arguments for (relatively) open borders. I will argue that all three approaches lead to the same basic conclusion: there is little justification for restricting immigration. Each of these theories begins with some kind of assumption about the equal moral worth of individuals. In one way or another, each treats the individual as prior to the community. These foundations provide little basis for drawing fundamental distinctions between citizens and aliens who seek to become citizens. The fact that all three theories converge upon the same basic result with regard to immigration despite their significant differences in other areas strengthens the case for open borders. In the final part of the essay I will consider communitarian objections to my argument, especially those of Michael Walzer, the best contemporary defender of the view I am challenging.

Aliens and Property Rights

One popular position on immigration goes something like this: 'It's our country. We can let in or keep out whomever we want.' This could be interpreted as a claim that the right to exclude aliens is based on property rights, perhaps collective or national property rights. Would this sort of claim receive support from theories in which property rights play a central role? I think not, because those theories emphasize *individual* property rights and the concept of collective or national property rights would undermine the individual rights that these theories wish to protect.

Consider Robert Nozick as a contemporary representative of the property rights tradition. Following Locke, Nozick assumes that individuals in the state of nature have rights, including the right to acquire and use property. All individuals have the same natural rights—that is the assumption about moral equality that underlies this tradition—although the exercise of those rights leads to material inequalities. The 'inconveniences' of the state of nature justify the creation of a minimal state whose sole task is to protect people within a given territory against violations of their rights.[2]

Would this minimal state be justified in restricting immigration? Nozick never answers this question directly, but his argument at a number of points suggests not. According to Nozick the state has no right to do anything other than enforce the rights which individuals already enjoy in the state of nature. Citizenship gives rise to no distinctive claim. The state is obliged to protect the rights of citizens and noncitizens equally because it enjoys a *de facto* monopoly over the enforcement of rights within its territory. Individuals have the right to enter into voluntary exchanges with other individuals. They possess this right as individuals, not as citizens. The state may not interfere with such exchanges so long as they do not violate someone else's rights.[3]

Note what this implies for immigration. Suppose a farmer from the United States wanted to hire workers from Mexico. The government would have no right to prohibit him from doing this. To prevent the Mexicans from coming would violate the rights of both the American farmer and the Mexican workers to engage in voluntary transactions. Of course, American workers might be disadvantaged by this competition with foreign workers. But Nozick explicitly denies that anyone has a right to be protected against competitive disadvantage. (To count that sort of thing as a harm would undermine the foundations of *individual* property rights.) Even if the Mexicans did not have job offers from an American, a Nozickean government would have no grounds for preventing them from entering the country. So long as they were peaceful and did not steal, trespass on private property, or otherwise violate the rights of other individuals, their entry and their actions would be none of the state's business.

Does this mean that Nozick's theory provides no basis for the exclusion of aliens? Not exactly. It means rather that it provides no basis for the *state* to exclude aliens and no basis for individuals to exclude aliens that could not be used to exclude citizens as well. Poor aliens could not afford to live in affluent suburbs (except in the servants' quarters), but that would be true of poor citizens too. Individual property owners could refuse to hire aliens, to rent them houses, to sell them food, and so on, but in a Nozickean world they could do the same things to their fellow citizens. In other words, individuals may do what they like with their own personal property. They may normally exclude whomever they want from land they own. But they have this right to exclude as individuals, not as members of a collective. They cannot prevent other individuals from acting differently (hiring aliens, renting them houses, etc.) . . .[4]

Migration and the Original Position

In contrast to Nozick, John Rawls provides a justification for an activist state with positive responsibilities for social welfare. Even so, the approach to immigration suggested by *A Theory of Justice* leaves little room for restrictions in principle. I say 'suggested' because Rawls himself explicitly assumes a closed system in which questions about immigration could not arise. I will argue, however, that Rawls's approach is applicable to a broader context than the one he considers. In what follows I assume a general familiarity with Rawls's theory, briefly recalling the main points and then focusing on those issues that are relevant to my inquiry.

Rawls asks what principles people would choose to govern society if they had to choose from behind a 'veil of ignorance,' knowing nothing about their own personal situations (class, race, sex, natural talents, religious beliefs, individual goals and values, and so on). He argues that people in this original position would choose two principles. The first principle would guarantee equal liberty to all. The second would permit social and economic inequalities so long as they were to the advantage of the least well off (the difference principle) and attached to positions open to all under fair conditions of equal opportunity. People in the original position would give priority to the first principle, forbidding a reduction of basic liberties for the sake of economic gains.[5]

Rawls also draws a distinction between ideal and nonideal theory. In ideal theory one assumes that, even after the 'veil of ignorance' is lifted, people will accept and generally abide by the principles chosen in the original position and that there are no historical obstacles to the realization of just institutions. In nonideal theory, one takes account of both historical obstacles and the unjust actions of others. Nonideal theory is thus more immediately relevant to practical problems, but ideal theory is more fundamental, establishing the ultimate goal of social reform and a basis for judging the relative importance of departures from the ideal (*e.g.*, the priority of liberty).[6]

Like a number of other commentators, I want to claim that many of the reasons that make the original position useful in thinking about questions of justice within a given society also make it useful for thinking about justice across different societies.[7] Cases like migration and trade, where people interact across governmental boundaries, raise questions about whether the background conditions of the interactions are fair. Moreover, anyone who wants to be moral will feel obliged to justify the use of force against other human beings, whether they are members of the same society or not. In thinking about these matters we don't want to be biased by self-interested or partisan considerations, and we don't want existing injustices (if any) to warp our reflections. Moreover, we can take it as a basic presupposition that we should treat all human beings, not just members of our own society, as free and equal moral persons.[8]

The original position offers a strategy of moral reasoning that helps to address these concerns. The purpose of the 'veil of ignorance' is 'to nullify the effects of specific contingencies which put men at odds' because natural and social contingencies are 'arbitrary from a moral point of view' and therefore are factors which ought not to influence the choice of principles of justice.[9] Whether one is a citizen of a rich nation or a poor one, whether one is already a citizen of a particular state or an alien who wishes to become a citizen—this is the sort of specific contingency that could set people at odds. A fair procedure for choosing principles of justice must therefore exclude knowledge of these circumstances, just as it excludes knowledge of one's race or sex or social class. We should therefore take a global, not a national, view of the original position. . . .

Those in the original position would be prevented by the 'veil of ignorance' from knowing their place of birth or whether they were members of one particular society rather than another. They would presumably choose the same two principles of justice. (I will simply assume that Rawls's argument for the two principles is correct, though the point is disputed.) These principles would apply globally, and the next task would be to design institutions to implement the principles—still from the perspective of the original position. Would these institutions include sovereign states as they currently exist? In ideal theory, where we can assume away historical obstacles and the dangers of injustice, some of the reasons for defending the integrity of existing states disappear. But ideal theory does not require the elimination of all linguistic, cultural, and historical differences. Let us assume that a general case for decentralization of power to respect these sorts of factors would justify the existence of autonomous political communities comparable to modern states.[10] That does not mean that all the existing features of state sovereignty would be justified. State sovereignty would be (morally) constrained by the principles of justice. For example, no state could restrict religious freedom and inequalities among states would be restricted by an international difference principle.

What about freedom of movement among states? Would it be regarded as a basic liberty in a global system of equal liberties, or would states have the right to limit entry and exit? Even in an ideal world people might have powerful reasons to want to migrate from one state to another. Economic opportunities for particular individuals might vary greatly from one state to another even if economic inequalities among states were reduced by an international difference principle. One might fall in love with a citizen from another land, one might belong to a religion which has few followers in one's native land and many in another, one might seek cultural opportunities that are only available in another society. More generally, one has only to ask whether the right to migrate freely *within* a given society is an important liberty. The same sorts of considerations make migration across state boundaries important.[11]

Behind the 'veil of ignorance,' in considering possible restrictions on freedom, one adopts the perspective of the one who would be most disadvantaged by the restrictions, in this case the perspective of the alien who wants to immigrate. In the original position, then, one would insist that the right to migrate be included in the system of basic liberties for the same reasons that one would insist that the right to religious freedom be included: it might prove essential to one's plan of life. Once the 'veil of ignorance' is lifted, of course, one might not make use of the right, but that is true of other rights and liberties as well. So, the basic agreement among those in the original position would be to permit no restrictions on migration (whether emigration or immigration).

There is one important qualification to this. According to Rawls, liberty may be restricted for the sake of liberty even in ideal theory and all liberties depend on the existence of public order and security.[12] (Let us call this the public order restriction.) Suppose that unrestricted immigration would lead to chaos and the breakdown of order. Then all would be worse off in terms of their basic liberties. Even adopting the perspective of the worst-off and recognizing the priority of liberty, those in the original position would endorse restrictions on immigration in such circumstances. This would be a case of restricting liberty for the sake of liberty and every individual would agree to such restrictions even though, once the 'veil of ignorance' was lifted, one might find that it was one's own freedom to immigrate which had been curtailed.

Rawls warns against any attempt to use this sort of public order argument in an expansive fashion or as an excuse for restrictions on liberty undertaken for other reasons. The hypothetical possibility of a threat to public order is not enough. Restrictions would be justified only if there were a 'reasonable expectation' that unlimited immigration would damage the public order and this expectation would have to be based on 'evidence and ways of reasoning acceptable to all.'[13] Moreover, restrictions would be justified only to the extent necessary to preserve public order. A need for some restrictions would not justify any level of restrictions whatsoever. Finally, the threat to public order posed by unlimited immigration could not be the product of antagonistic reactions (*e.g.*, riots) from current citizens. This discussion takes place in the context of ideal theory and in this context it is assumed that people try to act justly. Rioting to prevent others from exercising legitimate freedoms would not be just. So, the threat to public order would have to be one that emerged as the unintended cumulative effect of individually just actions.

In ideal theory we face a world of just states with an international difference principle. Under such conditions, the likelihood of mass migrations threatening to the public order of any particular state seems small. So, there is little room for restrictions on immigration in ideal theory. But what about nonideal theory, where one takes into account both historical contingencies and the unjust actions of others?

In the nonideal, real world there are vast economic inequalities among nations (presumably much larger than would exist under an international difference principle). Moreover, people disagree about the nature of justice and often fail to live up to whatever principles they profess. Most states consider it necessary to protect themselves against the possibility of armed invasion or covert subversion. And many states deprive their own citizens of basic rights and liberties. How does all this affect what justice requires with regard to migration?

First, the conditions of the real world greatly strengthen the case for state sovereignty, especially in those states that have relatively just domestic institutions. National security is a crucial form of public order. So, states are clearly entitled to prevent the entry of people (whether armed invaders or subversives) whose goal is the overthrow of just institutions. On the other hand, the strictures against an expansive use of the public order argument also apply to claims about national security.

A related concern is the claim that immigrants from societies where liberal democratic values are weak or absent would pose a threat to the maintenance of a just public order. Again the distinction between reasonable expectations and hypothetical speculations is crucial. These sorts of arguments were used during the nineteenth century against Catholics and Jews from Europe and against all Asians and Africans. If we judge those arguments to have been proven wrong (not to say ignorant and bigoted) by history, we should be wary of resurrecting them in another guise.

A more realistic concern is the sheer size of the potential demand. If a rich country like the United States were simply to open its doors, the number of people from poor countries seeking to immigrate might truly be overwhelming, even if their goals and beliefs posed no threat to national security or liberal democratic values.[14] Under these conditions, it seems likely that some restrictions on immigration would be justified under the public order principle. But it is important to recall all the qualifications that apply to this. In particular, the need for some restriction would not justify any level of restriction whatsoever or restrictions for other reasons, but only that level of restriction essential to maintain public order. This would surely imply a much less restrictive policy than the one currently in force which is shaped by so many other considerations besides the need to maintain public order.

Rawls asserts that the priority accorded to liberty normally holds under nonideal conditions as well. This suggests that, if there are restrictions on immigration for public order reasons, priority should be given to those seeking to immigrate because they have been denied basic liberties over those seeking to immigrate simply for economic opportunities. There is a further complication, however. The priority of liberty holds absolutely only in the long run. Under nonideal conditions it can sometimes be justifiable to restrict liberty for the sake of economic gains, if that will improve the position of the worst-off and speed the creation of conditions in which all will enjoy equal and full liberties. Would it be justifiable to restrict immigration for the sake of the worst-off?

We have to be wary of hypocritical uses of this sort of argument. If rich states are really concerned with the worst-off in poor states, they can presumably help more by transferring resources and reforming international economic institutions than by restricting immigration. Indeed, there is reason to suppose more open immigration would help some of the worst-off, not hurt them. At the least, those who immigrate presumably gain themselves and often send money back home as well.

Perhaps the ones who come are not the worst-off, however. It is plausible to suppose that the worst-off don't have the resources to leave. That is still no reason to keep others from coming unless their departure hurts those left behind. But let's suppose it does, as the brain-drain hypothesis suggests. If we assume some restrictions on immigration would be justified for public order reasons, this would suggest that we should give priority to the least skilled among potential immigrants because their departure would presumably have little or no harmful effect on those left behind. It might also suggest that compensation was due to poor countries when skilled people emigrate. But to say that we should actually try to keep people from emigrating (by denying them a place to go) because they represent a valuable resource to their country of origin would be a dramatic departure from the liberal tradition in general and from the specific priority that Rawls attaches to liberty even under nonideal conditions.[15]

Consider the implications of this analysis for some of the conventional arguments for restrictions on immigration. First, one could not justify restrictions on the grounds that those born in a given territory or born of parents who were citizens were more entitled to the benefits of citizenship than those born elsewhere or born of alien parents. Birthplace and parentage are natural contingencies that are 'arbitrary from a moral point of view'. One of the primary goals of the original position is to minimize the effects of such contingencies upon the distribution of social benefits. To assign citizenship on the basis of birth might be an acceptable procedure, but only if it did not preclude individuals from making different choices later when they reached maturity.

Second, one could not justify restrictions on the grounds that immigration would reduce the economic well-being of current citizens. That line of argument is drastically limited by two considerations: the perspective of the worst-off and the priority of liberty. In order to establish the current citizens' perspective as the relevant worst-off position, it would be necessary to show that immigration would reduce the economic well-being of current citizens below the level the potential immigrants would enjoy if they were not permitted to immigrate. But even if this could be established, it would not justify restrictions on immigration because of the priority of liberty. So, the economic concerns of current citizens are essentially rendered irrelevant.

Third, the effect of immigration on the particular culture and history of the society would not be a relevant moral consideration, so long as there was no threat to basic liberal democratic values. This conclusion is less apparent from what I have said so far, but it follows from what Rawls says in his discussion of perfectionism.[16] The principle of perfectionism would require social institutions to be arranged so as to maximize the achievement of human excellence in art, science, or culture regardless of the effect of such arrangements on equality and freedom. (For example, slavery in ancient Athens has sometimes been defended on the grounds that it was essential to Athenian cultural achievements.) One variant of this position might be the claim that restrictions on immigration would be necessary to preserve the unity and coherence of a culture (assuming that the culture was worth preserving). Rawls argues that in the original position no one would accept any perfectionist standard because no one would be willing to risk the possibility of being required to forego some important right or freedom for the sake of an ideal that might prove irrelevant to one's own concerns. So, restrictions on immigration for the sake of preserving a distinctive culture would be ruled out.

In sum, nonideal theory provides more grounds for restricting immigration than ideal theory, but these grounds are severely limited. And ideal theory holds up the principle of free migration as an essential part of the just social order toward which we should strive.

Aliens in the Calculus

A utilitarian approach to the problem of immigration can take into account some of the concerns that the original position excludes but even utilitarianism does not provide much support for the sorts of restrictions on immigration that are common today. The fundamental principle of utilitarianism is 'maximize utility,' and the utilitarian commitment to moral equality is reflected in the assumption that everyone is to count for one and no one for more than one when utility is calculated. Of course, these broad formulations cover over deep disagreements among utilitarians. For example, how is 'utility' to be defined? It is subjective or objective? It is a question of happiness or welfare as in classical utilitarianism or preferences or interests as in some more recent versions?[17]

However these questions are answered, any utilitarian approach would give more weight to some reasons for restricting immigration than Rawls's approach would. For example, if more immigration would hurt some citizens economically, that would count against a more open immigration policy in any utilitarian theory I am familiar with. But that would not settle the question of whether restrictions were justified, for other citizens might gain economically from more immigration and that would count in favor of a more open policy. More importantly, the economic effects of more immigration on noncitizens would also have to be considered. If we focus only on economic consequences, the best immigration policy from a utilitarian perspective would be the one that maximized overall economic gains. In this calculation, current citizens would enjoy no privileged position. The gains and losses of aliens would count just as much. Now the dominant view among both classical and neoclassical economists is that the free mobility of capital and labor is essential to the maximization of overall economic gains. But the free mobility of labor requires open borders. So, despite the fact that the economic costs to current citizens are morally relevant in the utilitarian framework, they would probably not be sufficient to justify restrictions.

Economic consequences are not the only ones that utilitarians consider. For example, if immigration would affect the existing culture or way of life in a society in ways that current citizens found undesirable, that would count against open immigration in many versions of utilitarianism. But not in all. Utilitarians disagree about whether all pleasures (or desires or interests) are to count or only some. For example, should a sadist's pleasure be given moral weight and balanced against his victim's pain or should that sort of pleasure be disregarded? What about racial prejudice? That is clearly relevant to the question of immigration. Should a white racist's unhappiness at the prospect of associating with people of color be counted in the calculus of utility as an argument in favor of racial exclusion as reflected, say, in the White Australia policy? What about the desire to preserve a distinctive local culture as a reason for restricting immigration? That is sometimes linked to racial prejudice but by no means always.

Different utilitarians will answer these sorts of questions in different ways. Some argue that only long-term, rational, or otherwise refined pleasures (or desires or interests) should count. Others insist that we should not look behind the raw data in making our calculations. Everyone's preferences should count, not merely the preferences someone else finds acceptable. I favor the former approach, a reconstructive or filtering approach to utility, but I won't try to defend that here. Even if one takes the raw data approach, which seems to leave more room for reasons to restrict immigration, the final outcome is still likely to favor much more open immigration than is common today. Whatever the method of calculation, the concerns of aliens must be counted too. Under current conditions, when so many millions of poor and oppressed people feel they have so much to gain from migration to the advanced industrial states, it seems hard to believe that a utilitarian calculus which took the interests of aliens seriously would justify significantly greater limits on immigration than the ones entailed by the public order restriction implied by the Rawlsian approach.

The Communitarian Challenge

The three theories I have discussed conflict with one another on many important issues but not (deeply) on the question of immigration. Each leads on its own terms to a position far more favorable to open immigration than the conventional moral view. It is true that, in terms of numbers, even a public order restriction might exclude millions of potential immigrants given the size of the potential demand. Nevertheless, if the arguments I have developed here were accepted, they would require a radical transformation both of current immigration policies and of conventional moral thinking about the question of immigration.

Some may feel that I have wrenched these theories out of context. Each is rooted in the liberal tradition. Liberalism, it might be said, emerged with the modern state and presupposes it. Liberal theories were not designed to deal with questions about aliens. They assumed the context of the sovereign state. As a historical observation this has some truth, but it is not clear why it should have normative force. The same wrenching out of context complaint could as reasonably have been leveled at those who first constructed liberal arguments for the extension of full citizenship to women and members of the working class. Liberal theories also assumed the right to exclude them. Liberal theories focus attention on the need to justify the use of force by the state. Questions about the exclusion of aliens arise naturally from that context. Liberal principles (like most principles) have implications that the original advocates of the principles did not entirely foresee. That is part of what makes social criticism possible.

Others may think that my analysis merely illustrates the inadequacy of liberal theory, especially its inability to give sufficient weight to the value of community.[18] That indictment of liberal theory may or may not be correct, but my findings about immigration rest primarily on assumptions that I think no defensible moral theory can reject: that our social institutions and public policies must respect all human beings as moral persons and that this respect entails recognition, in some form, of the freedom and equality of every human being. Perhaps some other approach can accept these assumptions while still making room for greater restrictions on immigration. To test that possibility, I will consider the views of the theorist who has done the most to translate the communitarian critique into a positive alternative vision: Michael Walzer.

Unlike Rawls and the others, Walzer treats the question of membership as central to his theory of justice, and he comes to the opposite conclusion about immigration from the one that I have defended:

> Across a considerable range of the decisions that are made, states are simply free to take strangers in (or not).[19]

Walzer differs from the other theorists I have considered not only in his conclusions but also in his basic approach. He eschews the search for universal principles and is concerned instead with 'the particularism of history, culture, and membership.'[20] He thinks that questions of distributive justice should be addressed not from behind a 'veil of ignorance' but from the perspective of membership in a political community in which people share a common culture and a common understanding about justice.

I cannot do full justice here to Walzer's rich and subtle discussion of the problem of membership, but I can draw attention to the main points of his argument and to some of the areas of our disagreement. Walzer's central claim is that exclusion is justified by the right of communities to self-determination. The right to exclude is constrained in three important ways, however. First, we have an obligation to provide aid to others who are in dire need, even if we have no established bonds with them, provided that we can do so without excessive cost to ourselves. So, we may be obliged to admit some needy strangers or at least to provide them with some of our resources and perhaps even territory. Second, once people are admitted as residents and participants in the economy, they must be entitled to acquire citizenship, if they wish. Here the constraint flows from principles of justice not mutual aid. The notion of permanent 'guest workers' conflicts with the underlying rationale of communal self-determination which justified the right to exclude in the first place. Third, new states or governments may not expel existing inhabitants even if they are regarded as alien by most of the rest of the population.[21]

In developing his argument, Walzer compares the idea of open states with our experience of neighbourhoods as a form of open association.[22] But in thinking about what open states would be like, we have a better comparison at hand. We can draw upon our experience of cities, provinces, or states in the American sense. These are familiar political communities whose borders are open. Unlike neighborhoods and like countries, they are formally organized communities with boundaries, distinctions between citizens and noncitizens, and elected officials who are expected to pursue policies that benefit the members of the community that elected them. They often have distinctive cultures and ways of life. Think of the differences between New York City and Waycross, Georgia, or between California and Kansas. These sorts of differences are often much greater than the differences across nation-states. Seattle has more in common with Vancouver than it does with many American communities. But cities and provinces and American states cannot restrict immigration (from other parts of the country). So, these cases call into question Walzer's claim that distinctiveness depends on the possibility of formal closure. What makes for distinctiveness and what erodes it is much more complex than political control of admissions.

This does not mean that control over admissions is unimportant. Often local communities would like to restrict immigration. The people of California wanted to keep out poor Oklahomans during the Depression. Now the people of Oregon would like to keep out the Californians. Internal migrations can be substantial. They can transform the character of communities. (Think of the migrations from the rural South to the urban North.) They can place strains on the local economy and make it difficult to maintain locally funded social programs. Despite all this, we do not think these political communities should be able to control their borders. The right to free migration takes priority.

Why should this be so? It is just a choice that we make as a larger community (*i.e.*, the nation state) to restrict the self-determination of local communities in this way? Could we legitimately permit them to exclude? Not easily. No liberal state restricts internal mobility. Those states that do restrict internal mobility are criticized for denying basic human freedoms. If freedom of movement within the state is so important that it overrides the claims of local political communities, on what grounds can we restrict freedom of movement across states? This requires a stronger case for the *moral* distinctiveness of the nation-state as a form of community than Walzer's discussion of neighborhoods provides.

Walzer also draws an analogy between states and clubs.[23] Clubs may generally admit or exclude whomever they want, although any particular decision may be criticized through an appeal to the character of the club and the shared understandings of its members. So, too, with states. This analogy ignores the familiar distinction between public and private, a distinction that Walzer makes use of elsewhere.[24] There is a deep tension between the right of freedom of association and the right to equal treatment. One way to address this tension is to say that in the private sphere freedom of association prevails and in the public sphere equal treatment does. You can pick your friends on the basis of whatever criteria you wish, but in selecting people for offices you must treat all candidates fairly. Drawing a line between public and private is often problematic, but it is clear that clubs are normally at one end of the scale and states at the other. So, the fact that private clubs may admit or exclude whomever they choose says nothing about the appropriate admission standards for states. When the state acts it must treat individuals equally.

Against this, one may object that the requirement of equal treatment applies fully only to those who are already *members* of the community. That is accurate as a description of practice but the question is why it should be so. At one time, the requirement of equal treatment did not extend fully to various groups (workers, blacks, women). On the whole, the history of liberalism reflects a tendency to expand both the definition of the public sphere and the requirements of equal treatment. In the United States today, for example, in contrast to earlier times, both public agencies and private corporations may not legally exclude women simply because they are women (although private clubs still may). A white shopkeeper may no longer exclude blacks from his store (although he may exclude them from his home). I think these recent developments, like the earlier extension of the franchise, reflect something fundamental about the inner logic of liberalism.[25] The extension of the right to immigrate reflects the same logic: equal treatment of individuals in the public sphere.

As I noted at the beginning of this section, Walzer asserts that the political community is constrained by principles of justice from admitting permanent guest workers without giving them the opportunity to become citizens. There is some ambiguity about whether this claim is intended to apply to all political communities or only to ones like ours. If states have a right to self-determination, broadly conceived, they must have a right to choose political forms and political practices different from those of liberal democracies. That presumably includes the right to establish categories of second-class citizens (or, at least, temporary guest workers) and also the right to determine other aspects of admissions policy in accordance with their own principles.[26] But if the question is what *our* society (or one with the same basic values) ought to do, then the matter is different both for guest workers and for other aliens. It is right to assert that *our* society ought to admit guest workers to full citizenship. Anything else is incompatible with our liberal democratic principles. But so is a restrictive policy on immigration.

Any approach like Walzer's that seeks its ground in the tradition and culture of *our* community must confront, as a methodological paradox, the fact that liberalism is a central part of our culture. The enormous intellectual popularity of Rawls and Nozick and the enduring influence of utilitarianism attest to their ability to communicate contemporary understandings and shared meanings in a language that has legitimacy and power in our culture. These theories would not make such sense to a Buddhist monk in medieval Japan. But their individualistic assumptions and their language of universal, ahistorical reason makes sense to us because of *our* tradition, *our* culture, *our* community. For people in a different moral tradition, one that assumed fundamental moral differences between those inside the society and those outside, restrictions on immigration might be easy to justify. Those who are *other* simply might not count, or at least not count as much. But we cannot dismiss the aliens on the ground that they are other, because *we* are the products of a liberal culture.

The point goes still deeper. To take *our* community as a starting point is to take a community that expresses its moral views in terms of universal principles. Walzer's own arguments reflect this. When he asserts that states may not expel existing inhabitants whom the majority or the new government regards as alien, he is making a claim about what is right and wrong for *any* state not just our own or one that shares our basic values. He develops the argument by drawing on Hobbes. That is an argument from a particular tradition, one that may not be shared by new states that want to expel some of their inhabitants. Nonetheless, Walzer makes a universal claim (and one I consider correct). He makes the same sort of argument when he insists that states may not legitimately restrict *e*migration.[27] This applies to all political communities not just those that share our understanding of the relation of individual and collective.

Recognition of the particularity of our own culture should not prevent us from making these sorts of claims. We should not try to force others to accept our views, and we should be ready to listen to others and learn from them. But respect for the diversity of communities does not require us to abandon all claims about what other states ought to do. If my arguments are correct, the general case for open borders is deeply rooted in the fundamental values of our tradition. No moral argument will seem acceptable to *us*, if it directly challenges the assumption of the equal moral worth of all individuals. If restrictions on immigration are to be justified, they have to be based on arguments that respect that principle. Walzer's theory has many virtues that I have not explored here, but it does not supply an adequate argument for the state's right to exclude.

Conclusion

Free migration may not be immediately achievable, but it is a goal toward which we should strive. And we have an obligation to open our borders much more fully than we do now. The current restrictions on immigration in Western democracies—even in the most open ones like Canada and the United States—are not justifiable. Like feudal barriers to mobility, they protect unjust privilege.

Does it follow that there is *no* room for distinctions between aliens and citizens, no theory of citizenship, no boundaries for the community? Not at all. To say that membership is open to all who wish to join is not to say that there is no distinction between members and nonmembers. Those who choose to cooperate together in the state have special rights and obligations not shared by noncitizens. Respecting the particular choices and commitments that individuals make flows naturally from a commitment to the idea of equal moral worth. (Indeed, consent as a justification for political obligation is least problematic in the case of immigrants.) What is *not* readily compatible with the idea of equal moral worth is the exclusion of those who want to join. If people want to sign the social contract, they should be permitted to do so.

Open borders would threaten the distinctive character of different political communities only because we assume that so many people would move if they could. If the migrants were few, it would not matter. A few immigrants could always be absorbed without changing the character of the community. And, as Walzer observes, most human beings do not love to move.[28] They normally feel attached to their native land and to the particular language, culture, and community in which they grew up and in which they feel at home. They seek to move only when life is very difficult where they are. Their concerns are rarely frivolous. So, it is right to weigh the claims of those who want to move against the claims of those who want to preserve the community as it is. And if we don't unfairly tip the scales, the case for exclusion will rarely triumph.

People live in communities with bonds and bounds, but these may be of different kinds. In a liberal society, the bonds and bounds should be compatible with liberal principles. Open immigration would change the character of the community but it would not leave the community without any character. It might destroy old ways of life, highly valued by some, but it would make possible new ways of life, highly valued by others. The whites in Forsythe County who want to keep out blacks are trying to preserve a way of life that is valuable to them. To deny such communities the right to exclude does limit their ability to shape their future character and destiny, but it does not utterly destroy their capacity for self-determination. Many aspects of communal life remain potentially subject to collective control. Moreover, constraining the kinds of choices that people and communities may make is what principles of justice are for. They set limits on what people seeking to abide by these principles may do. To commit ourselves to open borders would not be to abandon the idea of communal character but to reaffirm it. It would be an affirmation of the liberal character of the community and of its commitment to principles of justice.

Notes

1. The conventional assumption is captured by the Select Commission on Immigration and Refugee Policy: 'Our policy—while providing opportunity to a portion of the world's population—must be guided by the basic national interests of the people of the United States.' From *U.S. Immigration Policy and the National Interest: The Final Report and Recommendations of the Select Commission on Immigration and Refugee Policy to the Congress and the President of the United States* (1 March 1981). The best theoretical defense of the conventional assumption (with some modifications) is Michael Walzer, *Spheres of Justice* (New York: Basic Books, 1983), pp. 31–63. A few theorists have challenged the conventional assumption. See Bruce Ackerman, *Social Justice in the Liberal State* (New Haven: Yale University Press, 1980), pp. 89–95; Judith Lichtenberg, 'National Boundaries and Moral Boundaries: A Cosmopolitan View' in *Boundaries: National Autonomy and Its Limits*, ed. Peter G. Brown and Henry Shue (Totowa, NJ: Rowman and Littlefield, 1981), pp. 79–100, and Roger Nett, 'The Civil Right We Are Not Ready For: The Right of Free Movement of People on the Face of the Earth,' *Ethics* 81:212–27. Frederick Whelan has also explored these issues in two interesting unpublished papers.
2. Robert Nozick, *Anarchy, State, and Utopia* (New York: Basic Books, 1974), pp. 10–25, 88–119.
3. Ibid., pp. 108–113. Citizens, in Nozick's view, are simply consumers purchasing impartial, efficient protection of preexisting natural rights. Nozick uses the terms 'citizen,' 'client' and 'customer' interchangeably.
4. Nozick interprets the Lockean proviso as implying that property rights in land may not so restrict an individual's freedom of movement as to deny him effective liberty. This further limits the possibility of excluding aliens. See p. 55.

5. John Rawls, *A Theory of Justice* (Cambridge, MA.: Harvard University Press, 1971), pp. 60–65, 136–42, 243–48.
6. Ibid., pp. 8–9, 244–48.
7. The argument for a global view of the original position has been developed most fully in Charles Beitz, *Political Theory and International Relations* (Princeton, NJ: Princeton University Press, 1979), pp. 125–76, especially 129–36 and 143–53. For earlier criticisms of Rawls along the same lines, see Brian Barry, *The Liberal Theory of Justice* (Oxford: Clarendon Press, 1973), pp. 128–33 and Thomas M. Scanlon, 'Rawls's Theory of Justice,' *University of Pennsylvania Law Review* 121, no. 5 (May 1973): 1066–67. For more recent discussions, see David A.J. Richards, 'International Distributive Justice,' in *Ethics, Economics, and the Law*, eds. J. Roland Pennock and John Chapman (New York: New York University Press, 1982), pp. 275–99 and Charles Beitz, 'Cosmopolitan Ideals and National Sentiments,' *The Journal of Philosophy* 80, no. 10 (October 1983): 591–600. None of these discussions fully explores the implications of a global view of the original position for the issue of immigration, although the recent essay by Beitz touches on the topic.
8. Respecting others as free and equal moral persons does not imply that one cannot distinguish friends from strangers or citizens from aliens. See the conclusion for an elaboration.
9. Rawls, *Justice*, pp. 136, 72.
10. Compare Beitz, *Political Theory*, p. 183.
11. For more on the comparison of mobility within a country and mobility across countries, see Joseph H. Carens, 'Migration and the Welfare State' in *Democracy and the Welfare State*, ed. Amy Gutmann (Princeton: Princeton University Press, 1987).
12. Rawls, *Justice*, pp. 212–13.
13. Ibid., p. 213.
14. For statistics on current and projected levels of immigration to the U.S., see Michael S. Teitelbaum, 'Right Versus Right: Immigration and Refugee Policy in the United States,' *Foreign Affairs* 59 (1980): 21–59.
15. For the deep roots of the right to emigrate in the liberal tradition, see Frederick Whelan, 'Citizenship and the Right to Leave,' *American Political Science Review* 75, no. 3 (September 1981): 636–53.
16. Rawls, *Justice*, pp. 325–32.
17. For recent discussions of utilitarianism, see Richard Brandt, *A Theory of the Good and the Right* (Oxford: Oxford University Press, 1979); Peter Singer, *Practical Ethics* (Cambridge: Cambridge University Press, 1979); R.M. Hare, *Moral Thinking* (Oxford: Oxford University Press, 1981); and Amartya Sen and Bernard Williams, eds., *Utilitarianism and Beyond* (Cambridge: Cambridge University Press, 1982).
18. For recent communitarian critiques of liberalism, see Alasdair MacIntyre, *After Virtue* (Notre Dame: Notre Dame University Press, 1981) and Michael Sandel, *Liberalism and the Limits of Justice* (New York: Cambridge University Press, 1982). For a critique of the critics, see Amy Gutmann, 'Communitarian

Critics of Liberalism,' *Philosophy and Public Affairs* 14 (Summer 1985): 308–322.

19. Walzer, *Spheres*, p. 61.
20. Ibid., p. 5.
21. Ibid., pp. 33, 45–48, 55–61, 42–44.
22. Ibid., pp. 36–39.
23. Ibid., pp. 39–41.
24. Ibid., pp. 129–64.
25. I am not arguing that the changes in treatment of women, blacks, and workers were *brought about* by the inner logic of liberalism. These changes resulted from changes in social conditions and from political struggles, including ideological struggles in which arguments about the implications of liberal principles played some role, though not necessarily a decisive one. But from a philosophical perspective, it is important to understand where principles lead, even if one does not assume that people's actions in the world will always be governed by the principles they espouse.
26. Compare Walzer's claim that the caste system would be just if accepted by the villages affected (ibid., pp. 313–15).
27. Ibid., pp. 39–40.
28. Ibid., p. 38.

17 The Morality of Secession

ALLEN BUCHANAN

The Strategy

First, I will articulate a variety of arguments that purport to justify secession, or rather, secession under certain circumstances. For the most part these arguments rely on familiar and widely endorsed moral principles and values. However, I will endeavour to exhibit the logical structure of the arguments more clearly than is usually done, and I will subject their implicit moral and factual assumptions to careful scrutiny. Some of these prosecession arguments are flawed and some are of only limited application, but others are more compelling. The cumulative effect of these arguments is to establish a strong case for a moral right to secede. . . .

The Pure Self-Determination or Nationalist Argument

One of the most familiar and stirring justifications offered for secession appeals to *the right of self-determination for 'peoples,'* interpreted such that it is equivalent to what is sometimes called the *normative principle of nationalism.* It is also one of the least plausible justifications.

The normative nationalist principle, as I understand it, states that every 'people' is entitled to its own state, or, as Ernest Gellner puts it, that political and cultural (or ethnic) boundaries must, as a matter of right, coincide.[1] In other words, according to this understanding of the normative nationalist principle, the notion of self-determination is construed, in a very robust way, as requiring complete political independence—that is, full sovereignty.

The United Nations officially endorses the right of self-determination in several documents. For example, General Assembly Resolution 1514 bravely declares that 'all peoples have the right to self-determination; by

---

Extract from Allen Buchanan, *Secession: The Morality of Political Divorce* (Westview Press, 1991), pp. 27, 48–74 (minus 51–2, 62–3, 69–70). Reprinted by permission of Westview Press, Boulder, Colorado.

virtue of that right they freely determine their political status and freely pursue their economic, social and cultural development.' The phrase 'freely determine their political status', lacking any qualifying language, suggests that 'self-determination' here is to be understood in the robust sense, as requiring or at least allowing complete political independence. This in turn seems to commit the UN, in its affirmation of the right of self-determination, to the view that every 'people' has the right to secede if secession is necessary for achieving complete political independence.

The United Nations Charter (Article 1, paragraph 2, and Article 55), the United Nations International Covenant on Civil and Political Rights, and the United Nations International Covenant on Economic, Social, and Cultural Rights also proclaim a right of self-determination for all peoples.

An immediate difficulty, of course, is the meaning of 'peoples.' Presumably a 'people' is a distinct ethnic group, the identifying marks of which are a common language, shared traditions, and a common culture. Each of these criteria has its own difficulties. The question of what count as different dialects of the same language, as opposed to two or more distinct languages, raises complex theoretical and metatheoretical issues in linguistics. The histories of many groups exhibit frequent discontinuities, infusions of new cultural elements from outside, and alternating degrees of assimilation to and separation from other groups. More disturbingly, if 'culture' is interpreted broadly enough, then the normative nationalist principle denies the legitimacy of any state that exhibits cultural pluralism (unless all 'peoples' within it freely waive their rights to their own states). Yet cultural pluralism is often taken to be a distinguishing feature of the modern state, or at least of the modern liberal state. Moreover, if the number of ethnic or cultural groups or peoples is not fixed but may increase, the normative nationalist principle is a recipe for limitless political fragmentation.

Nor is this all. Even aside from the instability and economic costs of repeated fragmentation, there is a more serious objection to the normative nationalist principle, forcefully formulated by Ernest Gellner.

> To put it in the simplest possible terms: there is a very large number of potential nations on earth. Our planet also contains room for a certain number of independent or autonomous political units. On any reasonable calculation, the former number (of potential nations) is probably much, *much* larger than that of possible viable states. If this argument or calculation is correct, not all nationalisms can be satisfied, at any rate not at the same time. The satisfaction of some spells the frustration of others. This argument is furthered and immeasurably strengthened by the fact that very many of the potential nations of this world live, or until recently have lived, not in compact territorial units but intermixed with each other in complex patterns. It follows that a territorial political unit can only become ethnically homogeneous, in such cases, if it either kills, or expels, or assimilates all non-nationals.[2]

With arch understatement, Gellner concludes that the unwillingness of people to suffer such fates 'may make the implementation of the nationalist principle difficult.' Thus to say that the normative nationalist principle must be rejected because it is too *impractical* or *economically costly* would be grossly misleading. It ought to be abandoned because the *moral costs* of even attempting to implement it are prohibitive.

It is crucial to see that this criticism of the principle of self-determination is decisive *only* against the strong version of that principle that makes it equivalent to the normative nationalist principle, which states that each people (or ethnic group) is to have its own fully sovereign state. For the objection focuses on the unacceptable implications of granting a right of self-determination to all 'peoples,' *on the assumption that self-determination means complete political independence, that is, full sovereignty.*

However, as a number of writers have noted, the notion of self-determination is vague or, rather, multiply ambiguous, inasmuch as there are numerous forms and a range of degrees of political independence that a 'people' might attain. For example, under some conditions, a group might consider itself to have achieved its goal of self-determination if it secured the right to use its own language as an official language of the state, or if its territory was recognized as a province or state within a federation, or if the group's representatives were accorded a veto over constitutional changes or over important areas of federal legislation. 'Self-determination' need not mean full sovereignty, and hence to recognize a right of self-determination does not itself commit us to affirming that every group to which the principle of self-determination applies has a right to secede.

If the alleged principle of self-determination of peoples is either too vague to be of much use or implausible (when specified so strongly as to entail a right to complete independence and hence secession), what accounts for its popularity and longevity? My hypothesis is that the moral appeal of the principle of self-determination depends precisely upon its vagueness. It is a kind of placeholder for a range of possible principles specifying various forms and degrees of independence. These more specific principles do not express a substantive fundamental value, called self-determination. Instead, the moral force for any particular specification of self-determination depends upon the more basic values that implementing it might serve in a particular context. Once these more basic values are identified, it should be possible to dispense largely with the principle of self-determination, with its dangerous vagueness, and to concentrate on more direct arguments in favor of secession (or in favor of more limited forms of political independence).

Under certain conditions, achieving a greater degree of self-determination may be the only practical way for a group to protect itself from (1) destruction of its culture, (2) literal genocide, or (3) various injustices falling under the general heading of ethnic discrimination, including violations of civil and political rights that ought to be guaranteed to all citizens regardless of ethnicity, as well as what was referred to earlier as discriminatory redistribution. As we are concerned here with arguments to justify secession, I take up in upcoming sections of this chapter (1) the argument from cultural preservation and (2) the argument from self-defense, as justifications for that extreme form of self-determination which secession entails. Argument (3) has already been dealt with in part, under the heading of the argument from discriminatory redistribution. One point of that discussion was that whether or not the liberal doctrine of justified resistance to the state has clearly recognized it, discriminatory redistribution is a serious injustice and ought to be included among the grounds for justified resistance. It was also noted that whether resistance to discriminatory redistribution may justifiably take the form of secession depends, in the end, upon whether the need to eliminate the injustice of discriminatory redistribution is sufficient to establish a valid claim to territory on the part of the secessionists (and to override whatever claims to territory others may have to the seceding area).

Similarly, whether injustice in the form of violations of the civil and political rights of members of ethnic groups justifies not only revolution, as liberal doctrine concedes, but also secession, along with the taking of territory that the latter entails, will depend upon two things: first, whether there is any other practical and morally acceptable way of avoiding these injustices that does not involve the taking of territory; and, second, if there is not, whether the practical necessity of seizing territory in order to avoid injustice generates a valid moral title to that territory. These complex issues deserve special attention and will be taken up later. For the present, however, this conclusion can be proffered tentatively: The argument from self-determination may be understood either as appealing to self-determination for all peoples or ethnic groups as a fundamental value or as something instrumentally valuable for securing other, more basic values, such as cultural preservation, survival, or justice. If the former, then the principle of self-determination must be rejected, at least insofar as the principle is interpreted so strongly as to entail a right to secede. If the latter, then the argument from self-determination can be dropped in favor of an examination of those arguments to which it reduces.

Before we proceed to those arguments, it is worth noting an important connection between the nationalist argument for secession and the argument from discriminatory redistribution.[3] As observed earlier, not just the worse off but the better off, too, may claim to be victims of discriminatory redistribution and seek to escape the continuation of this injustice by seceding. It is on precisely this ground that many Slovenes, for example, advocate severing their region from the poorer and less developed areas of Yugoslavia.

Yet the same people may well accept policies within their own region that distribute wealth from the rich to the poor. What this suggests is that whether a group views itself as a victim of discriminatory redistribution will depend in part upon how it conceives of the boundaries of its own identity—whether it regards those to whom some of its resources are being transferred by government redistribution policies as *its own people* or as an alien group. Thus whether the reunification of Germany will succeed may depend in large part upon whether West Germans see the massive transfers of wealth from themselves to East Germans as redistribution to another people or as redistribution among one people, a matter of the wealthier members of a family helping their less fortunate relatives. The greater the identification of the benefactors with the recipients, the less likely the benefactors are to see themselves as suffering the injustice of discriminatory redistribution.

So, on the one hand, the presence or absence of a sense of distinct ethnic identity can determine whether or not discriminatory redistribution even becomes an issue, and hence whether it comes to fuel a secessionist movement. On the other hand, a policy of discriminatory redistribution can contribute to the emergence of a group's sense that it is distinct and to its desire to form an independent state: The members of a group may come to construct a common identity in part out of the recognition that they are all victims of the same enemy. The process by which a group becomes a force striving for a state of its own is usually a complex one in which a political and literary elite forges a strong sense of identity by convincing people that the economic disadvantages they suffer are the result of ethnic discrimination, and continued discrimination may impede assimilation, preventing a disadvantaged group from losing its ethnic distinctness. And when the members of a group perceive that they are barred from economic advancement available to others, the goods that membership in their distinct ethnic culture provides to them may become all the more important. This circumstance in turn may lead them to seek political autonomy in order to preserve their distinctive culture.

In some cases, however, a secessionist movement may be motivated by the desire to preserve a distinctive culture even when the members of the group in question are no longer the victim of discriminatory redistribution or other forms of discrimination. This may in fact be the case with Quebec. Some, perhaps the majority of Quebecois advocating secession do so on grounds of cultural preservation, not discriminatory redistribution or another injustice, although most would probably maintain that they have suffered serious discrimination until very recently. For this reason the issue of cultural preservation is worth considering, in its own right, as an independent argument for secession, even though in many cases the perceived need to preserve a culture will be closely tied to the grievance of discriminatory redistribution.

Preserving Cultures

Some have contended that by itself the need to preserve a culture can justify secession. Again Quebec can serve as a case in point. The Meech Lake Accord, as was already noted, contains a special provision recognizing French Canada as a 'distinct society,' and one reason given for including it was that doing so was thought to be necessary for the preservation of French Canadian culture. To frame the argument in this manner, however, may be too impersonal, too abstract. Its true force lies in the idea that the members of a culture who believe that their culture is threatened with disintegration feel that their very identities are imperiled, that in losing their culture they will in some sense lose themselves, or a significant part of the selves they value most.

To evaluate this justification for secession, two undertakings are required. First, we must explore the value of cultural preservation and try to chart its scope and limits. Second, we must ascertain whether there are other, less drastic measures than secession that can help provide sufficient protection for a culture. What counts as sufficient protection will depend upon how valuable the preservation of a culture is, and that in turn will depend upon what constitutes the value of a culture.

On the view endorsed here, the chief value of culture is more accurately characterized as the value of *cultural membership*. In other words, a culture is valuable first and foremost because of its contribution to the lives of the individuals whose culture it is. A culture's value will be enhanced, of course, if it also enriches the lives of others who are not members of it but who benefit from indirect contact with it.

The key point is that whatever value a culture has is its value *for individuals*. It is extremely important to emphasize, however, that this does not assume a conception of value that is 'individualistic' in any unacceptable sense of that much abused term. To say that culture is good (and only good) by virtue of the contribution it makes to the lives of individuals is not to assume that the good of those individuals is egoistic or purely self-regarding, nor that cultural membership is only an instrumental or extrinsic good for them. None of this is implied, although critics of liberalism's 'individualism' often suggest that it is.

There are two ways in which cultural membership can contribute to the good of an individual. In only one of them does cultural membership not qualify as an intrinsic good. And in neither does the good of cultural membership depend upon any assumption that the individual is egoistic or that her good is exclusively self-regarding. First, as we have already seen, Kymlicka has correctly noted that membership in a cultural community can be vital for the individual because it provides her with a meaningful context for choice.

This important point warrants more elaboration than Kymlicka gives it. The culture not only makes *salient* a manageably limited range of alternative goals, rescuing the individual from the paralysis of infinite possibilities; it also does so in such a way as to endow certain options with *meanings* that allow the individual to *identify with* and be *motivated by* them. Finally, the culture serves to *connect* what otherwise would be fragmented goals in a coherent, mutually supporting way, offering ideals of wholeness and continuity, not only across the stages of a human life but over generations as well. Without the context for meaningful choice supplied by a culture, the individual may feel either that nothing is worth doing because everything is possible or that life is a series of discrete episodes of choice, each of which is diminished in value because of its utter unconnectedness with the others. The landscape of choice may seem so flattened and featureless that movement seems pointless, and the sense that one's life is a journey in which milestones can be reached may evaporate. With some simplification, we can say that the first source of the value of culture is that it provides an appropriate *structure* for the individual's pursuit of the good life. To repeat: Nothing in this account of the first source of the value of culture assumes that the content of the individual's goals is egoistic or purely self-regarding.

What Kymlicka neglects to observe—and what renders his view vulnerable to charges of excessive individualism—is that cultural membership is valuable also because, at least for most individuals, *participation in community* is *itself* an important ingredient in the *content* of the good life, not just a part of its structure. Participation in community, for many people, at least, is a fundamental intrinsic good, not merely a structural condition for the successful pursuit of other goods or a means of acquiring them. In many cases the community that is most important in the individual's life will be a cultural (as opposed to a political, professional, or aesthetic) community. Nothing in liberalism or its understanding of human good precludes it from acknowledging this basic truth.[4]

Proponents of the argument under scrutiny must go farther than the statement that cultural membership, and hence the preservation of culture, is a good. They must show that there is a *right* to cultural preservation and that this right justifies secession. However, this alleged right, if it exists, cannot be a right to cultural *stasis*—a right to preserve a culture just as it is at present. The basis of the alleged right is the good that cultural membership achieves for individuals, and this good does not require an unchanging culture.

For the same reason, an appreciation of the value of cultural membership cannot by itself even support a right to the continued existence of any particular culture. What is important is that an individual be able to belong to a culture, some culture or other, not that he be able to belong, indefinitely, to any particular culture.

Of course, in practice this distinction will frequently be of little consequence because an individual whose culture disintegrates will sometimes not be able to become a fully participating member of another culture. This may be the case with some members of indigenous populations, including some North American Indians. The impact of white culture and technology in some instances may have rendered the traditional culture unviable, or at the least has so damaged it that membership no longer provides great benefits to the individual but instead imposes many serious liabilities. Yet for a number of reasons, including a shameful record of injustice and neglect, those whose cultures have been most severely damaged also have been barred from genuine assimilation into the culture the whites brought.[5] However, this is not always so. In some cases individuals can leave the sinking ship of one culture and board another, more seaworthy cultural vessel.

Tragically, the members of a dying culture may not always be willing to abandon it and give their allegiance to a new way of life, even when one is available to them.[6] The following type of case, which may be all too common, creates a dreadful moral dilemma. Consider the indigenous culture mortally wounded by the onslaught of 'civilization,' because the material base for its fundamental ways of life has been destroyed. (Such was the case with the destruction of the bison herds upon which the Plains Indian cultures were built.) Without this material base, which cannot be restored, the culture may not be able to supply in sufficient degree the goods that make cultural membership valuable and whose preservation provides grounds for secession or other forms of political autonomy, or even for according the group special rights. Indeed, any attempt to prolong the life of the moribund culture will not only fail but will also make the members of the group worse off by impeding their assimilation into the 'civilized' culture. Yet the members of the group remain steadfast in their desire to try to preserve the culture. They are like people who refuse to be rescued from their sinking lifeboat because it is *their* craft and because any other vessel seems alien and untrustworthy to them. Instead, they demand that we provide them with timbers and pumps (special group rights, greater autonomy, and/or other resources) to shore up what we have every reason to believe is a doomed vessel. The dilemma is this: Should we respect their preferences and render aid that we reasonably believe will only be detrimental to them, or should we act so as to promote their well-being even though this means rejecting their choices?

Notice that there is a dilemma here even for the strongly antipaternalistic. Even if one is willing to allow competent choosers to bring ruin upon themselves, it is quite another matter to provide them with resources to pursue a path that will prevent their children, and successive generations as well, from achieving the goods of membership in a viable culture. This problem deserves far more attention than can be given here. Despite the complications it introduces, the chief point I wish to make is that there is a limitation on the right to preserve a culture: Because the value of cultural membership is not limited to membership in one particular culture, and because individuals whose culture is damaged will in some cases be able to affiliate successfully with another culture (at least if they are given the resources to do so), there is, strictly speaking, no right to the perpetual existence of any one particular culture.

There is another reason why the right to cultural preservation cannot be understood as the right to whatever is necessary, including secession, for each and every culture to survive indefinitely. As was seen in our assessment of the pure self-determination or nationalist argument for secession, there simply may not be sufficient usable space and other resources for every culture to have its own autonomous territory. And the cultural preservation argument, as an argument for secession, assumes that the culture requires its own autonomous territory if it is to survive.

Yet another important limitation on the alleged right to cultural preservation is that some cultures may be so pernicious as to warrant no protection at all, much less the protection afforded by granting them their own territory. Indeed, some cultures are so heinous that they may be and should be destroyed. It would be little short of bizarre to say that the Nazis had a right to preserve their culture, even if one quickly added that this right was overridden by the fact that the culture in question was a genocidal barbarism erected on a tissue of grotesque lies and racist mythology. (Nazism, which included distinctive conceptions of the family, of the individual's relationship to society, and of virtue, and which also possessed its own peculiar aesthetic and art forms, does seem to qualify as a culture.) Such a culture has no right to preserve itself. So if there is a right to cultural preservation, it may be ascribed only to cultures that are not beyond the moral pale.

Finally, it is important to understand that the argument from cultural preservation assumes that the need to protect a culture is of such moral weight as to *generate* the valid territorial claim that justified secession requires. This argument, then, does not *begin* with a preexisting claim to territory. Instead, its *conclusion* includes such a claim.

In this regard the argument from cultural preservation for secession is to be contrasted with the argument from rectificatory justice to be considered below. The latter argument justifies secession as the reappropriation of territory that was unjustly taken (as in the case of the U.S.S.R.'s annexation of Lithuania, Latvia, and Estonia) and hence relies on a *preexisting* territorial claim. If the need to preserve a culture is to count as an independent justification for secession, then, it must be shown that at least under certain conditions this need generates a valid claim to territory in the absence of a historical entitlement to territory (as in the argument from rectificatory justice). In other words, if the argument is to succeed, it must at minimum establish that autonomous control over territory is *practically necessary*—that it is the only effective way to preserve the culture.

Keeping in mind these limitations on the right to preserve a culture, we must next ask whether there are other, less costly ways in which the existence of a culture may be protected. And as our special concern is with the place of secession in liberal theory, we must try to determine what resources a liberal order in particular has for protecting imperiled cultures while still accommodating them within its borders. Because the argument from cultural preservation assumes that under certain circumstances control over land is necessary for cultural survival, the questions to pose are these: (1) How might a group achieve forms of control over land other than the full control of territorial sovereignty that secession entails? (2) Would such alternative forms of control suffice to provide endangered cultures with whatever protection they are entitled to?

There are at least two major mechanisms for control over land (short of secession) available within a liberal framework. The first already exists within all liberal societies: *the laws of property and contract.* These laws enable members of groups, including cultural groups, to pool individual property into collective, jointly owned property. Throughout the history of liberal societies certain groups have done just this, and they have done so in part out of a recognition that collective control over real property was necessary for the survival of their distinctive shared goals and ways of life. Examples are plentiful, but only two will be mentioned here: religious orders (which establish monasteries and convents) and groups such as the Nature Conservancy (which purchase land in order to prevent it from being developed in ways that threaten wildlife habitat). In brief, the individual rights of property and contract fundamental to liberal societies can be used to create group rights that can afford communities a significant degree of control over land and natural resources. Of course, the property rights that groups can acquire in this way fall short of the territorial sovereignty that successful secession brings; but in some cases at least, the former, more limited type of control may suffice. Whether it does will depend upon the nature of the cultural group and the relationship between the survival of its distinctive features and the degree of control its members are able to exercise over land.

Some (like Kymlicka) believe that the resources of ordinary contract and property law are not always sufficient to provide endangered cultures with adequate control over land and resources. Accordingly, they propose a second form of control not already found in all liberal regimes: *special group rights*. These rights might be of several different sorts. But in each case they would be designed to provide special protections for vulnerable minority cultures. For example, as we have already noted, Indians may be granted the right to establish longer residency requirements for non-Indians in areas occupied by Indians in order to prevent the formation of voting majorities that would enact laws that erode Indian culture. Or tribes might be given the right to require that their children be taught their native language in public school and might be guaranteed public funds for doing so. Neither of these approaches, however, deals directly with the issue of control over territory and its influence on the preservation of culture.

In contrast, minority cultures may be protected by according them *special group property rights*. This can be done by granting minority group governmental units (e.g., tribal governments for Indians) the authority to enact special property laws that place restrictions on the ability of individuals or groups within the minority community to alienate land. As we have seen, this in effect is the right to restrict the ordinary individual right to private property, by limiting the individual member's liberty to buy and sell property.

Put more positively, granting such a right to a minority group or its governmental unit amounts to empowering it *to create new collective property rights directly*, rather than by members of the group forging them through cooperative exercises of their ordinary individual property and contractual rights. If the special right accorded to the minority governmental unit allows the creation to these new collective property rights (or restrictions on preexisting individual property rights) through majority voting procedures or any method other than unanimity, then protecting the territory and hence the culture by this method may prove easier than relying on ordinary contractual and property rights, because the latter require the voluntary agreement of *all* concerned. Avoiding the requirement of unanimity can be a distinct advantage of special group property rights over individual property rights. (But the cost of securing this advantage, of course, is that the individual is deprived of her power to veto decisions concerning the use of land through the exercise of her individual property rights.)

Yet another way to protect a minority culture would be to empower the minority to impose obstacles to entry into its territory by nonmembers and to impose exit costs on members who wish to leave. For example, instead of forbidding the sale of Indian lands to non-Indians, tribal governments might simply enact a surcharge on real estate transactions involving non-Indians as well as a special tax on non-Indians who rent land or dwellings on Indian territory. And in order to discourage Indians from leaving areas in which they are concentrated and, hence, from contributing to a situation in which they lack the population mass to sustain their culture, tribal governments could impose exit taxes an/or tax the profits on sales of property by members when they leave the territory.

What all of these methods have in common is that they are attempts to sustain conditions thought to be necessary for the preservation of a minority culture. Each involves granting the group in question, acting through its government, the right to restrict the rights otherwise held by individuals. Some methods grant groups varying degrees of control over territory, short of territorial sovereignty. To the extent that these special rights to restrict rights are exercised by majority rule within the group they can be seen as instances of the group *binding itself*—that is, limiting the freedom of its members for the sake of preserving the collective good of sustaining the culture. Self-binding can be a valuable means for preserving values.

So far we have noted only how special rights to limit the entry and exit of *people* into the cultural minority's territory, and how special rights to create limits on the alienation of land from the group's territory, can help protect a culture. But some cultural minorities complain that it is the intrusion of alien lifestyles and alien culture themselves that threaten the survival of their cultures.

However, if the reason a cultural minority seeks secession is to control its own borders in order to limit alien cultural influences, then in principle this goal might be achieved by less drastic measures than secession. For example, a tribal government or the government of a territorially concentrated religious community such as the Amish or Mennonites might be granted the authority to enact laws that create barriers to the entry of cultural influences that threaten to undermine the community's values. Some communitarian authors, including Michael Sandel, have proposed precisely this measure. Sandel suggests that a community ought to be empowered to protect itself against a type of activity that 'offends its way of life,'[7] such as the dissemination of 'pornography' within its area. In other words, just as there are ways of protecting the territorial base of a culture other than by establishing complete territorial sovereignty through secession, so there are other ways of protecting a community's culture from destructive alien cultural influences.

These differing possibilities raise an important and perplexing question for liberal political theory—one that to my knowledge has never before been posed, much less answered. From the standpoint of liberal values of freedom and tolerance, is it preferable to empower local communities *within* the state to restrict individual rights (e.g., to private property, or to freedom of expression) or to allow (or require!) communities that seek to do so to secede, to separate from the state?

The initial response is likely to be: Obviously it is more consonant with liberal values to allow the group in question to secede than to compromise individual freedom and toleration within the liberal state! Yet from a liberal standpoint, the second alternative has one clear advantage: *If* the liberal state retains ultimate control over entry to and exit from illiberal enclave communities within its borders, then individuals will have some freedom of choice to participate in these communities or not. Conversely, if illiberal communities are allowed or encouraged to secede, the liberal state's recognition of their sovereignty implies a presumption that those communities will control access to and exit from their territory. Even if liberalism champions the right to emigrate, the recognition of sovereignty that goes along with acceptance of secession at least implies a greater degree of *de facto* control over entry and exit than is possible if the group stays within the liberal state.

So, at least from a liberal point of view, there is a presumption in favor of *non*secessionist methods for preserving minority cultures—even if some of these methods involve limitations on liberal individual rights. And as we have just seen, there are a number of measures, from special property laws, to minority language rights, to constitutional rights of nullification and group veto, that can help to preserve minority cultures, without the radical step of secession. For this reason the cultural preservation argument for secession is of limited force. The burden is upon its proponents to show the inadequacy of strategies for cultural preservation that employ combinations of individual rights and various special minority group rights. Only if these alternatives are inadequate, or if the state refuses to utilize them, can the need to preserve cultural identity justify secession. Whether or not a right to secede, rather than some combination of individual and other group rights, will best protect minorities admits of no general answer. It will depend upon the particular circumstances.

Another, more fundamental limitation of the argument from cultural preservation should be acknowledged. So far I have argued only that there are alternatives to secession for preserving cultures and that liberalism favors some nonsecession alternatives, other things being equal. Later, when antisecessionist arguments are explored in detail, we will examine a serious challenge to the idea that a group has a right to secede when the goal of secession is to establish an illiberal state *that limits the opportunities of its citizens to exit from it*. There I will elaborate an argument that I merely sketch at this point: At least from a liberal point of view, the obligation to protect future generations from a regime that violates their rights while allowing them no escape from it can rebut what would otherwise be a sound justification for secession. The force of this argument stems from a distinction between allowing competent individuals to destroy their own freedom and allowing them irrevocably to deprive others of their freedom without their consent.

It was emphasized earlier that if the argument now under consideration is to be an independent justification for secession, it must show that, at least under certain conditions, a group's need to preserve its culture can *entitle it to territory*; that is, this need can *generate* a valid claim to territory where none previously existed. There are two cases to distinguish. The state from which the cultural preservationists are attempting to secede may have valid title to the seceding territory, or it may not. In the former case it is implausible to say that the need to preserve a culture, even when other means fail, justifies overturning the state's territorial claim and transferring title, as it were, to the secessionists. Any such principle would be unacceptable for at least two reasons. First, it treats valid territorial claims too lightly, according them too little substance. Second, because the notion of a culture and hence of a cultural group is so expansive and vague, the principle is a recipe for intolerably excessive international instability and thus is subject to the same objection that was raised against the 'people's right of self-determination,' or normative nationalist principle, encountered earlier. Therefore, the principle that the need to preserve a culture can overturn a state's valid claim to territory ought to be rejected.

So if the argument from cultural preservation is to have any prospect of success, as an independent argument for a *right* to secede, its application must be restricted to the second type of case, that in which the state from which secession is attempted does *not* have a valid claim to the seceding territory.

Of course, more than this is needed if the argument is to be fully convincing: The area in question must not be subject to a valid territorial claim by any third party either. For it is obviously not enough for the secessionists to establish that the state has no valid claim to the territory. To make a strong case that their need to preserve their culture entitles them to the territory, they must also show that no other group or state has a valid claim to it.

We can now pull together the various conditions that would have to be satisfied if the argument from cultural preservation is to succeed in justifying secession as a matter of right. (1) The culture in question must in fact be imperiled. (2) Less disruptive ways of preserving the culture (e.g., special minority group rights within the existing state) must be unavailable or inadequate. (3) The culture in question must meet minimal standards of justice (unlike Nazi culture or the culture of the Khmer Rouge). (4) The seceding cultural group must not be seeking independence in order to establish an illiberal state, that is, one which fails to uphold basic individual civil and political rights, *and* from which free exit is denied. (5) Neither the state nor any third party can have a valid claim to the seceding territory.

The principle on which the fifth condition rests is this: The need to preserve a culture, though it is a morally significant interest, is not as weighty as either a grievance of injustice against the state or the need to protect a group against literal extinction, and it cannot *overturn* (override or extinguish) a valid territorial claim and generate a new one for the group in question. At most, it can generate a new valid claim to territory for the group whose culture is imperiled if the territory in question is *not* the subject of a valid territorial claim by anyone else. The principle that underlies condition (5) seems plausible because it recognizes that groups have a morally significant interest in preserving their cultures without giving excessive priority to that interest.

Are all of these conditions met in the case of Quebec? Conditions (3) and (4) no doubt are. Conditions (1), (2), and (5) are much more problematic. . . .

Quite independent of the particular case of Quebec, the analysis has also advanced a set of five conditions that must be satisfied if secession on grounds of cultural preservation is to be justified. As these conditions together impose very significant constraints, the conclusion to be drawn is that the argument from cultural preservation, like a number of the other prosecession arguments already canvassed, is of rather limited utility. Only rarely will the need to preserve a culture justify secession.

Self-Defense

Although the distinction between a group's right to preserve its culture and its right to defend the very existence of its members against lethal aggression is sometimes blurred by rhetoric about 'cultural genocide,' there is a great difference. Even when the right to preserve a culture does not offer a compelling justification for secession, the right of self-defense can do so, under certain circumstances.

'Defense' here implies an effort to protect against a lethal threat, a deadly attack by an aggressor. Not every effort at self-preservation is a case of self-defense because what endangers may not be an attack by an aggressor.

(It might be, for example, a natural disaster.) Hence the concept of a right of self-*defense* is distinct from and narrower than that of a right of self-*preservation.*

The common law, common-sense morality, and the great majority of ethical systems, both secular and religious, acknowledge a right of self-defense as including a right to use force against an aggressor who threatens lethal force. For good reason this is not thought to be an unlimited right: Among the obvious restrictions on it are (1) that only that degree of force necessary to avert the threat be used, and (2) that the attack against which one defends oneself not be provoked by one's own actions. If such restrictions are acknowledged, the assertion that there is a right of self-defense is highly plausible. Much more problematic is the assertion that the right of self-defense includes a right to use force *against an innocent third party* in order to defend oneself against deadly attacks from a second-party aggressor. Each of these limitations, including the last, is pertinent to the alleged right of groups to defend themselves.

The argument under consideration has two variants. The first, in which a group wishes to secede from a state in order to protect its members from extermination by that state itself, is the most obviously compelling. Under such conditions the group may either attempt to overthrow the government, that is, to engage in revolution; or if strategy requires it, the group may secede in order to organize a defensive territory, forcibly appropriating the needed territory from the aggressor, creating the political and military machinery required for its survival, and seeking recognition and aid from other sovereign states or international bodies. Whatever moral title to the seceding territory the aggressor state previously held is *invalidated* by the gross injustice of its genocidal efforts. Or, at the very least, we can say that whatever legitimate claims to the seceding territory it has are *outweighed* by the claims of its innocent victims. We think of the aggressor's right, in the former case, as dissolving in the acid of his own iniquities, and, in the latter, as being pushed down in the scales of the balance by the greater mass of the victim's right of self-defense. Whether we say that the evil state's right to territory is invalidated (and disappears entirely) or merely is outweighed, it is clear enough that in these circumstances its claim to territory should not be an insurmountable bar to the victim group's seceding, if this is the only practical way to avoid its wrongful destruction.

The second variant of the argument makes the more controversial claim that to defend itself against an aggressor a group may secede from a state that is not itself the aggressor and that it may do so even if, as will often be the case, the use of force is involved. This amounts to the assertion that a group's need to defend itself against literal genocide can *generate* a claim to territory of sufficient moral weight to override the claims of those who until now have held valid title to it and who, unlike the aggressor state in the first version of the argument, have perpetrated no injustice to invalidate or override their title.

Perhaps the closest analog to this would be the common-law *defense of necessity*, according to which property rights may be infringed if doing so is necessary to avert some great evil. For example, I may trespass on your land to prevent a serious crime. But the chief difference, of course, is that in the case of secession from one state to avoid a threat to survival from another, there is not so much an infringement of a property right as the denial of one property right and its replacement by another. A concrete though hypothetical example will be useful.

Suppose the year is 1939. Germany has inaugurated a polity of genocide against the Jews. Jewish pleas to the democracies for protection have fallen on deaf ears (in part because the Jews are not regarded as a nation—nationhood carrying a strong presumption of territory, which they do not possess). Leaders of Jewish populations in Poland, Czechoslovakia, Germany, and the Soviet Union agree that the only hope for the survival of their people is to create a Jewish state, a sovereign territory to serve as a last refuge for European Jewry. Suppose further that the logical choice for its location—the only choice with the prospect of any success in saving large numbers of Jews—is a portion of Poland. Polish Jews, who are not being protected from the Nazis by Poland, therefore occupy a portion of Poland and invite other Jews to join them there is a Jewish sanctuary state. They do not expel non-Jewish Poles who already reside in that area but, instead, treat them as equal citizens. (Note that from 1941 until 1945 something rather like this occurred on a smaller scale. Jewish partisans, who proved to be ferocious and heroic guerrillas, occupied and defended an area in the forests near Brody, Poland, and in effect created their own ministate, for purposes of defending themselves and others from annihilation by the Germans.) Unless one holds that existing property rights, including the right of Poland to keep all its territory intact, supersede all other considerations, including the right of an innocent people, utterly lacking in effective allies, to preserve its very existence from the depredations of mass murderers, one must conclude that the Jews would have been justified in appropriating the territory necessary for their survival.

The force of the self-defense argument derives in part from the assumption that the Polish Jews who create the sanctuary state *are not being protected by their own state, Poland*. The idea is that the state's authority over territory is granted to it so that it may provide protection for its citizens—all its citizens—and that its retaining that authority is conditional upon its providing that protection. In the circumstances described, the Polish state is not providing protection to its Jewish citizens, and this fact voids its territorial authority.[8]

If this line of reasoning is cogent, then we have another illustration of a point made earlier during the discussion of the argument from discriminatory redistribution. In some cases, even where secessionists have no historical title to the territory they desire, and hence no basis for justifying secession as the reclaiming of what was wrongfully taken, weighty moral considerations favouring secession, in this instance the right of self-defense, may be sufficient to generate a new title to territory, thus transforming existing property rights and thereby justifying the taking of territory that secession necessarily involves.

It would be a mistake to assume that this type of case is fanciful simply because it is hypothetical. One of the strongest arguments for recognizing a Kurdish state or an Armenian state may be that only this status, with the territorial sovereignty it includes, will ensure the survival of these peoples in the face of genocidal threats. So there can be and indeed are situations in which the right of self-defense grounds a right to secede.

Rectifying Past Injustices

This is perhaps the simplest and most intuitively appealing argument for secession and one that has obvious application to many actual secessionist movements, including those currently in progress in the Soviet Union. It contends that a region has a right to secede if it was unjustly incorporated into the larger unit from which its members wish to separate. The act of unjust incorporation may have occurred in either of two ways: The seceding area may have been directly annexed by the currently existing state, or it may have been unjustly acquired by some earlier state that is the ancestor of the currently existing state. The Baltic Soviet Republics, as we have already seen, exemplify the first scenario. The secessionist movement in Bangladesh is an instance of the second. Bangladesh, along with other regions in the Indian subcontinent, was incorporated into the British Empire by conquest. When colonial rule ended, Pakistan, consisting of East and West Pakistan, was created. East Pakistan, taking the name Bangladesh, later seceded from Pakistan and, with the help of India's military, won its independence by force.[9] This second scenario raises its own special issues. Here it will be more fruitful to focus on the simpler first scenario, because it provides the most direct and compelling illustration of the argument from rectificatory justice.

That argument's power stems from the assumption that in these cases secession is simply the reappropriation, by the legitimate owner, of stolen property. The right to secede, under these circumstances, is just the right to reclaim what is one's own. This simple interpretation is most plausible, of course, in situations in which the people attempting to secede are literally the same people who held legitimate title to the territory at the time of the unjust annexation, or at least are the indisputable descendants of those people (their legitimate heirs, so to speak). But matters are considerably less simple if the seceding group is not closely or clearly related to the group whose territory was unjustly taken, or if the original group that was dispossessed did not have clear, unambiguous title to it. But at least in the paradigm case—one in which the seccessionists are the group that was wronged or at least are the indisputable legitimate successors to it—the argument from rectificatory justice is a convincing argument for a moral right to secede. (The difficulty, which we will explore later in some depth, is that the history of existing states is so replete with immoral, coercive, and fraudulent takings that it may be hard for most states to establish the legitimacy of their current or past borders.)

Under some circumstances, however, the considerations of rectificatory justice which establish that there is a right to secede are not sufficient to show that those who have the right ought to exercise it or that they ought to exercise it now. Here, as with other rights, there can be compelling moral reasons for not doing what one has a right to do, or for postponing the exercise of one's right in order to avoid inconvenience or even catastrophe for oneself or others. To repeat: Sometimes one ought not to do what one has a right to do.

The appeal of the argument from rectificatory justice is so strong that one might be tempted to assume that it provides the *only* conclusive argument in favor of secession. And some writers have in fact argued that a sound justification for secession must always be founded on a claim of rectificatory justice—on the assertion of a right to recover territory that was unjustly appropriated by another at some earlier point.[10] Let us call this *the historical grievance version of the territoriality thesis*. The territoriality thesis states that every sound justification for secession must include a valid claim to territory. In other words, it must be the case that the secessionists have a right to the territory in question. The historical grievance version asserts that the valid claim to territory that every sound justification for secession includes must be grounded in a historical grievance concerning the violation of a preexisting right to territory.

As the survey of prosecessionist arguments thus far suggests, this view on the justification of secession is too restrictive. It is one of the main theses of this book that there are some cases in which secession is justified even in the absence of a historical grievance about the unjust loss of territory. Although the historical grievance version of the territoriality thesis is wrong, it contains a grain of truth. The grain of truth is that a sound justification for secession must include a justification for taking the seceding territory, and that the simplest, most obviously compelling justification for taking the seceding territory is that doing so is merely reappropriation by the owners of what was wrongly taken from them. The error is the assumption that the secessionists' taking of territory can be justified only by establishing that it is a reappropriation of property that was previously wrongfully taken by others. The point is that there are other ways in which secessionists can establish valid title to the territory. We have just seen one instance of this: the hypothetical example of a Jewish sanctuary state in Poland in 1939.

But regardless of whether that particular example convinces, it is worth observing that there have been a number of major secessionist movements that have not based their claims on historical grievances about unjust seizure of territory. Furthermore, and much more important, at least some of these are cases of secession that are widely thought to be justified. For example, the American Revolution was a successful attempt by a part of the British Empire in North America, which included Canada as well, to secede from that empire. (As noted earlier, it was not strictly speaking a revolution, since no attempt was made to overthrow the British government but only to free the American colonies from its control.) Yet this secession was not based on any appeal to a historical grievance concerning the wrongful taking of territory. . . .

It may in fact be the case that existing *international law* tends to accord legitimacy only to those secessionist movements that can establish a historical grievance regarding unjust loss of territory (regardless of whether international law explicitly endorses the historical grievance thesis or not). But it begs the moral question to assume that existing international law is above criticism. If there are sound justifications for secession that do not make the right to secede derivative upon a right to rectify past unjust takings of territory, then there will be a case for modifying international law regarding secession. But here I wish to emphasize that whether or not the argument from rectificatory justice is the sole justification for secession, it is, at least in its most direct application, a plausible one. The next argument for a right to secede, the argument from consent, though initially plausible, makes the opposite error of those who assume that only a historical grievance concerning territory can justify secession: It overlooks the importance of establishing a valid claim to territory altogether.

Consent

Works of political philosophy contain a number of different arguments from consent, and they are seldom clearly distinguished from each other. One of the few political philosophers who has even briefly discussed secession, Harry Beran, first argues that consent is a necessary condition for political obligation and then infers from this thesis about consent that there is a right to secede.[11] His idea is quite simple: Unless the right to secede is acknowledged, groups will sometimes remain subject to the state's power without consenting to it. So if one agrees that consent is a necessary condition for legitimate political authority, then one must recognize a right to secede. Merely allowing people the option of emigration as a way of withholding consent is insufficient because in many cases either emigration will be prohibitively costly or there will be no opportunity to relocate in a state that is any more satisfactory.

This view can be attacked in two ways: By criticizing the thesis that consent is necessary for political obligation, or by denying that if consent is necessary for political obligation, then there is a right to secede when consent is lacking. I shall do both: First I will argue that consent is not a necessary condition for political obligation, and then I will show that even if it were, much more would be needed to show that there is a right to secede.

The thesis about the connection between consent and obligation is not the highly implausible claim that a citizen must consent to each and every law or policy, that he or she may accept or reject every law or policy at his or her discretion. This latter view is a denial of the existence of political authority, not an account of a necessary condition for its existence.

The more persuasive thesis about consent is that persons are under a general obligation to obey the laws of the state only if they consent to be governed by it, that they tacitly consent by accepting the benefits which the state confers on them, *and* that *not renouncing* these benefits counts as *accepting them.* Chief among these benefits are the personal security and freedom that life under the rule of law provides. Consent is said to be tacit in that no written or oral statement by the individual or group is thought to be necessary.

As a number of critics of this view have observed, the difficulty is not with the idea of tacit (or implicit) consent *per se* but with the assumption that what counts as tacit consent is merely refraining from renouncing benefits.[12] On Locke's version of the consent view, merely continuing to reside within the borders of the state while enjoying its benefits constitutes tacit consent. Because some of the most important benefits (such as security from attack from without) are *public goods*, available to all within the borders of the country if they are available to any, the only way to 'renounce' them (without changing the borders of the country) may be to cease residing there.[13]

The problem is that although cases of tacit consent do exist, this does not seem to be one of them. We are justified in saying that someone tacitly consented to something only where certain rather special conditions of a rule-governed, conventional sort obtain. For example, a person who already possesses appropriate authority, such as the chairperson of a meeting, announces that a certain course of action will be taken unless there is an objection, there is adequate opportunity for objections to be raised, members of the group can object without untoward costs, there is an understanding as to what counts as objecting, and so on. Merely continuing to reside in a country, and thereby enjoying the benefits provided by the state, is a far cry from satisfying anything like these sorts of rather specific conditions.[14]

Furthermore, as the legal scholar Lea Brilmayer has pointed out, if the foregoing example of tacit consent is apt, there is an even more fundamental difficulty. If silence or continued participation in the aforementioned meeting is to count as consent to the course of action in question, the person proposing or initiating the action must *already possess authority* over the group. But if this is so, when whatever else the notion of tacit consent can explain, it cannot explain that person's authority. Similarly, it is hard to see how tacit consent could explain political obligation, that is, the obligation to obey political authority, if the conditions for tacit consent include the assumption that political authority already exists.[15]

These and other dissatisfactions with the consent thesis have led some theorists to conclude that the real issue is *fairness*, not consent. They contend that political obligation rests on a moral *duty of fair play*. The state, through the contributions of other citizens, provides me with important benefits. My continuing to enjoy these benefits without obeying the laws that make them possible would be unfair to my fellow citizens. But if I do renounce these benefits, then my obligation ceases.

Most criticisms of the fair play approach have concentrated on showing that it fails as an account of what is *sufficient* for being politically obligated. The libertarian philosopher Robert Nozick, for example, has argued that merely continuing to receive benefits is not sufficient for being obligated to the benefactor. His point is that, as a general account of how we come to be obligated, this is much too strong: If it were correct, others could obligate us simply by imposing benefits on us.[16] Or, more accurately, we would be morally bound to obey those who imposed the benefits or to contribute to the continued production of those benefits or to take whatever steps are necessary, no matter how costly to us, to ensure that we no longer partook of those benefits. Nozick rightly concludes that this is an unacceptable account of the genesis of obligations.

Our concern, however, is with the thesis that accepting or refraining from renouncing the benefits the state provides is a *necessary* condition for being politically obligated. Even if this thesis is granted, we are a long way from having a justification for secession, for two reasons: first, there are other ways of renouncing the benefits of political association than by seceding; and, second, even if political obligation is severed by refusal of benefits, more is required to justify secession than the severance of political obligation. A valid claim to territory must also be established: It must be shown that the secessionists have a right to the territory.

The most obvious alternative to secession as a way of renouncing the state's benefits is emigration. However, as has frequently been noted, for many people emigration will at best entail severe costs. Even if a favorable alternative country exists and will receive such people, the costs of relocating may be high. But in many cases the situation is much worse than that: The only option may be emigration to an equally or more uncongenial state. Worst of all, there are some individuals—for example, some recent refugees from Vietnam, the 'boat people'—who can find no country willing to admit them. So whatever plausibility the fair play approach has as an argument in favor of secession depends upon the assumption that emigration is not a morally acceptable alternative for renouncing the benefits of cooperation. For if both ways of renouncing benefits were freely available, then there would be no case for secession, since secession not only involves renouncing the benefits of continued membership in the political association but also entails the taking of land.

This brings us to the second gap between the fair play principle and the right to secede. The fair play argument for secession would do only part of the job of justifying secession even if it were wholly unobjectionable. It would not by itself touch the territorial use because it does nothing either to establish the secessionists' claim to territory or to refute the antisecessionists' charge that secession is a wrongful taking of the state's land. Similarly, even if various objections to the consent argument could be successfully met, the most that argument would establish is that those who do not consent are not obligated. It would not show that they may appropriate territory, and hence it would not show that secession is justified. The consent and fair play arguments can at most demonstrate the conditions under which the state no longer has authority over people; they cannot show when the state no longer has control over territory. So arguments from consent and fair play, contrary to initial impressions, cannot even *in principle* justify secession.

For the same reason, even if it could be shown that either tacit consent or receipt of benefits is *sufficient* for political obligation, the fundamental issue of territorial sovereignty would remain untouched, as would that of the state's authority if the latter is taken to include authority over land as well as people. Tacit consent or receipt of benefits would be *sufficient* for political authority—where political authority includes territorial sovereignty—only if territorial sovereignty were already assumed.[17]

This simple but important point can be illustrated as follows. Suppose that a group of people illegally and unjustly came to occupy a piece of land claimed by another group. Suppose that the members of the first group tacitly consent to be governed by the political apparatus established by this group. Or suppose that the first group provides benefits to its members, which they accept, making no effort to renounce or avoid them. Whatever obligations are thereby generated among members of the first group, the question of which group has legitimate title to that piece of land remains unresolved. So regardless of what position we take on either the tacit consent view or the fair play view, each of which can be construed as stating either necessary or sufficient conditions for political obligation, these views provide no arguments for (or against) secession, contrary to what some writers, including Beran, have assumed.

Summary: The Case for a Right to Secede

... Although some prosecession arguments fail, including the argument from consent and the pure self-determination argument, and others, such as the self-defense argument, the argument from cultural preservation, and the argument from the limited goals of political association, are of very limited application, a variety of considerations taken together make a strong case for a moral right to secede under certain circumstances. Among the strongest arguments and most widely applicable arguments for a right to secede are the argument from rectificatory justice and the argument from discriminatory redistribution. Under extreme conditions, secession may also be justified on grounds of self-defense and, perhaps more controversially, in some cases where it is necessary for the preservation of a culture. . . .

Notes

1. Ernest Gellner, *Nations and Nationalism* (Oxford: Blackwell, 1983), p. 2.
2. Ibid., p. 2.
3. *Editor's note*: Discriminatory redistribution occurs when governments implement 'taxation schemes or regulatory policies or economic programs that systematically work to the disadvantage of some groups, while benefitting others, in morally arbitrary ways'. According to Buchanan, the desire to escape from such exploitation is a common, and morally legitimate, grounds for secession. He argues that a government's exercise of power 'is only legitimate if it refrains from exploiting one group for the benefit of another', and that violating this condition 'in effect voids the state's claim to the territory in which the victims reside'. Buchanan cites the American Revolution as paradigmatic instance of a

secessionist movement grounded in charges of discriminatory redistribution (Buchanan, *Secession*, pp. 40, 44).

4. Allen Buchanan, 'Assessing the Communitarian Critique of Liberalism,' *Ethics* vol. 99, no. 4, 1989, pp. 867–871.
5. This is not to suggest, however, that assimilation was never attempted. See David H. Getches and Charles F. Wilkinson, *Federal Indian Law*, 2d edn. (St. Paul, Minn.: West Publishing Co., 1986), pp. 111–122; and F. Cohen, *Handbook of Federal Indian Law* (Charlottesville, Vir.: Michie Co., 1982 edn.), pp. 127–143.
6. I am indebted to Dale Jamieson for clarifying this point to me.
7. Michael Sandel, Introduction, *Liberalism and Its Critics*, edited by Michael Sandel (New York: New York University Press, 1984), p. 6.
8. This is not to imply that the titles of private Polish citizens to the land in question are thereby voided. However, the founders of the Jewish sanctuary state could argue that all that is required is that private landowners be compensated for their losses and that their land be returned if the danger passes.
9. E.S. Mason, R. Dorfman, and S.A. Marglin, *Conflict in East Pakistan: Background and Prospects*, cited in Subrata Roy Chowdhury, *The Genesis of Bangladesh* (New York: Asia Publishing House, 1972), p. 11, no. 18.
10. This was the view of Lea A. Brilmayer, who has since acknowledged that 'one can imagine' secession might be justified on other grounds. See Brilmayer, 'Secession and Self-Determination: A Territorialist Reinterpretation,' *Yale Journal of International Law*, vol. 16, issue 1, January 1991. However, one needn't rely on imagination—history suffices: The case of the secession of the American Colonies from the British Empire illustrates the point that secession on grounds of discriminatory redistribution is justifiable.
11. Harry Beran, *The Consent Theory of Political Obligation* (New York: Croom Helm, 1987), pp. 37–42.
12. For an especially lucid and well-argued criticism of consent theory on this point, see John Simmons, *Political Obligation* (Princeton, N.J.: Princeton University Press, 1979), pp. 75–100.
13. A public good is a desired state of affairs that requires the contribution, which involves a cost, of all or some members of a group. The public good produced is available to all members of the group, the exclusion of noncontributors being impossible or impractical.
14. Simmons, *Political Obligations*, pp. 75–100.
15. Lea Brilmayer, 'Consent, Contract, and Territory,' *Minnesota Law Review*, vol. 74, no. 1, October 1989, pp. 6–10.
16. Robert Nozick, *Anarchy, State, and Utopia*, pp. 90–95.
17. Brilmayer, 'Secession and Self-Determination: A Territorialist Reinterpretation,' pp. 186–187.

Guide to Further Reading

1. Surveys of Minority Rights

There are now a number of general surveys of the rights of minority cultures around the world, illustrating the many forms or models of cultural pluralism:

CAPOTORTI, F., *Study on the Rights of Persons Belonging to Ethnic, Religious and Linguistic Minorities* UN Doc. E/CN 4/Sub.2/384 Rev. 1 (United Nations, New York, 1979).

GLAZER, N. and MOYNIHAN, D. P. (eds.), *Ethnicity: Theory and Experience* (Harvard University Press, Cambridge MA, 1975).

GURR, TED, *Minorities at Risk: A Global View of Ethnopolitical Conflict* (Institute of Peace Press, Washington, 1993).

HANNUM, HURST, *Autonomy, Sovereignty, and Self-Determination: The Adjudication of Conflicting Rights* (University of Pennsylvania Press, Philadelphia, 1990).

HOROWITZ, D. L., *Ethnic Groups in Conflict* (University of California Press, Berkeley, 1985).

MAYBURY-LEWIS, D. (ed.), *The Prospects for Plural Societies* (American Ethnological Society, Washington, 1984).

MCGARRY, JOHN and O'LEARY, BRENDAN, 'The Political Regulation of National and Ethnic Conflict', *Parliamentary Affairs* 47/1 (1994): 94–115.

SIGLER, JAY, *Minority Rights: A Comparative Analysis* (Greenwood, Westport, 1983).

SOWELL, THOMAS, *Preferential Policies: An International Perspective* (Morrow, New York, 1990).

WIRSING, R. (ed.), *Protection of Ethnic Minorities: Comparative Perspectives* (Pergamon, New York, 1981).

YOUNG, CRAWFORD (ed.), *The Rising Tide of Cultural Pluralism* (University of Wisconsin Press, Madison, 1993).

2. Minority Cultures in the Western Political Tradition

The status of minority cultures was a source of considerable debate within the liberal tradition in the nineteenth-century and the first part of the twentieth. For examples of this debate, see:

ACTON, LORD, 'Nationalism', in J. Figgis and R. Laurence (eds.), *The History of Freedom and Other Essays* (Macmillan, London, 1922—first published in 1862).

MILL, J. S., 'On Nationality', in *Considerations on Representative Government* (various editions—first published 1861).

BARKER, ERNEST, *National Character and the Factors in its Formation* (Methuen, London, 1948—first published in 1927).

ZIMMERN, ALFRED, *Nationality and Government* (Chatto and Windus, London, 1918).

For contemporary commentary on these debates, see:

AJZENSTAT, JANET, *The Political Thought of Lord Durham* (McGill-Queen's University Press, Montreal, 1988).

PAREKH, BHIKHU, 'Decolonizing Liberalism', in Alexsandras Shiromas (ed.), *The End of 'Isms'? Reflections on the Fate of Ideological Politics after Communism's Collapse* (Blackwell, Oxford, 1994): 85–103.

For some of the classical texts on minority cultures in the Marxist tradition, see:

MARX, KARL AND ENGELS, F., *The Russian Menace to Europe*, eds. Paul Blackstock and Bert Hoselitz (Free Press, Glencoe Illinois, 1952) [a collection of Marx and Engels' magazine and newspaper articles relating to ethnocultural conflicts].

LUXEMBURG, ROSA, *The National Question: Selected Writings*, ed. H.B. Davis (Monthly Review Press, New York, 1976).

LENIN, V. I., *Questions of National Policy and Proletarian Internationalism* (Progress Publishers, Moscow,1970).

STALIN, JOSEPH, *Marxism and the National Question* (Progress Publishers, Moscow, 1953).

For recent commentary on the Marxist tradition, see:

CONNOR, WALKER, *The National Question in Marxist-Leninist Theory and Strategy* (Princeton University Press, Princeton, 1984).

NIMNI, EPHRAIM, *Marxism and Nationalism: Theoretical Origins of a Political Crisis* (Pluto Press, London, 1994).

For the status of minority cultures in the Western political tradition more generally, see:

HOBSBAWM, E. J., *Nations and Nationalism since 1780: Programme, Myth and Reality* (Cambridge University Press, Cambridge, 1990).

MCNEILL, WILLIAM, *Polyethnicity and National Unity in World History* (University of Toronto Press, Toronto, 1986).

MCRAE, KENNETH, 'The Plural Society and the Western Political Tradition', *Canadian Journal of Political Science* 12/4 (1979): 675–88.

3. Contemporary Theoretical Approaches

There are few full-length books about the place of minority cultures within normative political theory. There are, however, an increasing number of edited collections which include significant contributions by political theorists. These include:

BAKER, JUDITH (ed.), *Group Rights* (University of Toronto Press, Toronto, 1994).

FRESCO, M. F. and VAN TONGEREN, P. J. M. (eds.), *Perspectives on Minorities:*

Philosophical Reflections on the Identity and the Rights of Cultural Minorities (Tilburg University Press, Le Tilburg, 1991).

FRIED, CHARLES (ed.), *Minorities: Community and Identity* (Springer-Verlag, Berlin, 1983).

HORTON, JOHN (ed.), *Liberalism, Multiculturalism and Toleration* (St. Martin's Press, London, 1993).

KUKATHAS, CHANDRAN (ed.), *Multicultural Citizens: the Philosophy and Politics of Identity* (Centre for Independent Studies, St. Leonard's, 1993).

For general theoretical discussions of cultural pluralism within contemporary political theory, see:

ADDIS, ADENO, 'Individualism, Communitarianism and the Rights of Ethnic Minorities', *Notre Dame Law Review* 67/3 (1992): 615–76.

GRAY, JOHN, 'The Politics of Cultural Diversity', in *Post-Liberalism: Studies in Political Thought* (Routledge, London, 1993).

GUTMANN, AMY, 'The Challenge of Multiculturalism to Political Ethics', *Philosophy and Public Affairs* 22/3 (1993): 171–206.

HABERMAS, JÜRGEN, 'Constitutional Struggles for Recognition', *European Journal of Philosophy* 1/2 (1993): 128–55.

KYMLICKA, WILL, *Multicultural Citizenship: A Liberal Theory of Minority Rights* (Oxford University Press, Oxford, 1995).

MARGALIT, AVISHAI and HALBERTAL, MOSHE, 'Liberalism and the Right to Culture', *Social Research* 61/3 (1994): 491–510.

NICKEL, JAMES, 'The Value of Cultural Belonging', *Dialogue* 33/4 (1994) 635–42.

PHILLIPS, ANNE, *The Politics of Presence* (Oxford University Press, Oxford, 1995).

RAZ, JOSEPH, 'Multiculturalism: A Liberal Perspective', *Dissent*, (Winter 1994): 67–79.

RICKARD, MAURICE, 'Liberalism, Multiculturalism, and Minority Rights', *Social Theory and Practice* 20/2 (1994): 143–69.

SPINNER, JEFF, *The Boundaries of Citizenship: Race, Ethnicity and Nationality in the Liberal State* (Johns Hopkins University Press, Baltimore, 1994).

TAYLOR, CHARLES, 'The Politics of Recognition', in *Multiculturalism and the 'Politics of Recognition'*, ed. Amy Gutmann (Princeton University Press, Princeton, 1992): 25–73.

VAN DYKE, VERNON, *Human Rights, Ethnicity and Discrimination* (Greenwood, Westport, 1985).

YOUNG, IRIS MARION, *Justice and the Politics of Difference* (Princeton University Press, Princeton, 1990).

4. Topics in the Rights of Minority Cultures

There is now a growing literature on specific topics relating to the rights of minority cultures. These include (a) the right to self-determination; (b) the rights of immigrants and refugees; (c) the rights of indigenous peoples; (d) collective rights; (e) language rights; (f) ethnonationalism.

(a) For discussions of the principle of self-determination, and related issues regarding secession and federalism as tools for accomodating ethnocultural diversity, see:

BARRY, BRIAN, 'Self-Government Revisited' in *Democracy and Power: Essays in Political Theory I* (Oxford University Press, Oxford, 1989): 156–86.

BERAN, HARRY, *A Consent Theory of Political Obligation* (Croom Helm, New York, 1987).

BINDER, GUYORA, 'The Case for Self-Determination', *Stanford Journal of International Law* 29 (1993): 223–70.

BRILMAYER, LEA, 'Secession and Self-Determination: A Territorialist Reinterpretation', *Yale Journal of International Law* 16/1 (1991): 177–202.

BUCHANAN, ALLEN, *Secession: The Morality of Political Divorce* (Westview Press, Boulder, 1991).

BUCHEIT, LEE, *Secession: The Legitimacy of Self-Determination* (Yale University Press, New Haven, 1978).

GAUTHIER, DAVID, 'Breaking Up: An Essay on Secession', *Canadian Journal of Philosophy* 24/3 (1994): 357–72.

HANNUM, HURST, 'The Limits of Sovereignty and Majority Rule: Minorities, Indigenous Peoples, and the Right to Autonomy' in Ellen Lutz et al. (eds.), *New Directions in Human Rights* (University of Pennsylvania Press, Philadelphia, 1989): 3–24.

HOWSE, ROBERT and KNOP, KAREN, 'Federalism, Secession, and the Limits of Ethnic Accommodation', *New Europe Law Review* 1/2 (1993): 269–320.

PHILPOTT, DANIEL, 'In Defense of Self-Determination', *Ethics* 105/2 (1995): 352–85.

WALZER, MICHAEL, 'The New Tribalism', *Dissent* (Spring, 1992): 164–71.

(b) For discussions of the morality of immigration and refugee policy, including questions about the justification for limiting immigration, or the legitimacy of expecting immigrants and refugees to integrate culturally, see:

BADER, VEIT, 'Citizenship and Exclusion: Radical Democracy, Community and Justice', *Political Theory* 23/2 (1995): 211–46.

BARRY, BRIAN and GOODIN, ROBERT (eds.), *Free Movement: Ethical Issues in the Transnational Migration of People and Money* (Harvester Wheatsheaf, London, 1992).

CARENS, JOSEPH, 'Membership and Morality: Admission to Citizenship in Liberal Democratic States', in W. Brubaker (ed.), *Immigration and the Politics of Citizenship in Europe and North America* (University Press of America, Lanham MD, 1989): 31–50.

CARENS, JOSEPH, 'The Rights of Immigrants', in Judith Baker (ed.), *Group Rights* (University of Toronto Press, Toronto, 1994): 142–63.

GALLOWAY, DONALD, 'Liberalism, Globalism, and Immigration', *Queen's Law Journal* 18/2 (1993): 266–305.

GUNSTEREN, HERMAN R. VAN, 'Admission to Citizenship', *Ethics* 98/4 (1988): 731–41.

HUDSON, JAMES, 'The Philosophy of Immigration', *Journal of Libertarian Studies* 8/1 (1986): 51–62.

KING, TIMOTHY, 'Immigration from Developing Countries: Some Philosophical Issues', *Ethics* 93/3 (1983): 25–36.

RESCHER, NICHOLAS, 'Moral Obligation and the Refugee', *Public Affairs Quarterly* 6/1 (1992): 23–30.

WALZER, MICHAEL, 'The Distribution of Membership', in Peter Brown and Henry Shue (eds.), *Boundaries: National Autonomy and its Limits* (Rowman and Littlefield, Totawa, 1981). Reprinted as 'Membership' in Michael Walzer, *Spheres of Justice: A Defence of Pluralism and Equality* (Blackwell, Oxford, 1983): 31–63.

(c) For discussions of the rights of indigenous peoples, including claims to land and to self-government, and their relation to Western political theory, see:

BOLDT, MENNO and LONG, J. (eds.), *The Quest for Justice: Aboriginal Peoples and Aboriginal Rights* (University of Toronto Press, Toronto, 1985).

BUCHANAN, ALLEN, 'The Role of Collective Rights in the Theory of Indigenous Peoples' Rights', *Transnational Law and Contemporary Problems* 3/1 (1993): 89–108.

CLINTON, ROBERT, 'The Rights of Indigenous Peoples as Collective Group Rights', *Arizona Law Review* 32/4 (1990): 739–47.

MACKLEM, PATRICK, 'Distributing Sovereignty: Indian Nations and Equality of Peoples', *Stanford Law Review* 45/5 (1993): 1311–67.

PENZ, PETER, 'Development Refugees and Distributive Justice: Indigenous Peoples, Land and the Developmentalist State', *Public Affairs Quarterly* 6/1 (1992): 105–31.

TULLY, JAMES, 'Aboriginal Property and Western Political Theory', *Social Philosophy and Policy* 11/2 (1994): 153–80.

(d) For discussions of the concept of 'collective rights', and its relation to more familiar ideas of individual rights, see:

GALENKAMP, MARLIES, *Individualism and Collectivism: the Concept of Collective Rights* (Rotterdamse Filosofische Studies, Rotterdam, 1993).

GARET, RONALD, 'Communality and Existence: The Rights of Groups', *Southern California Law Review* 56/5 (1983): 1001–75.

MACDONALD, IAN, 'Group Rights', *Philosophical Papers* 28/2 (1989): 117–36.

MCDONALD, MICHAEL (ed.), *Collective Rights*, special issue of the *Canadian Journal of Law and Jurisprudence* 4/2 (1991): 217–419.

SANDERS, DOUGLAS, 'Collective Rights', *Human Rights Quarterly* 13 (1991): 368–86.

VAN DYKE, VERNON, 'Collective Rights and Moral Rights: Problems in Liberal-Democratic Thought', *Journal of Politics* 44 (1982): 21–40.

(e) There has been very little written about language rights within political theory. For a collection of essays which raise some of the normative issues involved, see:

SCHNEIDERMAN, DAVID (ed.), *Language and the State: The Law and Politics of Identity* (Les Editions Yvon Blais, Cowansville, Quebec, 1991).

For overviews of language policy issues around the world, see:

FISHMAN, JOSHUA, *Language and Ethnicity in Minority Sociolinguistic Perspective* (Multilingual Matters Ltd., Clevedon, 1989).

LAPONCE, J. A., *Languages and their Territories* (University of Toronto Press, Toronto, 1987).

WEINSTEIN, BRIAN, *The Civic Tongue: Political Consequences of Language Choices* (Longman, New York, 1983).

WEINSTEIN, BRIAN (ed.), *Language Policy and Political Development* (Ablex Publishing, Norwood NJ, 1990).

(f) The issue of minority rights is inextricably bound up with the phenomenon of nationalism, both because some minorities see themselves as 'nations', and so mobilize into nationalist movements, and because the process of building nation-states has often involved efforts to assimilate minority cultures. Until recently, the phenomenon of nationalism was largely ignored by political theorists. For recent discussions, see

MILLER, DAVID, 'In Defense of Nationality', *Journal of Applied Philosophy* 10/1 (1993): 3–16.

POOLE, ROSS, 'Nationalism and the Nation-State in Late Modernity', *European Studies Journal* 10/1 (1993): 161–74.

TAMIR, YAEL, *Liberal Nationalism* (Princeton University Press, Princeton, 1993).

WALZER, MICHAEL, 'Nation and Universe' in G. B. Peterson (ed.), *The Tanner Lectures on Human Values* 11 (University of Utah Press, Salt Lake City, 1991): 509–56.

For useful historical and sociological studies of nationalism, see:

ANDERSON, BENEDICT, *Imagined Communities: Reflections on the Origin and Spread of Nationalism* (New Left Books, London, 1983).

CONNOR, WALKER, *Ethnonationalism: The Quest for Understanding* (Princeton University Press, Princeton, 1993).

GELLNER, ERNEST, *Nations and Nationalism* (Blackwell, Oxford, 1983).

YUVAL-DAVIS, NIRA, 'Gender and Nation', *Ethnic and Racial Studies* 16/4 (1993): 621–32.

Many of the most influential accounts of nationalism (including all of the authors just listed) are excerpted in:

SMITH, ANTHONY and HUTCHINSON, JOHN (eds.), *Nationalism* (Oxford University Press, Oxford, 1994).

5. International Law

Some of the most important developments regarding the rights of minority cultures have occurred at the level of international law, as indigenous peoples and other minority groups have actively lobbied for greater international recognition and protection for minority rights. For overviews of these developments, see:

BERTING, JAN et al. (eds.), *Human Rights in a Pluralist World: Individuals and Collectivities* (Roosevelt Study Center, Middleburg, Netherlands, 1990).

CRAWFORD, JAMES (ed.), *The Rights of Peoples* (Oxford University Press, Oxford, 1988).

DINSTEIN, YORAM and TABORY, MALA (eds.), *The Protection of Minorities and Human Rights* (Martinus Nijhoff, Dordrecht, 1992).

LERNER, NATAN, *Group Rights and Discrimination in International Law* (Martinus Nijhoff, Dordrecht, 1991).

THORNBERRY, PATRICK, *International Law and the Rights of Minorities* (Oxford University Press, Oxford, 1991).

6. Case Studies

There is an enormous literature on ethnocultural groups and conflicts in various countries. For overviews, see the collections listed under Section1 above. What follows is a very selective list of some recent works which examine ethnocultural issues within various Western and Commonwealth countries in a theoretically informed way, highlighting the normative issues involved.

(a) For discussions of minority cultures within the United States, including the land and self-government rights of Indian tribes, the language rights of Hispanic minorities, and voting rights and affirmative action policies for African-Americans, see:

BARSH, R. and HENDERSON, J., *The Road: Indian Tribes and Political Liberty* (University of California Press, Berkeley, 1980).

GLAZER, NATHAN, *Ethnic Dilemmas: 1964–1982* (Harvard University Press, Cambridge, Mass., 1983).

GROFMAN, BERNARD (ed.), *Controversies in Minority Voting: The Voting Rights Act in Perspective* (Brookings Institute, Washington,1992).

GUINIER, LANI, *Tyranny of the Majority: Fundamental Fairness and Representative Democracy* (Free Press, New York, 1994).

KARST, KENNETH, *Belonging to America: Equal Citizenship and the Constitution* (Yale University Press, New Haven, 1989).

MINOW, MARTHA, *Making all the Difference: Inclusion, Exclusion and American Law* (Cornell University Press, Ithaca, 1990).

O'BRIEN, SHARON, 'Cultural Rights in the United States: A Conflict of Values', *Law and Inequality Journal* 5 (1987): 267–358.

SANDEL, MICHAEL, 'Freedom of Conscience or Freedom of Choice' in James Hunter and O. Guinness (eds.), *Articles of Faith, Articles of Peace* (Brookings Institute, Washington, 1990): 74–92.

SVENSSON, FRANCES, 'Liberal Democracy and Group Rights: The Legacy of Individualism and its Impact on American Indian Tribes', *Political Studies* 27/3 (1979): 421–39.

WALZER, MICHAEL, *What It Means To Be An American* (Marsilio, New York, 1992).

(b) For discussions of minority cultures in Britain, primarily recent immigrants from former British colonies, see:

HORTON, JOHN (ed.), *Liberalism, Multiculturalism and Toleration* (St. Martin's Press, London, 1993).

MODOOD, TARIQ, *Not Easy Being British: Colour, Culture and Citizenship* (Trentham Books, London, 1992).

PAREKH, BHIKHU, 'British Citizenship and Cultural Difference', in Geoff Andrews (ed.) *Citizenship* (Lawrence and Wishart, London, 1991): 183–204.

POULTER, SEBASTIAN, 'Ethnic Minority Customs, English Law, and Human Rights', *International and Comparative Law Quarterly* 36/3 (1987): 589–615.

RICH, P., 'T. H. Green, Lord Scarman and the issue of ethnic minority rights in English liberal thought', *Ethnic and Racial Studies* 10 (1987): 149–68.

(c) For discussions of the rights of minority cultures in Canada, including Aboriginal peoples, the Québécois, and immigrant groups, see:

BOLDT, MENNO, *Surviving as Indians: The Challenge of Self-Government* (University of Toronto Press, Toronto, 1993).

EISENBERG, AVIGAIL, 'The Politics of Individual and Group Difference', *Canadian Journal of Political Science* 27/1 (1994): 3–21.

TAYLOR, CHARLES, *Reconciling the Solitudes: Essays on Canadian Federalism and Nationalism* (McGill-Queen's University Press, Montreal, 1993).

TURPEL, M. E., 'Aboriginal Peoples and the Canadian Charter: Interpretive Monopolies, Cultural Differences', *Canadian Human Rights Yearbook* 6 (1989–90): 3–45.

WEBBER, JEREMY, *Reimagining Canada* (McGill-Queen's University Press, Montreal, 1994).

(d) For minority cultures in other Commonwealth countries, see:

CARENS, JOSEPH, 'Democracy and Respect for Difference: the case of Fiji', *University of Michigan Journal of Law Reform* 25/3 (1992): 547–631.

DEGANAAR, J., 'Nationalism, Liberalism, and Pluralism' in J. Butler (ed.), *Democratic Liberalism in South Africa: Its History and Prospect* (Wesleyan University Press, Middletown, 1987): 236–49.

KUKATHAS, CHANDRAN (ed.), *Multicultural Citizens: the Philosophy and Politics of Identity* (Centre for Independent Studies, St. Leonard's, 1993).

MACDONALD, IAN, 'Group Rights in South Africa: A Philosophical Exploration', *Politikon* 15 (1988): 19–30.

MULGAN, RICHARD, *Maori, Pākehā and Democracy* (Oxford University Press, Auckland, 1989).

SELASSIE, ALEMANTE, 'Ethnic Identity and Constitutional Design for Africa', *Stanford Journal of International Law* 29/1 (1993): 1–56.

SHARP, ANDREW, *Justice and the Maori: Maori Claims in New Zealand Political Argument in the 1980s* (Oxford University Press, Auckland, 1990).

An interesting historical survey of policies regarding minority cultures throughout the Commonwealth is provided in:

HANCOCK, W. K., *Survey of British Commonwealth Affairs: Volume 1: Problems of Nationality: 1900–1936* (Oxford University Press, London, 1937).

Index